THE
BIPERSONAL
FIELD

THE BIPERSONAL FIELD

Robert Langs, M.D.

Clinical Assistant Professor of Psychiatry
State University of New York, Downstate Medical Center
and
Visiting Staff Psychiatrist
Long Island Jewish-Hillside Medical Center
Glen Oaks, New York

JASON ARONSON, INC.
New York

ISBN: 0-87668-246-8

Library of Congress Catalog Number: 75-42530

typeset by Nestor Latronico
New York, N.Y.

Manufactured in the United States of America

to Charles, Bernard
and Sandra

But often, in the din of strife,
There rises an unspeakable desire
After the knowledge of our buried life;
A thirst to spend our fire and restless force
In tracking out our true, original course;
A longing to inquire
Into the mystery of this heart which beats
So wild, so deep in us—to know
Whence our lives come and where they go.

Matthew Arnold
1852

CONTENTS

Contents

The Patient's Attempt to Resolve the Interactional Pathology of the Bipersonal Field • Psychotherapeutic Techniques Related to Dreams • The Comprehension of the Latent Content of a Dream • Dreams as Reflections of Unconscious Fantasy and Unconscious Perception • The Functions of Dreams Within the Bipersonal Field

The Therapist's Incomplete Interpretations • Their Intrapsychic and Interactional Implications • The Intrapsychic and Interactional Consequences of an Ongoing Unrepaired Frame • Sectors of Therapeutic Misalliance and the Development of a Misalliance Cure • The Therapist as a Pathological Container for the Patient's Contents • Communicated Memories • Their Relationship to Unconscious Fantasies and Unconscious Perceptions • A Shift in the Bipersonal Field Toward the Patient's Intrapsychic Conflicts • The Patient's Efforts to Projectively Identify into the Therapist

Interactional Symptoms and Resistances • The Therapist's Interventions as Products of the Bipersonal Field • Attempts to Resolve a Misalliance • The Therapist's Attempts to Drive the Patient Crazy • The Adaptive and Maladaptive Aspects of the Therapist's Containing Functions • Psychosomatic Symptoms and Containing Functions

PREFACE

The step from my initial clinical treatise, *The Technique of Psychoanalytic Psychotherapy* (Langs, 1973a, 1974), to the present volume may at first glance seem more a leap across an impassable chasm than the pursuit of a relatively uncharted but negotiable trail. The illusion of distance and disparity is undoubtedly exaggerated by the fact that the present volume is appearing some months before my companion study of the psychoanalytic literature on the patient-analyst interaction (Langs, in press a). This work will reveal the pathways I have traveled through the literature over the past two years to arrive at the present point in my thinking. On the other hand, the very crucial clinical byways that have brought me to this juncture are only hinted at in my recent papers (Langs, 1975a, b, c), although the direction of my clinical thinking is in evidence.

In my two volume work on technique, I adopted, based on my empirical experiences, a strong adaptational approach—

one that I term the adaptational-interactional viewpoint. It is possible to find in that work my early ventures into the interactional dimensions of psychotherapy—and psychoanalysis—although it took several years of difficult but exciting clinical research to bring them to the present point of explicit articulation. Along the way, my recent papers have reflected efforts to probe some of the clinical consequences of this approach—while the present book is a bolder statement of its great potential.

As I have indicated elsewhere (Langs, in press a), upon the completion of my volumes on technique, my deepening clinical observations of the psychoanalytic and psychotherapeutic interactions led me into vast and relatively unexplored territories. These forays prompted the initiation of a new clinical volume. In the course of developing this work, I turned to an extensive study of the psychoanalytic literature, and soon became absorbed in the reading of many important contributions and in the discovery of many unknown and valuable papers. The literature proved to be so filled with riches, much of which had not been adequately tapped or appreciated, that I spent considerable time abstracting, criticizing, and reformulating this crucial body of work (Langs, in press a).

In this context, I want to specifically single out and acknowledge the paper by Madeline and Willy Baranger (1966) from which the title of the present volume has been taken. In my search for a metaphorical and figurative concept with which to describe the interplay between the interactional and the intrapsychic realms, and between the patient and the therapist or analyst, I found the bipersonal field concept to be extremely viable. And while I do not entirely subscribe to the Barangers' delineation of this area, and have attempted to modify and enrich the concept, and to develop aspects that were not covered in their presentation, I remain deeply indebted to them for the basic conceptualization and its great clinical and theoretical value.

Having completed my investigation of the psychoanalytic literature, I was eager to provide clinical material that would substantiate and expand the many ideas I had crystalized. There had, after all, been a constantly deepening interplay between my exploration of the literature and my ongoing clinical observations. I felt uncomfortable with the initial impression that so many of my new formulations had been derived from the elaboration—however original—of the ideas of others. In actuality, my own clinical studies had played an equally decisive role in the development of my thinking. In casting about for a solution to this dilemma, I turned to the most recent series of tapes that I had made for Jason Aronson, Inc. It appeared that it might be feasible to transcribe and update this material, and that these transcriptions might prove to be a rather exciting means by which I could offer some pertinent clinical observations.

It soon became evident that I had found a most unusual and rewarding vehicle for the presentation of psychoanalytic ideas. The seminars transcribed here had originally been selected to explore the basic dimensions of psychoanalytic psychotherapy; and they had done so entirely through clinical presentations drawn from extensive process notes. Each of the five presentations had been selected because it dealt with a major aspect of psychotherapeutic technique. However, the clinical material brought us back repeatedly to issues related to the therapeutic interaction—and this area became the overriding focus of our discussions.

The original recordings of these seminars were edited primarily to protect the anonymity of the patient and the therapist, and to afford me an opportunity to elaborate occasionally upon some of the spontaneous comments made in response to the presentation. It is to be stressed that the clinical material was always presented sequentially, and that this provided us with an opportunity both to make and to validate predictions and formulations as we went along. This aspect has not been altered in the present transcriptions, although they have

been further edited to affort additional anonymity to both patient and therapist, and to offer me a final opportunity to update and clarify my ideas.

For me, the original seminars and their subsequent rework-
ing was a most stimulating and gratifying experience. By dis-
pensing with formalities and the usual concer for thorough
systematization, these presentations offer a series of living patient-therapist interactions that truly breathe life into theory,
and excitement into learning and teaching. The presenting
therapists came from several different settings; all were in the
process of learning psychotherapy. The discussants were their
colleagues; and their patients were being seen under the aus-
pices of one or another clinic. I wish to offer my tribute and
gratitude to these dedicated therapists and to the patients
with whom they worked. The therapists candidly shared with
me their struggles with their patients. They inevitably revealed their vulnerabilities and at the same time, their
strengths. For their part, the patients displayed a rich unconscious perceptiveness and creativity, and it was they who especially guided me toward enriching insights.

While this book is based entirely on material drawn from
psychoanalytic psychotherapy, I wish to state explicitly my
belief that this work is equally relevant to the psychoanalytic
situation. Without attempting here to establish my thinking
on the differences and similarities between these two therapeutic modalities (See Langs, in press a), I do wish to indicate
that, while I fully recognize significant distinctions between
the two forms, my own empirical observations have led me to
conclude that there are many crucial areas of overlap. In particular, the study of the therapeutic interactions in psycho-
analysis and psychotherapy indicates that the basic intrapsychic and interactional processes that prevail in each situation
are essentially comparable, and that there is a need to establish a well-defined—and thereby therapeutic—bipersonal
field for both treatments. Almost all of my present clinical
writings are based on the psychotherapeutic situation because

the clinical material currently available to me for publication derives solely from that modality (See Langs 1975 a, b, for clarification). I have no doubt whatsoever that similar presentations drawn from the psychoanalytic situation would lead to formulations comparable to those developed in this volume —to which certain specific qualifying distinctions would have to be added.

I wish to express my appreciation to Alice Rosenthal, who supervised the editing of this book, and to Letty Grierson, who did the immediate and most helpful editorial work. Sheila Gardner carefully and efficiently transcribed these tapes, while Anita Hunter and Jason Aronson encouraged their development. Above all, the participants in these seminars made this book possible.

I conceive of this volume as a major contribution toward the integration of the interactional dimension into classical psychoanalytic theory and technique (See Langs, in press a, for a full acknowledgment and discussion of earlier efforts in this direction). To the extent that the work that unfolds in these seminars presents new ideas, there is bound to be controversy, and this is healthy for psychoanalysis. At a time when many within and without the field believe that psychoanalysis has lost the vitality derived from discovery and active controversy, I would also like to think that this volume will stand with those works that demonstrate how far from the case this is.

Finally, it occurs to me as I complete this preface that it is quite fitting that this initial study of the therapeutic interaction take the form it does, a form which affords a view of the multileveled interactions between the patient and the therapist, the presented and his colleagues, and the seminar group and myself. It is my fervent hope that the reader too will be drawn into this interaction and will benefit deeply from the experience.

Robert Langs, M.D.
Rosyln Heights, N.Y.
January, 1976

Chapter 1

CREATING A THERAPEUTIC BIPERSONAL FIELD

THE THERAPEUTIC INTERACTION IN AN INITIAL HOUR •
THE INTERACTIONAL AND INTRAPSYCHIC CONSEQUENCES
OF A PREMATURE TERMINATION AND CHANGE IN THERA-
PIST • ISSUES RELATED TO THE FRAMEWORK OF THE PSY-
CHOTHERAPEUTIC SITUATION • DEALING WITH INTRA-
PSYCHIC AND INTERACTIONAL RESISTANCES • THE
INTRAPSYCHIC PATHOLOGY OF THE PATIENT AND THE IN-
TERACTIONAL PATHOLOGY OF THE BIPERSONAL FIELD

L:* Today's seminar is on the subject of the initial session in psychotherapy. It is my intention to allow the patient who will be presented to us—and hopefully the therapist as well—to teach us some of the fundamental techniques related to the first hour, and to show us something about the development of the therapeutic relationship and the bipersonal field in which it takes place. As we listen, then, let's try to consider not only some of the usual clinical issues that come up in the first hour, but let's also keep an eye on the unfolding relationship between the patient and the therapist, on their interaction and on the ways in which the two of them develop the therapeutic setting. With this as our orientation, and with a readiness to consider other issues as they are introduced by the patient and therapist, let us begin with the presentation.

T: I introduced myself to the patient in the waiting room and then said we would walk to my office, which was

* L=Langs; T=Presenting Therapist; D=Discussant

some small distance away. We started down the hall and she looked around and said, Oh, is this a new paint job? She was referring to the hallway we were walking along, which has actually been painted very recently, and she said, I guess it really must be, because I used to come here before, in a way, to see Dr. X—this referred to her previous therapist who had transferred this patient to me when he left the clinic. So, I said something to her like, So, there have been changes here since you came last time?

L: Okay, so there was an exchange of words in the hallway on the way to the first session. Let's search for some principles of technique related to it. First of all, what did you have in mind as you responded?

T: Well, I thought she was saying that her therapy had been interrupted and this was the way she used to walk with her former doctor, and now implicitly she was saying she had a new person, a new therapist, and that the first thing she noticed was the new paint. I was sort of new also. So, I don't know what purpose I had for my answer . . . I guess I was just sort of agreeing with what she had said—that things were different now.

D: Without picking up on the affect that she was bringing out? What affect was it—was it anger, hurt, disappointment?

L: What do you mean?

D: Anger, hurt, disappointment . . .

L: Would you have said something about her having feelings of that kind in the hallway?

D: No.

L: Oh. Let us just orient ourselves by commenting on what the therapist did. I'll try to spell out a couple of principles. The therapist chose, while listening to the material, both in terms of its manifest and latent content, to simply take it on the surface, and rather than be silent, she decided to respond to the surface qualities of the patient's comments with some kind of reality response of her own—in order to convey to the patient a sense of cordiality. I think that is a matter of personal preference to most therapists. I think some would be quite silent in response to these comments, and unless the patient asked a specific question, they could both be comfortable in that silence. Other therapists might want to say something like: Well, yes, they just recently repainted it. This would be addressed to the reality and would convey what has been termed a human response.

Now, if we are going to be thinking of the development of the framework of the therapeutic relationship and the creation of a therapeutic bipersonal field, there will be a preference for a response in which the therapist either maintains his silence or at most nods to the patient. I think it would be rather awkward to indicate to the patient that you would only discuss whatever is on her mind once the two of you were in the office, although you might want to do so if the patient attempted to carry on conversations like this again and again. But when you have in mind the creation of a special therapeutic climate, you begin to realize that your responses must have some other basis than social amenities, and that there are some basic technical principles involved.

I don't want to anticipate too much at this point, but I will point out that you have two initial tasks that many have seen as being in opposition, although this does not have to be the case. On the one hand, you want to set up an atmosphere of cordiality, while on the other hand you have to create conditions of necessary frustration in order to develop a viable bipersonal field. There are also certain essential limits and boundaries needed in psychotherapy. Clinically, I have found that treatment must be established within a definitive framework, and if you don't develop it and indicate its nature from the outset, there will be repercussions—that I promise you; that any patient will promise you.

I will add, too, that this basic concept of setting clear-cut limits is one of the most unpopular ideas that I have developed from my clinical observations. It immediately seems both petty and rigid to most therapists, but I hope that the clinical material that we will be hearing will help each of you to decide whether this idea is arbitrarily rigid —as I am certain it is not—or if it is supported by our own repeated clinical observations and reflects the actual needs of the patient.

However, let me add that if the therapist decides to respond just briefly with a remark or two that is on the surface seemingly innocuous, based on the belief that it would be overly severe to ignore the patient's comments —a position we need not accept—he then has a therapeutic responsibility. And this is perhaps one of the most crucial points; what is this responsibility? What is the therapeutic task that has to be carried out? I would say that it is important that this be established in the very first session.

D: I think that it has to be pursued once they get to the office—looked into in more depth.

L: We'll take that as the point. The patient will almost never bring it up again. That will be it, as far as the patient is consciously concerned. The therapist has the responsibility to communicate implicitly to the patient that, while he or she has every intention of being cordial, there are certain boundaries to the relationship. I believe that they are absolutely crucial to the psychotherapeutic situation and that you have an entirely different experience with the patient, depending on how you set up these boundaries—and I will demonstrate that to you when we get to it. So, in order to create the proper setting, my general inclination is to recommend that you be as relatively silent outside of the session as possible; to respond only if you have to, and then with some small comment. But, you must be certain to get back to it in the session—and to do it in a particular way. If you do it in a very offensive way, you will say implicitly to the patient, What was this business about the paint in the hall? Come on. No more of that stuff. Or you can implicitly say to the patient, Look, this is psychotherapy, and in psychotherapy everything that comes up in the treatment has to be explored, has to be spoken about. Now, you, for whatever reason, made some comments before we got to the session, before the session began—what comes to mind about it? If you don't do this, you are letting the patient unconsciously know that you sanction an extension of the relationship beyond the confines of the office, into the hallway. This indicates that you are willing to extend the boundaries and this will create a particular climate. We will see with this patient what happens when you do this, though it also depends on how you happen to deal with it. In principle, one tries to be relaxed, and one tries to be relatively silent, recognizing that this is an extension of the boundaries that has unconscious meanings to the patient.

So, we listen for manifest and latent content from the beginning. Let's try to develop possible meanings for this particular communication. In order to do so, we want to translate the manifest content into the latent content, and for that we need the context; that is, we need a very basic concept here, that of the *adaptive context*. This refers to the main event—inner and outer experience—that the patient is adjusting and responding to, which is here, of course, that it's a first session with a new therapist. This contains many implications related to being transferred, the previous realistic hurts, their extension into unconscious fantasies, and the fantasies and conflicts evoked by beginning with a new therapist. So, the session itself is one adaptive context for every first hour; it is part of the adaptive context that we use in order to understand the patient's communications.

Notice, too, that we are alrealy dealing with a basic ground rule regarding the framework of psychotherapy, that is, where the patient and therapist communicate. So, in the context of this first session and the transfer, let's speculate about some of the unconscious meanings of this communication from the patient. First, we might recognize that her remarks have to do with the hospital, so that you know she is not far from talking about her conscious and unconscious fantasies about that situation; she is talking about the new paint, and things not being familiar. That is the content, but there is another point. She spoke of these things before she got to the office, so in addition to the content we have the location; what could the unconscious meanings be of the fact that the patient made these comments on the walk to the office?

D: Testing—like testing the limits?

L: Testing the limits, yes. That's one thing that patients do from the beginning.

D: Maybe in some way, the patient by talking in the hall was attempting to establish some relationship with the therapist other than a therapeutic one.

L: Right, so it's both of these; both comments are related. Now, if we put these two ideas together, we'd say: the patient is communicating an unconscious wish to have a relationship with the therapist that extends beyond the usual boundaries of the therapeutic relationship. Now, in the light of the fact that she just got "kicked out" of the office of a previous therapist, who totally deserted her, you can begin to get a feeling that maybe this isn't to be taken so casually, because it may very well and probably does have a very deep, unconscious meaning. Maybe she's saying: I've just been destroyed by another therapist; will you at least give some special compensation?

So you see how the least little thing in psychotherapy can have very deep meanings, and how we don't take lightly anything that goes on between the patient and the therapist. It could be the crucial communication and it usually is, you see. So the patient is asking, will I be able to get something special, and she is sort of testing out how you will respond. Will you set the boundaries by not answering her; will you answer her and not set boundaries and give her this gratification? If you do answer, in order not to be totally cold right off, will you later establish the boundaries and let her know what they are; or will you not do so?

Now I realize that I am commenting rather extensively before we hear much material from the patient. I'm doing this because we have not been over the principles of technique pertinent to this area before, and because perhaps if we establish those principles clearly, we will have a chance to see if the material from the patient supports them. I can tell from your faces that you are somewhat taken aback by this lengthy commentary on a seemingly innocuous remark made in the hallway on the way to a first session. Of course, if the patient herself does not on some level and in some important way refer to this interchange during her session, I will seem to have made quite a fuss about something relatively minor. However, my own clinical experience indicates that virtually every single patient in psychotherapy will test out the boundaries and framework of the therapeutic situation—the bipersonal field—in the first session and actually throughout treatment.

In fact, there is another important factor here in addition to this patient's apparent wish to obtain special reparation for the hurt contained in the ill-timed loss of her first therapist—which you will note is actually a modification of the framework in itself, since it constitutes a premature termination of the treatment based on the needs of the therapist rather than on a mutually agreed upon and appropriate termination based on the needs of the patient. The patient's attempts to quickly modify the framework may well be designed as a means of disrupting the therapeutic work and deriving inappropriate de-

fensive reinforcement from the therapist. Let's just keep
that in mind and see if we can document this idea with
this particular patient. I might mention that Viderman
in a recent paper (1974) has also discussed this very phenomenon, of testing the frame as it occurs in psychoanalysis. So, let's keep an open mind and see if the framework of the bipersonal field is a crucial component or
not, and then we can decide whether we can deal with it
relatively naively or whether we will have to utilize some
clear-cut, therapeutic, technical principles in order to
establish and maintain it.

I want to also make clear that recognizing the importance of the framework is not meant to convey that the
therapist should adopt a stern or anxious approach. If
you develop a clear idea of the therapeutic importance of
the framework—something that we will discuss as we go
along—then you are able to recognize that impingements
on the part of the patient in this area have extensive therapeutic implications, and that it is possible for the therapist to respond in keeping with some sound therapeutic
principles and to be quite firm and yet non-destructive.
As therapists, we must quickly learn that therapeutic
humanness and concern has some very special characteristics.

So, in principle, a kind of accepting facial expression
might serve the purpose of conveying a human response,
while simultaneously indicating implicitly to the patient
that you have the capacity to develop boundaries and to
create a necessary framework for the therapeutic interaction. If, on the other hand, you have responded verbally, it is essential to the development of this very sensitive area—and we will see just how sensitive patients are
to the nuances of the framework—to bring up this outside interchange in the session. In this way, you reestablish the boundaries and avoid a misalliance effected by
this discussion in the hallway, one that affords the patient transference gratifications such as the satisfaction

of her erotic or symbiotic unconscious fantasies and wishes. You are also thereby conveying to the patient the special quality of the therapeutic relationship, designed for the special interactional experience that will take place within the bipersonal field. You are creating a special situation that enables the patient to convey derivatives of unconscious fantasies and introjects related to the intrapsychic conflicts on which her neurotic or other symptoms are based, a situation that renders such derivatives available for the kind of therapeutic work toward insight and inner change that can occur in psychotherapy.

Here, we are already talking about the means through which the therapist begins to develop a proper kind of therapeutic alliance with his patient—another subject that we should get into as we go along. Well, I've gone on for quite a bit, but I did want to establish a generally predictive framework for our listening. Now, let's get back to some clinical material.

T: I gave the patient directions where to meet me in the future, and we went into my office. The patient sat down and right away started talking. She asked, Do I have to come twice a week? I wasn't expecting it. I only came once a week with Dr. X. I don't think I need it now. I wanted it with him, but it couldn't be arranged then and most of the problems that I started with seem to be a lot better so now I don't really think I need twice a week.

Actually, she had been assigned to me for twice weekly therapy and had been informed of this by the clinic.

L: And you said to her, Look, you're my first patient. What do you want from me? Nobody cooperates with me. (Laughter.) All right. How would you deal with this? (Pause.) That's the manifest content; anybody have any thoughts about latent content and other implications?

D: Some negation? Also, she wanted a close relationship with the former therapist, but she's also saying, Now that

I've got a relationship with you, and you want me to come more often, I'm not ready yet for such a close relationship.

L: When we discuss these problems, you'll find that I will ask of you to always develop the adaptive context and the patient's response to it. You know, just identifying fantasies is not sufficient; it really doesn't tell us enough; it doesn't do the job. So you're saying that the adaptive context may be her anxieties about the therapist and getting to know the therapist. Is there any other way of thinking of this material?

D: She might have been hurt. Her former therapist had left her, so perhaps she's not so willing to extend herself into a deeper relationship than she had before.

T: She had wanted twice a week with her first therapist but they couldn't arrange it.

D: So she was not willing to extend herself as much as formerly.

L: Right, she's saying that the adaptive context is not only the anxiety of meeting her new therapist, but also is the reaction to her former therapist. But what's the most striking quality?

D: That she had wanted therapy twice a week and now she is saying she doesn't want it twice a week.

L: Yes, but what quality? You're talking about the quality of guardedness. I think there is a different quality: the one I made the joke about, which is what?

D: She was testing the therapist.

L: Testing? What else? Testing can cover a lot of territory. Let's be more specific. How did you feel? I preempted your feelings.

T: She seemed provocative to me.

L: Yes, she's being provocative. Isn't that the most striking aspect? How did you feel when she came in and said, Do I have to come twice a week; what's this whole business about twice a week? And here you've been told, See her twice a week—which she probably knows on some level. How did you feel?

T: She came in and she sort of threw this at me. That . . . who needs you twice a week? I'm not even sure I want to see you once.

L: Okay, so you felt provoked and rejected right off. The first level, not that it necessarily has to be the most meaningful one, should be how you feel. Start there, because what you are experiencing of course is in some way related to what the patient wants you to experience. Now, you may distort this, and you may experience subjectively things that may go beyond what the patient wants you to experience. Distortions come from your own idiosyncratic reactions and your own problems, but by and large, there is always a kernel of truth in your subjective reactions. If that valid nucleus of your inner response gets confirmed in the material from the patient, then you can interpret something based on it to the patient. Unless it's an emergency, which is what this begins to shape up as. Then you'll have to do it just based on how you feel, with less material from the patient. But we have some time here; we'll see. The point is that she comes in like gangbusters. She's attacking, she's angry, she's trying to provoke, she's trying to give you a difficult time. So what does that have to do with the adaptive context that you were developing?

D: She was dropped by her previous therapist, and I wonder if this is a displacement of anger from the previous therapist.

L: Yes, unless she didn't like your answer about the paint job, I think we have every reason to believe that this patient is in a rage over what happened with her previous therapist. Now, your concept that this rage toward Dr. X has been displaced onto the present therapist is a sound one. You are describing a basic intrapsychic mechanism and defense of the patient—displacement. Actually, this mechanism is basic to the development of transference expressions—a concept that we will soon discuss.

However, while displacement is the key intrapsychic mechanism, there is also a central interactional mechanism that is demonstrated here. While I don't want to get into an extensive discussion, let's at least introduce the concept. Interactionally, this patient appears to be making an effort at *projective identification*. Now, why do I say that? Well, projective identification is an interactional effort to put one's own inner contents into someone else, in order to manage these inner contents externally and to possibly benefit from the efforts at management undertaken by the other person. Notice that I am stressing that it is an interactional effort—an actual attempt to generate some kind of inner state and response in another person. I am not saying that the patient will create a state that is identical to his own in that other person; the object has a full opportunity to accept or reject what is being placed into him, and to process these contents according to his own needs. Notice too that this is a different concept from a projection, which is an intrapsychic mechanism—as is displacement—in which an individual attributes to someone else aspects of his own inner state and contents without making actual, interactional efforts to put these contents into the other person.

Now, with this patient we could hypothesize something like the following: she has been dumped by her previous therapist and she feels angry, helpless, and abused. She comes into her session with her new therapist and immediately balks at a proposed arrangement for the frequency of her sessions. She is, as we agreed, giving the therapist a hard time and actually attempting to create in the therapist an inner state that is not unlike her own. She is attempting to put into the therapist her own anger, frustration, and helplessness—and you can be sure that she will observe how the therapist handles the contents that she has been asked to contain.

I bring all of this up because I think that this is a situation in which you can get a feeling for an effort at projective identification, and we can see if the patient's associations confirm this type of interactional effort. It is always important to validate any formulation with the patient's subsequent association, and this is especially true in regard to interactional mechanisms and the subjective responses of the therapist. It is also important that the therapist be aware of what the patient is attempting to put into and stir up within him, so he can interpret such efforts at projective identification, rather than unconsciously sharing them with the patient and thereby creating a sector of misalliance—a shared blind spot or pathological interaction—and become involved in what Grinberg (1962) has called a projective counteridentification. But, things are getting a bit too complex for this early in the session and in our study of the therapeutic interaction.

So, let's pause now and get some perspective. Implicit in what I am saying is that from the outset, the patient's communications are determined by her adaptive tasks—the adaptive context. While many things may have happened since the patient terminated with her previous therapist, we find it safe to assume that one adaptive context for her reactions in this initial session with her present therapist is her experiences with Dr. X. We are therefore attempting to comprehend the initial communications from the patient in this context, and to determine its unconscious sources and meanings. This does not imply that we will neglect any more surface and realistic considerations, since we will be prepared for additional conscious reasons why this patient wants to be seen just once weekly. However, we will not simply accept such surface thinking and will attempt to understand her response in depth. Here we are taking an adaptational and interactional approach to our understanding of the patient, and we will find that this is consistently necessary in every psychotherapy.

There is, however, an additional point that we shouldn't overlook in what is often a welcome focus on a previous therapist—namely, any possible contribution to this initial problem from the present therapist. I had earlier suggested that the therapeutic bipersonal field, in which the patient and therapist will interact, depends on a secure and clearly defined framework. I had indicated that patients are extremely sensitive in this area, and that they actually welcome such a framework since it serves their therapeutic hopes, and yet they attempt to break it because of the anxiety entailed in going through a true therapeutic experience. However I have postulated that as soon as some implicit issue regarding the framework arises, it will become an important adaptive task and context for the patient.

So, while we may all think that the patient had the frequency of her sessions on her mind long before she met her present therapist, the fact that she begins her session by raising another issue related to the framework actually indicates that this entire area is of great concern to her. I can tell you from repeated clinical experience that this is rather typical and by no means the exception; that is, once an issue regarding the frame of the bipersonal field has arisen, the patient will very often begin a session with some allusion to a component of the framework—the ground rules and boundaries of the psychotherapy. This happens so consistently that I already feel confident that the patient is indeed working over the therapist's response to her efforts in the hall to immediately modify the framework and boundaries of the therapeutic relationship.

In this context, I want to also point out that it is best not to read a patient's chart, since this contaminates the one-to-one relationship, violates the confidentiality of the previous therapy, and is a unilateral modification of the frame. It provides the therapist with secrets that he must then conceal from the patient. It is preferable that the new therapist experience his relationship with the patient directly, allow the material to unfold from the patient, and recognize that he will be hearing a mixture of reality and fantasy and that his job will be to unravel the extent to which there is veridical perception and the extent to which the patient's unconscious elaborations and distortions have influenced her view of the prior therapy.

So, you listen to the patient, and respect what you hear. And I don't mean just consciously; I mean unconsciously as well. But all sorts of things go on with therapists in training and none of it is that great or that nice to experience for the patients. So on top of everything else a new therapist may inherit a sudden termination. Goodbye; my time is up; I've used you, I've spent you, and now I'm throwing you into the garbage. There'll be somebody to pick you up in six weeks or so.

And this is the patient you have in front of you. Now what do you expect, a saint? If she is a saint, then, you'd better start worrying about reaction formations. But somehow she has to adapt to it; she has to work it out. And there is no way she is going to do it nicely.

You can expect hell from all of your transfer patients. But if you remember that this is an adaptive context, then you are in a sound position. Instead of responding by saying, Goddam it, either you come twice a week or forget it, you can do some interpreting. That immediately shows the patient you're not being destroyed and you're not angry and not rattled, but you are capable of understanding. Then suddenly it strikes the patient that you're not like the other louse who abandoned her, but there is nothing in the world that is going to convince her of this distinction except a correct intervention—and this situation will need one quite soon.

Parenthetically, notice the language that I used. I called the first therapist a louse and maybe should have called him a bastard, and I said that he threw the patient into the garbage. Why did I talk this way? Well, whatever your personal fantasies may be, I do this in order to indicate how the therapist should think in his sessions with the patient. As he's attempting to define the adaptive context and to ascertain the patient's conscious and unconscious fantasies, he should be feeling and thinking, and doing it in plain language—because that is the stuff out of which fantasies are made. And while we attempt to maintain our self-boundaries as we engage in trial identifications with the patient, and attempt to empathize with his feelings and fantasies, our thinking should not be encumbered with technical notions but should flow plainly and directly. You will find throughout these seminars that I will attempt to use language in keeping with my own impressions of the inner state of the patient, and I might add that this is also the stuff out of which meaningful interpretations are made.

So, we're rather quickly involved here in a study of the relationship between interpretation and interaction—the connection between offering the patient cognitive insights and being a constructive figure for introjective identification. But let's not pursue that for the moment; let's get back to this patient's initial reaction: what heading does this come under? You read the section in my book (Langs, 1973a) on the goals of the first session. What are the goals and how does this relate to them?

D: Establishing the ground rules.

L: Definitely; it's related to the ground rules of psychotherapy, but what else?

D: Establishing the proper climate of treatment.

L: And related to that, establishing a sound therapeutic relationship—a therapeutic alliance. Here, notice that I'm stressing the importance of a valid interpretation in the creation of a sound alliance. When a previous therapist has been traumatizing, it is essential that the present therapist implicitly and inherently distinguish himself from his hurtful colleague. This is vital for the alliance, and it cannot be done through efforts at direct reassurance, which implicitly and unconsciously are inappropriate interventions and display a similarity to the previous therapist rather than serving as a means of making this distinction.

Coming back to this material, what else in this patient's behavior touches upon a goal of the first hour?

D: Not to create a misalliance.

L: Yes, but for the moment, I wouldn't put it quite that way.

D: Does the goal have something to do with engaging the patient?

L: Let's go back to the patient's behavior; what's the technical term for it? (Pause.) Well, it's usually called transference. There's another word that would come after it in terms of this particular behavior and what it represents.

Before you answer, since I have called her behavior— her refusal of twice weekly sessions—an expression of transference, let me clarify my meaning: often, what we term transference has significant nontransference elements. To the extent that this response on any level represents a reaction to the therapist's modification of the framework in his talk with the patient in the hallway, it has an unconscious veridical basis—a nontransference component. We would then have to wait and see the extent to which the patient is responding in a manner that is in keeping with the unconscious meanings of this transgression, and the extent to which she has unconsciously elaborated it through intrapsychic distortion. It seems likely from the intensity of her reaction that there is a large intrapsychic and distorted component, and that therefore, even in this particular context, this response is primarily transference-based. But it is best, then, to speak first of reactions to the relationship with the therapist, and to afterward sort out the transference and non-transference aspects.

The second consideration related to the transference component here concerns the displacement that we have postulated from the previous therapist. This is a type of transference that has been described by Sandler and his associates (1969, 1973) and by myself (Langs, in press). The displacement that accounts for the distortion has been made from a relatively recent figure—the previous therapist—onto the present therapist. We would postulate, however, that beyond the previous therapist lies an early childhood, parental figure. We want to be clear regarding our use of the term transference and its specific referrents, since most writers and analysts are quite vague in this regard. Remember that transference basically refers to an unconscious fantasy or introject that is inappropriately connected to the therapist. These unconscious processes may be expressed in some direct response toward him or the behavioral consequences may be displaced so that they are expressed toward another person. For the moment, the main point that I want to make is that the therapist must have the patient's associations in order to determine the latent content and unconscious basis for a reaction of the patient; only then can he clearly claim that it is primarily a transference response and identify its underlying nature.

So, for the moment, we are terming this a primarily transference reaction in what I call the classical sense of the term (Langs, in press), but we still have not identified another important feature of this response. What is it?

D: Acting in?

L: You're close, but it's not quite acting in. Acting in generally implies a gross enactment or behavioral transaction between the patient and the therapist within the session. Here, the patient is just saying something about what she wants. But, what does transference always become?

D: Resistance?

L: Resistance! This is what resistance is; what the word means. This isn't any welcome communication. What could be a clearer example of resistance than saying, I only want to come half the time? This is what resistance is about. Resistance can be much more subtle. But it can't be much more blatant—unless it is goodbye; that's the ultimate resistance. It's resistance. And one of the goals in the first session is to deal with resistance—if you wan to have a patient. Actually, that is usually the area of the first intervention. You help the patient with his resistances, and to modify them. So here's a patient who tells you that the first goal with her is going to be dealing with a resistance. Now, that's all very pretty in the way of principles, but how the hell are we going to do it? She hasn't said anything about the previous therapist; she hasn't said anything to help us. She's just come in with this complaint, and then fallen silent. What do you do?

Now, while we are thinking about how we are going to deal with this resistance, let's review some of the other goals of the first session. We want to get to a diagnosis and an assessment of the patient's problems and their background. We want to know something about the patient's assets and his liabilities. We want to find out if there are any acute problems, especially acute depressions and intense anxieties, and especially any type of suicidal possibility or potential; and we want, as we are discussing here, to pick up any of the patient's major resistances and deal with them, primarily through some kind of general, interpretive-like intervention. Often we have to limit ourselves to a confrontation with an evident resistance, so that we indicate to our patient that we are aware of his objections to treatment and of any major impediment that is unfolding; that very awareness can often be helpful. The discussion we are having also goes along with the assessment of preformed attitudes and fantasies of the patient which may have transference and nontransference qualities. We also assess the patient's capacity to work in therapy, in terms of her conscious co-operativeness but also in terms of the extent she communicates derivatives of unconscious fantasies. Over all, we are attempting to establish the therapeutic alliance and we will culminate any initial session with specific recommendations to the patient and, if these are accepted, with the delineation of ground rules of the therapy. Now, let's get back to the patient.

T: Here I said something.

L: Okay, before hearing the therapist's intervention, what might some of you have said here?

D: Well, you might make a confrontation to the patient related to her anger and to the way in which she is resisting or obstructing treatment.

D: That seems a bit premature and the patient might experience it as joining battle with her.

L: Yes, if the therapist intervenes without sufficient material to make a general interpretation, and responds with a confrontation, he is risking a sector of misalliance in which he and the patient exchange aggressive commentaries. As soon as the therapist joins battle in this way, he loses, and in fact, the patient might gain a misalliance cure. By that I mean that the patient would have her hostile transference needs gratified; she would thereby experience an interaction that repeats something inappropriate in her relationship with her previous therapist, and undoubtedly in her childhood with her parents. In this way her inner world—her hostile introjects— would be confirmed in the outside world—the responses of the therapist. In addition, if the therapist does become angry, the patient can justifiably put her own intrapsychic anger, and the conflicts and anxieties attached to it, into the therapist and find relief. The momentary alleviation of conflicts and symptoms in this kind of way is a phenomenon that I have termed a *misalliance cure* (Langs, 1975a).

D: I think it would be premature and really unnecessary to accept the decrease in sessions at this point.

L: I would agree with that. If the therapist waits a while, I feel confident that the patient will provide her with the derivatives related to this therapeutic problem that could enable her to formulate an interpretation. Even an empathic statement regarding the change from one therapist to another is premature, since it is not in the material from the patient for the moment.

The point is that we all agree that this resistance comes at the therapist before she knows anything about what is going on. We should have certain hunches about what is happening, based on our general knowledge of human beings and especially of patients, but we really don't know. Well, when we don't know, what do we do? First of all, we're silent—our basic and often unappreciated mainstay. And if there is a gap, or we feel that we must intervene, we ask the patient to fill us in. Actually, by being silent we are nonverbally asking the patient to tell us more, and doing it in a way that I prefer. That is, through our silence we're asking the patient to go on with her free associations—with her saying whatever comes to mind. This is basic to psychotherapy and is part of the framework and ground rules. Sure, there are some differences between the free associations that we get from patients in therapy and from those in analysis, but the basic request to the patient to say whatever comes to mind—to free-associate—still remain an essential component of the therapeutic situation if we are going to establish the kind of bipersonal field in which structural change through insight and constructive identifications will occur for the patient. So, our silence implies to the patient that she should continue to say whatever comes to mind.

Now, in the face of the adaptive context related to the initiation of the therapy—and these early resistances are also a major therapeutic context—we can safely assume that the patient's associations will have some relationship to these problems, and will help us to understand what is going on in the patient in connection with them. In fact, if the patient simply goes on with further reality rein- forcements, further concrete reasons for wanting to be seen once a week, we would meet considerable defensive- ness. However, we see that she is beginning to shift away from the realities, and we hope that she will continue in this direction. You see, if she goes on to manifestly talk about other things, we will be in a position, by using the adaptive context as an organizer, to derive latent content related to her wanting to come just once a week. The therapist's silence is an implicit directive to the patient to communicate in this way.

However, if you feel that the situation is awkward, and the patient becomes silent, then you can say to her some- thing like, You apparently have some very strong feelings about this. Before we decide anything, why don't you say whatever is on your mind, and we'll see where it goes.

You just want to get her to talk some more; that's all you have to do. You don't have to intervene in any other way at this point. The session is far from over. You don't challenge her and join battle, because then you're going to be destructive like the first therapist. Let's just get her to talk. I assure you that if she talks, she will give us the derivatives that we need. You must learn something from the very beginning. As resistant as the patient is, as much as she wants to destroy therapy, she wants even more to be cured. Patients—and therapists to some extent—are always divided like that. Now, one patient in a thousand will be so defensive that he really wants to destroy treat- ment, but you'll know that in a hundred ways and he'll still give you a couple of clues. Remember, our patients will let us know. In essence, you show patience, tolerance, and a wish to understand; then you wait for the patient to communicate further. So, how did you deal with it?

T: I said, Well, you've just come in and you obviously have some very strong feelings about this, so let's explore it a little further.

L: Okay, so that's what you did do. You said, let's explore it further. Which is fine. Let's see what happens.

T: So she says, Oh, it's really just a waste of time; if I come twice a week, it takes me an hour to get here and then I have to spend the time for the session and it takes me an hour to get back, and the whole day is taken up by this. And if I come twice a week, that means two days like that and I could use one of them to go to the beach. And also, if I came twice a week, then I have to not work an extra day. And I have a job and I'm going to go to school and I would like some time for myself. And she sort of hesitated. And she said: I think I made progress before. I couldn't go to school before, but now I'm back in school. And I'm working. I'm still somewhat confused about my boyfriend, but I'm still seeing him. And she sort of stopped. And she said, I moved out though. I was living with him but I moved back with my mother. So things seem to be going very well. And the she stopped.

L: So, what do you hear now? Just briefly.

D: Two things. Number one, she simply furthered the resistance. She simply went on to say, twice a week is bad, costs me time and effort, and all that. But then, she also said she's getting better; I really don't need it. But then she said, Well, I do have problems now; I still have problems with my boyfriend. Which is perhaps a derivative of wanting to be cured.

L: Yes, anything else?

D: Well, also in terms of the first session, it's kind of like bringing in another person to play off the relationship with the therapist—whatever that may stir up. So that's my point then. I left my boyfriend and I'm with my mother, which is: I left my male therapist and now I'm with a female therapist.

L: Well, let me just put it a little bit differently. The first
     thing she does then is she tries to reinforce the reason for
     the one session, the resistance, with further pieces of re-
     ality. And I would suggest that you have to respect some
     of these realities. You don't ever deny that it has uncon-
     scious meaning and that the unconscious motives are
     crucial, but if she has enough reality then the chances are
     that you're not going to modify her decision. In other
     words, if she is working, going to school, and it takes
     three hours for the session, you're going to be hard
     pressed—unless she gives you clear derivatives—to show
     and convince her that these other things are also operat-
     ing. But she then suddenly mentions something else,
     which has to do with the hypothesis that I offered: her
     previous treatment. Now, of all the things that she brings
     up, she brings up her previous treatment. She does also
     bring up her boyfriend and her mother, which we are go-
     ing to take cognizance of, but she says that the previous
     treatment helped her return to school, to get a boyfriend,
     and things are fine because she left the boyfriend and
     she's back with her mother. So, you begin to wonder—
     what does all that mean? So she starts off with the real-
     ity and hammers it home a little bit more. But now, she
     gets on to other things. So, she's starting to communicate
     her unconscious fantasies and motives.

         In response to the deepening of her communications,
     there is more that we can begin to formulate. First, no-
     tice the form of this deepening. We have for the moment
     a central adaptive context related to the transfer from
     one therapist to another, out of which the issue of the fre-
     quency of the sessions has arisen. I will leave aside for the
     moment the secondary adaptive context related to the
     patient's concerns about the boundaries of her relation-
     ship with this therapist, because it will complicate the
     discussion. Let's just be clear that it becomes a second
     adaptive context that is undoubtedly related to the first
     —the loss of Dr. X and the transfer to a new therapist—

and that we would ultimately, in interpreting the patient's response to these adaptive contexts, show her the connections between the two.

But, in the adaptive context of the transfer, the patient says that she wants to come just once a week. This creates a therapeutic context that organizes the therapist's listening, but it is one that has unconscious meanings that can only be understood in terms of the basic adaptive context available to us—the transfer. The patient first spells out a whole bunch of realistic reasons for wanting just a single session each week, and then she begins to talk about other things. It is this shift that we welcome, because it will be a means through which the patient will indirectly communicate her reactions to the transfer. By knowing the adaptive context and realizing that it is the organizer of the patient's reactions and communications, we can connect the themes in her associations to the adaptive context, and it is in this way that we arrive at latent content. This is really what we mean when we speak of *unconscious fantasies*—the working over of a given adaptive context through displacements, so that the adaptive efforts occur unconsciously. This is also our definition of *derivatives*—expressions of a given unconscious fantasy that are more or less disguised. You can review the relevant sections in my book (Langs, 1973a).

Now, getting back to this material, it has some hints—derivatives—of the unconscious fantasies and stirrings within this patient. She's telling us that at a time when her therapist was prematurely terminating her treatment, she left her boyfriend. Now, right off, we can say that this sounds like she was acting out the very thing that she was experiencing in the treatment, making that familiar shift from the passive victim to the active perpetrator. It also sounds like—that is, we are hypothesizing—a flight to the safety of her home and to the ties of her mother at a time when she was being traumatized. We have to remember that this apparently occurred before she knew she was going to have a woman therapist, so that we don't overinvest the return to her mother with unjustified meanings—it's important to stick with the material. However, it does hint at unconscious fantasies of revenge on the therapist, and this is in keeping with her decision not to have the twice-weekly treatment that had been recommended to her. For her, having one session a week is now, in part, a displaced revenge on her hurtful former therapist.

Now, with our sensitivity to interactional mechanisms, we can also suggest another component to her leaving her boyfriend. Remember, interactional mechanisms supplement intrapsychic mechanisms; the two realms interact and reinforce each other. Interactionally, it may very well be that the patient left her boyfriend in order to put into him her own feelings of helplessness, rage, abandonment, and the like. In that way, she could now manage this constellation of feelings outside of herself, and she would also have an opportunity to see how the boyfriend managed such hurts. This last effort has been written about by Wangh (1962), and he called it *the evocation of a proxy*—an effort to stir up and mobilize a set of responses in another person at a time when they are lacking in the subject. Here, the patient finds that she is deficient, let's say, in the necessary adaptive and ego resources needed to deal with the trauma of the loss of her therapist and the anxieties and conflicts that it is stirring up inside her. She put a similar problem into the boyfriend and borrows from him—introjectively identifies with—any adaptive resources reflected in his handling of it.

Now, we're getting rather speculative and probably will have little chance in this material to validate these ideas, so I won't take them further. However, notice that we had reason to postulate something quite similar to this kind of projective identification and evocation of a proxy in the patient's immediate refusal to see this ther-

apist twice a week. In fact, this may help us to understand why this was the very first thing she said—she
wanted to come at you suddenly and abruptly, because
this was a quality of what had happened to her and of
what is still disturbing her.

Coming back to basics, notice that as far as our making an assessment of this patient's ability to work effectively in therapy, we are learning something important
about her dynamic conflicts, her defenses, and even a little bit about the continuing problems that make her want
to go on with her treatment. We're also beginning to see
that she has the capacity to communicate meaningful
derivatives of unconscious fantasies; this kind of unconscious cooperation, so to speak, is a very important and
often overlooked dimension of the therapeutic alliance.
All right, it is time to get back to the clinical material;
let's see where she goes.

T: Her last sentence was, So things seem to be going well.
And then I asked her what she thought she would like to
continue working on now. She said that she felt she had
made some progress . . .

L: Well, you know, when she said, Things are going well,
she had left her boyfriend and gone back to her mother—
I would not have interrupted her at that point. I would
have been wondering just how well things were going and
suspecting that some problems were beginning to show
up indirectly. In addition, you were beginning to get derivatives and, on another level, she was beginning to talk
more freely. I think we see here your own struggle in
shifting your style as a therapist from an emphasis on
getting facts and focusing on reality, to getting derivatives and focusing on unconscious components, like unconscious fantasies and introjects. You have to begin to
value the indirect communications from your patients. If
you don't get derivaties related to her motivation for
wanting just one session, all the facts and surface
thoughts in the world are not going to give you a twice-a-

week patient, which is undoubtedly what she needs to be. So, she's starting to talk; let her talk. She's giving you material. She's offering something with latent meaning in talking of the struggle with the boyfriend, mother, and the rest.

T: She said, Well, I don't expect all my problems to be solved and my life to be perfectly smooth. That would be boring. I think I'm just a normal kid with a few problems. So I asked her if she could tell me a little bit about them and what was troubling her and what those difficult areas still were. And she said, Well, it's just so hard to repeat; it's very boring. I've already talked about it and don't the records say it all? So I said, It sounds like you feel frustrated having to start all over with a new person and covering what you feel to be old ground.

So she said, Yes, I do. Then she sort of stopped and said, Well, before, I couldn't do my school work. I had broken up with my old boyfriend, Bill, because I felt used. Then I moved in with a new boyfriend—Albert. I still liked Bill, though. And I thought about him a whole lot, but I didn't see him because I didn't want to be unfaithful to Albert. Finally, I moved back with my mother.

I wanted to find out more about that, so I said, How did that come about?

L: Up until this point, I think that what you did was quite good. That is, you took the wind out of her sails. You identified her feeling upset about the previous treatment; you showed some understanding of what was disturbing her—and it enabled her to communicate more to you. Now, came the crucial material. You see, out of your positive and empathic responses came the derivatives that you needed to understand what was going on unconsciously within her. That's a very crucial sequence. Then, in order to understand and evaluate your last intervention, we have to formulate the latent meaning of what she said. So, who will try to do this?

D: She mentioned something about looking at her records.

L: Yes, the question came up about looking at her records. And the therapist chose to ignore that and to simply point out that the patient was frustrated in having to repeat herself. Now, many would feel that this is an adequate way of dealing with that question. I myself would prefer a different kind of response, something to the effect that what would be crucial to her treatment is what transpired between the two of you. I would not answer her question directly, since to do that would actually be a way of modifying your anonymity; it is a self-revelation rather than an interpretive intervention. I would want to be secure in knowing that I had not looked at this patient's records and my communications with her would ultimately convey this implicitly to her. Even the manner in which I would respond to this particular comment would begin to express to the patient that I believed in the total confidentiality of our relationship and that I would maintain it however possible.

Actually, this is a complicated area, since this patient is being seen in a clinic and there are inevitable modifications in this aspect of the framework. After all, you are presenting her session here. However, you are actually involved in one of the two modifications of confidentiality that I think have justification—the other is a therapist's references to his patients to his own therapist or analyst. But remember that these reports will, because they relate to an essential part of the framework, result in some compromise of the bipersonal field, and of the therapeutic interaction, and even of the therapeutic outcome. You are presenting this material in an effort to learn how to do psychotherapy, and there is really no other way to learn this profession.

So, it is actually in the best interests of the patient to be hurtful—it's that kind of a compromise. Not that you ever tell the patient directly that you are presenting her case to a supervisor, or to someone else; that self-revelation would only further damage the framework, through a destructive modification of your anonymity. But nevertheless you are aware of the fact that you are presenting this material to someone, and that there is an interaction between yourself and a supervisor; this realization has an influence on what transpires between you and the patient. All of this is implicitly present in your interaction with the patient. Further, if the patient were to imagine that she is being presented to a supervisor, while again you should not respond with a direct clarification since that would also be a modification of the framework through a self-revelation, you could not treat her fantasies or beliefs that you are indeed making such a presentation as a piece of irrational craziness or transference distortion. You would have to work with it in a way that recognizes that the patient actually has many reasons to suspect that this is the case. The transference component would come solely through any subsequent distortions that the patient makes of this valid belief.

This is all very tricky and difficult, especially for a beginning therapist. Even more experienced analysts have problems in this area; that's why we need some ground principles, even though they are relatively lacking in the literature. Your goal is to establish a secure framework for the bipersonal field and the therapeutic interaction that is to take place within it. You want to secure this framework to the greatest extent possible.

Her reference to her records is far from innocuous. It's another comment related to the framework and the boundaries of your relationship with her; so it is becoming evident that this is of great concern to her. Now, some of this comes from the conversation in the hall, but something else undoubtedly set that off as well. It must be coming in part from the premature termination of her first treatment. That is a traumatic modification of the framework, in that it is an untimely termination of her treatment—something not at all in her interest—and a modification of an implicit component of the frame that implies that you will continue therapy until the patient has adequately resolved her intrapsychic problems. There may be other things that prompted her concern with the frame, and we should remember that every patient in therapy will test out that area from the outset.

You should also realize that if you were to indicate that you had indeed reviewed the record of her previous treatment, you would be telling her quite plainly that her therapy with Dr. X was not at all subjected to total confidentiality. In addition—and this is quite crucial—you would be indicating that you participated in a violation of confidentiality, and this will in turn create a negative and destructive image of yourself that the patient would subject to introjective identification and then work over. All of this is overlooked by therapists who think in a naive way that they ought to know as much as they can about a patient. Actually, more important than any information that you would learn from a record related to the patient —and I seriously doubt that anything written there could be really significant or more important than what transpires between you and the patient—is totally overshadowed by the necessity of establishing a secure and proper framework for the therapeutic process. These policies have been followed in the past because the importance of the framework has not really been appreciated.

Now returning to what happened between you and the patient, your intervention actually adheres to the principles that I just spelled out, and the way in which you intervened showed considerable sensitivity. This is why you received a considerable reward in what followed. But then, if you have panned gold, you have to know how to recognize it. Now what is the gold here?

D: Change came up. She began to talk about numerous changes and her feelings about change. For example, she said she had a boyfriend and she had felt used—something we postulated before. You said that when the therapist leaves a patient, the patient feels used. And then she went on to another boyfriend and she was faithful to him. She didn't try to get back to the other one. Then another change—to her mother.

L: Okay, so how would you boil it down—you are picking up on the important segment of the material. What are the unconscious communications contained in it?

T: Well, she said that she went to the new boyfriend because she felt used by the old one, but she continued to think about the old one even while she was with the new one, because he was very important to her.

L: Right, you're identifying derivatives. That's the first thing. You're telling me that each of these are derivatives of both her fantasies and her perceptions related to the first therapist. Mind you, they're both. Because I would not call "being used" an unconscious fantasy. I think, if anything, it's more a perception than a fantasy of what happened. She was used; let's not kid ourselves. Remember too—you can only decide what is fantasy if you know what is reality. There is always a mixture of the two and you must know which is which. If you said to this patient, you had this fantasy that you were being used here—implying, you're crazy, you're insane, and you must modify that—you would be doing a great injustice to her. A great injustice. If on the other hand, you said something to her about feeling used, you could then clarify how she extended that experience intrapsychically. You could then put your addendum this way: You felt used, like a boyfriend who sleeps with you and discards you. That is her elaboration of the therapist's misuse of her. You were used in a certain sense, and for you it had a sexual meaning—that last is the fantasy component. You must always be able to delineate your comment in terms of the reality aspects and then get to the fantasy element. You are thereby separating out transference from nontransference, fantasies from reality, and helping the patient to develop her capacity to make distinctions regarding inner and outer reality, and about what is distorted and non-distorted. Here, you might want to look at my papers on the patient's unconscious perceptions of the therapist where I go into the issue of the extent to which the patient's communications related to the therapist are veridical, and the degree to which they are not (Langs, 1973b, 1975c).

Now, since I have been thinking along with this patient in very plain words—I do not think in technical terms except occasionally when I am abstracting something that has developed, or discussing it in a seminar such as here —I want to try to convey this patient's central unconscious perception of fantasy as I think she's experiencing it. I want to do this so that you can see how we take an adaptive context and the patient's associations, as she shifts away from that context on a manifest level to talk about something else, and put it all together in a meaningful way and formulate what we call an unconscious fantasy—more correctly, an admixture of reality and fantasy. So, the patient may be thinking something like this: My previous therapist used me. He took me as he would a girlfriend and used me to his satisfaction, and then he discarded me. But even though he used and abused me, I still think of him; I still have great loyalty to him. I am not like he is—I don't do things like he did. I'm loyal; if I'm with one person, I stay with that person. I don't dump him; I don't discard him. Oh, I will leave him if he hurts me, but somewhere in my heart I'm still loyal to him. But even so, I know something about loyalty and despite these feelings, I don't hurt the person that I'm committed to; I'm not unfaithful.

Now, it is only by appreciating the sequence of events, and the interaction between this patient and both her former and her present therapists, that we are able to really understand the unconscious meanings of the patient's communications. We haven't as yet connected them to an intrapsychic problem within the patient, or even begun to trace out their genetic roots. And there is good reason for this: right now the major pathology of the field has been developed from the first therapist's hurtful termination of this patient.

Now, in saying that, let me introduce the concept of the bipersonal field here since it's a way of conceptualizing the psychotherapeutic relationship and interaction that I will use throughout these seminars. I actually developed this group of ideas by observing sequences of the kind that we have just heard. The term *bipersonal field* is one that I have borrowed from the Barangers (1966) who used it in a paper on insight in psychoanalysis. I had already begun to think of the therapeutic situation as taking place within a frame and within a container, and the bipersonal field concept really interdigitated beautifully with the clinical formulations that I was developing at the time.

In essence, this concept indicates that psychotherapy takes place within a clearly defined physical and psychological field or space—something that Viderman (1974) also recently wrote about. This field is defined by the framework which not only sets off the therapeutic situation from all other realities, but also gives it its specific characteristics, attributes, and powers. The two polarities of the field are, of course, the patient and the therapist, and the processes within the field relate to their interaction. Their interaction takes place along what I have called the interface of the bipersonal field, and the location of that interface depends on the moment-to-moment contributions to the field from both the patient and the therapist.

I am not going to develop this concept very much more until we have some further specific clinical material, since I don't want this to get too abstract. The present situation with this patient does, however, bring up one immediate reward that comes to us from this conceptualization. We don't have any preconceived notions about the pathology of the bipersonal field—that is, we don't necessarily assume that the main contribution to this pathology will come from the patient, although we certainly hope that it will. We are prepared to find moments when the therapist places more pathology into the field than the patient, and even perhaps find that the patient at such times—almost always unconsciously—will incorporate this pathology and attempt to modify it—which is tantamount to an unconscious effort to cure both himself and the therapist. In fact, I think we are seeing such a process in this very material. I would have to call it an unconscious attempt to cure the clinic and, to some extent, the previous therapist, more than any apparent effort for the moment to assist the present therapist with something destructive that she has done.

This is not a very surprising development—the patient still has work to do with what happened to her with Dr. X. What makes this particularly interesting for the moment is that we cannot say that this is based on a countertransference problem within Dr. X, although it may have been compounded by such difficulties. It is only countertransference in its broadest sense of all unneeded traumas to the patient, in that it may not stem from unresolved intrapsychic conflicts within Dr. X, but have been dictated by the realities of his commitment to work for a given period in the clinic—and nothing else. However, for the patient, this is hardly any compensation.

This is again where the bipersonal field concept helps us. The former therapist's departure clearly disturbed the bipersonal field of both therapies, and the patient now has a need to resolve that disturbance—including those aspects of this disruption that she has introjected. And she undertakes these therapeutic efforts rather exquisitely by the two means that are available to her, the same basic tools that are at the disposal of the therapist: by an unconscious—that is, indirect—general interpretation (remember that the therapist is in a position to offer more specific and, of course, conscious interpreta-

tions to the patient; these are two of the differences between himself and the patient within the bipersonal field
—and there are many other differences and similarities
that we will get to later) and at the same time by offering
herself as a model for positive introjective identification
—a curative model.

The general interpretation went something like this: I
want you to realize that Dr. X has not been a person of
integrity. He has done something inappropriate that he
should learn to manage and control. He has been inappropriately destructive.

Now, in addition, the patient is saying something to
the therapist about Dr. X having been seductive and using her like a girlfriend, but it is not clear as yet where
this comes from and what it means. The overall effort is
what I have called *unconscious interpretation*. The adaptive context is the therapeutic misalliance evoked by Dr.
X's premature termination of her therapy and in a sense,
the intervention constitutes the patient's efforts to have
him—in the form of the present therapist—modify this
destructive interaction through insight. Now, I am well
aware that for the moment this does not touch upon an
intrapsychic conflict and a neurotic piece of behavior by
the therapist, and this is all to the good since we will have
many opportunities to discuss this more usual type of
problem. What you can see here is that for this patient,
the premature termination of her therapy was a senseless
act and is something very much like a neurosis—it is inappropriate to reality in that it totally ignored her needs.

Now, in conveying all of that to this therapist, the intervention implies that the patient has understood something about Dr. X, and on that level she already offers
herself as a model of a good therapist. This model is reinforced by the content of her associations—her intervention—which submits to the present therapist—as well as
to the memory of Dr. X—a constructive image for introjective identification, with which the patient undoubtedly

hopes to modify the possibility that this therapist will behave in any way similar to the destructive Dr. X.

As if things were not complicated enough already, let's also remember that at the same time that the patient is offering herself as a curative model, and is offering therapeutic interventions, she indicates that she had made an introjective identification with the destructive part of Dr. X, which undoubtedly reinforced her own inner destructiveness, and she left her boyfriend. We see here something that is absolutely characteristic of both the patient and the therapist, although hopefully it will be in different proportions for each of them. There is the wish to cure and be cured, and there is the wish to remain ill and to do harm. In fact, even in the patient's or therapist's most destructive communications and hurtful interactional efforts, there is a kernel of therapeutic intention and hope.

Let's also get back to some of the further clinical issues that we can clarify here. We can return to the *therapeutic context* which, as you know, I have defined as the principle current therapeutic task for the therapist (Langs, 1973a). Earlier, we had identified this task as the patient's initial resistance regarding coming to therapy twice a week. Having now obtained very meaningful derivatives of unconscious fantasies and motives for the patient's wish to reduce the frequency of the sessions, we are in a position to interpret these to the patient. We have kept the therapeutic context in mind and have organized it around a central adaptive context, and are now in a position to intervene. If the therapist takes this step at this point, she can repay the patient's therapeutic endeavors with a therapeutic effort of her own. Her correct interpretation would offer the patient an opportunity for cognitive insight and a chance to see that this therapist is indeed different from the hurtful Dr. X—a chance for a positive introjective identification. On a practical level, it would enable the patient to recognize that in addition to the realities that bother her about twice-a-week therapy, there are a number of unconscious contributions to this tentative decision.

So, let's get to how we would intervene. I might have done so at this point, although with the patient offering me such important and loaded associations, I undoubtedly would have waited a bit more. Still, at this juncture you could have said something like this: In addition to the realistic problems that you anticipate if you were to come twice a week to therapy, there seems to be another reason why you want to come only once a week. You have been talking about loyalty and abandonment, and this must have something to do with the way your treatment with Dr. X ended. It seems that you're very hurt and really very angry about what happened. You feel that you were used, and that Dr. X used and then discarded you. You know, you're really telling me that this is no way to be. You're saying that therapists should be loyal as you are. But most of all, you seem to have been very deeply hurt once, and you apparently want to protect yourself from being hurt like that again in your therapy with me. And I think this is another reason why you don't want to commit yourself to a more intense relationship with me and are trying to protect yourself from it right off.

So, you see, we take the unconscious fantasies and perceptions—remember not to overlook the patient's valid unconscious perceptions—this totality of her unconscious communications, put it together with the adaptive context, and relate it to the therapeutic context. In this way, you arrive at the correct intervention.

Up to this point in the session, I think that you, as therapist, did what you had to do in order to further the development of the material. You said, let's explore and the patient started to give derivaties—just as I promised she would. You made an empathic intervention, and she gave you better derivaties—also as I promised. When you're right, you'll get good responses and the material will thicken—you'll get more and it will have depth. Then you're in a position to understand more and to do more for the patient. It is really a very gratifying kind of experience, but eventually it takes you to the point where unconscious processes and communications—the realm of interpretations—comes into play.

Now, when you have material with important latent content, you must deal with it on that level. Your having reached this point is undoubtedly why you got into some difficulty, and I can assure you, that many therapists have a similar problem. And that is why I say that here, asking her why she went to her mother, unconsciously indicates to the patient that you are out of touch with the deeper processes within herself and contained in her communications. You see, an incorrect intervention conveys a great deal to the patient about what's going on inside of yourself—the therapist. We won't go into that topic at this point since I am sure we will have better opportunities to discuss the many ramifications of errors in technique.

All we want to note here is that the nice things that you had been doing were undone a bit when you didn't appreciate what she had given you. You didn't understand the context, you see, and this is something that she now knows. And here, she was beginning to warm up to you and I think she was beginning to like you, and now you've suddenly changed and she will sense that. Patients are constantly, consciously and unconsciously, processing your interventions and even your silences, and as we will see again and again, they come to appreciate a great deal of what is going on inside of their therapists. They make all sorts of unconscious hypotheses, and again, mostly on an unconscious level, attempt to validate them in a manner that is not unlike the therapist's efforts to validate his own hunches and hypotheses, although the therapist should be doing this with a greater degree of conscious awareness. The validating process undertaken by both patient and therapist is a crucial component of pyschotherapy; but again, we will discuss that later on when the material from a patient permits.

I am once again attempting to help you appreciate what is going on interactionally here, because it's only in that way that you will understand what goes on intrapsychically with this patient. So, she was warming up to you and now you're suddenly . . .

D: Like her old therapist. (Laughter.)

L: Yes—same clinic, same game. Okay, let's see if the patient does indeed pick some of this up. You can take that as a prediction—her responses will shift now. I think that the comment about your becoming like her old therapist may be quite pertinent; she's bound to be quite sensitive about that. Let's see if it's reflected in the material.

T: I asked her how it came about that she went back to her mother. And she said, Well, I just decided one day to do it. I don't know why. It just came to me. I told my boyfriend, I have something to tell you and since I had said that, I had to go ahead and tell him. 'Cause I had said that I wanted to talk to him about something special. So I had to go ahead and tell him. I told him and he just said okay, and so I moved out. And I felt like I had to do that. But I do still see him even though I am living with my mother.

So then I asked the patient how long she had been with her mother. She said, About a month.

L: Now comes the point where someone will say, Langs tells me to never talk. But you can see the difference in the quality of the material: the patient is becoming more intellectualized and shifts toward communications filled with minor details and having less depth. Not that these associations are by any means barren. Notice how she says that she wanted to talk to her boyfriend about something special. That little derivative is really her disguised and displaced way of saying exactly what I had just discussed with you—that she (the patient) had communicated something very special to you and that it would have been extremely helpful if you had been able to pick it up and interpret it.

Now her association and my direct and conscious comment may seen like coincidence to you, but I can assure you that this type of parallel will appear over and over again. So long as you are in touch with the conscious and unconscious flow of the interaction between the patient and the therapist, you will find that the patient unconsciously perceives many aspects of it—including the implications of her own communications. And while she will then certainly elaborate these perceptions according to her own unconscious fantasies, or even distort her perceptions to some degree based on her own intrapsychic needs, she will let you know about many valid unconscious perceptions. Patients have, as I will say again and again, an enormous degree of unconscious perceptiveness and creativity.

Actually, this material enables me to introduce a few more complications. At this point, we could say that the patient was becoming resistant again. And in the past, we would be attempting to understand the intrapsychic anxieties and conflicts within the patient that prompted these excessive defenses and this resistance; and it would be more than likely that we would not consider the interactional aspect at all. Now, you can be sure that if a patient uses intellectualizing and isolating defenses, this is part of her own defensive style and has been prompted in part by her own intrapsychic needs and conflicts. But I would submit to you that you cannot really understand this resistance without the bipersonal field concept and an understanding of the interaction that occurs within it. In fact, if you interpreted this as a defense based entirely on the patient's intrapsychic conflicts, it is my belief that you would be inappropriately placing the entire responsibility on the patient at a point when you yourself had contributed to her defense in important ways.

You see, the patient shifted to more intellectualized material right after you began to ask more intellectualized and reality-oriented questions. You become interested in little facts and stuff, and the patient, who is always looking to mobilize her own defenses, joins you in intellectualizing. Now, if we think of this as the bipersonal field, we could say that both you and the patient contributed to the defenses of the field and to the resistance within the patient. We are seeing a living example, then, of an *interactional resistance*.

We also see a sector of misalliance shared by the patient and therapist, and their common efforts to split off the piece of the field that contains the true adaptive context—the transfer of this patient from one therapist to another. And notice, it was at the point where the patient was beginning to communicate her feelings about this transfer in depth that you began to ask your surface questions. We can suspect that this is no coincidence. In fact, when you begin to assess a resistance of the patient within the bipersonal field and attempt to discover your contributions to it, you should go back to the point at which you helped the patient to develop her resistance and explore what she was talking about at the time. You investigate your reactions to whatever she was communicating at that juncture, and it tells you something of the adaptive context for your countertransference-based response.

Without going into it in any detail for the moment, the interactional approach has convinced me that errors in technique, such as the ones we have just seen, stem from countertransference problems, to which may be added lack of knowledge. That's why I do not think it's a coincidence that as the patient was becoming more intensely involved in her relationship with you and in her feelings about her previous therapist, something prompted you to begin to ask superficial questions that took her away from these areas.

So you see, we have here what I have termed an interactional defense or resistance that emerges both in the intellectualized quality of the patient's associations and in the reality-oriented type of interventions that you are now making. The splitting off of the unconscious allusions to the transfer from one therapist to another has been termed a *bastion* by the Barangers (1966). This refers to a split-off part of the field that is walled off by repression, denial, and other defenses in both the patient and the therapist. I believe that this way of thinking gives us a more sensitive picture of what is going on, and that it makes a great deal of difference since it determines the manner in which you deal with the resistance.

As I said, if you think of this solely in intrapsychic terms, you will hold the patient responsible for the blockage, intervene accordingly, and the patient will become angry, because on some level she will know that you have contributed to the problem. She will not be able to confirm your intervention with her validating process, and she will feel that you are blaming her and not accepting your own responsibilities in this situation. She will sense that you are placing some of your problems into her— projectively identifying them into her. And she will react to those efforts by introjecting or refuting them. In all, this will create a neurotic vicious circle that will prove disruptive for both of you.

Earlier, I had mentioned something about the interface of the therapeutic interaction within the bipersonal field. Notice how this interface has shifted from unconscious communications related to the pathology placed into the field by the previous therapist through his premature termination of this patient's therapy and her working over of these problems, to a far more surface point, in which defenses predominate. And notice too that the interface has received contributions from both the patient and the therapist, and that both have caused this shift in location.

Now, technically, this discussion indicates that when your patient becomes defensive, you examine both her ongoing intrapsychic conflicts and motives, and your interaction with her. You examine what is going on within yourself and you attempt to determine whether you interventions—or failures to intervene—have promoted these defenses or not. Here, you might begin to realize that you lost sight of the therapeutic context that relates to this resistance, and disregarded the adaptive context as well. You might then have sensed that she had begun to produce meaningful derivatives related to the transfer from Dr. X to yourself, and it was at that point that you began to ask the kind of questions that you did. This would enable you to intervene positively at this new point, both directly and indirectly.

For example, you would certainly stop asking these minor questions and give the patient an opportunity to eventually produce some new and meaningful derivatives. That is, you would in actuality desist from contributing to the defensiveness of the bipersonal field and to the way in which you were reinforcing the patient's intrapsychic defenses. Remember this point: with interactional problems, rectification comes first. Once she's left on her own, I can assure you that her curative motives would begin to take over and that she would again make efforts to reach you. This is a consistent observation: patients will accept misalliances initially, and then they will attempt to modify them; and therapists will generally do something similar.

Actually, I think that simply stopping such questions would suffice, but if it didn't, you might then intervene and say something like this to the patient: You had begun to talk about your feelings about what happened with your previous therapist and about the issue of loyalty and disloyalty, and the whole problem of being used. Apparently, some of my questions led you toward other concerns and you began to describe some of the little details of your life. It seems that you welcomed the opportunity to get away from those other feelings.

In this way, you implicitly accept some responsibility for the patient's defensiveness, and then indicate her own need for these defenses as well. You keep your explicit acknowledgment of your role to a minimum, and talk of if essentially in terms of the patient's perceptions of you, rather than through any type of self-revelation. You can see how the interactional approach affects our technique, and we'll see more of that later. Here, it influenced the specific general interpretation of the patient's resistance —a most important step in resolving such difficulties.

So here I see the shaping up of a misalliance between yourself and the patient, and the creation of a bastion. In addition to avoiding her feelings about the previous therapist and yourself, the two of you are sharing resistances related to dealing with the whole problem of the frequency of her sessions. You're inviting her to talk about other things that are for the moment unrelated to these important adaptive and therapeutic contexts. And you can see that both of you find some momentary relief at this point, since her current associations are less loaded with affect and have a lesser potential to create anxiety in either of you. The patient will go along with you, but eventually she will attempt to help you to modify the misalliance. But is she doesn't do this fairly quickly or if you don't get to work, she won't come twice a week.

So we're back to a consideration of early resistances, and actually to the therapeutic alliance. You can see how complicated contributions to this alliance can be, and how the alliance has a lot to do with many things that go beyond the patient's and therapist's relatively autonomous ego functions and their capacities to relate maturely to each other, and to trust. Here we have had an unconscious undermining of the therapeutic alliance, and that's why I have called such an interaction a sector of therapeutic misalliance (Langs, 1975a). So, both patient and therapist for the moment are attempting to cure or deal with their anxieties through intellectual defenses. Let's see what happens.

T: Okay. So I asked her how long she'd been with her mother. And she said, About a month. And I said, Your former therapist, Dr. X, has been gone that long. And she said, Yes, I wondered if it had something to do with him —my leaving my boyfriend. Dr. X didn't know it. It happened right after I stopped seeing him. I wonder if I had to do it, somehow. But I really don't understand all that. And I answered, It sounds like you've been having a lot of thoughts about what happened.

L: Okay, now you're getting back to it—and so is the patient, which is fine. I would even say that this is your own conscious or unconscious effort to modify the bastion and the misalliance, and the shared interactional resistances. So you did the curative work, which is excellent. In fact, the rapidity with which you connected her moving in with her mother to the termination of her therapy with Dr. X doesn't even bother me, as it might otherwise have done. You see, I would have rather preferred to let the patient go on, and to associate and lead the way. If you have faith in the patient's wish to communicate, you will obtain everything from her that you need for your interventions. But the situation was one in which the resistances had been reinforced and you found a fine way of getting back on the track. Maybe you didn't realize it, but you were implicitly modifying the therapeutic misalliance—rectifying it more than explicitly interpreting its basis. But here, the rectification should suffice quite nicely. Please continue.

T: And she said, I really got to like Dr. X. I really thought he helped. I wondered if he liked me. One day I asked him. I knew he wouldn't say no, but I thought he wouldn't say yes, either. And he said, Well, what do you think? And I said, You might not like me because I was unfaithful to my boyfriend and did bad things. He said it wasn't up to him to judge me, but to help me understand my actions. And she added, I mean I wasn't in love with him or anything, but I did want to know if he liked me. I also asked him where he was going. I asked him . . .

L: Yes, I was going to say it, but the patient says it so beautifully for me. She unconsciously and indirectly offers the proper response to her own question—the interpretation that the therapist needed. She connects her interest in knowing whether the therapist liked her with his leaving her. And he should have intervened not by answering her question, nor by saying that he could not answer it, but by offering a valid interpretation: You are deeply hurt by my abandoning you and by my being unfaithful. You see it as a bad thing and now you're asking for something special to compensate for the way in which I've hurt you. Just notice, in passing, what appears to be an introjective identification again, in that the patient takes in the therapist's unfaithfulness to her and lives it out with her boyfriend. So you see, you stick to the adaptive context and to the therapeutic context, and you understand latent content by connecting the patient's associations to these contexts. Then you're in a position to interpret unconscious elements rather than working on the surface and saying something that is actually useless and even destructive to your patient.

Now notice again that I'm getting much more active, because the patient is communicating in depth once more. And again we see that when the therapist intervenes in a valid way, the patient does indeed modify her defenses. She once more produces meaningful derivatives that will ultimately help us with the main problem at hand—her resistance and her thoughts of coming just once a week. And notice too that the patient has indeed come back to the termination of her previous therapy, and that she has now told us a great deal more about what happened—material that we can readily use in interpreting to her.

And we begin to hear that issues related to the framework and boundaries of the therapeutic relationship actually did come up in other ways with Dr. X, in addition to the premature termination. In fact—and I won't attempt to document it here since it relates to the previous treatment—this material enables me to point out something that I have observed repeatedly, and will be able to demonstrate more directly to you later on. At the time when this patient was becoming more and more disturbed about what was happening between herself and her therapist, and her anxiety and depression was mounting, notice what she did. She attempted to modify the framework—she attempted to effect what I have called a *framework cure*. And if the therapist does indeed reveal any of this personal information, he will be sharing with her such a cure and this will be the means through which both of them will attempt to alleviate their separation anxieties and guilt.

This is absolutely typical and something that you should remember: a modification in the framework can provide a form of misalliance cure in the face of mounting difficulties. Probably here the cure would be based on the special transference gratifications involved in the self-revelations of the therapist, and on the feelings of fusion that the patient will be able to experience by finding out that her therapist liked her or told her where he was going. There would be a shared denial of the separation—and vacations and terminations are frequently times when both the patient and therapist are likely to modify the frame. In fact, I suspect that some of this patient's symptom relief was actually based on one or another aspect of misalliance and framework cures. Maybe we will be able to document some of this before this session is over.

Now, there's another aspect that I want to call to your attention because it is so characteristic. We see evidence here of what might be called an intense, erotic or possibly even erotized transference. However, if the behavior of Dr. X is, as we would suspect, characteristically of the kind that the patient is describing here, we can quickly see that this erotic transference neurosis has an important interactional component—that it is also an interactional neurosis. Now, again, I am presenting many interactional concepts here and it would take a lot of time to develop each of them. I simply want to acquaint you with these basic ideas and concepts, because I am certain that we will have every opportunity to develop them later in these seminars. But you see, the principle is always the same—the intrapsychic problems are reinforced, and interact with those that stem from the therapeutic interaction.

Also, when a patient talks about her previous therapist, do not be drawn into sharing another kind of misalliance, in which the focus is entirely on the prior therapist and the latent implications for the present therapeutic relationship are defended against and missed. This material may be the harbinger of a homosexual transference and a homosexual interactional neurosis with the present therapist, one that may already be taking shape. Some of this may have come from the very early modifications in the boundaries that stemmed from their talk in the hall—I can assure you that I have seen this type of consequence develop repeatedly.

Perhaps now, with all these references to the framework and boundaries, you will begin to realize that I was not being petty, and that this is really a very sensitive area for every patient. A poor framework implies a lack of boundaries and promotes an erotic or erotized transference. In fact, the therapist who has difficulty in maintaining the framework often has his own erotic or erotized countertransference problems, which then interact with these propensities within the patient.

Well, forgive me for wandering a bit, but the material

has become most interesting. In getting back to what is happening in this session, you can see that the therapist has been rewarded by being able to bring the patient back to her previous termination and by showing some understanding of what the patient is feeling. Once the patient begins to sense that the therapist is in touch with her unconscious communications and her intrapsychic anxieties and conflicts, she offers further helpful material. So again we see that our understanding of the latent content of the patient's associations can only develop by first conceptualizing the dyadic interaction within the bipersonal field. We should get more now; let's see what happens.

T: The patient said, I asked him where he was going.

L: This, by the way, is typical. I will say a little bit more before we hear what actually happened. First of all, you can see how this is related to the conversation in the hall. The effort to break the boundaries at the time of desertion. It's right there. And the acting out toward the boyfriend shows you that there was a lot that was unresolved. By the way, this is the juncture at which I would bring up the walk in the hall—and one other thing. You see, you've got two tricky problems. You've got to establish the twice-a-week therapy and you've got to interpret the patient's rage and wishes for revenge. Just as she left the boyfriend she wants to leave you. She's giving you a very easy surface interpretation. Then, once you have interpreted that, you should go back and reestablish the boundaries. Otherwise that will be another reason why she won't come twice a week—because the homosexual fantasies and anxieties vis-à-vis the therapist will be uncontrolled if there aren't boundaries; without a clear-cut frame, the patient will fear their actual gratification. This is why she needs both. She needs the intervention related to her revenge on the other therapist, and she must have clear-cut boundaries. If you don't establish both, then you're not going to have a patient. You could

make a correct interpretation here and miss the boundary problem. And you'd never understand. You'd think:
Gee, I did a good job; how come she didn't come twice a
week?

This is basic. We must create a therapeutic bipersonal
field with a proper relationship and clear-cut boundaries.
And we must also be capable of then interpreting to the
patient. These are the dual factors in cure through inner
change and insight. The relationship itself is not enough,
but one must have a relationship where the boundaries
are well defined and where there is no or absolutely minimal transference gratification; where there is a positive
identification with the therapist, so that the patient will
accept interpretations and want to understand them,
rather than be concerned about the infraction of the
boundaries which create anxieties and misalliances.
Once infractions of the boundaries have been corrected
and analyzed—which is an important therapeutic experience in itself—the therapist can interpret in other areas
and give the patient additional cognitive insights. This
approach affords the patient positive identifications
through the relationship, and creates the proper back-
drop against which derivatives of the patient's intrapsychic conflicts can unfold and against which interpretations can be made in a meaningful way. Relationship and
interpretation. And notice how well the patient knows it.
Having obtained something interpretive about the connection between her behavior and the previous termination, she now comes back to the boundary problem.

D: Boundaries?

L: The boundaries of the therapeutic relationship and the
bipersonal field. They were extended into the hall
through their conversation. And if you allow this to remain and if you don't interpret it, you're saying to the patient: I want gratification from you that goes beyond the
therapeutic aspects of our relationship and you offer
something in kind to her. And that has only one meaning

in the light of this material: it is an actual form of homosexual intimacy. Matters are different, however, if you
say to the patient: You wanted to know where Dr. X was
going. That reminds me of your wanting something outside of the office with me, that is, the conversation we
had in the hall. What comes to mind about it? Following
that, you could interpret her anger and her need to control it, and her wish to repair her sense of hurt by having
something extra from you. In this way, you would be offering her some understanding and securing the frame.
At the same time, you would be saying implicitly to her:
Here we will have reasonable and necessary limits and
there will be a definitive framework to our relationship.
We will not be uncontrolled and you can count on it.

As you will see later on, the framework is essential in
providing a bipersonal field in which the patient can develop some general ego strength and face her specific intrapsychic conflicts. The frame—the setting—is a crucial
contributor to the ego resources that the patient develops
through a secure therapeutic hold. This is important because the patient is talking about how she goes from one
boyfriend to the other—how she acts out and is impulsive, and doesn't know how to control herself. So you're
implicitly saying to her, Here, we have controls; and you
will have me as a controlled person to identify with. By
managing the framework, you let her know that you can
manage your own intrapsychic tensions, and she will introject these adaptive capacities.

So remember, we keep an eye on both dimensions—
the cognitive-interpretive, and the interactional with its
introjective identifications. Each has its separate consequences and each becomes structuralized in its own way;
although I am beginning to realize that cognitive insights
will merge with incorporations of the good therapist,
while positive introjective identifications get worked over
into cognitive insights. I expect that we will be able to see
these developments more clearly in a later presentation.

I think it is also rather evident by now that all of this does take place in psychotherapy—and in any therapeutic relationship. These are important processes and contents available in the psychotherapeutic bipersonal field; they must be considered if you want to do a good job in psychotherapy. Sure, there are distinctions between psychotherapy and analysis—there is little doubt about that; but it is becoming clear to me that the vast areas of similarity have been largely overlooked. We won't get into that now; my main point is that I hope that I am demonstrating in a convincing way the need for a sound framework in psychotherapy, and the extent to which these identificatory and interpretive processes actually do take place.

All of this also leads me to point out that you can't modify a patient's psychopathology just by being a good person to him. If you could do that, you could forget about all of this complicated stuff that we are struggling with today, and just go into your sessions and be a nice guy or gal, and you wouldn't have to interpret anything. Unfortunately, that won't work; it will only take you so far and no further—and actually not very far at all. The patient has a right to expect something more than that, and he does; and if you do not convey it, he actually won't think that you're a nice person after all, no matter how sweet you are—your niceness or goodness has to be expressed through well-timed interpretations.

On the other hand, you cannot just interpret out of the blue to the patient, without having created a meaningful and viable relationship. You also have to secure the framework of the bipersonal field so that your interpretations have their intended meanings and effects. If you do something inappropriate or destructive in your behavior with the patient, he will act out much as you have done, and there will be a therapeutic misalliance despite the verbal correctness of your intervention.

So you see, none of this material is coincidence. In general, though, the patient is not omnipotent and his unconscious perceptions are indeed colored by his intrapsychic fantasies and elaborated through them. But he does, as I said, show an enormous degree of unconscious sensitivity and perceptiveness. The therapist has to scrutinize the patient's associations for these unconscious perceptions, and this is extremely difficult for any therapist to do since it threatens his narcissism and his entire psychic equilibrium—which is part of the reason why all of this has been so largely overlooked.

In fact, there are situations where the patient will offer the therapist erroneous unconscious perceptions that are designed to further his own neurotic needs, but these can only be determined after extensive efforts at validation that include a further study of the patient's associations and of the therapist's subjective reactions. So it's not that the patient is always correct; it's just that he has many correct and valid things to communicate, and the therapist can make great use of them. Also, no patient knows everything about you, even though they do know a great deal. No patient knows every fantasy that you have had— or even most of them—and every therapist is grateful for that. So patients do know a great deal, especially without direct awareness; they are not omnipotent, but they are exquisitely and powerfully perceptive.

I would therefore say that it is quite meaningful that this patient comes back to the boundary issue in this session. She's given you enough derivatives about her anger, now she comes back to the boundaries: I wanted to know whether he liked me; I wanted to know where he was going. She does this because that's the unfinished job. It's as though she's saying, I've given you enough derivatives for you to know that I'm angry and want revenge, now I'm going to have to come back to the boundary problem, because you don't seem to be interested in that at all.

You see, it's not coincidence. I pick it up because it's

in the patient's material. So the patient and I are working together. What I can do consciously, she is doing unconsciously. I really believe in the curative needs of the patient and his unconscious sensitivity.

This, too, goes under the heading of the patient's efforts to help the therapist—to cure the therapist of a blind spot, of an area that the therapist has missed, and of the inner difficulty within the therapist that has led to this blind spot. This is a constant part of the patient's interaction with the therapist; it's based on the patient's exquisite unconscious awareness of the things stirring within himself, and within the therapist to some degree, particularly those aspects of the therapist's difficulties that are expressed in their interaction and placed into the bipersonal field. Eventually these disturbances in the therapist are introjected by the patient—as we will discuss later on.

Finally, I want to stress that in addition to the patient's efforts to cure the therapist, these communications also contain her own unconscious fantasies and distortions. I an emphasizing here the aspect that has to do with valid perception and efforts to help the therapist who has to be helped in order that he may in turn help the patient. I'm emphasizing that part because it has been relatively neglected and most readily defended against by this therapist and by analysts in general.

Let's continue now.

T: And she had wanted to know also, Would Dr. X ever tell her? And he had said, Yes. And she asked, Will you tell me now? And he said, Yes; but then he was quiet.

L: See again—another reference to testing the frame. He said, Yes. He was going to violate the boundaries. Now can we guess why he was doing this? I've already offered some hints.

D: His own guilt?

L: Of course. Guilt, and his pathological needs. We all suffer . . .

D: When patients leave us.

L: Patients leave us and we leave patients. All of our prob-
    lems get stirred up. So we're looking for a misalliance if
    we haven't managed the anxieties. The inherent human
    need for misalliance is so enormous, it is never, ever re-
    solved in any of us, because it has to do with inevitably
    unresolved problems and with death. None of us want to
    die; none of us want to accept it; we're going to fight it to
    the last, and we're going to fight it in our work; we're go-
    ing to fight it with our patients. And the need for misal-
    liance also has to do with wishes for symbiotic fusion—
    and more. So we're going to constantly have to struggle
    against our wishes for misalliances, you see; especially
    at times of separation. So he says, Yes. Now whether he
    did it or not, the patient then wants to find out not only
    whether this therapist would gratify her inappropriately,
    but also if he shares her anxieties. You can see now how
    unconsciously critical that walk in the hall was: the
    boundary issue pervades the patient's communications.

       In concluding this seminar for today, I'll be brief since
    we will continue with this patient next time. We've seen
    the importance of dealing with the adaptive and thera-
    peutic contexts even in the first session, and the impor-
    tance of derivatives of unconscious fantasies, particularly
    as they relate to early resistances in a first hour. This
    therapist neglected to some extent the important goal of
    establishing the patient's need to continue her treatment
    and really did not, as yet, adequately interpret the un-
    conscious dimension of the patient's wish to reduce the
    frequency of the sessions. Empirically, this wish is usual-
    ly tantamount to wanting to terminate treatment, so that
    one must analyze and interpret such a wish as a major
    resistance; to comply with it is often a prelude to actual
    termination.

       We've seen the importance of both interpretation and
    establishing a sound relationship with proper boundaries
    in initiating treatment. We see that the boundaries repre-

sent the therapist and if they are extended without rectification later on—without analysis of the extension and
correction of it—this can create anxieties that contribute
to acting out among other problems.

The last thing that we have seen is a good illustration
of modifying one's goals in a first hour according to the
patient's needs. The main need here has been to get to
the early resistances and the reaction to the transfer,
rather than obtaining any lengthy history from this patient. This has been done in this hour, but as I said, we
would have liked to have seen more of an effort to find
out why the patient wanted to continue treatment; this is
a basic part of establishing the therapeutic alliance. The
other basic contribution to the therapeutic alliance
would be, not some expression that you're going to be a
nice therapist or something of that sort, but the establishment of the proper boundaries and a valid interpretation based on the very clear derivatives from the patient. It is only these measures that will establish a sound
therapeutic alliance; the other approach will seem seductive and inappropriate to the patient and rightly so—it
will actually interfere with the alliance. Well, with these
comments, we will conclude for today.

Chapter 2

SOME INTERACTIONAL CONSEQUENCES OF A MODIFIED FRAME

THE THERAPIST'S ANONYMITY AND THE BASIC GROUND RULES OF PSYCHOTHERAPY • THE INTRAPSYCHIC AND INTERACTIONAL CONSEQUENCES OF ALTERATIONS IN THE FRAMEWORK OF THE BIPERSONAL FIELD • SOME INTERACTIONAL PROCESSES AND MECHANISMS • MISALLIANCE CURES • THE HOLDING FUNCTION OF THE FRAME • THERAPEUTIC AND NONTHERAPEUTIC REGRESSIONS • THE INTERFACE OF THE THERAPEUTIC INTERACTION • THE PATIENT AS A MIRROR FOR THE THERAPIST WITHIN THE BIPERSONAL FIELD

L: We will pick up today where we had left off last week—at the point where the therapist had asked her patient about the many thoughts that she apparently had about her former therapist.

T: The patient said, I really got to like Dr. X; I thought he helped. I wondered if he liked me. One day I asked him if he did. I knew he wouldn't say no, but I thought he probably wouldn't say yes. He said, Well, what do you think? I said, You might not like me because I was unfaithful to my boyfriend and I've done some bad things. He said it was not for him to judge me but to help me understand my actions. I mean, I wasn't in love with him or anything, but I did want to know if he liked me. I asked him where he was going, would he tell me. He said, Yes. But then he was silent. I thought that was sort of strange. So I said, **Well, where are you going? He said he was going to Southern California—to the Coast.**

L: Technically, then, how does one deal with a question of this kind?

D: There must be a lot of fantasies in the patient about this; maybe she is wondering where the therapist will be, so that possibly she can get in touch with him.

D: I really wonder what benefit there would be for the patient to have this particular bit of information.

L: The benefit that's described in the literature is that you're being human about it and not overly frustrating to the patient; this type of separation is a very hurtful thing. **And let's assume that Dr. X had already obtained a lot of material from the patient. Let's assume that, even though it's probably not correct. Some therapists ask,** why not at some point let the patient know that you're leaving the area and that that's where you'll be? This at least lends a certain human element to the situation and really isn't harmful in any particular way, and at least you have not left the patient completely frustrated and hanging nowhere, feeling that you were really very hard-headed about it.

D: But what kind of patient are you discussing?

L: Any ambulatory outpatient, although I suspect that most of these basic principles apply to every patient and to every therapeutic interaction.

D: The therapist must be human, but gratifying the patient with direct answers can interfere with the patient's motivation to work in therapy. So I think that the patient should be frustrated.

D: If the patient asked the question just before I was leaving on vacation, and there was no time to analyze and explore it, I would not want to frustrate the patient for several weeks. I would be inclined to answer such a last-minute query.

L: You can be sure that your patient would soon pick this up about you, and use it to act out with you, because it is an unconscious invitation for collusion and misalliance. In addition, he will have learned that you maintain the framework under usual circumstances—if indeed you do that—and that, but under pressure, you modify it. The timing will in no way change the many ramifications of a break in the frame.

Let me discuss this topic a bit further. Perhaps the most important reference to this subject in the literature is the monograph by Leo Stone (1961) entitled *The Psychoanalytic Situation*. While Stone wrote about analysis, we can consider his ideas in terms of their relevance to the psychotherapeutic situation. As I mentioned before, these issues are important in psychotherapy and there is a need to develop principles related to the framework in this situation too. Let me try to state Stone's position as clearly as I can. I will try to briefly summarize it for you.

He begins by reviewing Freud's (1912a, 1912b, 1913, 1914, 1915) basic papers on technique. He refers to a rule that Freud developed regarding the need to appropriately frustrate the patient. What ground rule or concept is used to characterize this need to frustrate the patient in certain ways, in order to motivate him to work in treatment. And I would say that it is also done in order to preclude certain adaptive solutions that would then interfere with the adaptation we are looking to effect—namely, structural change. After all, if you allow for a resolution of a problem in one way, that's the resolution—the patient won't go looking for another solution. That's characteristic of human beings. So, if you solve a problem by gratifying a wish, then you will not help the patient solve it in any other way. Gratifying the wish is not structural change; it's gratification, and it's not a resolution of whatever is neurotic in that wish. But what was the rule that Freud delineated? (Pause.)

The rule of abstinence. I'm sure you have heard of it. It states that analysis—and I will add here, psychotherapy—should be conducted in an atmosphere of reasonable deprivation. Now Stone makes the point that Freud himself (1919) wrote that the patient will have to be given some gratification. And of course, now comes the question: what kind? Well, Freud felt that sometimes there would have to be compromise and noninterpretive satisfactions—from the analyst to the patient. He was concerned that you can overdo the frustration. If you read his case histories, he was offering such gratifications all the time. He was always doing things that were extra-analytic. In fact, it's a remarkable thing to know that the man who wrote the case histories (1905, 1909a, 1909b, 1918), and did the kind of work that he describes there, wrote these papers on technique. They reflect two different kinds of thinking, except for the fact that this was his interpretation of his own ground rules.

Stone points out that the question still comes up as to what is appropriate gratification for the patient. It was his contention that if you unduly frustrate him, you create unnecessary regression. And that's where the problem does indeed come in. What is undue frustration? In other words, what gratifications is the patient entitled to? And that's something we're going to be talking about all year because it is still a controversial issue.

And since we're probably not going to be able to verify our position here to any great extent, because this relates largely to an interaction that occurred with the patient's previous therapist, I will not offer a lengthy discussion at this point so we can get back to the clinical material. I don't want to offer a general answer based on past clinical experience; I want us to learn from each patient presented to us the extent to which frustration is important, and the extent to which it should be compromised. Remember, we are dealing here with transference gratifications—gratifications of the patient's pathogenic unconscious fantasies—that some analysts believe to be necessary in order to maintain the therapeutic alliance or to keep the patient in treatment. Whether this is the way to accomplish these goals is something, as you know, that I seriously question.

But let's use the material that we have up to this point. We know something of the context in which this request occurred; we heard the associations that surround it in the present and past sessions; and on this basis, we could make some comments about this issue of frustration. Let me put it this way, With this material from the patient, what do you think the answer is?

D: The context seemed to be whether the therapist was going to care for her, was going to like her, almost . . .

L: Almost what? She used another word . . .

D: Love?

L: Yes, do you love me? Do you love me? and if you look at the cluster of her associations in this hour, you can see that she meant this as the love of a man for his girlfriend, with its amorous and sexual implications. And in the context of a therapeutic relationship, this is a kind of neurotic love, and is different from the actual type of love —used in its broadest sense—that the therapist can and must offer to his patient. So she is already saying that the therapist had two choices: to respond in a loving way in her sense, or to do so in what should have been his sense —with a therapist's love. And she really makes clear that it is the modification in his anonymity—in the necessary frustrations—that would convey the sexualized and neurotic form of love. And this is always the case—the therapist's appropriate love is expressed by maintaining the boundaries.

So, you have to distinguish these two types of love because, as I said, the therapist in one sense of the word, should love his patient. There's no question about that. This is a controlled, or what is called a sublimated, kind of love; it is expressed through concern and the wish to take care of and cure the patient. It is expressed through establishing the proper climate for the treatment and in all of the therapist's interpretive endeavors.

In contrast, she's told you about a different kind of love. If we remember the previous associations to her question and make use of the sequence, we see that it has indeed to do with the love between a boyfriend and girl-friend. So her material does help us answer this question in a manner that communications from many patients, when understood in depth, have done.

Now, in this context, her associations also suggest that she's talking about a mother's kind of love as well—a mother who had cared for her, allowed her to live with her, and provided for her in that way. This is a reminder that there are also differences between maternal love and the therapist's love, and in the boundaries between the patient and each of these figures in her life.

Coming back to the main focus, let me say it again: the patient is asking the therapist what type of love he has for her. And she says that if it is indeed erotic and neurotic, he will tell her where he is going. And if he doesn't have this kind of love, he won't do that; he will offer an inter-pretation and a secure frame instead. So the answer lies in the sequence of the patient's associations. And what did the therapist do?

D: He tells her that he's going to California.

D: He gratified her and told her that he loved her. And while she can't go to California—to the Coast—she is going to the beach.

L: How do you like the reference to the beach? It now takes on meaning. And how do you know she can't go to Cali-fornia? Are you telling her she can't go?

D: Well, I'm assuming that she couldn't.

L: She isn't there right now. Right. She isn't in California, but that doesn't mean she can't go. Freud said something very cogent about all of this in his papers on technique; his writings contain the kernels of almost everything that was developed later on in this area. It's really an amazing thing. And he said something related to the concept of misalliance which I am so intrigued by and am writing about (Langs, 1975a). Well, as I review the literature I find that anybody who really got into the patient-analyst relationship and interaction really knew about this phenomenon. Without going into detail, what we mean by a *therapeutic misalliance* is a situation in which the patient and therapist join together in an interaction not designed primarily for inner change and conflict resolution through structural change within the patient. The interaction has as its conscious, and more often unconscious, purpose some other goal, such as bypassing such inner change, offering substitutes for adaptive inner change that are maladaptive, and offering pathological defenses to the patient—and to the therapist as well.

It's a well-known concept in various forms. And Freud knew it too. He (1915) put it very beautifully: he said there are certain patients—he was talking about women and this was in a paper on transference love—who want their love gratified. And he said he didn't mean only in the gross ways of going to bed with the patient, he meant in very subtle ways too. Those are the most dangerous, you see. And if you do so, he wrote, then the patient has her cure, but the analyst doesn't have his. Which I think is putting it beautifully, just beautifully. His cure—the analyst's cure—is structural change in the patient. The patient's cure is really not a cure; it's what I call a *misalliance cure*, it's a continuation of the neurosis and of the interaction that was pathogenic. And this is a striking example of the offer of such a cure, where instead of interpreting an aspect of the patient's separation reaction, in terms of her wishes for fusion, a reparative gift, and a shift in the boundaries, the therapist gratifies the patient's neurotic—yes, inappropriate and neurotic—needs. Racker (1968) in particular wrote that at the moment when the patient asks for a misalliance—he called it a *vicious circle*—the only appropriate response by the therapist is a correct interpretation. That is the key to preventing a misalliance.

Now, I want to explain this; I want to say a little bit more because there are so many facets that I haven't touched upon. The patient is saying to the therapist, Do you love me? And she's really talking about two different kinds of love. One is love as a therapist who wants his patient to grow and change within; that's one kind. The other is really the love of the parent who made her sick; the parent who created whatever it was that led her to drop out of school—we don't have the genetic material. But it was a love that was seductive, incestuous, and disruptive of her functioning, you see. Now, in choosing to tell her where he is going to practice, he is giving her, not the therapist's love, but the pathogenic love. And you have to see this; this is so crucial to the situation.

The real expression of love as a therapist would have been an interpretation, that she is feeling hurt, she's having very intense feeling toward him; she's deeply hurt by his abandoning her, not only as a lover but as a mother—this is another reason she went back to live with her mother. As a lover and a mother she wants him, out of his inevitable guilt—he could introduce it if it was in the material—out of his inevitable guilt of abandoning a patient in the middle of a treatment, she wants him to make amends in a way that would be destructive, by apologizing and by granting her something special. This intervention would offer her relief through insight and a positive introjective identification—through accrued strength and adaptive mastery.

Direct answers to her questions, in contrast, might relieve the frustrations for the moment, and perhaps ease the therapist's disturbance and his difficulties in helping the patient to resolve the loss, but it would interfere with a valid intrapsychic resolution of both the patient's and the therapist's separation anxieties. Giving the patient a tie to the therapist is, as I pointed out before, a modification of the framework and offers her both a framework and misalliance cure—remember that. For the patient, the relevant conflicts might have to do with problems related to separating from her mother; we know that she went back to her mother at the time of her termination. Maybe her mother had difficulty in letting her go, and this is a therapist who also can't let go of her. This becomes a repetition of a neurotic pattern and interaction, and what Racker (1968) has called a vicious circle. It means that the interaction within the bipersonal field is now repeating a previous pathogenic interaction, rather than creating the conditions under which the effects of the earlier disturbing relationship can be modified.

But notice, a good deal of this is speculation, and this is typical when the framework has been modified. Once the conditions of the bipersonal field have been altered, you don't get the genetic and other derivatives that you need to comprehend the patient's intrapsychic conflicts. However, this much we can say: the therapist modified the framework, and in a sense he acted out. The therapeutic hold was damaged and the frame no longer offered the patient a general sense of security or ego strength. The patient incorporated the therapist's problems with controls and management, and acted out herself. I think we do have some clues now as to why the patient went back to live with her mother and left her boyfriend—it undoubtedly had something to do with the therapist's behaviors and interventions; and upon this, the patient built her own contributions. A premature termination by a therapist is a terribly traumatic experi-

ence, but if the therapeutic relationship and the treatment situation is otherwise handled adequately, it can
generally be worked through with a minimum of disruptive response on the part of the patient. However, if it is
compounded by modifications in the framework, you can
expect chaos—something that I've termed a *nontherapeutic regression* in that it is extremely difficult to analyze and derive therapeutic benefit from. It presents a
very difficult therapeutic situation, especially because
the therapist is usually unaware of his own contributions
to the patient's regression.

I really don't want to overstate things here because we
do not have the material from the sessions between Dr. X
and this patient, through which we could further validate
this discussion. I realize that I am working in a way that
is uncharacteristic of me, but I offer these ideas so that
you can begin to think about some important issues in
psychotherapy. We do have some material from the patient in the present session related to this discussion, and
we may be able to get some additional degree of confirmation of my ideas as we go along.

But before getting back to the session, I want to complete my general discussion of these issues and the comparison of my position with that taken by Stone. It is my
impression that Stone would agree with this therapist,
that it's perfectly all right to answer this patient directly
on two conditions—if you have analyzed the implications
of the question as fully as possible, and it is your best
clinical judgment that it would be overly frustrating not
to respond. To put that last point another way, you have
decided that such a revelation will really not significantly
distort the patient's transference responses to you, and
in fact, might enable them to unfold more clearly.

As you can gather, I do not agree with this position,
because I do not think that the therapist can ever change
the inappropriate qualities of this kind of gratification,

and because it becomes an alternative to working out a more adaptive solution to the patient's—and the therapist's problems, such as the separation anxieties that we are discussing here. I do not agree with Stone because I have learned something of the therapeutic importance of a sound frame, and because I agree with Milner (1952) and Viderman (1974) who have pointed out that a secure frame is essential for the development of a transference neurosis.

While I won't get into the issue of the extent to which the patient experiences something approaching a transference neurosis in psychotherapy, I will say this much: I have considerably modified my thinking since writing my book on technique (Langs, 1973a, 1974). There clearly is a workable and analyzable version of what has been called the transference neurosis in the patient's relationship to the therapist in psychotherapy. Actually, a careful scrutiny shows that this is a mixture of fantasy and reality, transference and nontransference, but what is essential to recognize is that the patient in psychotherapy really does intensely invest in his relationship with his therapist, and to a large extent his intrapsychic problems emerge in connection with this relationship. And furthermore, the psychotherapist is in a position to explore, analyze, and resolve these reactions in his patient in the course of the psychotherapy. In fact, if he wants to do a really effective job, this is where he will have to do a large part of his work, because this is where the patient is reacting and adapting, and it is actually where the patient is expressing both his neurosis and his ego strengths.

But we're getting into many side issues and I ask your forgiveness for introducing so many different important dimensions of psychotherapy at this time. As I said, my main goal for the moment is to identify some of the basic problems that we will be studying repeatedly in these seminars. Don't worry about sorting out the details, or even remembering each of these problem areas; we will be returning to them often enough so that they will eventually take on some meaning.

Now, when Stone says, How much frustration? and suggests that anonymity can get to be absurd, my response centers around the important therapeutic functions of the frame and of these appropriate frustrations which are a part of that frame. And I have not found that a secure maintenance of the frame is experienced by the patient as any kind of rigidity, although many therapists and analysts have wanted to see it that way. It creates a safe place for the analyzable unfolding of the patient's inner sickness. Actually, the regression that stems from a secure frame does not derive from excessive frustration—it has an entirely different basis—one that I will discuss with you later on. In essence, the regression has to do with the emergence of the patient's most severe psychopathology within a well-managed frame. This is what I have called a *therapeutic regression* because it is readily analyzable and touches upon the patient's most important inner problems. And the patient's material will show you quite clearly that this kind of regression is not based on feeling unreasonably frustrated at all, but that it stems from fear of a necessary therapeutic task. In addition, we have to remember that the patient does not get well through being less frustrated in inappropriate ways, and that he derives his greatest gratification in psychotherapy, and in analysis, through a correct interpretation from a therapist who has done it in a meaningful, caring way. The patient doesn't get better through revelations that go beyond the boundaries of the relationship—that actually creates therapeutic misalliances and is a disservice to him.

And as I have already told you, the whole situation gets very tricky in that a modification in the boundaries can offer the patient a temporary framework cure and a period of symptom relief. But this I can guarantee you: a careful in-depth listening to the patient's material at these times will show you that this is a form of misalliance cure, that it has been derived from shared pathological defenses and gratifications between the patient and therapist, and that while the patient welcomes the temporary relief, he deeply resents the inappropriate basis for it. Remember, it is not only a question of the therapist's fulfillment of his role through a capacity to properly frustrate the patient, but it is also the matter of recognizing the difference between the many implicit gratifications offered to the patient through a proper therapeutic relationship, a set of well-managed ground rules and boundaries, and valid interpretations on the one hand, and the explicit gratification of giving the patient something that goes beyond these satisfactions on the other. These explicit manipulations ultimately have a pervasive negative effect on the patient and are the basis for negative incorporative identifications with the therapist, and many other detrimental reactions.

I think that the basic fallacy in the thinking of Stone and others who take such a stance is that they do not listen to the manifest, and especially, the latent content of the patient's associations after such self-revelations and infractions of the boundaries of the relationship. They do not take the altered frame as their adaptive context. But, if you use the basic psychoanalytic method of searching for derivatives of unconscious fantasies and reactions to an intervention through careful attention to the material that follows, you will consistently find that the deviation not only has unconscious meanings to the patient, but that it has negatively affected the patient's perception of the therapist; it has a very deep actual and realistic disturbing impact on the patient.

Stone says in a footnote that he doesn't believe in the

patient's unconscious perceptiveness—that must be an important factor in his thinking. However, if you listen to the material from the patient after you've modified the frame once or twice, you will find that he doesn't appreciate your deviation and the seeming gratification. This is because on some level, usually unconsciously, he knows that the therapist has acted out of guilt or out of some other problem related to his inability to bear the anxiety involved.

Remember, the patient has his own capacities for empathy and identification, and for what has been termed for the therapist trial identification. He has a capacity for introjective identification, he takes in many things from the therapist, and he samples them consciously and unconsciously. He does his own processing of the communications from the therapist, and much of it is unconscious, especially early in treatment. So he has the means of unconsciously sensing that the therapist has acted through some countertransference difficulty, and we can always demonstrate this process within the patient by carefully examining his associations and responses to the therapist at the time. In fact, the therapist who is out of touch with his own countertransference problems can use the material from the patient to alert himself to their presence. This is another observation that comes from thinking of psychotherapy as occurring within a bipersonal field—an occurrence that takes place at any point in the bipersonal field is reflected in alterations at every point in the field. This is the old concept of the patient as a mirror for the therapist, one that Margaret Little (1951) so exquisitely described. So, the therapist can utilize the patient's material as well as his own subjective experiences in attempting to sort out any countertransference reactions on his part.

Of course, I could say considerably more and hopefully validate it if we had additional material, but even those few communications from this patient have set me off, because the issues are so important and the implications for psychotherapy so crucial. But let's move on to another aspect of the ground rules and the frame that is pertinent here, and briefly consider it. To save time, I will identify it for you—it is the therapist's anonymity. Freud (1912b) put it this way: the analyst should be like a mirror with his patient and play back to him only that which the patient communicates. So, the therapist should maintain his anonymity on various levels, including facts about his private life, such as where he's going once he leaves the clinic. We must remember that this is not meant in some totally absurd, impersonal sense. It was meant to convey a tenet related to the manner in which reflections from the therapist interfere with the interaction; with the projections from the patient, and with the therapeutic properties of the bipersonal field. We could now even add that such self-revealing responses convey unconscious fantasies within the therapist, which would then complicate the interaction, the relationship, and the therapeutic outcome. They also reflect difficulties in the therapist's capacity to manage his own inner state.

So, let's pull some of this together. In commenting on this aspect of Stone's very important monograph, which made many positive contributions that I'm not going to detail here since they're not pertinent to the immediate discussion, I've taken issue with one aspect. That aspect relates to modifications in the basic rules of technique, and we should recognize that ultimately the rebuttal can only come from clinical observation. I haven't alluded to such data in my discussion, but suggest that even this material may give us some explanation of the kinds of responses that patients have to these modifications in technique, and the extent to which they do indeed help to create misalliances rather than therapeutic alliances, and promote pathogenic and pathological resolutions rather than adaptive solutions. We're touching here on the

ground rules of therapy; they are designed to create a
treatment situation—a bipersonal field—in which the
patient's neurotic needs and wishes are not gratified, and
are thereby converted into verbalized associations and
other behaviors that can in turn be analyzed in a manner
that will help the patient resolve his inner difficulties.
There are indeed many gratifications in the psychotherapeutic relationship, but the central gratifications stem
from the pursuit of insight, the positive qualities of the
relationship, and the ultimate achievement of conflict
resolution and inner change for the patient.

Gratifications of this other kind—in which the therapist tells the patient where he is going, by which he un-
does an aspect of the separation, the hurt, and the frustration for both himself and the patient—offer an unconscious tie; in doing so he has actually done two detrimental and related things. First, he has gratified the patient's
inappropriate need to deny the separation, to hold onto
him, and thereby temporarily covered over all of the related unresolved inner conflicts in the patient—and
probably in himself. So he has provided a misalliance solution—*a misalliance cure*; *a framework cure*— instead
of giving her the opportunity to associate to the separation and express her frustration, and convey all of the derivative associations, fantasies, and memories with which
they are linked. This would provide her with an opportunity for cognitive insights related to her separation problems so that in the future she could master them more effectively without neurotic resolutions.

Secondly, he has to some extent modified the boundaries of the relationship, and has done so in a seductive
way. This conveys to the patient his own inability to tolerate the frustration of the separation and his own unconscious belief that the patient cannot tolerate it. He
has therefore offered himself as a model of someone who
has difficulty with separation reaction, so that in a vari-

ety of ways he's offered a pathogenic interaction and a pathogenic introject or figure for identification to the patient. And we can confidently postulate that part of the reason that this patient left her boyfriend and went back to her mother was the failure—her failure—to achieve with her therapist's help cognitive insights into this area, and the additional effects of the pathological introjective identification with the therapist—an identification, if we remember her ealiest associations, that she struggled against. She attempted to offer a different manner of resolution, to some extent, by talking about being faithful and not betraying others. Now we know that this had much broader implications. We see too that the therapist's communication of where he would be going unconsciously reflected many other facets that played into the patient's difficulties rather than providing her an opportunity to resolve them.

So, it is for reasons such as these that I take a rather firm stand regarding the ground rules of psychotherapy. Certainly, in emergencies, one is prepared to modify ground rules in the interests of preserving, let's say, the patient's life when the patient is suicidal, or there's some acute regression. But by and large, adherence to the basic ground rules does two things: first it provides the patient with the maximal opportunity to analyze a particular conflict and offers the therapist the maximal opportunity to interpret the unconscious fantasies, memories, and conflicts related to the particular situation—the realm of cognitive insight and inner change. Second, it offers an optimal, constructive model of the therapist as an individual for identification, as someone who can tolerate frustration, maintain appropriate boundaries, and adhere to the therapeutic task. Maintaining the framework has a whole variety of very positive implications which are severely compromised when the therapist steps beyond the boundaries, beyond the basic ground rules of the treatment situation. It is always a dual, detrimental influence. It interferes with the communication of unconscious derivatives, with the so-called transference illusion, with the therapeutic alliance, and with the opportunities to interpret; and it offers pathogenic, negative, destructive, so-called *bad introject*, which the patient will incorporate. She will then both work on these with an eye on their resolution and use them for her neurotic needs.

So, we see now that these basic issues can come up in a first session—and this is especially true with a transferred patient—and we realize that they often come up at termination. There's a common tendency among therapists to deviate at times of termination, out of their own anxieties, rather than accept the opportunity to maintain the boundaries and to interpret the patient's very basic and deep separation anxieties. A good deal of this hasn't been validated from the material presented to me, but you can turn to my book (Langs, 1973a, 1974) and review the vignettes related to the ground rules and their deviation, and see how these ideas are supported again and again.

Now, the rejoinder often is, Well, that was true for this situation, but does that mean that it's always this way? My answer is, I've never seen it to be otherwise.

Lastly, this is a request by the patient for the therapist to extend the boundaries of the relationship, and I've always found that this occurs at extremely meaningful moments in the therapy, and that it has very deep meanings of the kind that we're starting to develop here. And again, you can do the most for the patient in terms of using your special capacities and especially your unique ability to offer interpretations, which nobody else can do.

D: Also, Freud talked about the therapist as a surgeon— that was his model—and when the surgeon starts an operation, he puts aside all of his feelings in order to perform that operation.

L: You see, the surgeon and mirror models had been over-
stated, and this is what Stone was reacting to when he
pointed out that the analyst is not a mirror in the sense of
being inanimate or inhuman; such a concept would be
absurd. The therapist is not a mirror; he is a human in-
strument—a human being. He observes and momentarily incorporates the communications from his patient. He
then works them over—he metabolizes them—and he se-
lectively conveys to the patient whatever he learns about
him through this process. The surgeon model has to do
with the need to remain appropriately detached while humanly involved.

But humanness is not to be equated with gratifying the
patient directly. One of the most striking patterns in the
analytic literature is that as soon as someone discovers
that there is what they call a real relationship between
the patient and his analyst—I prefer to term this aspect
the nonstransference component of the total therapeutic
relationship—and he realizes that there is something going on in the therapeutic interaction beyond transference, he immediately suggests that you have to gratify the
patient in certain extra-therapeutic ways in order to be
and to prove that you are human. The logic of that absolutely escapes me; plus the fact that if the writer did
something of this kind just once and listened to the material afterwards, he would soon know better. And yet analysts modify the frame and they don't listen to their patient's unconscious responses, and almost everybody does
this type of work, over and over again—with certain rare
exceptions. Greenacre (1959) speaks in favor of maintaining groun rules, even though she deviates occasionally, and there are a few others who see therapeutic value in
maintaining the frame—but they are for the moment
largely unheard voices in the wilderness.

D: About just technique in general: I was once told by a supervisor that when a patient asks a reality question like,

are you married? do you have any children? where are you going for your vacation? he advised answering something to this effect: I will answer that, but let's talk about it first.

L: Well, I think I've answered your question, haven't I? I apparently didn't reach you. What was I saying? What's the answer as far as I'm concerned?

D: Well, to make the interpretation. But the implication in this way of presenting it to the patient is that at the end of the interpretation, the therapist would say to the patient, Well, I'm actually going to California.

L: Yes, I think my position on that is clear. If I'm still ambiguous, I'll say it. First of all, you are saying to the patient: Let's fake the frustration. I'm going to pretend that I'm not going to answer you until you tell me what you have on your mind, then I'll answer you.

      The point is that if the patient knows that he is going to be gratified and that his defenses are going to be reinforced, of his neurotic wish will be gratified, then he will not produce the derivatives necessary to resolve anxiety or depression or conflict that is disturbing him, as it's related to the question that he wants to know about— the therapist's marital status, or where he's going on vacation, or any other personal fact. To reveal such information interferes with the image of the therapist, and with the patient's opportunity to project derivatives onto him. It interferes with the patient's wish to do any sort of therapeutic work regarding the conflicts that are involved. And it interferes with the image of the therapist, presenting him as someone not capable of creating a situation of appropriate frustration, as someone who has his own personal countertransference-based on unresolved needs to gratify the patient and not to analyze. So again, it has its effects in two areas: it interferes with the unfolding of the necessary derivatives of unconscious fantasies, and it interferes with the patient's image of the therapist, producing incorporative identifications with a damaged therapist. And remember too, the interactional approach tells us something of the importance of external reinforcements to the patient's intrapsychic defenses. This really is a very important and relatively misunderstood area.

It used to be and still is quite common for one to hear that the analyst, and especially the psychotherapist, can do anything that he wants to do in reality as long as he analyzes it. What I'm saying is that this is not so. The reality has an impact; it contributes to sectors of misalliance; it provides gratification of inappropriate fantasies and needs; it provides inappropriate defenses and interferes with the opportunity for insight; and it interferes with positive, constructive identifications with the therapist.

So you see, the technical principle has to be that these wishes—these efforts to modify the boundaries—must, not out of inhumanness but out of therapeutic necessity, be frustrated. And they have to be analyzed. Again we come back to the fact that the therapist's humanness is most meaningfully expressed in his ability to create the proper therapeutic situation, one in which the patient can resolve his intrapsychic conflicts through insight— through the interpretation of derivatives. Anything that deviates from this basic stance, even if it's done in the name of humanness, is ultimately destructive and for that reason inhuman.

All right, let's get back to our clinical material and see how much of this we can verify from this patient.

T: So then she was quiet, and I said that she seemed a little sad. Well, then she got furious at me. She said, People often tell me I look sad when I'm just sitting quietly. I hate it. I'm not sad.

L: Okay, let's try to understand that. So she got furious. Let's get back now to what's going on between you and her. We had formulated a lot of this last week. We have to reformulate and then try to understand her reaction to your comment. Here you were trying to be so nice and sympathetic—supportive if you will. She didn't appreciate it. Why do you think she was telling you all of this? What was she communicating? What have we discussed?

D: The therapist's abandoning her?

L: Yes . . .

D: There's one more element to that. In addition to that happening, it seems as if she was pointing out that she got something from her former therapist. Her former therapist in the end said, I love you, and she's wondering, perhaps, what you're going to do.

L: Yes, what else? (Pause.)

Well, we said something about her giving you material about why she wants to reduce the number of sessions: her sense of hurt; her sense of anger; her identification with the destructive therapist who disrupted things very suddenly and very quickly. We also said something about the conversation with the new therapist in the hall, if you remember, and I had suggested that she had quickly brought up the issue of the boundaries of the relationship, and we saw that, as the session went on, this actually was a very crucial issue in this patient's mind. Now we want to get back into our impressions of the therapeutic interaction—to what is happening within this bipersonal field between the patient and the therapist, and how the field is being structured or modified. It is essential that we follow the interaction because without a sensitivity to it, we will be unable to comprehend the patient's associations.

Now, in the context of this patient's concerns about the boundaries of her relationship with you, and her associations to what has taken place in her previous therapy, I would suggest that she may have taken your comment about her seeming sad as a kind of seductive intervention that made you appear to her much like her previous therapist. Now, this is just a hypothesis, but notice that we would be hard pressed to understand her reaction to what you said, without being in touch with her interaction with you and the flow of her associations.

But there is another thing that may be going on here. As I had said, she is communicating her unconscious fantasies and feelings to you in a very rich way. And I think that she may be angry with you because you're not picking them up, even though it is a first session. That may be a part of it—that she wants you to realize that your response is not what she needs; she's letting you know that very quickly. All right, let's go on; let's see where the session goes.

T: So I said she sounded irritated at me for saying what she didn't want to be told by others. And she said, Yes, what do you know about me. I don't feel like I relate to you at all. You're just a lady sitting there. I wanted to come here . . .

L: See, what do you know about me? She's starting to criticize. And notice something else. Here is a confirmation of what I said a moment ago. Namely, that the patient was offering derivatives concerning the things that were disturbing her and she felt that you weren't relating to them. And we're very much aware now that this first session is focusing more on the transfer from one therapist to another, than on the patient's problems in any other area. Now in an initial session in which a transfer is not an issue, the patient would actually begin the interaction, as a rule, largely with her outside problems on her mind. She would also of course begin to consciously and unconsciously experience her interaction with the therapist, and this would begin to shape her communications, even in a first hour.

It is here that I want to mention again the *interface* of the therapeutic interaction as it occurs within the bipersonal field. The interface may be conceptualized as the resultant of all of the vectors placed into the bipersonal field by the patient and the therapist, and I think of it as having many important characteristics. First of all, it tells us something about the ways in which the therapist and patient are interacting and how the therapist influences the patient's communications—and the reverse. The interface has a location in the bipersonal field that tells us which of the two participants, from moment to moment, is exerting the greater influence on what is being communicated. It has stability or variability, depending on the extent to which the patient or the therapist is consistently the major determinant of the location of the interface. And of course, it varies according to the input from both the patient and the therapist, reflecting both pathological and nonpathological contributions. Lastly, the interface is open to outside influences that are funneled either through the patient or the therapist—and more rarely through a third party directly.

Now without attempting to really clarify this concept here, since we will have an opportunity to look at it more closely later on, we can see that the therapist's intervention significantly influenced what the patient went on to say. Much of the interface of this interaction has been determined by the patient's experiences with her previous therapist, and some of it has been influenced by the discussion in the hall. At this specific moment, it appears to me that the interface is being significantly influenced by the patient's unconscious perceptions of the therapist's failure to appreciate and understand the latent content and the many implications of her associations.

Actually, this type of fluctuation of the interface will occur in any first session, even when the transfer elememt is not a factor. We can use this particular session to highlight the extent to which in any first session there can be a crucial dynamic interaction, with very important resistances that must be dealt with in a meaningful and even interpretive way to whatever extent possible. This is needed for the treatment to develop properly, and for a secure bipersonal field to be established. Patients have an inherent capacity to be unconsciously perceptive in any session; unconsciously they are exquisitely in touch with the nature of the therapist's interventions and his failures to intervene. Now while this may make some of you quite uncomfortable, this unconscious sensitivity can actually be used to great advantage by a therapist who is in touch with it.

T: The patient said, I wanted to come here today, but I didn't really know what it would be like. And then there was a knock on the door. (Laughter.) And I thought, Oh God, a knock. I guess I tried to pretend it wasn't there, but there was another knock right away. So I said, Excuse me, and I got up and opened the door. It was the social worker from Aftercare and she said, A patient of yours is flipping out in the cafeteria. (Laughter.) . . . And come immediately. So I said, I'm with a patient. Please ask the patient to try and get hold of himself and I'll see him in a few minutes. Have him come and sit here and wait out-side the door—on the bench. (Laughter.)

L: Talk about staging.

T: The social worker from Aftercare was quite irritated and said, But you have to come right away. And I said, Well, I can't, so just tell the patient that I will see him in a few minutes, and have him sit outside on the bench. And then I sat down.

D: What part of the session was this?

T: Oh, there was about ten minutes left . . . So the present patient said, I should leave and let you talk to that poor person. (Laughter.) Somebody who needs it more than I do. So I said, You're not sure that you deserve my atten-tion, and she said . . .

L: This is a particular style of intervening, you know, this
      business of echoing what the patient says, and I really
      want to try to teach you not to use it. It's particularly
      false—very flat—at this point. You can see that what you
      say to a patient depends on what you hear and how you
      formulate what the patient is communicating. It does
      take time to do that, but echoing the patient is like hav-
      ing heard nothing but the manifest content.

      Here was a reality, a very disturbing reality: a coinci-
      dental event that was bound to have very deep repercus-
      sions. So, you do not want to intervene so quickly and ba-
      sically, your first job is to listen to the patient, see where
      she goes, and keep in mind the interruption as her adap-
      tive context. At some point, if the patient did not include
      her conscious thoughts during the interruption, you
      should ask her what came to mind as she heard the con-
      versation. If necessary, this is something you should ac-
      tively invite. You made a comment already, but you want
      to hear what it stirred up in her. You know you're in
      trouble. This business of a patient of yours flipped out
      isn't going to help. But, the one thing that can help is
      your honestly being willing to explore her reaction and
      to allow her to express her fantasies and feelings about it.
      You're not omnipotent, you're not totally responsible for
      everything your patients do, even though I sometimes
      make you feel that way. And it's almost true, but you're
      not completely responsible. The patient also has his
      share of responsibility. The therapist does have a special
      burden though, and the attitude that makes the differ-
      ence is being comfortable and exploring it with the pa-
      tient.

      And here, that particular kind of intervention really
      will only, I think, irritate her even more, because it has a
      very mechanical quality, and it's sort of out of touch with
      all that's stirring in the patient. After all, she's telling you
      that she wants to come just once a week, and that she's

feeling hurt; and she's telling you about her anger at her previous therapist and her wanting to pay you back for him as she did by moving out on her boyfriend—these are all communications that require interventions; they relate to her inner pain. It was this kind of help that she was seeking, and in fact, I think that unconsciously she is now saying that she really wants to come twice a week, and that if you'll just make a correct interpretation or two, she'll do it. But now I'm afraid that she will feel that you don't understand her, and that it looks as though you don't understand another of your patients either. Things aren't going too well. So this is the time for something else. Particularly, first getting the material from the patient. Remember that as a principle: make sure that you have as much material as you can get, and particularly when there is a coincidental occurrence, you want the associations from the patient. You might want to read Weiss' (1975) paper on such events too.

T: Then she said, I really don't want to come twice a week; I don't need it; it's ridiculous. My friends would ask who I saw on the two days I'd have sessions. I'd say, Well, I see my shrink and they'd say, What, are you that sick? So, then I asked her . . .

L: Now, who would like to tell me what this comment is about?

D: She wants some reassurance after what happened with the other patient.

L: Yes, that's another way of looking at it. What else? What's the adaptive context of this comment?

D: What just happened?

L: Yes, start thinking like this patient, like a human being. What do you begin to think when you hear this knock and this conversation?

D: I may flip out in a cafeteria myself someday.

L: Yes, what else? That's one part of it, and what's the other part?

D: Especially if I'm a patient of this doctor.

L: Yes, why?

D: Because I have an incompetent doctor. And she may not attend to me if I needed her—as she did with the other patient.

L: Yes, that's part of it . . . What else?

D: Therapy is destructive—it doesn't help.

D: My doctor is no good.

L: Yes. What do you mean—therapy? You mean, my doctor. See how we all use defenses. The thought would be, maybe my doctor is crazy, maybe she doesn't know what the hell she's doing. And here she finds a way of saying it. My friends will think that I'm sick—crazy.

Now, let's trace this out. With all that went on before, we had a major job to do—to intervene about her wanting to come once a week. Then comes the shocker. But if you stay in touch with it and you're not frightened by it, then you can still intervene—and even have more to say. On the surface, you could point out that after the interruption she came back to wanting to come once a week. At least on the surface, you could do that. You could say, You must be kind of scared about coming to see me, what did you think when you heard all of that? She's bringing you right back to it.

You see, it isn't only her fear for herself now, it's her fear for her doctor. And notice again how it comes up. Here we see how exquisite the interaction is. The patient is like a barometer and will fluctuate in identifications with you—as you are and as he perceives you. I'm not eliminating unconscious fantasies; they're very crucial, but they are evoked by a reality stimulus and they relate to unconscious perceptions. Now, if you heard—okay, you're lying on your analyst's couch and somebody knocks on the door. You've got to come quickly; one of your patients is about to flip out. (Laughter.) What are you going to think about this guy; what did he do? Now, again, it isn't that he's totally responsible or maybe you begin to think he is; you start to wonder: where am I; what's going on? Now, you suddenly have an image of this guy as not knowing how to take care of his patients, not knowing what to do, and allowing his patients to go crazy and maybe driving them crazy to boot.

Now, what have I done? I've offered you a trial identification with this patient. Having experienced it, we have to reconstitute our self-boundaries and examine it. We constantly make this shift back and forth—identifying with the patient and sometimes with his objects, and then cognitively assessing and exploring our subjective experience. Let's do it here. Suddenly, this patient talks about how they're gonna think she's crazy. So you see, she has picked this up from her perception of the therapist at this moment. Sure, she's also reflecting her own anxiety about going crazy in her treatment with this therapist, and she may also be remembering her previous therapist and his craziness. The entire constellation prompts her to renew her thoughts about coming once a week.

Now, maybe some of you feel that in her mind, being seen twice a week means that she's crazy and being seen once a week means that she isn't. Somewhere, she may have this fantasy. But if we are following this therapeutic interaction, this response to a disturbance in the bipersonal field—an intrusion vector—and if we recognize the adaptive context for this portion of the patient's associations, then I think that the most powerful contribution to her renewed thoughts about once-weekly therapy stems from this patient's conscious and unconscious perceptions of her therapist and her extension of these perceptions in her inner fantasies. She has picked something up from her view of this therapist and has placed it inside of her—she fears that she will be seen as crazy.

Now we really don't know what happened to that other

patient. Maybe somebody came along and belted him. But remember, the patient doesn't know either. She is with the therapist for the first time and she has had a complicated experience with her first therapist, who apparently both seduced and abandoned her. I think it's likely that the earlier experience also contributed to this patient's reaction, and that in retrospect all of this might even indicate that the patient experienced her previous therapist's interventions as unconscious efforts to drive her crazy. You see, the patient's reactions are always overdetermined; based on her ongoing, cogent associations, we attempt to sort all of this out—to get at manifest and latent content. And notice again how powerfully this reaction in the patient is determined by a direct experience with the therapist—even in psychotherapy.

Now, let's recognize another point—how the patient brings up her responses to what just happened. She doesn't come out and say directly to the therapist, you know, I heard what was said to you, maybe you'd better tell me a little more about your credentials—I'm beginning to be a little bit frightened, especially after what happened with my first therapist. No, she says, I'm not going to come twice a week because my friends will think I'm crazy. Now if you're in touch with this, you begin to recognize that the patient, as I said, is continually unconsciously perceiving, mixing in her own fantasies, but constantly taking you in from moment to moment. So here an unconscious perception of the therapist is expressed as a comment by the patient about herself. This is what is called *incorporative* or *introjective identification*. I don't think it's a great mystery or so difficult to conceptualize. When people hear those words, they get frightened and wonder what the hell they mean. The same thing happens with projective identification. It's really not so difficult. You just stay in touch with the adaptive context, with the patient's interaction with yourself, and with the many indirect and unconscious implications of what transpires, and you'll be able to recognize these mechanisms quite easily.

So, in introjective identification, the patient takes a trait of the therapist, or an aspect of the therapeutic interaction, based on a reality nucleus and his elaboration of it in fantasy, and he takes it in and becomes that himself. He takes the contents and attributes as his own, and experiences them—directly or indirectly—as such. And it's just so basic; it goes on all the time.

Now, if the therapist tries to make an interpretation at such a moment, what's going to happen? Would you listen to a looney? You've got to first correct the disturance in the relationship—in the patient's perception of the therapist. If she makes an interpretation in any other area now, the patient is going to run scared; there is no way anything you could say could get confirmation, unless you break the neurotic interaction first. That is, here she believes that she's with a crazy person, like her mother perhaps, or like somebody else who is sick; and she's caught up in it. So you must say to her something like this, Based on what you just heard, you seem frightened of me and you wonder if I'm destructive or sick. You say that that's how your friends will think of you, but I think that after what just happened, that thought expresses your concern about me. And maybe some of what happened with Dr. X has added to that anxiety. And notice that it was right after the interruption that you mentioned again wanting to come just once a week. You can see now that in addition to whatever hardship is actually involved, it has something to do with your fear of treatment and your concerns about my ability to help you.

Notice that technically you have dealt with several adaptive contexts with this intervention—the traumas of the previous treatment, the anxieties related to initiating this therapy, and the acute anxieties evoked by the interruption. And you have also dealt with the main therapeutic context: the patient's wish to reduce the sessions—the central resistance. So you take this interruption and the anxiety that is placed into the bipersonal field, into both the patient and the therapist, and you turn it to considerable therapeutic good. And in doing this, you have simultaneously offered the patient some cognitive insight related to a central resistance and modified her image of you as someone who is sick or crazy. You are making sense to her. She then has an opportunity to make an incorporative or introjective identification with a good and helpful figure. Not only have you shown her that you have a capacity to understand, but you also have implicitly indicated your own capacity to manage the anxieties that the interruption had evoked in you, and the anxieties that come from the patient's renewed indication that she only wanted to see you once a week as well. And this is the only way that you could break the neurotic vicious circle that was developing with this patient, based on your earlier failures to intervene, and on the implications of the interruption.

We can now come back to your more surface comment, that the patient didn't feel that she deserved your attention anymore. A better translation would be that she didn't want your attention anymore; she wanted to get out of your sphere of influence. And this is even more interesting, because your comment had the quality of an invitation to her to become depressed, and we could postulate that the intervention was a reflection of your own depression and sense of failure. After all, you must have felt upset and sad to hear all this, in front of this patient and at this time. It must have been a terrible experience for you, and you handled it in part by attempting to place your sense of despair into the patient. That is a projective identification on your part—something that is, as you can imagine, far from uncommon in therapists. This projective identification probably contributed in an important way to the patient's taking your sickness into herself. In addition, I would suggest that her wish to see you only once a week is in part an effort to reject the projective identification, and to get some distance from you.

Well, I've probably gone beyond conceptualizations that we will be able to readily confirm from this patient since you're getting close to the end of the session, but I hope that it has helped each of you to think about some important interactional mechanisms that I will have a lot to say about later on.

T: I didn't make any sort of comment, except of support and reflecting back that she felt that coming twice a week meant that a person was more ill.

L: Yes—in tune in a way, maybe unconsciously—but you just didn't say which person.

T: She repeated, I don't think I'm sick; I'm just a normal kid with just a few problems. And I asked her if she ever thought that twice a week sessions was simply more intensive treatment, rather than meaning a person was sicker, and she said, No, she never did think of that but that it seemed to make some sense.

L: This is called an appeal to the therapeutic alliance, which I don't utilize. This type of direct appeal to reason is certainly not to be preferred to the correct interpretation. Unfortunately, the entire session lacks a correct interpretation and such an intervention would have had a far more positive effect in terms of developing a secure therapeutic alliance than any sort of shift to manifest content and logic. The factor that is crucial is that the direct appeal ignores the very powerful unconscious elements; it ignores the communications of the patient—something the patient will sense—and it attempts to really cover the therapist's ignorance.

T: Then the session was over and I asked her to come in for the second scheduled session of the week, since she had

been scheduled for twice a week, and said we could continue to discuss it further. I also told her that I would
take a vacation approximately seven weeks from now.

L: That I would not have done. In this session, I really feel
that the interests of the patient would require not telling
her that. I think it's a disservice to the patient at this deli-
cate point—to do it. Otherwise I would have done so, if
the therapy was established—no question about it. And
did she agree to come back for the second session?

T: No, that was the time she was going on vacation too, so
she was very happy.

L: Oh, she was thrilled—so glad to hear it. I wonder?
       The fact that this patient was transferred from one
therapist to another, and that she was being seen in a
clinic, should not have deterred this therapist from firmly
structuring the psychotherapy. We see that unfortunately
the therapist failed to return to the extra-therapeutic
contact; that she failed to interpret some of the unconscious motives and fantasies related to this patient's wish
to reduce the sessions from twice to once a week; that in
the absence of such interpretations she resorted to what
would technically be called a manipulation, a direct
request and directive to the patient to come in for the second hour that week; and that she also failed, in conclud-
ing this hour, to structure the treatment situation—the
bipersonal field. In doing so, she's created difficulties
that would undoubtedly have to be dealt with subsequently in this therapy.
       So let us remember that regardless of the conditions
under which a patient is seen in the first session, toward
the end of that session, it is a therapist's responsibility
to acknowledge that the patient seems to be having certain kinds of problems. This is said very simply, without
technical language, and in this case, the therapist would
have said briefly that the patient still seemed to be having
some difficulties and in particular, some anxieties about

the development of the treatment on a twice a week basis, and that she should avail herself most definitely of the opportunity to explore these difficulties, and that overall the therapist felt that she could be helpful. This establishes one aspect of the framework for the treatment— the commitment on the part of the therapist.

From there, the therapist should spell out something regarding the fee, even if it is set by the clinic policy. She should take over all responsibility for the treatment, and not contribute directly to what is called *the splitting of the transference*. This concept is actually broader in that it entails all feelings, reactions, perceptions, and fantasies that the patient has regarding treatment and the therapist, and therefore includes both transference and nontransference components. It refers, however, to the extent to which a clinic situation offers a set of realities to which the patient can assign certain of his responses to psychotherapy to clinic personnel and policies while experiencing other aspects of his reactions to treatment more directly with the therapist. Any participation in this type of defensiveness on the part of the therapist will create an important sector of misalliance.

So, the therapist should establish the patient's fee, the frequency of the sessions, the time of the sessions, and she should offer the patient an opportunity to ask questions if necessary. The patient's responsibility for the session, and the therapist's policy regarding vacations should also be spelled out. In all, the goal is to establish a clear-cut framework for the psychotherapeutic interaction and to develop a well-defined bipersonal field.

It must be more than evident that my own clinical experience has indicated quite unmistakably that a sound psychotherapeutic process takes place within a clearly structured treatment situation, and that such a framework is absolutely essential. Since this is one area that I will be discussing throughout these seminars, I will wait for further clinical material before elaborating. Here, since we are studying a first session, I simply want to stress that in addition to the usual, somewhat nondynamic, though basic, considerations regarding a first session —in terms of the fundamental goals of assessing the patient's need for therapy and establishing a basis for treatment—we should realize that a very meaningful interaction is initiated.

So, in addition to offering a formal set of ground rules, the therapist's behavior and communications implicitly indicate a whole series of additional nonarticulated boundaries and conditions under which the treatment will take place. It is in this realm that he establishes his neutrality, his concern for the patient, his anonymity, his relative passivity, and his basic role as a listener who will intervene only when therapeutically indicated by the communications from the patient. In this way, the therapist is conveying information to the patient regarding the nature of their relationship and the therapeutic situation, and this will be an unconscious factor in the patient's decision regarding treatment. To the extent that the therapist has been successful in indicating implicitly to the patient the unique qualities of the therapeutic bipersonal field, the patient will begin to sense, and to process on some level of awareness—often largely unconsciously— these special conditions. He will gradually come to understand that the therapeutic field has characteristics that set it off from the rest of reality, and that it offers a unique opportunity for the interactional unfolding of the patient's inner problems, under conditions that maximally foster the availability of derivative expressions of these inner disturbances, and in a manner that renders them available for interpretation and alteration through understanding and identification.

While it certainly takes a long time to create a secure bipersonal field, it is important to realize that its nature is being conveyed to the patient even in the first sesssion. There is too much of a tendency to think of the first hour as different and separate from the remainder of the therapeutic experience, and as a result to consider a separate set of relatively deviant principles as a basis for the therapist's behavior and interventions in that session. There is no sound basis for such an approach, and the patient himself will certainly not split off his experiences in the first hour from the rest of his interaction with the therapist. Unconsciously, he will in fact be disturbed by all unneeded modifications in technique and will often attempt to exploit them. Some of this need to deviate seems to come from unresolved "stranger anxieties" within the therapist, and many recommendations have appeared in the literature in the guise of ill-advised modifications that have been advocated as a means of establishing the therapeutic alliance. Anyone who looks at the patient's responses to such manipulations in any depth will quickly discover how antithetical they are to a sound therapeutic alliance.

Finally, this material has demonstrated that all understanding of the patient's associations must take place within a comprehension of the therapeutic interaction— even in the first hour. By studying the initial session of a patient who has been transferred from one therapist to another, this component has been easily demonstrated. It is, however, an aspect of every first hour and when early resistances come up, they should always be considered within the adaptive contexts that have unfolded in this initial interaction. To truly appreciate what is going on intrapsychically, we must first know what is happening interactionally; in psychotherapy, as in analysis, this is the basic ongoing vehicle for understanding the patient.

So, with these remarks, we will conclude for today. I want to thank our therapist for a most interesting presentation; actually, you showed considerable sensitivity to this patient's plight and probably did as much as you could this early in your training. It's really not out of any wish on my part to be critical that I have tried to show you that empathic and surface responses just turn out to be insufficient. I'm really speaking for the patient and for what the patient needs. Unfortunately—or fortunately, since I hope you experience it as something that is welcome—this means that you will have to learn how to understand the patient in some depth and how to offer really valid interpretations to her. Concern is not enough, though you must have that; you must also learn to become that very special person who offers an understanding of unconscious processes to the patient. I do think that you have provided us with a good start along that road.

Finally, I want to say again that I am well aware that I have mentioned so many aspects of psychotherapy in this pair of seminars that we could devote an entire year to them—and we will. I hope that it hasn't been too overwhelming for you, and I want to reassure you that we will be considering all of this over and over again. I wanted you to get a feeling for the complexities of the therapeutic interaction and process in psychotherapy, and I wanted to demonstrate the extent to which you can indeed be in touch with unconscious processes within the patient in this therapeutic modality, and that you can deal with them as well. Thank you again for an excellent presentation.

Chapter 3

TECHNICAL ERRORS AND THE THERAPIST'S PROJECTIVE IDENTIFICATIONS INTO THE PATIENT

THE MEANS AND IMPLICATIONS OF PROJECTIVE IDENTIFI-
CATIONS BY THE THERAPIST • AN EXCHANGE OF PROJEC-
TIVE IDENTIFICATIONS BETWEEN THE PATIENT AND THE
THERAPIST • ASPECTS OF THE THERAPIST'S INNER STATE
REFLECTED IN HIS MANAGEMENT OF THE FRAME • THE
THERAPIST'S PATHOLOGICAL AND NONPATHOLOGICAL
CONTAINING FUNCTIONS • THE PATIENT'S UNCONSCIOUS
PERCEPTIONS OF THE THERAPIST'S DIFFICULTIES • THE PA-
TIENT'S USE OF THE VALIDATING PROCESS • THE INTERAC-
TIONAL NEUROSIS

L: Let's begin right off with a new patient and with our presentation for today, and see where it takes us.

T: The patient I will present is a woman in her late forties,
who had several children late in life because of difficulties in conceiving. She had had a number of operations
and entered treatment because of a fear of losing control
of her anger, sexual problems in her marriage, and a general sense of disillusionment. Briefly, her early history is
that she had several siblings, saw her mother as extremely harsh, and spent many years searching for love and
clinging to those who loved her. She tends to be too nice
to everyone. She had had previous therapy, privately,
about ten yeas earlier and she had been seen in a different clinic for about a year when she was transferred to
here. I had seen her for about two months at the time of
the session that I will present. First, I will briefly describe
the hour before the one I plan to discuss.

She started talking at once, asking me to change her hours in September—a month hence. The reason she gave was that her mother-in-law was baby-sitting for her children early in the morning and felt it would be cold and dark, and she no longer wanted to sit. She asked for a midday hour, since her husband was free at that time and could stay with the children. She also said that her mother thinks that she does not need therapy. Her mother said she could talk to her and to her husband, so why did she need a psychiatrist? Her husband agreed and thought that the therapy was a big waste of money. She then said that this made her very angry, because her husband had been in treatment for a long period of time.

From there, she went on to talk about the psychiatrist that she had seen ten years ago, and said that at that time she had been in the hospital and later went to see him. One of her gynegologists had suggested she wasn't able to have a baby because of an emotional problem. She went to this psychiatrist and he told her that everything was going to be fine, that now she was going to have a baby, and that she had made the right decision to come to therapy. And one day she told him that she was pregnant and he said this was terrific and that she was going to have a nice, healthy baby. The next thing that happened was that she went to the hospital and had a miscarriage. The psychiatrist came to visit her while she was there and he said to her, You know why you are sick? You're sick because you want to be sick. She then told me that she became very angry and left therapy.

Then she started telling me about her husband not satisfying her in lovemaking, and that she had this fantasy when they made love—it was like she was making love to herself. She told me another fantasy, that while she was making love to her husband, this other man was making love to her. And he was very nice and sweet and spoke very softly to her. In general, these were the issues in the previous session.

L: Who would like to discuss this session?

D: One thing that strikes me is that the therapist was either silent or he hasn't mentioned his own comments.

L: Yes, that is an excellent place to begin. Had you said anything to her in the session?

T: Yes . . .

L: Before you tell us your interventions, give us a chance to try to sort out this material without them. What happens? Can we formulate this material? Well, we see that an issue related to the ground rules has come up, and then we hear something about her previous treatment and the many ways in which the ground rules—neutrality, anonymity, the location of the interaction, and probably a lot more—had been modified by her first psychiatrist. And we hear that the patient is angry and dissatisfied with her husband and that she's having fantasies of making love to herself or having some other man do it.

Now, perhaps you share with me a feeling that there is something rather hollow with this formulation. It's really quite confined to the surface—to the manifest content and themes. Oh, we could add some notion that maybe her anger at her first psychiatrist is displaced from her present therapist, but that's only a hunch based on our knowledge of the ways in which patients displace these kinds of things. And we could also speculate that maybe her sexual fantasies have something to do with her therapist, but that also comes from previous clinical experiences and not from something that is clear-cut in this material. So, it doesn't hang together and in point of fact, I really don't think that we can say what's going on.

Now, two things are missing from this material: a clear-cut adaptive context, and the interaction between the patient and the therapist. Oh, the adaptive context may have something to do with her wish to change the hour, but that is really not clear at all. And even if it is the adaptive context, without knowing how the therapist responded to this request, we are really unable to appreciate the latent content of these associations. If he had agreed immediately to change the hour, we might think of this material in one way, and if he had refused to do so, we would think of it quite differently. And as you can see, I'm already suggesting that the adaptive context may in part have something to do with the therapeutic interaction and relationship, and I am indicating that without knowing the transactions within this bipersonal field and the extent to which the framework of the field has been secured, we can't get any feeling for what is going on inside this patient, consciously or unconsciously.

For example, let me indulge in a brief exercise. If the therapist had agreed to change the hour immediately, without exploring it, the patient might be unconsciously communicating her veridical unconscious perception of the inappropriate way in which he went about changing the hour without clarifying the situation first, and analyzing the implications of the request for the patient. She may also be implying that she felt she had seduced the therapist. You see how tentative we have to be without actually knowing what transpired.

On the other hand, if the therapist had refused outright, the associations would indicate that the patient felt he had been destructive, and her seductive fantasy would take the form of an effort to repair his hurt. There are, of course, many other possibilities, but the point that I'm trying to establish is that without knowing the actual therapeutic interaction, you really cannot determine the intrapsychic state and fantasies of this patient. And this is always the case: we can only approach the intrapsychic and the patient's unconscious fantasies and perceptions through a deep appreciation of the therapeutic interaction. In a way, the therapist's omission, which implies a belief that you can understand material from a patient without knowing anything about the interaction, has given us a chance to see how this is simply not the case.

T: Well, the patient kept asking me whether her fantasy was normal. And she kept repeating that I probably thought it was sick. I had responded by asking her to clarify her fantasy, and by saying that I wasn't sure what was fantasy and what was reality. She said that it was hard for her to stop the fantasy and that she liked it, and that she was frustrated with her husband and had created an imaginary lover, although in reality she was making love to herself. She then said she wondered what my thoughts about her were, and she speculated that I thought she was sick, or that maybe I thought that her fantasies were normal, as her husband said they were. I asked her more about the man who was making love to her and she said that it was nobody, no one specific.

She then brought me back to the question of the change in the hour, and I told her that I would think about it, because I wanted to hear more from her, but that I felt that she seemed to have a valid request and that I would look into making the change.

L: Well, does this help us? What can we now add?

D: It looks to me as though the therapist was revealing something about himself when he told the patient that he couldn't distinguish fantasy from reality.

D: The patient may be attempting to seduce the therapist by trying to modify the boundaries of their relationship.

L: It is true that this is a form of modifying the boundaries of the framework, but not in the sense that we usually think of such modifications. Actually, this is more an effort to change one aspect of their agreement within the established ground rules—the time of their sessions. Even so, the question of some kind of unconscious seduction should be kept in mind.

D: Her request to change the hour might even tie up with

her fantasy that she is not getting any gratification from her husband at home; maybe her wish to change the hour is an attempt to obtain some special kind of gratification from the therapist.

D: Somehow, the session seems to reflect some difficulty in the therapist, in that he did not develop his interventions to the patient around a central adaptive context, such as the change in the hour. Also, he did not connect the patient's associations to the change in the hour, and he seemed to randomly search after different aspects of her associations.

D: Maybe the references to the previous therapist reflected a negative image of her present therapist that is also being displaced onto her husband. Maybe she has also related it to herself, because she spoke about what a fool she is.

L: It is my impression that we are hearing so many divergent comments for two reasons: we don't know what has been going on in the therapeutic interaction over the recent sessions, and especially in the previous hour; and we really don't have a clear picture of the sequence of this particular session. As a result we don't have a central adaptive context, and we end up making random speculations. So, for the moment, let's focus on the technical issues related to the ground rules, and develop the principles that we will need as to how to handle a request like this, to change the hour of her sessions.

D: In principle, you'd wait for some more material or unconscious derivatives related to why she wants to change the hours. And then perhaps you would both maintain the ground rules and use that as material for an interpretation.

L: Now you say maintain the ground rules? That is, you would not change the hours?

D: He doesn't answer the question. He says, Tell me more about it.

L: He doesn't answer it initially—he asks for more material and he gets further associations. Then what do you do?

D: I'm not sure, but perhaps you make an interpretation.

L: You try to make an interpretation; what else do you do?

D: Isn't there also a reality problem?

L: Yes, you also have to deal with the reality. The point is that you have two tasks: the first is to assess the reality, and to get a clear picture of that, and to give the patient time to convey it to you before you make any sort of a commitment. Once you say to the patient that she has made a valid request, you have changed the conditions of the interaction. You've already agreed that the patient's request is valid—before you've heard her out. You really have no basis for saying that, so she knows that you're saying something that you really aren't in a position to say. She knows that you've already agreed with her, long before you've heard the whole story, and she's going to recognize that about your communication.

So, you see, a premature comment like that has a two-fold effect. It says that you're ready to go along with her, before you hear her out, and that you are already inclined to accept her request. Then she has an entirely different job to do than she would have had if you had maintained your neutrality. She doesn't have to tell you that much about the unconscious meanings because you've already agreed to participate. If you maintain the matter as an open one, where you're not going to commit yourself because you really don't know, you'll be amazed at the surprises that come up. As it turns out she had said to her mother-in-law, you really don't want to babysit for me, do you?

T: Well, she had told me about it before. This is not the first time it's come up. It came up in the previous session too.

L: So, it's been on her mind.

T: Yes, and I knew about the reality before then too.

L: Okay, so I'm just talking about how, in principle, the therapist has to maintain this as an open question in order to do two things: to assess the reality and to ascertain the unconscious meanings of the request. Now, if the reality turns out to be valid, then the therapeutic stance is that it's reasonable, and if I can change the hour, I will; and whatever meanings the patient then gives to the change are her fantasies about it. But, if the reality is not valid, you have another kind of situation: what would be indicated is that the therapist should not go along with it, and should interpret the fantasies that the patient is trying to live out as a kind of acting out. Here, if you do go along with the request, the unconscious meanings are gratified, and you have a sector of misalliance.

Let me clarify this point. If you go along with the change in hour because there is a sound reason for it, it will gratify certain unconscious fantasies in the patient. But the therapist has not made the change primarily to afford the patient these gratifications, and any belief that she has that this is the case can be treated and analyzed as a distortion. On the other hand, if the reality is not appropriate, then you are basically gratifying a neurotic fantasy and wish of the patient, and you are living out something with her that constitutes a neurotic gratification.

As I have discussed with you before, it is clear that whenever you modify a ground rule there is an unconscious, inappropriate neurotic gratification for the patient and the therapist. It's a shift in the boundaries; there will be some gratification. If there is a realistic reason for doing it, then that gratification can be worked out. If there isn't, then you have a different situation. You've simply gratified her, and the resolution of that situation is much more difficult and it leaves a mark. It means that you had a need to gratify certain of her un-

conscious fantasies and defenses, just as she had a similar need. The two of you have formed a misalliance.

So, in listening to the material from the patient, this
determination will color your understanding and intervention. Because if she has an airtight reason for changing the hours, and then comes up with the fantasy that
this makes you her secret lover, well, that's a distortion
of this situation. You haven't done it in order to conspire
with her to become her lover; you've done it because
there is a reality need and you are helping her to continue
the treatment. If, on the other hand, she simply manipu-
lated you, and it turns out she could get somebody else to
sit very easily, then you have indeed—on one level—
joined her in a secret love pact.

So, you listen for the reality and for unconscious meanings, and you intervene with a particular tone, depending
on what you discover in each area. All right, so now we'll
listen to the next session.

D: It would appear that the sequence in which the patient
brings up the change in her hours, and then goes on to
talk about how she has this secret lover who's gratifying
her, reveals an unconscious meaning of the request and
her wish for you to comply. If you do comply, it will be
necessary to point out this seductive meaning to her. Actually, in this session, you could have intervened, and
said to her something to the effect that this request has
some such implication.

L: We didn't hear enough details of the session, so I really
can't say how or if I would have done that. The therapist
might have made an intervention in this area, and said
that the request for the changed hour is in some way a request for a kind of gratification that stirs up fantasies
about lovers. However, she hasn't made very much of a
bridge between the two situations, and she hasn't clearly
related the therapist to her fantasies. The intervention
seems premature. It's more the kind of thing, at least

based on the brief presentation of that hour, that one would keep in mind and eventually definitely expect to interpret.

It's going to come up again. So, in terms of anticipating the particular session that we are about to hear, there can be no question that one of the adaptive contexts for the patient—and therapist—will be this unresolved question about the change in hours and the fact that the therapist has not already agreed to do it. But she does anticipate his compliance and I think she will also respond to that.

D: Well, you pointed out that perhaps he agreed to do it before finding out the facts.

L: He had said that he had heard about it in other sessions —we don't know.

D: But then she later talked about her previous therapist, who told her that her pregnancy was going to be fine, telling her these things when he didn't really know the facts and had no way of knowing.

L: Well, yes, but we don't know if this is really valid without knowing the facts. But there is another point about that. Now, let's just develop one more point because I want to get to the next session. This is a remarkably consistent observation: a situation in which the patient is asking for any sort of modification in the boundaries of the relationship—the framework—evokes two things in the patient: first, references to other variations in the boundaries, and second, the wish, if you do it once, you'll do it again and again. You'll see this all the time: once you gratify a modification in the framework, no matter how bona fide the indications, there will be requests for more of the same. That's another thing to keep in mind as a prediction.

But notice what she does, and it's so beautiful. In this session, where she's asking for a change in the ground rules, she remembers a time when her previous therapist visited her in the hospital and modified the ground rules of the relationship—that the patient and therapist meet only in the therapist's office. And what is her comment about that deviation in technique? I think it's very clear. That he was a destructive, horrible therapist, and that the deviation was part of his destructiveness. Sure, she's talking about his grandiosity and manipulativeness, but she's also commenting on his deviation in technique. She seems to sense that he was doing these things to gratify his own unconscious needs, and not out of any considera-tion of her. In fact, as I mentioned before, his outbursts of anger was another modification in the framework; it shattered his neutrality. And you know what she did after that—she left therapy. You can be certain that there are many patients who leave treatment because the therapist has unnecessarily modified the framework.

From this, you can see that if you don't have an air-tight reality as a basis for making a modification in the ground rules, the patient will feel that she has seduced you, that you had wanted to be seduced, that you grati-fied yourself, and that you are destructive. It evokes this kind of image; that's why you have to have a very clear-cut reason. Then you can say that these reactions are dis-tortions because there is the reality; and if there isn't re-ality, they're not distortions, they're perceptions.

Two last points about all of this: the first is related to the management of the ground rules. While the material doesn't fully illustrate it, let's at least establish from the hints that we have here, and from the many other obser-vations that we've already discussed, that the manage-ment of the ground rules is a crucial dimension of the treatment situation and of the patient-therapist relation-ship. The way in which the therapist manages these ground rules reflects his identity and the state of his own intrapsychic conflicts and controls, and the patient is constantly testing this and monitoring it. The way in which the therapist manages these ground rules affects the way in which the patient projects onto the therapist the so-called transference dimension—the patient's intrapsychic projections onto the therapist—and it also affects the patient's unconscious perceptions of the therapist. The therapist who cannot handle the ground rules and maintain secure boundaries will be correctly perceived as one who is not in control of himself and as one who is destructive, as this patient describes her previous therapist.

And the second point is something to keep in mind always. It comes up when a patient refers back to a previous therapist in a very negative, destructive way. First, look at the basis for this image: we have references to so-called supportive treatment, and we get a feeling for how manipulative, destructive, and inappropriate such treatment may be. But second, when the patient is referring negatively to a past therapist, we must always suspect that there is something in the way of a disturbance in the present patient-therapist relationship. In some way this material, as do all communications to the therapist, alludes to some mixture of unconscious perceptions and fantasies about this therapist. We must always suspect that the patient is unconsciously letting the therapist know that she sees him as destructive and that possibly in some way he is actually being destructive. We must remember this because we must constantly search for the truth in the patient's communications and for the unconscious perceptions that they contain. We must not presume that they contain solely or mostly distorted fantasies—and are therefore transferences—and deny the realities that the patient is perceiving. In particular, the therapist should not simply consider this material to be related to the previous therapist, but should attempt to search for what the patient is communicating in regard to the present treatment situation and in regard to her relationship with him in the present. He searches both himself for subjective clues as to what the patient could be sensing and perceiving as destructive, and he searches the further material from the patient for clues as to what is prompting these communications now.

As I mentioned earlier, it's an extremely common thing for patients to refer to themselves in critical ways when the latent material actually alludes to unconscious perceptions and criticisms of the therapist. And secondly, a patient will allude to previous therapists, and to others who have been destructive, at a time when the patient is not only having unconscious fantasies about the therapist's being destructive or is trying to protect herself from the unconscious sexual fantasies concerning the therapist, but also when she is dealing with valid unconscious perceptions of actual destructiveness or seductiveness in the therapist. We'll keep this in mind and we'll see if anything develops later that will help us to verify these possibilities. Now, let's hear the next session.

T: This time she came in, lit up a cigarette, and said, You remember what you told me last time, how I had misunderstood you? Well, how did I misunderstand you?

L: I heard all of your interventions; I missed that one. You see why it's important to know the therapeutic interaction—it's where the patient is at. It is what the patient is reacting to and it will often be the key to understanding what is actually going on inside of her.

T: Well, she was referring to a comment that I had made when she said something about her psychiatrist's visit to the hospital and his having said that she was sick because she wanted to be sick. I had questioned her, said something like, This is what he said? I raised a question that the patient felt indicated that I didn't believe her, and she got angry. This all happened at the end of the hour and I had concluded by saying, Well, you could have misunderstood me. But the patient had left angrily and she now began the next session by referring back to what had happened. She said, You remember what you told me last time? Before I left, you said that I misunderstood you. Well, tell me now, how did I misunderstand you?

L: Yes, well, and you said that this patient's problem is that she's too nice to everybody. I couldn't believe that for a second. Now, when we see her in operation, it's an absurdity. It really is. More than that, this just makes me wonder what was going on previously in this therapy. All right, go ahead.

T: Then she was really pressing me, telling me that she was really angry. And I even noted that she started the session not as she usually did, with talking, but she lit a cigarette and looked very nervous while she was doing it.

L: You said this to her?

T: No, no. That's what I observed.

L: Oh. So you didn't say anything.

T: She said it, and I answered that it seemed she'd been thinking about it—about what I had said. Yes, she said, I have been thinking about it because I felt that you said that the other psychiatrist was right in saying that I am sick because I want to be sick. And that you said that I'm coming to you because I just want care and love.

D: That isn't clear.

T: This had come up in a previous session or two. The patient had talked about going to many doctors such as a gynecologist and others, and it was somehow established that she seemed to be going because she was looking for care and love, because her husband and mother didn't care. The patient had added that she hadn't betrayed her husband with another man. At that time, all I said was that maybe she was also coming here for care and love, because I was a doctor too.

And now she went on and said, I'm not coming here

looking for care and love. I meant doctors. I didn't say psychiatrists. I meant that I was frustrated, so I was looking for care from doctors not psychiatrists. And now you seem to want to tell me that there's nothing wrong with me, and that I'm just coming here to get the care and love that I miss at home. She was very angry while she was saying this. Then she went on talking about her mother; that her mother had told her the other day that she didn't think that she needed a psychiatrist.

L: I just want to say one other thing, since you wondered about the necessity of mentioning interventions. Here, I wanted to try to predict the contents and dynamics of the session you are about to report. So you read a session to set the stage for it; you leave out the last part of the session; you leave out your last intervention, and as a result there's no way you can predict the themes of the next session. I just want to show that to you in terms of the importance of knowing the antecedents of a session. As I said before, if you don't know what went on between the patient and the therapist, there's no way that you're going to predict or understand what happens next. You left out an intervention of yours which was clearly very significant, and the whole thing is completely out of kilter. I just want you to see that.

If you had told us what you had said, we would have had the chance to anticipate this hour. After all, what would have the greatest impact on this patient—her expectation of the change in hours, or this brief interchange at the end of the session? It is here of course that our sensitivity to human beings, and our empathic capacities, come into play, and there can be little doubt that this patient's feeling that you doubted what she had told you would have a major impact upon her. In fact, this is a very striking example of the extent to which a modification in the framework—here, it took the form of your not maintaining your neutrality—becomes a major adaptive context and task for the patient.

Now we can deal later with the question as to whether the patient correctly understood your comment, or distorted it, but I can assure this much: when the patient reacts in this kind of conscious way, and even when she reacts intensely unconsciously, the odds are overwhelmingly in favor of there having been a valid core to her perception of your intervention. We can even look to some validation of this thesis in what you did in presenting the session to us. First, you left out your interventions entirely, and second, when you reported what you had said to the patient, you left out what is clearly the most important intervention of the hour—at least for the patient, and she is probably right about that. These defensive behaviors on your part give us a clue that there is a countertransference problem at work. So notice that here in a rather unusual way, we have taken the conscious associations from the patient as a clue to a countertransference problem in the therapist, and then observed the therapist's behavior and found some confirmatory indications that this is the case. Usually, we are working on the patient's unconscious perceptions and the therapist's subjective experiences; so having this all out in the open gives you a chance to see it from a slightly different angle.

And there is another point. The speculation that I offered just a little while ago, that it may well be that this therapist has been somewhat hostile or destructive with this patient for some time, now has some degree of confirmation. For whatever reason, it appears that he has been working almost exclusively on the surface of her communications, and has been having some difficulty in appreciating the adaptive contexts for her associations, and the problems that she has been working over unconsciously. And without getting into the whole issue of countertransference in any depth, we can say that this has been in the service, to some extent, of some unresolved hostility on his part. Here, we sense another kind of misalliance, one of a sado-masochistic interchange.

In addition, it seems clear that this patient is well aware of her therapist's difficulties in understanding her, and that her complaint about this question at the end of session is not only an intense reaction to his modification of the framework and his neutrality, but is probably the culmination of a number of episodes in which she felt misunderstood and accused. After all, there was an accusatory quality to those earlier comments about her coming to treatment for love and care, comments that appear to have been made prematurely as far as we know from the little segment described to us. And in the session that we just heard, her associations to her previous psychiatrist seem now to have had unconscious implications not only for her request to change her hour, but also seem to be a vehicle through which this patient was attempting to alert the therapist to his unconscious hostility, and to interpret some of its narcissistic and grandiose qualities. She was implicitly showing the therapist, through a kind of confrontation or superficial interpretation, and through the use of a "bad" model, how inappropriate it is to behave in such a manner. In any case, your questioning her about what the psychiatrist said clearly indicated that you didn't understand the adaptive context of her associations and its unconscious meanings, and that you did not appreciate her therapeutic efforts. So you reacted in a particular way and the patient may well have had reason to have then perceived you as defending the other psychiatrist.

You can now see why this seemingly small interchange at the end of the hour had such a powerful effect on the patient. We would easily have been able to predict this as the overriding adaptive context for the coming hour. In fact, to offer you something to think about that I will not attempt to validate, it may very well be that the therapist's unconscious motives for leaving out his interventions were not only intrapsychically defensive, but actually constituted an effort to projectively identify his feelings of confusion and helplessness into us. And in her own way, the patient may have been attempting to place into the therapist her sense of grief and rage over her experiences with her previous psychiatrist, and even with her present one; and the therapist's response in turn may have been an effort to refute the patient's projective identification and to not contain it.

I know that this gets a bit complicated, but as I say, this last intervention may have been an effort at projective identification by the therapist who was attempting to place into the patient, quite inappropriately, some of his own confusion and anger. I know that I've gone out on a limb, but I want to get you thinking about these concepts, and we'll see if the material from the patient supports any of it. We'll get into these problems of projective identification and the therapist's containing functions later on, but I think there is already some justification for thinking about the interaction between patient and therapist as the crucial component of this particular bipersonal field. We certainly will not be able to understand what is happening intrapsychically within the patient without doing that.

So, your interventions are quite important and this patient teaches us that, by letting you know immediately how important it was to her. This is how she began the session. Please continue.

T: She said her mother told her the other day that she didn't need a psychiatrist, that everything was fine and . . .

L: That's going to help those who didn't immediately realize that, when she talked about how her mother and husband felt she didn't need a psychiatrist, she was really speaking about herself. In fact, you can now see the context for this particular communication. The therapist hadn't understood her and had said something hurtful.

He joined forces with this horribly destructive, omnipotent, terrible, boundary-breaking therapist, whose heritage I would surely not want to have on my back, and she's in a rage. And she's thinking about leaving treatment.

Now, in terms of the ground rules and boundaries of the relationship, you've presented them in a confusing way, but it sounds very much as though your question really did convey some doubt about the patient, and some modification in what should be neutral listening and intervening. So, she really isn't crazy in wondering why you would even question her about what her former therapist had said to her, you see. And in a way, that was not really a neutral comment; the basic ground rule that the therapist gears himself toward neutral intervention directed toward interpretations, was really modified through that comment. No matter how innocently you asked the question—Is that what he really said?—it is not a neutral query. Casting doubts on the patient evokes a very intense reaction.

From this material alone, we can now get a clinical feeling about one of the points that I made in my article on the framework (Langs, 1975b). I mentioned it a little while ago, and now we can really appreciate it. The manner in which the therapist handles the framework reflects the extent to which he is able to manage his own intrapsychic conflicts and inner state. This is something that the patient readily senses, and I myself learned about it from patients who were responding to modifications in the framework initiated by their therapists. And once it was pointed out to such a therapist in supervision, he was able to acknowledge that there was something unresolved within himself that had prompted the deviation. And what we see here is typical of certain inadvertent deviations—the therapist is being unduly critical. Now it's well beyond the province of this seminar to explore the therapist's associations to his intervention, and to trace out its unconscious meanings—we'll leave that to him. I'll be satisfied for the moment if you can all get a feeling that the therapist has behaved inappropriately, and that it has been expressed in an erroneous intervention that simultaneously entails a modification of the framework—the therapist's neutrality.

You can also sense a second point that I have tried to establish, namely, that errors in technique and in managing the framework are by no means innocuous and without effects on the patient. They are countertransference-based, disturbed communications from the therapist, since they are not based on a valid assessment of the therapeutic situation and the material from the patient. They have a considerable impact on the patient, as this young woman is so clearly demonstrating.

In terms of the bipersonal field, they constitute pathological disturbances that have been placed into the field by the therapist. And in terms of Bion's (1962, 1963) concept of the container and the contained, this erroneous intervention by the therapist is an unconscious effort to place into the patient—have her contain—aspects of his own inner disturbances, apparently in order to have the patient work them over. This containing function is an important one for both the patient and the therapist, and for the bipersonal field, although I am sure that you recognize that the therapeutic situation is designed for the containing of the patient's psychopathology far more than for that within the therapist, although his contributions along these lines are inevitable. For the patient, this is a valid part of the therapeutic process, while for the therapist, even though it can be turned to the therapeutic gains for the patient, it's a type of countertransference-based interactional effort that should be quickly modified and resolved.

Now, before we get too far afield, let's return to this patient and her therapist. For the moment, we don't exactly know why she brought up her previous psychiatrist prior to the present therapist's hurtful remark, although we do wonder if the latter hasn't been subtly or grossly destructive in the past, and if he hasn't also been unnecessarily modifying the boundaries of their relationship. The material from the patient certainly points in this direction, and clinically, I have rather consistently observed that the therapist who deviates once, will virtually always deviate again.

But what really creates a difficult situation is that at the time that the patient brings up her previous psychiatrist, and her struggle against her negative incorporative identifications with him, at that very moment, you behave in a manner that is on some level quite similar to his, and that fosters an unfortunate identification between you and him. This is something that you would want to detect very quickly and modify. You could do that, for example, by using the patient's conscious and unconscious perceptions of your destructiveness, and of the similarity between you and the previous psychiatrist —which she is already talking about—recognizing their implications and changing your stance—and doing a bit of self-analysis to insure that you won't be hurtful again. Then you could use this same material interpretively.

This is very crucial since you really cannot modify the patient's actual reasons to condense her image of you and the other therapist, without behaving therapeutically in a manner that distinguishes you from him. You can be fairly certain that this type of therapist has little capacity to understand unconscious processes within his patient and to interpret to her, so that your ability to interpret unconscious aspects of her reactions to your hurtful comment would take you a long way toward this goal. And remember this as well: despite the writing of Greenson (1967, 1972) and myself (Langs, 1974, 1975c), I would like to establish here that the basic therapeutic principle is not to directly acknowledge to the patient that you have made a mistake, but to *implicitly* accept responsibility. I have found that such self-revelations are treated as a further modification in the framework by the patient, and that they actually constitute an unnecessary added deviation in technique.

The therapeutic work with the patient is served by your implicit acceptance of the patient's perceptions of your error and your treatment of them, in which you accept responsibility and in no way suggest to the patient that her perception of the incident is distorted, crazy, or transference-based. In fact, no matter how the patient extends her perceptions of your error intrapsychically into all types of transference-based distortions, you must always maintain an awareness that she started with a fairly valid perception of yourself. So accepting her view of you as having been destructive, and understanding the basis for her anger, you could say something to the effect that she apparently perceived your comment as quite hurtful and as questioning her truthfulness, and that for these reasons she is quite furious and has done such and such—depending on where she will go from here. Only then, can you address yourself to any distortion or misuage that the patient develops in response to what has happened.

And as if all of this working through of the patient's reactions to your error weren't enough, you must also have the capacity to change the conflicts within yourself that prompted the countertransference response. If you are unable to do this, and I suspect that as yet you have not developed this capacity since we have clues that indicate that you have made hurtful comments of this kind before, it is rather apparent what will happen: you will get your hostility under control in one area only to express it in a new way. So, without your working through the unconscious conflicts and fantasies and introjects that have contributed to your error, it is more than likely that there will be a repetition of this kind of experience.

And as a little exercise, let me show you what would happen if you were able to explore your underlying countertransference difficulties and resolve them. For example, just by taking the material from this patient as a participant in the bipersonal field and as a reflector of both her own and your inner psychopathology, I could speculate that one function of your provocativeness is that it serves as a defense against some kind of erotic countertransference difficulty. I say this because this is what the patient is communicating—she is struggling with fantasies of this kind, and interactionally, while a great deal of it undoubtedly stems from her own conflicts in this area, some of it more than likely derives from unconscious perceptions of such problems within yourself. It is this mixture that I have termed *the interactional neurosis*—the neurosis of the bipersonal field, to which both the patient and therapist have contributed.

Now, I am not going to make any effort to validate this formulation for the moment, but only offer it to illustrate that no matter how much the therapist were to become consciously aware of his hostility and provocativeness toward this patient, his efforts to manage these impulses would fall short unless he was able to effectively get in touch with his unconscious needs for the hostility, as, for example, a protection against underlying erotic fantasies. I am well aware that this asks a great deal of the therapist, and that some of you are not as yet in therapy or analysis. I do not make the rules within the bipersonal field, and I do not create the conditions under which the field will function therapeutically. It is the patient and therapist who do this, and it is the patient who asks of the therapist that he be able to become aware of the pathology that he places into the field, and that he have the capacity to master it. Actually, once you become aware of the sensitivity of the patient to the therapist's countertransference expressions, and to some of the exquisite communicative qualities of the bipersonal field, you cannot fail to recognize the need for the therapist to master as much as possible his propensity to place pathology into the field and into the patient. I know that this sounds tough and demanding, but again I want you to remember that this has been communicated to me—and of course to others—by patients. And it is what the patient not only needs, but has a right to ask for.

So it is only in these ways that you can restore your capacity to understand the unconscious communications from this patient and your ability to interpret to her, and thereby shift your image from a destructive or so-called bad object, like the previous psychiatrist, to a far more constructive and so-called good object, who then offers the patient important opportunities for positive identifications. At the same time, by being able to manage and secure the framework, you offer the patient a secure hold for her therapeutic experience and inner growth.

Well, this material certainly has generated a great deal of thought; but now, let's get back to the session.

T: She said that her mother had also said that she didn't think she needed a psychiatrist any more, and that if she needed someone to talk to, she could talk to her instead. Then her mother-in-law said that she could not baby-sit anymore.

L: We see here a communality between the destructive image of the mother-in-law, the mother, and the therapist.

T: Her mother-in-law told her, Ask him, ask him if he's going to change the hours of the sessions and I was extremely angry with my mother-in-law. And I told her, Look, he doesn't talk. Don't you understand? That's my job; I do all the talking. He doesn't ask questions, you have to give the answers. By my mother-in-law doesn't understand. She is just like my husband.

L: Now, this is also quite common, and it relates to the continuous, ongoing identifications of the patient with her therapist. And we see an aspect of this identificatory process in this material. She is really getting at the whole hurtful business of the present therapist's comment about her former psychiatrist. She is now communicating her unconscious perceptions of the current therapist— and undoubtedly secondarily, the former one as well— and these current perceptions are based on the therapist's remarks as the previous session ended. And the material also indicates that the patient has introjected the anger of both therapists, especially the present one. She may also be reacting to his failure to say anything about the change in hours. But here, I think the main focus is on the therapist's hurtful comment to her. Would you please review the end of that previous session again?

T: I had merely asked a question about what the patient had said regarding the previous psychiatrist's comments. She had then said, Now I know what you're thinking about me. You think I came here for care and love, and nothing is wrong with me and that I'm perfectly normal. Right? Isn't that what you think? You think I'm just coming here for love and attention. Well, I'm not going to leave here right now. I can't. I know time—the session is over, but I can't leave here now with this thought in my mind. I must know what you really think about me. And don't tell me that we'll talk about it next time. You always do that. (Laughter.) At this point I said, Could it be that you misunderstood me? And then I repeated to her that our time was up. And she was visibly very upset. And then she said to me, So, you're going to leave me like this and I'm going to have to wait until next time in this state.

L: So, we now see how important it is to get the specific associations from the patient; it's not possible to formulate without them. And now we see that in the final interlude something else was involved. The patient raised an issue in regard to the ground rules—she wanted her hour extended. That shows you that the whole issue of the framework was very much on her mind. She could have reacted in a hundred different ways. Now, after what you just said, she responds by saying, I don't want to leave; I want a reparative gift; I want to extend the hour.

So you see, this patient is attempting to achieve a *framework cure* by having her hour extended, so that the disturbance within herself generated by the therapist's intervention can be brought under control. And in addition, by attempting to alter the framework herself, she is both trying to exploit the therapist's mismanagement of the frame for her own gain, and attempting to call to his attention his modification in this framework, in a manner that unconsciously may well be designed to have him intervene so as to restore the solidity of the frame. More than likely she knows that the therapist will remind her that the hour is over, and in a sense she will achieve some relief through his firmness. You also see here how the patient incorporates the therapist's mismanagement of the framework and then attempts to use it—both to further maintain her neurosis and also to cure it.

D: The patient felt accused of lying.

L: Yes, but you should see this in its broader context. Here, we have indications that the therapist has been modifying the framework and not maintaining his neutrality, that he's been having difficulties in dealing with his hostile impulses, and that in a sense this patient has been misused as an object of his aggression. It may very well be that the therapist has been disturbed by his difficulties in this area or by some other problems with honesty, and that he is attempting here to place these difficulties into the patient. So—and this is really a speculation—we may have here a projective identification by the therapist of some inner dishonesty or corruption, placing it into the patient to have her work it over, so that the therapist can manage these feelings outside of himself.

In any case, you can see here how technical errors and mismanagements of the framework can include projective identifications by the therapist into the patient. Actually, I am beginning to realize that the opportunity for such projective identifications ranks high among the unconscious motives for becoming a psychiatrist or psychoanalyst. The patient is very vulnerable in this regard and is actually not there to serve as a container for the therapist's pathological contents. There is little doubt, however, that this type of interaction does occur and that it has a great deal to do with efforts by the patient to cure the therapist—his sickness has been placed into her. But remember, such efforts are not part of her primary reasons for being in treatment.

So again, we can see why I have indicated that the working out of the therapist's problems should occur in his own treatment and not in the treatment of the patient. It constitutes a misuse of the patient and although it is inevitable at rare moments, repeated use of the patient in this way constitutes a major modification of the bipersonal field and a basic disruption of the therapeutic process; it shifts the interface too consistently toward the therapist's pathology. And you can see here that the patient reacts to this kind of misuse with anger and that this anger is a response not only to being attacked, but also to having some of the therapist's difficulties placed into her, and that it also reflects an incorporative idenfication with her destructive therapist.

And it is at this juncture that she makes a comment that is absolutely typical at times like this: I have to cure myself. Well, this is true in many senses of the word. She has to cure herself because she has a part of the sick therapist inside of her. She has to cure herself because the therapist is unable to, for the moment. And in all, she has to cure herself because the psychopathology of the bipersonal field has been places into her and she is, for the moment, left to her own therapeutic resources. Technically, you have not only raised an unnecessary question about the patient's veracity, you have also failed to appreciate the nature of her unconscious communications and you haven't made a much-needed interpretation. She not only unconsciously and consciously perceives some kind of difficulty in you, but she has also taken it in and is experiencing it within herself.

Actually, in that earlier hour, I would have intervened. While I have little doubt that if I had heard all of the material in recent weeks, the intervention would have included references to other modifications in the framework and other errors, let me just illustrate by concentrating on how I would have handled this material in the adaptive context of her request to change her hours. I would have pointed out to her that she saw my acknowledging the validity of this request as having accomplished some kind of seduction and sexualized gratification. And when she brought up the material about the psychiatrist who extended the boundaries of her previous treatment, I would have used it to demonstrate some of the unconscious meanings of a modification in the framework for this patient.

It all seems a bit hollow to me now, since I think this material very strongly suggests that she is unconsciously alluding to other alterations in the framework; otherwise, I would not expect her to convey such blatant derivatives, and to experience such intense anger. The point for us at this juncture is that your own communications made it clear to the patient that you did not appreciate the unconscious issues and adaptive tasks with which she was struggling. And it was because of this, and the modification of your neutrality, that she now conveys her unconscious perceptions that you didn't understand her, and she begins to wonder why she should stay in treatment at all. And she takes it a step further: since it appears that you are not going to cure her, she will have to cure her-self.

It reminds me of a presentation made to me just a few days ago, in which a similar therapeutic impasse pre-vailed: the therapist had been placing a considerable a-mount of his own pathology into the bipersonal field and into the patient, and he had not been able to adequately manage the framework. This patient went on to talk about how he would have to hypnotize himself if he was going to get better. Now, just as with your patient, such communications reflect not only valid unconscious per-ceptions and an appropriate depressive and self-curative response, they also clearly extend into a whole set of un-conscious fantasies about the process of cure and about the patient's own intrapsychic conflicts and introjects. Each patient will deal with a hurtful interlude according to his own personality and inner constellations. The pa-tient that I just mentioned became profoundly depressed, while your patient flew into a rage and directly chal-lenged you. But remember that before you can effectively deal with the intrapsychic component, you must be able to recognize and implicitly accept the patient's valid un-conscious perceptions. If you are not sensitive to this component, you will only be hurtful once again, and try to tell her that her whole response is transference-based and distorted. And then she'll feel that you are uncon-sciously attempting to drive her crazy, and unfortunate-ly, even that would have a veridical core to it.

Patients are seldom able to cure themselves, so if you're going to be able to help her achieve that goal, and if you are going to be able to cure her through your own interventions, you will have to understand her. And she will make every effort to help you get back on the beam. So let's see what happens next.

T: She was talking about her mother-in-law who was telling her to ask me to change the hours of the sessions and she

said, I told her that he doesn't talk, I do all the talking
and he doesn't answer a direct question; it's up to me to
give the answers. She doesn't understand how therapy
works. Then she told me, My mother-in-law is just like
my husband. You know what he told me the other day?
He said that I'm perfectly all right and that I don't need
any therapy. He said that we could also save some money.
You see, he really doesn't care. He needs the therapy, but
I don't need the therapy.

L: He needs the therapy . . .

T: She said, He's the one that can allow himself . . .

L: Just listen to this patient unconscious communications.
Look at how important the realities are in evoking them
and how crucial they are to understanding them. The
building blocks for unconscious communications are
both perceptions and fantasies, and even the fantasies
derive in large measure from distorted and undistorted
aspects of reality. And you can see how a patient works
over a given adaptive context and trauma directly and indirectly, and how much work she does with it through
displacement.
    So, let's be clear about the meaning of this material.
By identifying the adaptive context as her reaction to
your hurtful comments, we can then organize her associations and identify their latent content. And we see a
mixture of unconscious perceptions, unconscious fantasies, and their intrapsychic elaboration within the patient. And the patient says first, you don't talk. Now, often, the therapist in training who learns to be relatively
silent and to listen to the patient until he actually has e-
nough material to interpret him, tends to fear that the
patient will complain about this silence. And it is my
clinical observation that patients almost never complain
about the therapist's necessary and valid use of silence,
but that instead, they almost always complain when the
therapist does not intervene adequately. And the thera-

pist's failure to understand and to offer valid interpretations is, on one level, a form of silence, although often some very destructive elements are contained in that silence. But it is rather typical for patients to complain about their therapist's silence when he has been missing interventions or intervening inappropriately.

Next, comes the allusion to the need for her to give the answers—to cure herself—and I've already commented on that in some detail. She then goes on to say that her mother-in-law doesn't understand how therapy works. Here, she is not only unconsciously perceptive regarding your difficulties in treating her, she is also doing a kind of supervision. I'm afraid that she has said something to you in just a few words that puts together many of the points that I have tried to make to you with a hell of a lot more verbiage. Patients do tend to be more parsimonious than supervisors—at least that applies to me.

But beyond that, the questions we want to try to formulate are how it is that the patient is so unconsciously perceptive and sensitive to her own therapeutic needs, and how it is that she knows something of her need for interpretations rather than hurts, or so-called support. I have indications that this has a great deal to do with the *validating process* that occurs continuously within the patient, much of it on an unconscious level. It appears that the patient processes the extent to which your interventions are helpful, meaningful, and of value in her managing of her anxieties and inner woes. Patients do all sorts of processing, and while it may seem amazing to you, they very clearly indicate their preference for insight-oriented therapy.

The patient then goes on to make a connection unconsciously between her mother-in-law, and, by implication through the adaptive context, her therapist. Now heretofore, we would have thought that the patient was referring to two recent figures that have a bearing on some

kind of transference displacement. That is, that the patient was experiencing some type of distorted perception
or fantasy of the therapist, based on displacements from
her mother-in-law and husband, and we would immediately suspect earlier ties to her mother and father. We
might also think that the patient is projecting onto her
mother-in-law and husband her denial of any need for
therapy.

This is again where the conceptualization of the bipersonal field and the therapeutic interaction helps us to
formulate the matter somewhat differently and far more
accurately. Because, when the patient goes on to say that
the husband feels that she doesn't need treatment and
that she's all right, and that he really doesn't care, she is
only secondarily denying her need for treatment. In
terms of the central adaptive context and the therapeutic
interaction, she is primarily talking about the therapist
and doing so in a manner that reflects accurate perceptions of his interventions. Some of them, as we had been
told earlier, seemed to convey the hurtful and insensitive
qualities described by the patient, and these communications are therefore not primarily transference distortions.
They are what I have termed primarily reality-based, unconscious perceptions that have genetic links (Langs,
1973b). This is an important distinction in that under
these conditions the patient is not primarily distorting
her perceptions of her relationship with the therapist, but
is in actuality experiencing some type of pathogenic interaction with him one that in many ways repeats a past
pathogenic interaction as well. This is what Racker
(1968) has called a vicious circle and what I have termed
a therapeutic misalliance. The pathogenic past and the
patient's present pathological unconscious fantasies and
introjects are being reinforced and repeated in her interaction with the therapist; and while the patient will al-

ways add distortions to these actualities, their veridical core cannot be overlooked if we are going to do effective work with the patient.

You see, this means that rather than interpreting to the patient that she has this distorted and crazy idea that you want to get rid of her and that you don't care about her—interventions which, as I've said, would only further damage her capacity to distinguish fantasy from reality, and to resolve her intrapsychic conflicts—you have two other jobs to do. The first is to modify your actual contributions to the misalliance and to restore a proper therapeutic field and relationship. The second is to accurately intervene, in a way that would be helpful to this patient. Thus, here you would say that the patient has perceived your question of her as hurtful, and as an indication that you don't care about her or that you wish to be rid of her —tying it to her husband's comments and adding that it has apparently prompted thoughts of wanting to leave treatment. Notice again that you have implicitly accepted her perceptions, without explicitly confessing that you have been hurtful and apologizing. Clinical experience indicates that the patient is only further burdened by your apologies and that what she needs for her own intrapsychic reorganization is an implicit acceptance of her perceptions and a sound interpretation that shows that you have recovered, begun to modify your countertransference problems, and now understand her again.

So you begin to see why it is important to separate reality and fantasy in the patient's communications. Now, while they are always intermixed and there is no such thing as a pure perception or a totally distorted fantasy, we can separate those communications that are primarily veridical from those that are primarily distorted. And you can also see that it is only when you have sorted out the realistic components of the patient's communications that you can clearly identify the distorted and transference aspects—those parts that are related to unconscious fantasies and introjects.

I think that it should now be clearer to you that there are two basic intrapsychic mechanisms that, while they are clearly intermixed, can be separated for study: unconscious perception and unconscious fantasy. And I hope it is also becoming clearer to you why we can only approach the patient's intrapsychic fantasies and conflicts through a complete understanding of the therapeutic interaction. Without it, nothing makes sense and we go back to the days which I hope will soon be placed into the distant past, when almost all of the patient's communications were considered to be distortions and transference-based, with the exception of an occasional conscious remark or those components that were seen as contributing to the therapeutic alliance. We have a much more complicated and difficult job to do in understanding the patient in the ways that I am describing, but the therapeutic outcome will be far more effective.

Now, we finally come to the crowining association: He needs the therapy, but I don't need the therapy. The patient has taken in the communications from the therapist, has introjected his inner state as reflected in them, and has concluded that he needs the therapy, not her. While this is, of course, a distortion, in that the patient is utilizing the therapist's psychopathology to projectively identify her own difficulties into him, it is also quite true —for the moment, it is the therapist who most needs the therapy. And we will see how actively she develops therapeutic endeavors in this direction.

In the meantime, notice this much: that when the therapist places pathology into the field, he both attempts to use the patient as a container for his sickness and offers himself as what I have called a *pathological container* for the patient's own pathological contents. That is, he unconsciously offers himself as a vehicle for the projective identification of the patient's difficulties into himself, in a form that reinforces the patient's denial and other defenses, rather than in a form that is therapeutic. Here, we see something of the pathology of the therapist's containing function. And it is my impression that this is an important form of pathology, in that many therapists inappropriately and unconsciously attempt to absorb the patient's pathology into themselves on a pathological basis that does not enable the sick contents to be properly metabolized and interpreted; rather they create a hiding place for the patient's sickness. And on this basis many patients find temporary relief from their inner difficulties, and we have another important form of misalliance cure.

It is well to remember that the interactional processes of projective and incorporative identification have many important nuances that we have not as yet investigated. Here, I'm stressing something that I have not seen discussed in the literature—that the recipient of a projective identification is by no means totally passive. Instead, the object of a projective identification actually may invite such a process from the subject, or on the other hand, communicate reluctance to accept such processes into himself. In this interlude we see something of a pathological invitation to the patient to projectively identify her sickness into the therapist.

I know that this all seems rather complicated, but I hope that these processes are becoming clearer, and I can assure you that we will continue to examine them in our clinical material so that you can become better acquainted with them. They are crucial mechanisms in the therapeutic interaction with all patients, and are not confined to those who are relatively primitive. Projective identification, like projection—which is an intrapsychic defense without interactional intentions—is a universal mechanism and is used by individuals at every level of functioning.

Perhaps this needs a bit of clarification. As I mentioned before, projection is an intrapsychic defense without interactional intentions toward another person. It is a defensive mechanism through which the patient attributes aspects of his own inner contents to another person, in an effort to solve primarily intrapsychic conflicts. On the other hand, projective identification has explicit interactional components. It is an actual effort to put into another person the subject's intrapsychic contents and introjects. It is an attempt to have the other person contain these introjects and work them over. The subject does this in order to manage his own inner contents outside of himself, and to benefit from the placement of disturbing internal conflicts into others, as well as from the capacities mobilized in the other person in dealing with these particular contents. It is this that Wangh (1962) has called evocations of a proxy—an interactional effort to place contents into another person in order to have the object mobilize adaptive functions lacking in the subject —who will in turn introject the object's positive functioning. These efforts get more complicated, so I will stick for the moment to some basic definitions until we have additional material with which to illustrate them.

In mentioning all of this, it occurs to me that we could postulate that the end of the last session saw a particular kind of exchange of efforts at projective identification between the patient and this therapist. I would put it this way: for some reason, the patient was attempting to place into the therapist some of her own bad introjects, in the form of her communications about bad and destructive psychiatrists. Some of this may have been an effort to reproject destructive contents put into her by her present therapist earlier. We don't have sufficient material to decide this point.

But nonetheless, notice what happened. The therapist did not seem to be aware of what the patient was projectively identifying into him, and accepted the projective identification unconsciously—a process that Grinberg (1962) has called projective counteridentification. He then attempted to project these contents back into the patient by doubting the patient's veracity. As a result, she has inside her the pathological and destructive intojects that she is working over in this session. From this, I hope that you can see that these are truly interactional efforts and interactional mechanisms, with defensive and gratifying functions.

D: I am not clear about the use of the word identification in the term projective identification.

L: That's a good question and it touches upon an important source of confusion about this concept. As you know, in classical psychoanalysis, identification is a term that is generally used to describe a given person's taking in of attributes of another person. It is an unconscious process that leads to some inner change within the subject based on his perceptions of the object—it is an introjective process. On the other hand, as I understand it, the term identification in projective identification essentially describes the continued attachment of the subject to the contents that he has placed into the object. This is a point developed by Malin and Grotstein (1966) and they stress that the word identification here implies a continued investment by the subject in his projected contents. So you see, no introjective process or inner change in the subject is implied in this usage, although some writers have suggested that projective identifications lead to depletion of the subject based on the loss of inner contents. And if you think about it, the identification in projective identification also seems to imply an effort by the subject to evoke an identification with aspects of his in-

ner self on the part of the object. It is quite unfortunate
that the processes subsumed under the concept of projective identification have been so named; the term itself
has generated a great deal of confusion and resistance
solely on the basis of the language that has been used.
However, it is an established concept and if we understand its meaning, it provides us with an important
means of comprehending interactional occurrences.

In this context, let me stress that my emphasis on the
universality of the mechanism of projective identification
is not meant to imply that all patients use it to the same
extent. There is little doubt that certain patients, especially those who are narcissistic, borderline, and schizophrenic, tend to make more pervasive use of projective-
identification than do those who tend to be neurotic. I
am emphasizing the broad use of this mechanism so that
you will think of it as a potential dimension in every interaction, and not restrict it to your work with relatively
disturbed patients. I also want you to recognize that therapists—however disturbed or well integrated—are also
prone to use this mechanism.

Now, I realize that all of this sounds very Kleinian, and
that's generally frowned upon in some quarters nowa-
days. But it happens to be an historical fact that the
Kleinians were particularly sensitive to interactional
mechanisms, at a time when the classical Freudians were
focusing on intrapsychic operations. However, since the
Kleinians have developed these concepts based on
studies of the child's earliest primitive mental functioning, they tend to see these interactions in terms of the
primitive inner contents that are projected into another
person, introjected by that person, and reprojected back
into the original subject. Now, while such interactions
certainly do occur, there is another sequence that they
tend to ignore—one that takes into account external realities and actualities. It is this neglect of the role of reality that has subjected the Kleinians to considerable criti-

cism, as has their overriding emphasis on the more primitive aspects of these interactions, to the neglect of those that occur on more mature levels.

It will take us too far afield to sort out the more valuable and the more questionable aspects of the Kleinian position, and those of you who are interested can read Kernberg's fine paper on this subject (Kernberg, 1969), and you will have a chance to further study this aspect when my new book appears (Langs, in press a). Here, I would only stress that the Kleinians would tend to neglect the therapist's actually hurtful and destructive projective identifications into the patient in assessing her responses—although a careful reading of their clinical vignettes show that they do not do so entirely. They would think of this interaction primarily as some effort on the part of the patient to projectively identify into the therapist, based on her own primitive intrapsychic fantasies. One thing that I've noticed is that they do tend to disregard the projective identifications of the therapist or analyst in studying their sessions, but this is something that is overlooked by most analysts regardless of their background.

Just one last comment before we return to the clinical material. I had said something earlier about the therapist who, based on countertransference needs, offers himself as a nontherapeutic or pathological container for the patient's disturbed inner contents. I want to counterbalance this by noting that the therapist also has an appropriate function to contain the patient's pathological contents in order to introject these contents and metabolize them in a manner that generates understanding and interpretations. This is a function that should be appropriate to the patient's needs and well managed by the therapist. And as you can see, the appropriate containing functions of the therapist are expressed not only in the manner in which he listens and then intervenes, but also the ways in which he handles the framework. Modifications in the framework can actually express rejections of the patient's contents, as well as overly intense and pathological needs to take them in. Again, we are getting into complicated issues, so I think that it is time to get back to the material.

T: So, he (her husband) needs the therapy. See, he really doesn't care. He just says that he needs the therapy and that I don't need it. But, you know, my mother also says that I don't need the therapy. And my husband again says that I don't need it. But what do you say? What do you think? Do you think I need therapy? Please answer me; just this time; just this question. I know you don't want to answer me.

L: Lang's rule: one deviation begets another. Now she's asking you to, really, in a sense, deviate. Give her an opinion —not a neutral intervention geared toward an interpretation—an opinion and a nontherapeutic gratification.

D: How would you intervene here?

L: I would interpret the unconscious meaning of the request. I would say, You feel that I kind of strayed away from being helpful to you, that I asked a question that casts doubts on your veracity, so if I can extend myself in that way, then you feel that I should extend myself in another way and now repair the hurt by giving you some kind of direct reassurance and some kind of direct gratification. That is the correct intervention. It comes out of what we're formulating, and it deals with the interactional hurt and the framework.

You see, questions of this kind come up at a point where the therapist has been hurtful, and the patient wants a special kind of reparation because of his failure to interpret and to remain neutral. This material does not, as I hear it, center around a request to change the hours, as much as it does on this other issue. That's why

I'm convinced that you must have said it in a way that really questioned her truthfulness. If she were distorting your intervention so much, she would not have reacted as intensely as she did; this kind of intense reaction comes out of real hurt. Think of this when questions of this kind arise—especially that other one: I'm so anxious, won't you please give me medication? The request for medication, virtually without fail, comes at a moment when the therapist has been hurtful, and in addition, hasn't made the interpretations that the patient needs. She's got to have something: if his words can't cure her, she at least wants drugs not only for their possible psychopharmacological effects, but because they would afford her special gratification through both the medication itself and the extension of the framework—a factor in medication that is generally overlooked. After all, medication modifies the fundamental aspect of the framework related to the patient's verbal associations and the analyst's neutral and verbal interventions, and it even removes the cure of the patient to some extent from the bipersonal field. It certainly extends the boundaries of that field and significantly modifies the therapeutic nature of the interaction between the patient and therapist. What is needed here instead is a correct interpretation. We will stop now, but we continue with this patient next week.

Chapter 4

THE PATIENT'S AND THERAPIST'S EFFORTS TO RESOLVE A THERAPEUTIC MISALLIANCE

THE CONCEPT OF TRANSFERENCE AS AN ILLUSION • THE PATIENT'S UNCONSCIOUS INTERPRETATIONS TO THE THERAPIST • THE THERAPIST'S PROJECTIVE IDENTIFICATIONS • THE PATIENT'S INTROJECTIVE IDENTIFICATIONS • THE PATIENT AS SUPERVISOR TO THE THERAPIST • THE HIERARCHY OF INDICATIONS FOR INTERVENTIONS FROM THE THERAPIST

L: I will ask our therapist to quickly describe the session, up to the point where we will continue our study of the material.

T: (The therapist repeats the material of the session up to the patient's words: I know you don't want to answer me.)

L: Let's do something basic for the moment. In order to correctly formulate in a meaningful way, we must organize the material of any session around the main adaptive context; in that way we can determine the latent content. We have established that the two adaptive contexts for the present material are first, the fact that her mother-in-law will no longer sit for her and the therapist has not as yet shifted her hours; and second, that the therapist had made a hurtful comment, which implied his doubts of the patient's veracity. These two adaptive contexts will interweave and we can build our understanding of the latent content of this session around each of these adap-

tive contexts. Now, how could the material in this particular session be appropriately formulated around these
adaptive contexts?

D: She spoke in terms of a rationalization that everybody
else had provided for her. Her mother and her husband
said she didn't need treatment, and she was going to have
difficulty in reality in regard to getting the treatment, so
she asked the therapist, Won't you also please tell me
that I don't need treatment?

L: Well, you're close. You're almost there. She isn't asking
the therapist. She does say that the therapist seems to be
implying that she doesn't need therapy, but what is she
trying to do?

T: She's trying to convince me that she's sick; that she does
still need therapy.

L: Well, she's saying that, but she's also talking about how
other people feel she doesn't need therapy, which is in the
service of what?

D: Of defense?

L: Yes, what's the defense?

D: Denial?

L: Denial of what? Denial of the need for treatment—you
just about said it, but you didn't quite crystallize it. In
other words, she's mobilizing whatever she can, in a defensive effort to deny the need for something that she
might not be able to have. She's also trying to convince
you that she is ill, in order to see to it that you change the
hours. So, in the adaptive context of the threat posed to
her treatment, this material conveys the unconscious fantasy: If I can't be certain that you're going to continue
my therapy, then I'm going to prepare myself by denying
the need for it.

You see again how the so-called unconscious works.
how the hidden mind works: while she's denying the need
for treatment in one part, in another part she's trying to
tell you, Look, I'm really very crazy; you're not changing

the hours because you seem to think I don't need treatment; it's as if you think I'm perfectly fine and you might as well know that I'm not; I'm sick.

Now, let's get to the other context: the hurt by the therapist.

D: The patient seems to be trying to get back at him.

D: Her associations related to the husband and how selfish he is are really displaced from the therapist, who was selfish and not on her side, but on the side of the psychiatrist.

L: Well, for one thing notice that it's a lot easier for you to formulate the patient's associations around the adaptive context of her need to change the time of her sessions than it is to do it based on the adaptive context of the therapist's hurtful comment. With both, we have to know something of what is happening in the therapeutic interaction, but with the hurtful response, we are dealing with the patient's unconscious perceptions and introjection of the therapist's inappropriate interventions.

Since I offered a rather extensive discussion last week of the patient's associations in light of that particular adaptive context, I will only add a few additional comments here. In addition to her telling the therapist that if he doubts her truthfulness, he is the one who needs therapy, the patient points out that such an approach is quite selfish—the husband's selfishness—and this is quite true: it is not in the service of the cure of the patient, but in some sense involves the cure of the therapist. And she is scolding the therapist for his behavior, and at the same time attempting to help him. And I think that she probably will now offer some more extensive help to him; so let's be prepared for it.

And in the meantime, we should turn this experience around and realize that when we hear associations about people who don't know what they're doing, and about someone who needs help, and when we hear about others who are being destructive, we should start asking ourselves questions like, What did I do wrong now? And we begin to reassess our most recent interventions, or possibly our failures to intervene. At such times, the therapist should reevaluate the therapeutic interaction and the state of the framework, and investigate his subjective feelings and fantasies of late.

You can learn a lot from this patient if you are willing to listen to and monitor her associations in terms not only of unconscious fantasies about you—which of course they convey—but also, and this is far more painful, her unconscious perceptions of you. In fact, when you begin to do this effectively, you won't need any supervision—the patient will unconsciously do it all for you. So, let's see what happens here. Based on my experiences with these situations, I would anticipate an unconscious interpretation from this patient. What will it be? Anybody want to guess? (Pause.)

Well, it seems to me that it will depend on whether she wants to be genetic in her approach, and tell you that your hurtful intervention was based on a problem with your parents, or whether she will approach it in terms of your conflicts in relating to women. Well, we'll see. Perhaps, too, she will address herself to your difficulties in terms of some problem with aggression.

T: She said, My husband feels I don't need therapy; that he needs the therapy. My mother tells me that I don't need therapy, but please tell me just this once, what is it that you say? How do you feel? Do you think that I need a therapist?

L: If this was understood better and in depth, you could have made an intervention. Look. She's trying to put the therapist on the spot. She's asking for a noninterpretive intervention. She's asking for a repair of the hurt, and is saying, If you're insensitive and you're not saying where you stand on her request for new hours, repair the

hurts by giving her a gift, an opinion. Also, squirm a little; she's going to make it difficult for you. On that basis,
you could have said to her that she was angered about
the comment that you had made last session, she saw it
as insensitive and hurtful, and now she wants to put you
on the spot; and she wants some kind of special gratification to repair the hurt. See, that would be an intervention
in which you would show that you do not wish to continue
to participate in what is becoming a sado-masochistic
exchange—you hurt her; she's trying to hurt you; there's
a back and forth. Otherwise, you will not interrupt the
neurotic vicious circle between the patient and the therapist—the sector of misalliance. Her question is an effort
to perpetuate it, and anything other than an interpretive
response to her query would also further it.

Some writers have called this an attempt to act out or
act in, and to gratify transference fantasies. My own discussion has shown you that it's far more complicated in
that these efforts have both transference and nontransference components, and the total interaction has additional countertransference-based contributions from the
therapist. In terms of the interface of the bipersonal
field, the therapist has put a significant piece of pathology into the field and has moved the interface toward his
own inner disturbances for the moment, a development
that the patient is both using for her neurotic gain—for
example, by putting her own pathology into you—and
attempting to truly modify—by undertaking unconscious
curative efforts directed toward you.

All of this serves as a reminder that unconscious transference memories and fantasies, and past relationships,
are repeated and conveyed in psychotherapy to a very significant extent within the bipersonal field and therapeutic interaction. The model that many therapists are
taught to use suggests that transferences are expressed
primarily through the patient's fantasies, and usually via

conscious fantasies directly related to the therapist. Nothing can be further from the truth. Now, in discussing this problem of transference expressions, please be clear that I have already indicated that this patient is actually experiencing a mixture of transference and non-transference elements, in which unconscious veridical perceptions of the therapist's actual behavior play an important part.

Nonetheless, we should be aware that a careful reading of Freud (1914, 1920) on this subject shows that he was well aware of these efforts at evoking a repetition of the past on the part of the patient in his relationship with the analyst—or therapist. He was less mindful of similar efforts by analysts—and they are quite common. But, the most critical transference interpretation occurs at the moment in the patient's associations and behavior where the therapist, instead of responding in a way that might perpetuate the underlying fantasies and inner reality, or repeat in any way the interaction with the parent who had created the neurosis in the first place, offers a sound and sensitive interpretation—at that very crucial point. Even where you've been involved in a misalliance for a moment, if you can then step back and interpret, you then become entirely distinct from the pathogenic parent. The interactional experience is completely different from the one that fostered the patient's pathology and the patient experiences something new. She can effect an incorporative identification with you and she gains cognitive insight. Then she also is forced to expose the fantasies that she's been trying to live out with you; because you have not gratified them, they will be expressed in an analyzable form. It becomes an exquisite moment—moment of cure.

It is situations like this that will convince you that interpretations of the patient's unconscious fantasies and perceptions, as they are related to the therapist in terms of their transference and nontransference elements, are essential to psychotherapy. They will also convince you that on one level, every communication from the patient has a bearing on the therapeutic relationship and inter-action. Please do not misunderstand the implications of these comments. For one thing, I have stressed that these communications are a mixture of transference and non-transference, so I am not suggesting that the patient's as-sociations contain only transference-based distortions. Nor am I overlooking the therapeutic alliance which re-ceives contributions from the patient based on both transference and nontransference elements. And lastly, I am not suggesting that every intervention by a therapist will relate to the therapeutic relationship, although I am indicating that the therapeutic interaction, and the bi-personal field containing it, must be in order and proper-ly understood for interventions related to outside experi-ences to have salutary effects on the patient.

Returning to this moment in this patient's treatment, it is a reminder that sectors of misalliance are inevitable in every psychotherapy, and that their therapeutic and analytic resolution provide important insightful and pos-itive introjective experiences for both the patient and the therapist, although it is certainly the cure of the patient which should be uppermost. We do not want to forget that the psychotherapeutic situation is designed for the cure of the patient and not of the therapist, although the latter is in a position from time to time to make his own therapeutic gains through it. When the therapist inter-venes with a sound interpretation at a moment when a misalliance prevails, the consequent insight and introjec-tion have a significant effect on the specific unconscious fantasies, anxieties, and pathological introjects that re-late to the patient's symptoms. The patient is then in a position to adaptively manage and modify them. Identi-fication and insight—they are our two essential, inter-

acting, mutually interdependent and mutually depen-
dent therapeutic tools.

Finally, we can see something that has been readily
demonstrated in the classical psychoanalytic literature:
that in these attempts to repeat a past pathogenic interaction, transference becomes a resistance, the resistance
to recovery. But transference also becomes the crucial
means of revealing the past. It is both. However, I now
want you to recognize that what has in the past been
termed transference in this way is actually a mixture of
transference and reality, transference and nontransference, unconscious perceptions and unconscious fantasy.

D: The question here is about the use of the word transference. This is all real, this is all going on right at the moment and involves feelings and so on, and it involves accurate, current perceptions. How does it become transference?

L: A good question. In part you are touching on the whole
concept of transference as an illusion, which has been the
subject of considerable confusion. Many writers have
thought of transference as a fantasy expression, rather
than recognizing its many actual manifestations in the
direct relationship with the therapist or analyst, and in
living displacements outside of the therapeutic relationship. The valid core of the concept of transference as illusion refers to the manner in which a clear-cut delineation
of the framework of the therapeutic relationship and situation insures the patient that her transference wishes,
and their expression in the interaction with the therapist,
will be safeguarded from direct, nontherapeutic gratification. It is in this sense that Milner (1952), Viderman
(1974) and myself (Langs, 1975a) have indicated that it is
the ground rules and boundaries of the therapeutic relationship—the frame—that makes it feasible for the patient to experience an analyzable constellation of transference expressions—the so-called transference neurosis.

The illusion concept in no way implies that there is something unreal about the patient's transference-based feelings toward the therapist, although some have given it this implication. These experiences are quite real to the patient, but the specific quality that distinguishes them from all other such experiences is that they occur within the bipersonal field and there are safeguards for both the patient and therapist in regard to their inappropriate or direct gratification. And it may even occur to you that the concept is further confused by the observation that the patient, in addition to distorted, transference-based reactions to the therapist, experiences feelings and fantasies toward the therapist that have a major valid core to them. Certainly, we are no longer able to justify a concept of the patient's feelings toward the therapist that stresses their illusory and as-if qualities—we will have to be much more specific in establishing the valid meanings that we give to such a concept.

However, in turning to this material, it certainly has a transference element in the fact that the patient consciously and unconsciously perceived the hurt from the therapist, saw that he was having difficulty, and then extended all of this in some distorted way intrapsychically. For example, one transference element is the link to her husband. Now this therapist hasn't said to her—as far as we know—You know you don't need treatment. You should stop, and I don't give a damn about you. So she's already elaborating it a little bit. You'll hear more. The unconscious tie that she makes between her husband and the therapist points to more. I grant you that the material does not especially illuminate the transference element, but it's there.

Remember, we're going to basically define transference as that part of the patient's contribution to the relationship and interaction with the therapist—be it behavior, fantasies or perceptions—that is based on his path-

ological and distorting intrapsychic fantasies and introjects. And these in turn are based on past experiences
with early parental figures and on the internalization of
these experiences. The term transference has been extended, and I think somewhat legitimately, to include
other intrapsychic distorting components from the patient, such as is seen in projections of his own impulses
or fantasies, or of the internal figures within himself, and
even to include displacements from more recent figures,
like the husband in this case. The classical concept of
transference has been extended in these ways, especially
through the work of Sandler and his associates in Eng-
land (Sandler et al., 1969, 1973).

But, if we are going to define transference in terms of
distorting intrapsychic effects on the patient's relationship with the therapist, we would now have to include aspects that have been described almost entirely in the
writings of the Kleinians. After all, an effort at projective
identification by the patient into the therapist is based to
some extent on his intrapsychic pathology and involves
distortions. Similarly, distorting introjective identifications taken in by the patient belong somewhere to the
concept of transference as well. The difficulty is that
these are interactional mechanisms and do not fit the
classical concept of transference, in which intrapsychic
mechanisms prevail, especially displacement and repression. So we have some rethinking to do in regard to this
very fundamental concept, although I will not pursue the
Kleinian aspects here, in order to have time to get back
to the clinical material.

Just a few more words about the classical concept of
transference. Greenson (1967), in his book on analytic
technique, defines transference as essentially inappropriate, basically distorted, and deriving from the patient's
intrapsychic unconscious fantasies. From there, we have
to distinguish it from nontransference elements in the

patient's responses to the therapist. You see, the reality is there and then it gets extended in terms of the patient's intrapsychic fantasies. Remember, transferences do not come simply out of the patient's inner world; they are prompted by some reality—most often it is in the realm of the patient's relationship with the therapist, though sometimes it lies in outside relationships. This is a different concept from the notion that in the patient's reactions to and perceptions of the therapist there are reality elements. There are reality precipitants for basically intrapsychic transference reactions, and there are also essentially nontransference perceptive responses to the therapist, which are then extended within the patient in terms of transferences. Both go on, and each has different implications technically. Transferences have reality precipitants, and reality perceptions—conscious or unconscious—are extended in terms of transferences. There are always intermixtures too.

Actually, in addition to clarifying these basic definitions, and understanding how one deals differently with a basically transference-based and distorted reaction to the therapist, as compared to an essentially valid response that is subsequently distorted, there is another very difficult technical issue related to transference. I raise it despite the statement by Sandler and his associates (1969) that every analyst knows clinically the referents for the concept transference—that is, what a transference expression looks like. I do not think this is the case, and in fact, I think that this is a major area for clinical research.

I believe that we have a lot to learn about the manifestations of transference. For example, many analysts confuse unconscious transference fantasies, that may be expressed through a wide range of derivatives in the patient's interaction with the analyst and with outside persons, and manifest references to the analyst in the patient's associations. As a result, many analysts—and therapists—think of transference only when they hear references to themselves or very obviously displaced material that they can clearly connect to themselves. And for this reason they are very selective in their thinking about transference expressions, and often miss more disguised communications from the patient that contain transference implications.

A more careful listening, in which both transference and nontransference allusions to the therapist are constantly considered, and in which the adaptive contexts that stem from the ongoing interaction with the analyst or therapist are kept in mind, will demonstrate clearly that on some level virtually every communication from the patient has a transference component. Now it may very well be that some other aspect of the material predominates for the moment, and it may also be that despite the transference implications, you choose to intervene on another level. This is fine. However, we must learn to recognize unconscious communications related to the therapist and to realize just how pervasive they are —even in psychotherapy. I think we will do a lot better with our patients once this is clarified.

Let's get back to the clinical material and I hope to show you some transference elements in this patient's associations. Even when the patient has an actual reason to feel hurt and to want in turn to hurt you, you must not overlook the fact that she will inevitably extend her appropriate perceptions and responses intrapsychically into distortions based on her own neurotic needs. So eventually, we can be confident that the patient will express her neurosis even in her efforts to cure the therapist. As a result, we will be able to get back to the "analysis" of the patient's illness. However, in intervening, we will want to sort out these two components—the veridical and the distorted—and to quietly accept the patient's therapeutic endeavors while carefully interpreting the neurotic aspects of her reactions.

Now, your question about the realistic aspects of primarily transference-based reactions in the patient is a good one. It has been my experience that if you or a therapist asks a good question, based on the ongoing material from the patient, the patient will on some level answer it. Let's see if this does indeed happen.

T: She then said, I would not have come here just for love and attention. But, even if I had, isn't that really sick? Like the other day, last week, I had sex with my husband, and he came very quickly.

L: So, that's the second interpretation that she's offering to the therapist. I gave her three choices, and now she has selected the therapist's sexual conflicts—the husband came too fast. You see, the therapist spoke prematurely; he came too quickly. Get that under control, she is saying. Now, this material also reflects something of her own sexual difficulties, and her own sexual fantasies. Everything in the patient's communications is overdetermined and condensed. Here, we have the condensation of an unconscious interpretation to the therapist about his unconscious, or conscious, sexual anxieties, which led him to speak too quickly, to come prematurely, to hurt her, to not satisfy her, and all the rest. At the same time, this material reflects her own sexual difficulties—for example, the way in which she is sexualizing the relationship with the therapist. She's talking about how she is not here for love, which of course tells you what she's here for. And she has some sexual fantasies about the therapist that she wants gratified; that is also in this and her earlier material—the associations to the other man she thinks of during intercourse. She sees that this situation between herself and the therapist is a sexual one in which she's not being gratified. That's an unconscious fantasy; that's a transference element that we can trace out eventually beyond the husband to someone in her childhood, probably her father.

But, what I'm trying to teach you is that it's both transference and nontransference. If you make an error, if you do something hurtful, then listen to what the patient tells you about yourself. Learn from it. And listen also to what she says about herself. And in intervening, don't say to her, You know you have this crazy fantasy about my being hurtful. Nor do you say to her that you're sorry that you've been having disturbing sexual fantasies about her—that is a modification in the framework that would enormously frighten and burden the patient.

Instead, you wait until the patient's associations connect this material to you on some level, and then you intervene sensitively. I want to stress the need to wait until her associations begin to center on the therapeutic relationship, before saying anything at all, since in that way your comments will have a convincing effect on the patient and she will probably not utilize denial. And when the material does begin to coalesce, then you could, using the material to this point, say something to the effect that the patient has seen your questioning of her truthfulness as a kind of sick and premature remark. Now, you might let this suffice, rather than adding that she also seems to have some impression that you are sexualizing your relationship with her.

It is here that therapeutic tact and sensitivity comes into play, and I believe that there are a number of reasons not to add this to your intervention. For one thing, you have already picked up her unconscious perceptions of you to a sufficient degree to demonstrate both your recovered sensitivity and your ability to appreciate her valid efforts. In addition, I suspect that there is some truth in the patient's interpretation, and since it cannot be treated primarily as a distortion, I would not bring it up in the session with her, but would confine my efforts to myself, making every endeavor to detect and master my

own erotic countertransference. As I said, you can benefit greatly from the patient's therapeutic communications, but this should be done in the confines of your own
thoughts. Lastly, she might consider this idea of her perceiving you as sexualizing the treatment as an attempt on
your part to project, or even projectively identify, your
own sexual conflicts into her, and in fact, such an intervention might have exactly those qualities—which is another reason why I would not make it.

Here, I am trying to show you how you monitor the patient's associations and your own responsive, subjective
reactions for both veridical and distorted elements. And
as you develop them, you privately attempt to sort out
your proposed interventions, and decide on which aspects are appropriate to communicate to her, and which
are not. This is no easy matter, and you can be guided by
the patient's ongoing associations in this respect also.
That is, those formulations that her further associations
support can be more readily offered to the patient.

So, after indicating aspects of the patient's veridical
unconscious perceptions regarding your premature and
hurtful comments, I would then deal with the transference elements. You could therefore proceed to point out
to the patient that these experiences have prompted within her some apparently disturbing sexual fantasies about
you, as reflected in her thoughts about another man
while having intercourse with her husband, and in the
sexual way in which she conveyed her perceptions of you.

Now again let me make clear that I am simply offering
this as a model intervention, and that I do not believe
there is sufficient material to interpret the transference
element in the patient's associations at this juncture. Not
only do we not have the important genetic aspects, but we
do not have the thread in the patient's associations that
link the sexual material to the therapist. Without that, I
would be quite silent and in fact, would be making what I

have termed *silent formulations* and *silent interventions*. I would be working over these formulations and interventions and awaiting confirmation of them from the patient's material. Valid silent formulations should be confirmed by the patient before you verbalize their contents to her; and you can then intervene with a great deal more confidence.

It is important to have patience and to take your time. I can assure you that among the patient's deepest wishes are those related to getting well, and on this basis the patient is unconsciously cognizant of her responsibility to convey derivatives of her intrapsychic conflicts and fantasies to you. And she will do just that in all sorts of disguised ways, and if you have a clear picture of the adaptive context and the unconscious meanings of her communications, you will be able to intervene quite effectively at the proper moment. In a sense, as de Racker (1961) so exquisitely described, the patient will feed you the interventions she needs, and offer you the material that you need in order to be a good therapist. In fact, as I am showing you, she will do even more than that: she will even attempt to cure the obstacles within you to interpreting effectively. Begin to have faith in your patients and, as I said before, they will teach you all that you have to know about therapeutic technique. Now, let's hear some more.

T: She went on, Like the other day, last week, when we made love, and he came too quickly. He does this all the time. I said to him, Can't you slow down, because if you don't, you know what will happen. And you know what he said to me? He said, who cares?

L: Do you know what she was implying, what will happen?

T: She might lose control; she might leave therapy; she might go crazy, or something like that.

L: So you weren't really clear?

T: No.

D: Wasn't her question a rhetorical one?

L: She's threatening something and I'm wondering if the therapist was familiar with this kind of thing. There are all sorts of possibilities.

T: What she could be saying is, I might go crazy or I might leave treatment.

D: To her husband she's saying, I'll go to somebody else who comes more slowly.

L: Yes, it's apparent that she's saying something to both her husband and the therapist. The most obvious implied threat is that she'll find another man who can do it right. Notice too that she's saying that he does this all the time; this helps to confirm my suspicion that the therapist has been intervening in this kind of premature and hurtful manner for a while.

Also, notice the way in which the patient is able to use her husband, for the moment, for a projective identification of her sexual anxieties and conflicts. He lends himself to such a projective identification and invites it—an aspect that I had discussed earlier. And on this basis, for the moment, you would have some difficulty in interpreting to the patient her own sexual conflicts. So you can see how someone who offers himself to the patient as a pathological and inappropriate container for her disturbed contents can provide her with a form of misalliance cure—however temporary. Something similar, of course, is going on with the therapist, who has invited projective identifications into himself by the patient that are not for the moment therapeutic, but serve to rid her temporarily of her sexual anxieties and conflicts. This is an important form of misalliance cure, but like all such false cures, it can be turned to genuine therapeutic gain if the therapist recognizes it, no longer offers himself as such an inappropriate container—modifies the actuality—and then interprets to the patient what has been going on.

Getting back to some basics, this material also answers a question that is often raised, as to whether patients in psychotherapy free-associate. For me, free associating occurs in psychotherapy as well as in analysis, and is based on the fundamental rule that the patient should say whatever comes to her mind. Now, as I said before, there are differences in the attributes and qualities of the free associations of the patient in analysis, as compared to psychotherapy; but there is a vast area of similarity as well. In fact, the frequency of the sessions, and the position of the patient, are only two of the many variables that influence the patient's free associations. Some additional relevant factors are the nature of the patient's psychopathology, his relatively autonomous capacities, and a whole variety of attributes of the therapist as well. The point I want to stress is that sound insight psychotherapy can and should be based on the material and interaction that derives from permitting free association by the patient, and thereby securing an avenue for the communication of his unconscious fantasies and perceptions.

This concept is borne out here when the patient suddenly starts to talk about her husband in bed, as if the topic came out of nowhere. But notice how meaningful this shift in manifest content is for our understanding of the patient; she had been talking about her anger at the therapist and now she begins to talk about her sexual experiences with her husband. This shift in her associations conveys important unconscious fantasies and perceptions. It's the most valuable kind of sequence that you can get. If she went on and on about therapy, what would you learn? Would you learn that she sees it as a sexual experience? Would you learn that she thinks you have a sexual problem? You couldn't possibly.

So this is a patient who is gifted in unconscious communication. And try to be clear about the way in which you get to the latent content that the patient is conveying:

you establish the adaptive context and the patient talks about another manifest theme. She thereby conveys associations that are meaningfully related to the original adaptive context. She displaces and disguises the fantasies that pertain to this original context, and they appear as *derivatives*—disguised expressions of unconscious fantasies and perceptions. This is also what I meant when I pointed out earlier that unconscious fantasies can be viewed interactionally as the intrapsychic working over of an adaptive context or trauma through displacements.

T: From what you said before, she would continue in a vicious circle because I didn't make the correct intervention.

L: Well, yes.

D: She is saying that you have a sexual problem too.

L: She's describing the nature of the problem—for you and for her. What usually happens with patients is that they participate in, and then they attempt to modify, the misalliance. They accept it and then they don't want it. After all, a misalliance isn't going to cure her, and your having problems won't do it either. She accepts the gratification for a moment and then she tries to change the situation. She's now in the stage of trying to let you know how she perceives the misalliance, and your problems and hers—condensing them in these last associations. She's now working to resolve the therapeutic misalliance. She won't maintain it indefinitely, and neither will her therapist—hopefully. And the modification of the misalliance includes unconscious efforts to cure the therapist.

Actually, this woman communicates quite richly. This relates to a basic aspect of the therapeutic alliance that is not generally written about. It relates to the capacity of the patient to communicate derivatives of unconscious fantasies and perceptions. That is essential to the therapeutic process because it is where the patient's neurosis comes from. The therapist's part of the alliance in this area is his ability to understand and interpret such material. That's where his job comes in and if he can do that, patients will give him more material. If he can't, they become very despairing.

A second inherent part to a viable therapeutic alliance is the patient's willingness to interact with the therapist in a way that unconsciously repeats past traumas, and unconsciously conveys the pathogenic intrapsychic identifications that are within the patient. This affords the therapist the opportunity to modify these past interactions and to offer the patient new and constructive identifications. Ultimately, cognitive insight is necessary for the mastery of symptoms, but these interactional repetitions permit the patient to project and to projectively identify into the therapist, and to incorporatively identify with and take in the therapist's responses. These provide another important means of inner change, even though it generally doesn't modify specific intrapsychic conflicts. With certain patients, this kind of interactional modification is necessary for long periods of time, before the crucial modifications that can occur through the interpretation of derivatives of unconscious fantasies can be effected. Please continue.

T: The patient went on: And I said to him, You know what will happen if you don't? And do you know what he said to me? Who cares? He really just doesn't care at all. He just cares for himself. So at this point, I said, What will happen? Then she said, Oh, I told him about my fantasies. I told him how I feel that I make love to myself. And do you know what he said? He said, For women that's normal. But I said, You can do something about it. And you know what he did? He just walked away. You know how I feel? He really doesn't change. And I feel that I have little hope. This anger in me is just building up, and I feel very frustrated. I have little hope of our making it together. And do you know what my mother told me?

She told me that if I lose my husband, I will become a tramp, and that I will go on welfare. And you know, I'm a woman with children.

L: See, she gets next to the anger—in terms of her own anger and her perception of your anger. She gets very quickly to her despair: he won't change, so I have no hope. She'll live out her fantasies about you with her husband. You see, she's desperately trying to utilize a kind of masturbatory fantasy in order to preserve the object tie, and to control her impulse to go searching for a substitute for him—and for you.

T: But doesn't she have a real problem with her husband?

L: Oh, it's a real conflict, there's no question about it.

T: They were on the edge of divorce.

L: Yes. That's another, more realistic adaptive context. But again, if you simply hear this material in terms of her real problem with her husband, you will never discover, first: the way in which she's contributing to her husband's problems; and second: the way in which she's living out with her husband her conflicts with you. Then she will decide to leave her husband, at the point where she feels that you are absolutely hopeless and she's not going to get any help from you. The next time you hurt her, she'll leave him. These are some of the ways in which her unconscious fantasies and her unconscious perceptions involving you contribute to the manner in which she manages her other problems. And you discover to the amazement of all concerned that if you are able to change and if she is able to resolve her conflicts with you and, ultimately, the intrapsychic elaborations including the genetic aspects of these conflicts, suddenly she's reacting differently to her husband, and soon he picks it up, and the next thing you know, the husband is potent. And your whole picture of the patient's problem has been clarified: it turns out that this seemingly poor, innocent victim has been living out a whole complicated intrapsychic fantasy related to a displacement from you, which also has its root, again, in her own inner pathology and in her childhood. These ideas illustrate the concept of interactional contributions to acting out.

As soon as you start to focus on the reality problem, you immediately deny these additional sources of her reactions. Once you shift to that reality conflict, you're no longer dealing with neurosis, because if you have a husband who really can't satisfy you sexually, you do indeed try to do something about it. And you decide whether you want to live with him or whether you want to leave him— and there's nothing neurotic or inappropriate about that. But if you have a therapist who is hurtful and who isn't helpful, and you decide to leave your husband, that's a neurosis.

Freud (1926) in *Inhibitions, Symptoms, and Anxiety* said that if Little Hans was afraid of his father because he wanted to go to bed with his mother, that wouldn't be a neurosis. But he was afraid of horses, so there was a displacement and there was an inappropriate reaction that could only be understood through his intrapsychic conflicts and fantasies. If this patient is having fantasies about you, and she leaves her husband, that's what we mean by a neurosis. Her behavior is not appropriate to the situation; it's appropriate to another situation and the inner fantasies and perceptions that are related to it.

This is one of the greatest failings in psychotherapy— the therapist lacks a concept of neurosis and of the intrapsychic conflicts on which it is based. And instead of pursuing inner conflicts and intrapsychic fantasies and introjects and unconscious perceptions, he focuses on reality-based conflicts and their relatively inconsequential intrapsychic repercussions. And the whole therapeutic job is done on a manifest level that not only fails to enable the patient to modify her inner disturbance, but actually serves to reinforce it. And especially in situations of this kind—which are so very frequent—in which the intrapsychic conflicts relate to unconscious fantasies about, and perceptions of, the therapist, there is a special need within many therapists to confine themselves to the displaced problems with the husband. This enables the therapist to deny his own contributions to the patient's disturbance, and to fend off the unconscious communications related to him. The therapist uses the patient's outside difficulties, and the disturbances in those around her, to projectively identify his own inner difficulties into that outside situation. So, once again, theoretical misunderstandings go hand in hand with countertransference difficulties. Now, let's get back to the patient.

T: She continued, I feel this anger; it's rising in me, and it's getting a lot worse; he's not changing and I feel almost no sense of hope. I feel there's no way to go. And do you know what my mother told me? She told me I'm going to become a tramp; I'm going to become a whore. And I'm a woman with children. And tell me, why did she say that to me? Why me? And she said it with such real anger. Me. I never had anyone—except for one time when I was sexually molested as a teen-ager. The patient had mentioned this fact a few sessions before. Now she said, This was forced on me. Why me?

L: You can see why so few analysts, let alone therapists, have been willing to see the extent of the unconscious perceptiveness of the patient. She's already told you that you want to destroy her, that you have a sexual problem and that you're impotent, and now you're a rapist. Now who in the world wants to hear this kind of stuff all day long from patient after patient, particularly when it's partially justified and touches all kinds of sore spots? So we decide that this is all fantasy. It isn't that you've been coming on strong and you've been abusive; it's that she has this distorted fantasy. Her father was abusive and she's projecting it onto you. And this is actually your distortion and your protective fantasy.

Yet many analysts who are in search of the truth have been perfectly willing to live with that kind of mythology for a long time. And you can appreciate why. It's very hurtful to think of these things as valid—as perceptive—and to find the truth in them. It's really very difficult. It's narcissistically mortifying; it's anxiety provoking; it's depressing, and it's despairing. So we defend ourselves by saying it's all fantasy—all projections from the past. How nice. But it isn't true. And if it isn't true—and yet you think it is—you can't intervene properly and you cannot really help the patient, except by showing her that you're so inept and she's so smart—or by creating some other kind of misalliance. It hurts; it does. You've been dragged over the coals. Go ahead; let's see what she does.

T: And she went on: this was forced on me and I could tell you that I have been faithful to my husband all these years. And that, that's crazy; to put up with all this all these years is crazy. And my mother telling me that I'll become a tramp; this is the help that I'm getting from my mother . . .

L: Here comes the bad mothering theme and interpretation. I think that she's done with the therapist now, unless she can think of a few interpretations that I haven't formulated as yet. I would not be surprised.

You know, when a patient has been sufficiently traumatized and hurt by her therapist, there comes a moment when she really makes a massive effort to cure the therapist and the disturbance within the bipersonal field. The interface at this point is very close to the therapist and quite filled with vectors related to his pathology, and the patient is actually the active therapist at this moment —a not uncommon occurrence in a poorly managed therapy.

I'm not trying to be overly critical, but at this juncture in your training, when you have so much to learn and so many countertransference difficulties to get under control, you present a problem of enormous proportions for this patient. I am not speaking for myself at this point, but entirely for the patient, and I am translating her communications to you.

And again, let me remind you that in addition to these perceptive interpretations, she is certainly communicating aspects of her own intrapsychic conflicts and fantasies. You may have begun to think with all of my emphasis on the patient's unconscious perceptiveness that I have abandoned the basic model of psychotherapy as a situation in which the patient's intrapsychic conflicts and problems are explored and resolved. Nothing could be further from the truth. All I am saying is that we should investigate the contents of the bipersonal field and the therapeutic interaction, without prejudice as to who is putting into the field the main pathological elements; the therapeutic work will always occur at the interface created by the patient and the therapist. And I am saying that when this interface is determined largely by pathological vectors from the therapist, this is where the therapeutic efforts must focus.

And please be clear—I'm saying that this is necessary as a prelude to the original design of the therapeutic situation, and to the actual goals of treatment: namely, the cure of the patient. There's no way that you can bypass the therapist's contributions to the patient's pathology; they must be recognized, modified in actuality, resolved through self-analysis by the therapist, and analyzed with the patient. And then, when the therapist's pathological contributions to the bipersonal field are under relatively good control, the therapeutic interface will shift toward the patient and will receive its major vectors from the psychopathology of the patient. This is the expected model of psychotherapy, although, as you see, it is often not an actuality. These are all what I would call hard facts and they are painful to face, but the therapist and the patient can mature enormously by confronting them and dealing with them.

Now, we can also see that the patient is struggling with sexual fantasies, and impulses to act out sexuality. And it appears that some of these difficulties have both a current and genetic tie to her relationship with her mother, while other aspects stem from her interaction with the therapist. In a clear and typical mixture of unconscious perception and fantasy, this patient experiences—with whatever degree of validity—the therapist's hurts as an unconscious effort to push her into sexual acting out; and further, she is actually having some difficulty in maintaining her controls because of these pressures and because of the uncontrolled model offered by the therapist.

Certainly, she is also struggling with her own craziness, but she is, in addition, attempting to cope with what may be termed the craziness of the therapist. In all, as we see, both her depression and anxiety mount, and her potential for acting out intensifies. We have an excellent opportunity to observe what I have called an *interactional neurosis* and the pending development of *interactional symptoms* and *interactional acting out*. I have called it the interactional neurosis because there are significant contributions from both the patient and therapist, and you can see that the proportions vary from moment to moment. And the concept has clinical importance, in that exclusive exploration of these symptoms in terms of the patient's intrapsychic conflicts and fantasies will not resolve the problem; the contributions of the therapist must be recognized and modified as well.

So we see the exquisite therapeutic efforts of this patient, a small portion of which is self-directed and a larger portion of which is directed toward the therapist for the moment. And we see the extent to which all of this occurs on an unconscious level and can only be understood if we have a clear grasp of the adaptive context—here, the therapist's hurtful interventions.

And so she deals first with his more developed years when he, she suspects, suffered both sexual and agressive conflicts and disturbances; and then she comes down to basic problems like mothering and difficulties with a bad mother, who doesn't know how to adequately care for her child. You will notice that these unconscious interpretations are on a general level, and as I said earlier, lack the specificity of interpretations available to the therapist, because of the communications with which the patient must work. And you may all begin to realize the extent to which the therapist could benefit from these efforts on the part of the patient, although he has a great deal of work to do on his own.

Finally, when you hear themes related to bad mothering, you must always ask yourself if you have intervened badly, and if there is some problem in your basic therapeutic hold. And further, when you hear themes about people trying to drive the patient crazy—and you may remember that I had formulated an aspect of the therapist's effects on the patient in just those words—you should reassess the nature of your interventions with, and feelings toward, the patient. The patient's material should also be monitored for clues regarding her unconscious perceptions of the difficulties that you are having. And while there is an unlimited variety of possible themes, this patient seems to have touched upon the basic areas: bad mothering, sexual and aggressive conflicts, and problems with control and management.

T: And this is the help, she went on, that I got from my mother, when my husband even threatened to leave me for a while, and Dr. Y—her previous therapist in the clinic that referred the patient to the present therapist—said to me when my husband was threatening to leave me, I should stay away from my mother. And Dr. Y rarely said anything so directly to me; so when he said this, I really listened. The she stopped for a while and it looked as though she was thinking. She then said that all of her siblings have been in treatment at some time or another. So here I said, It seems that you're implying that your parents have something to do with this. She then said, Oh, yes, if you knew my mother, she's a real sergeant.

L: Here you focus on a reality issue and take her away from the whole theme with which she began the session—her reactions to you. And technically, your intervention, which is a kind of clarification or confrontation, is made entirely without an adaptive context. In addition, if you think about the intensity of her communications, you have curiously selected a relatively mild aspect for your comment, and you have put aside all of her allusions to sexuality and destructiveness.

However, in keeping with my discussion of your modification of your neutrality and of the frame, you might now notice that she's telling you that her previous therapist deviated in regard to his neutrality, and I would have liked to hear her associations to that, because she had earlier asked you to deviate and to make a similar comment. Her associations would have led you to its unconscious meanings for her. You take her away from that flow to imply something about her parents: Let's talk about your parents. It's much easier, but it will create a split off bastion of the bipersonal field.

Also, realize that by focusing on the reality issue, you're getting away from the manner in which the patient returns to the theme of psychiatric treatment, and to a deviation in the neutrality of the therapist. One deviation in neutrality has now brought up another such deviation. She talks about it in the past, but of course it has been stirred up in the present.

Notice, too, that we now know that your behavior is a

repetition of her mother's earlier controlling, destructive and dominating behavior; so, you have repeated the past in the present. As a result, there can be no therapeutic modification of the patient's internal representations of this past and the inner objects developed out of it, and no modification of the connections to her own inner, neurotic problems. So here we also see the difference between transference and nontransference in terms of their basic structure. Transference implies that the therapist has not in actuality repeated the past and the patient attributes such a repetition to him; nontransference implies that the therapist does indeed repeat this past and then the patient elaborates it according to her own intrapsychic fantasies. The implications for your interventions are crucial, but the effects of the interaction on the patient and her inner life are even more crucial.

T: She was talking about how her mother was a real sergeant. Then she talked about her childhood: how her mother was very unloving; how she was very uncaring; how she wasn't considerate; how she didn't care; and how she, the patient, went out of her way to try and please the mother, to try and get some nice response from her; and how her mother was so rigid and so inflexible; and how on Fridays she used to come home and do the cleaning, wash the floors, do the shopping and cook the meals. Her mother was just there really, just like a queen.

The patient had to clean the house, scrub the floors, do the cooking, and do the shopping, and she told me that she was never allowed to date on Friday nights, that she had to stay in. She went out of her way in many different ways to try and get a pleasing remark, some sort of approval from her mother, and she never got anything. She and her sister were very different. She then related a story about how late one night they were in their room with the lights out, and she was trying to go to sleep but couldn't. Their door was open and she heard noises coming from her mother's bedroom, and it was keeping her up. Then she called out, Mother, are you there? What are you doing? And she got no answer, except that her sister woke up and said, Shut up, let me sleep. And her sister never asked questions and things never bothered her as much as they seemed to bother the patient.

L: I've found this over and over again: whenever the patient gets around to the therapist's or the analyst's conflicts and problems in listening and in intervening properly, he almost always gets around to the primal scene. Patients intuitively recognize that the therapist and analyst are involved in a listening kind of procedure that mobilizes all of their own primal scene conflicts, and that errors in intervening reflect exhibitionistic problems related to that sphere. Of course, the patient is attempting to deal with her own primal scene conflicts as well, but once again, when the therapist's problems predominate, such material often conveys an unconscious interpretation related to the therapist's exhibitionistic and primal scene conflicts—as is the case here. Any therapist who has been in analysis and who hasn't gotten to his primal scene conflicts has some specific work to do.

T: This was the end of the session.

L: So, the hour ends with an extended plea for love and with reminders that she is trying very hard to do her job; she would simply like a favorable response from the therapist. Just remember that the pleasing remark and approval that she needs from the therapist is not the same as what she feels entitled to from her mother; it is as you would expect, a correct interpretation.

It appears then that this patient is attempting to be more specific than I had anticipated. She returns again to the area of sexual conflicts, as she suspects and perceives them on some basis—we don't have the earlier material—in the therapist, and as they intermix with her own difficulties in this area. And she goes back to a genetic aspect of her own sexual anxieties, and offers in this way a genetic clue for the therapist as well.

Now, I had not specifically anticipated her dealing with this particular aspect, although, once she gets to it, it is one that I have heard repeatedly and can recognize as valid. I'm not particularly disappointed, since this patient has helped me very nicely by bearing out my basic general predictions in a very exquisite and exciting manner.

The efforts with which she concludes this hour can however, serve as a reminder that we really can learn from our patients how to do psychotherapy, and that our patients can indeed be relied on not only as the source of our enlightenment, but as I said before, as the source of all that we will need for our interventions. Here it is evident that the therapist was unclear in regard to the organizing factor in this material—the adaptive context— and he did well to remain relatively silent. This at least enabled the patient to undertake her extensive unconscious therapeutic efforts on his behalf, and while it is clear that she is deeply hurt and disappointed that they have not been understood, as the hour approached its conclusion, he did at least affort her an opportunity to express herself and from that we learn a great deal.

So, now at last, we are going to hear the session that you wanted to present to us. Please begin.

T: At this session she comes in and sits down and doesn't say anything; she had trouble beginning. And I thought that this was very unusual because she generally sits down and starts right away with something. I waited about a minute or a minute and a half, and I said, It seems as though you're having difficulties talking today. And she was just silent, and then I said something to the effect that when we first started, I had told her that one of the things here in psychotherapy is that we have certain rules, and one of the rules is that we have to talk about whatever comes to mind. And she said, Rules! What do you mean by rules?

L: So, right off she says exactly what I was going to say—in her own way. And look at how sensitive she is, even though she hadn't heard our discussion. Here we've been focusing again and again on your own modifications of the framework—the ground rules. And she comes in and decides to show you how it feels; she will not comply with the fundamental rule of free association—the basic rule. Perhaps, she is doing this in order to draw your attention to the fact that you have modified the framework yourself, and to mobilize your awareness of it. In a sense, her behavior has certainly generated an unconscious interpretation on your part—namely, an intervention to the effect that the ground rules of therapy are being modified. Unfortunately, you did not fully state by whom.

Technically, it would have been best if you had been silent and had taken her initial silence as a clue that something was the matter, and immediately reviewed in your mind what had happened in the last session or two. Your would also attempt to determine the context of this response. Her silence is, of course, a resistance, but here, in keeping with our previous formulations, we would have to term this an *interactional resistance*, as well as one that is intrapsychic. By this I mean that you have significantly contributed to the patient's resistance by your own modifications of the framework; many resistances within the patient have both intrapsychic and interactional components. So, you might have been silent while you busily reviewed what had happened. And if you felt that you had to intervene, it would have been preferable to simply point out that she seems deeply absorbed in silence for the moment.

T: Just sit there silently? I waited about a minute and a half. It seems to me that it depends on the patient and the situation—it depends on the context.

L: There are definitely clinical situations where the therapist should remain silent; it depends on your understanding of the silence at the moment. Here, it seems that she
doesn't want to talk to you. She's been talking about not
being understood, so I suspect that she must be angry
about that. I would ask myself, what else is going on? So
I would be silent for a while, because I'm trying to figure
things out. Then I might intervene. And if she still remains silent, then I say to myself, okay, it's her scene.
She has a need to be silent. I'll sit back and try to understand its meanings and let's see where it goes. I would
have no hesitation. Then, if it got very very long, I might
then say something further, much like my initial comment. You have to learn to tolerate this kind of experience, to try to understand it, and to sense what the patient is living out with you—its interactional implications.

T: Then she said, Rules, what do you mean I don't obey
rules? And she became very angry and very agitated.
Then she didn't say anything. Then I said something
like, Well, it seems that talking about rules reminds you
of something else. Then she said, Well, there are rules
and there are rules. And maybe you didn't mean like dis-
obeying a rule in school. You know, I was thinking . . .

L: Now look, let's also try to think. Let's use the patient's
unconscious sensitivity. She wants to disobey the rules.
What could the unconscious meaning of that be? What's
the reason for that?

D: She wanted the therapist to deviate from the ground
rules by changing her hours and is upset that he hasn't
done it.

L: Right; she's concerned about changing her hours which,
as I said before, is not a deviation in the usual sense, although it is an alteration in the framework. In fact, I had
been thinking as I listened to the last session, that her re-

quest to change the hours may be filled with unconscious meaning, in light of the indications that the therapist has been modifying aspects of the framework, such as his neutrality, again and again. It served to remind me that the therapist must always review his own manage-ment of the framework when the patient presents a re-quest to modify the frame. Such requests will typically occur in response to his own alterations of the frame, and this will especially be the case when there are indications that the therapy is in difficulty. In a well-run treatment situation, where the framework is managed effectively and firmly, attempts to modify the frame occur when the patient is threatened by a therapeutic regression. That does not seem to be the case here.

So, in addition to her continued attempts to work through her responses to the therapist's hurtful com-ment, she is concerned about his failure to clarify the sit-uation regarding the change in her hours. And with both things on her mind she withdraws into what now appears to have been an angry silence. However, I suspect that she is most angry about your own failure to obey the rules, and that this is why this theme has appeared.

D: Perhaps she was again asking the therapist for some-thing.

L: Yes, but let's remember the context. When one issue about the ground rules comes up, the patient's associa-tions will go to other issues in the same area. This is ex-tremely characteristic and it can be utilized for your own understanding so that when you hear the patient alluding to some aspect of the framework, you check out all of its other components—the fees, the responsibility for the sessions, your own neutrality, anonymity, and use of neu-tral interventions geared toward interpretations, and the basic need for total confidentiality. Now, in a clinic, maintaining a sound frame is often a major problem, and the issue is usually joined when other problems related to the framework arise. However, it is well to remember that the modifications in the bipersonal field that occur in most clinics are often subjected to bilateral avoidance, and thereby create sectors of misalliance or isolated and sealed-off bastions of the bipersonal field.

T: She said, There are rules and there are rules. And maybe you weren't talking about rules like I had in school. And then she went on, You know I was thinking the other day about doctors, about all the doctors that I've seen and how I've hated them, and I'm just not able to forget it. Then she went on to talk about all these doctors, how they didn't care for her, how she hated them, and how they were only interested in her money. These doctors only look at everyone as a body and they looked at her and thought how much money they're going to get for doing an abortion. Will it be $500 or will it be $600, that's all that was in their heads. They didn't really care.

L: Her precious unconscious fantasies and perceptions. Okay, so what does that mean? She finally gets to some content. We know she hates doctors who don't care; we know she hates you. Her derivatives get less disguised. It's very clearly related to your unforgettable hurtful comment and your not having told her you'll change her hours. Then she brings in abortion. What does that communicate?

D: Death.

L: What kind of death? And let's put it into the form of an unconscious fantasy.

D: Being terminated prematurely?

L: Yes. When June comes, you're going to hear about everybody's abortion, because you're going to be stopping treatment prematurely. It certainly seems that the issue of her hours and of her continuing with you in therapy is uppermost. Remember, the premature termination is an abortion. Now, that image is a mixture of reality and fantasy. If you're dealing with it concretely, it isn't an abortion. But if you regard it figuratively, poetically, metaphorically—it is. It's an abortion. So this is what she's afraid of. That he's going to just abort her. He doesn't care. So notice how it comes up. Of all the millions of procedures she could have named—abortion. Just hear it. Because people communicate exquisitely; if you start to take seriously every little thread, you'll learn so much about them. Go ahead.

T: And she talked about the abortion, and all the money that they want from you. She said, They give you a time, and you just sit there.

L: Is there anybody who isn't convinced? They give you a *time* and you just sit there. It's so beautiful. She's not talking about the time of her session, but the time of her abortion. The condensation is just magnificent.

T: Nobody comes out, you sit there and you wait for hours. And then someone comes out and if you're not the person that has all this money to give him, then you just have to sit there some more. And good-bye. And they won't treat you.

L: She thinks that you're angry at her because you're underpaid here. (Laughter.) Now, to translate this witticism into a conscious insight, she is probably commenting on the fact that she does not pay you directly in the clinic. And beyond that, at this moment when she is, in a sense, at your mercy in regard to the time of her sessions, she is unconsciously and almost plaintively conveying the plight of the clinic patient—his deep sense of vulnerability and helplessness. You can see the intensity of the frustration that is growing in this woman.

T: She went on, He comes out and if you're not the one with the money, good-bye. Forget about it. And he will not treat you. He just behaves toward you like you're a nothing. And then she said, Did I ever tell you the story of when I was fifteen years old? Well, I was having trouble with my hip. And she sarcastically described how her mother took her to this local physician. And she said, He told me to get undressed. He said he had to see my whole body, and you know, at fifteen, I was very well developed. I had the body of a woman. And I asked for a sheet, and the doctor just said nothing. And my mother also said nothing. The doctor looked at me and smiled, and I got very angry but I just stood there and I did nothing.

L: Now, through somewhat less disguised derivatives, she is conveying her unconscious perceptions of you as a voyeur and as using her sexually. Of course, this is once again an amalgam of her unconscious perceptions of her plight here in the clinic, and of your misuse of her on the one hand, and her own fantasies and conflicts on the other— her willingness to exhibit herself and submit to you if you'll just change her hours. And as these derivatives become less disguised, we get the feeling that she is trying to reach you in one way or another, and through one interpretation or another. At the same time, she's trying to understand why you're holding back on the change in hours. She seems to feel that you do not even recognize or acknowledge her as a person. And she is also frustrated that you have not made use of her unconscious communications, either by getting around to the question of the time of her sessions, or by offering her a meaningful interpretation related to her perceptions of how hurtful you have been.

D: How come she doesn't ask more directly?

L: What do you think?

D: She's so afraid of him, or sees him as so uncaring. If she asks him directly, he'll directly clobber her over the head.

L: Yes, she is afraid of a direct inquiry, both because of a fear that she will be abused by the therapist, and a dread of her own wishes for masochistic gratification. On the

one hand, there is the wish to suffer, on the other the
wish not to. The patient is always divided. But remember
too that the therapist has doubted her truthfulness and
in actuality, he has been abusive on some level, and she
undoubtedly is afraid to confront him further with his
hurtfulness. Remember: she did deal with some of these
problems on a conscious level for a while, which is actually quite rare for patients. Most of the time they don't
communicate directly and this is a human characteristic.
We all often communicate indirectly through derivatives
and some of it has to do with the underlying conflicts and
fantasies, and the need for inner defenses and repression.
But there is also an interactional component related to
the fear of the object—the therapist. Actually, that's a
good question and one that deserves careful study. Let's
see if she adds to our answer to it.

T: She's talking about standing there without clothes on.
And she said, That doctor was staring at me. That old
bastard was just staring at me. She said, Do you know
what my friend David—that's how she referred to her
other psychiatrist ten years ago—said to me?

L: Notice—see how the derivatives become clearer. This
woman is just precious. Most patients won't give you
such easy derivatives related to a psychiatrist, but they
will all find ways of letting you know what you're doing
when you keep missing it. She's going to cure you by interpreting to you. She's going to cure you by giving you
clearer and clearer derivatives. Then you finally have to
say something.

T: She said, There were hours that I was just sitting there
with him, with my psychiatrist, and he was just telling me
about his problems and things about his life. (Laughter.)

L: Can it be any clearer? Who has the problem? I've just
finished writing a paper on the patient's efforts to cure
the therapist (Langs, 1975a), and I know what many ana-

lysts will say: they'll say that I'm making the whole thing up and that I've gone crazy. It's been said about other analysts who have gotten into this area, and the comment is made that psychotherapy or analysis is not for the cure of the therapist or the analyst, and that focusing on perceptions is simply a defense against dealing with the patient's unconscious fantasies. Many misconceptions arise at this point, and much of it has to do with the defensiveness of the analyst, who is actually attempting to get away from his patient's valid perceptions of him, and from his own unconscious conflicts.

But if you hear something like this, and you're willing to look at the data—the associations from the patient— then maybe you'll be convinced that this is really what the patient is struggling with. She is dealing with her unconscious perceptions of the therapist and her own inner elaborations of them, and you cannot understand her unconscious communications and conflicts without a clear idea of what is evoking them. That's why I feel that tapes of presentations like this are so magnificent—you can hear the sequence unfold bit by bit and experience your own struggle to understand what is going on from one moment to the next. And you can see how it helps if you conceptualize the therapeutic interaction as occurring within a bipersonal field and are not prejudiced right off in assuming who, for the moment, is sick and who is healthy, and who is putting the pathological contents into the field. You then have an opportunity to formulate and predict, an opportunity that has not been available from other models of the therapeutic relationship.

So here, she gets around to a therapist who really seems to have been crazier than her. And it would also be nice for you if you could say to yourself, as her present therapist, that she's just talking about her friend David —another modification in the framework in terms of the appropriate formalities that should be established be-

tween the patient and the therapist—and not about yourself. But she is also talking about you. And of course,
she's building out of that other situation, and her present
situation with you, a whole set of additional fantasies,
and we will deal with them once we have resolved the disturbances within yourself that have enabled her to legitimately put into you her own craziness for the moment.

So you see again where the container concept and projective identification come in, in that she had a first therapist who told her about his problems and offered himself as a pathological container for the patient's sickness.
A container who would absorb her craziness without understanding it and without ever interpreting it to her.
And you can be sure that that can be of some relief up to
a point, though unfortunately on a basically destructive
basis. And you can also be sure that there are many therapists who function in this kind of way. But at some
point, the therapist will attempt to dump all of the sickness he has absorbed back into the patient, and the patient will become infuriated or disillusioned, and will
leave treatment.

Now when she says that he told her his problems, we
certainly want to recognize that there may be distortions
here, and that only some of it is not distorted. But again,
it would be unfortunate if we dismissed this description
as an irrational transference fantasy, or simply a misrep-
resentation of the past. If you think about it, this image
is in keeping with other things that we've heard about
this psychiatrist—his noninterpretive comments to the
patient, his visit to her in the hospital, and his direct attack on her for her miscarriage. So, whatever she is adding to her perceptions of this first therapist based on her
own pathological unconscious fantasies, there appears to
be a large nucleus of validity in them.

This communication of hers is extremely important;
let me pause to say a bit more about it. Here I've been

commenting that the material over the last two sessions has revolved in a large way around the patient's unconscious perceptions of the present therapist—her unconscious perceptions that he is having difficulties and that he has significant countertransference problems—and that she is making a variety of efforts to alert him to the nature of his countertransference problems, and the underlying basis for them. She is involved in what Searles (1975), in a paper on the Patient as Therapist to the Analyst, has clearly described as a very major and important effort on the part of schizophrenic and nonschizophrenic patients to cure their therapists or analysts. Here, I have been formulating efforts on the part of this patient to pick up and communicate to the therapist the nature of his difficulties, and her endeavors to cure him of these problems. And I've gone on and tried to demonstrate a number of different interpretations on her part, and a whole variety of areas that the patient relates these difficulties to. Now I haven't asked the therapist to tell us whether these interventions, which I call unconscious interpretations, are correct and valid, because I feel that's the therapist's private matter. But based on what I know in general about therapists, and on what I have seen of this therapist's work, I would suspect that they are indeed quite valid, unconscious interventions.

So my confirmation has to come from the patient, and I've had to wait for it—patiently and hopefully. And what does the patient finally say? She finally gets around to a therapist who had clear-cut problems and who told these problems directly to her as patient. This alludes not only to the past therapist, but to the present therapist as well. That is, to the present therapist who has been unconsciously communicating his problems to the patient. I consider this to be validation of the thesis that I had offered. The patient gets around to a therapist with clear-cut problems, and to a situation where the therapist's problems took precedence over those of the patient. And I think this very clearly validates the formulations that have been offered in regard to the patient's unconscious perceptions of the therapist's difficulties and her unconcious efforts to help him. I am eager to hear more.

T: So she said, He told me about his problems.

L: Now you know why she was silent at the beginning of the session—she was waiting for you to start free associating. (Laughter.) Eventually, we come to understand these things.

T: Then she went on to say, I knew his whole life—talking of course about the other psychiatrist. And at the end of the session, I didn't know who should be paying, who should be charged for these sessions—me or him? (Laughter.)

L: Which are her prostitution fantasies, too. See how complicated it gets?

T: And I really wanted to charge him. But finally I was able to screw him . . .

L: Be warned: finally I screwed him.

T: And the patient remembered a time when she came to her therapist and said that she was nauseous and vomiting and was convinced that she was pregnant. The therapist had laughed at her and had called her gynecologist right in front of her, and the two had been laughing because they felt that it was impossible for her to be pregnant at the time. The patient asked him what was funny, and the therapist told her that he didn't feel that it was conceivable that she was pregnant. And the patient went on to describe how these symptoms actually turned out to be the first signs of a serious gastrointestinal illness that had necessitated hospitalization, and from which she had nearly died.

L: So now the material from the patient becomes quite morbid and somber. She reminds us how it is ultimately really quite tragic when the therapist is unable to recognize his own difficulties and his problems with his patient, unable to utilize the patient's efforts to assist him with these difficulties, and unable to be helpful. Sooner or later the therapist is seen as someone who cannot be trusted, who cannot be helped, and who cannot help; an intense depression sets in and there is a very morbid overcast to the entire situation.

This is also already a partial answer to why the patient doesn't communicate directly to such a therapist. There is no longer a feeling of trust or of safety—or even hope—and certainly the therapist who has been hurtful is hardly the one in whom the patient can confide.

T: She continued: And then there is the first gynecologist I had, the one who made the mistake in treating me. And because of him, I couldn't be helped later. And because of him, I had to have all these abortions. And you know, I probably could sue him. I was so angry and I still am, so incredibly angry. And I said to myself, if I'm ever going to see that man again I'm really, really going to let him have it. I was just so angry. And then she sat back and said, And you know what's funny? Do you know what's really funny? That I saw him. I saw him at the hospital once and I felt like smacking him, like smacking him right across his face. But we just looked at each other and I didn't say anything.

L: So, she adds more to her answer to our question about why she is not direct with the therapist—if she confronted the therapist directly, she would completely lose control. Here's another answer: the patient was afraid of losing total control of her rage and of ther wishes for revenge, so she has a need, then, to repress her perceptions and fantasies in order to protect herself from her fury—and from her depression and anxiety. So, the patient answers your pertinent question—probably because she is dealing with that very issue herself at this point.

T: I really hate doctors, she said, I really hate them just so
     much. And I'm telling you this because you said that I
     was going to them for care and for love. But I just really
     hate them. She stopped, and I said something to the ef-
     fect of, Well, I'm a doctor too.

L: You mean, hate me please? You see, without under-
     standing what she's so angry about, that isn't going to
     help.

T: I wanted to shift the focus.

L: Yes, but you could have done it by intervening in a differ-
     ent way—with an interpretation. Instead, you not only
     invite her hate, which is of course directed toward you
     already, but you also have made a kind of unconscious
     interpretation. Through your comment you are implicitly
     suggesting that much of this hate is directed toward you.
     The problem with that intervention is that the therapist
     should be offering conscious interpretations, not uncon-
     scious ones, as the patient most often does. Your inter-
     ventions have to be on a conscious level, in order to dem-
     onstrate to the patient your actual awareness of the
     meanings of her communication, and by implication,
     your capacity to manage whatever it is she is directing to-
     ward you. It would also show her that you have taken it
     all in and properly worked it over to the level of a con-
     scious insight. She needs that from you, in order to have
     that insight for herself on a conscious level where it fos-
     ters her adaptive resources; it also offers you as a model
     of someone who can do that kind of therapeutic work.

T: She said, Yes, they are doctors, and you're a psychiatrist,
     and you're trained to look at a person as a person, and to
     see what's on their mind, and not to look at a patient for
     money. You know, at the beginning, I really hated you
     and I was trying to prove something. I was trying to prove
     you wrong, and I said to myself, Why are you doing this
     to him? And then I guess I just started to really hate my-

self, and I said to myself, Why are you letting them do all of this to you? And I just really hated myself. And I was hating myself, I guess, because I didn't walk away. Like with the doctor who had examined my hip. I could have insisted that he gave me a sheet. And if he didn't, I could have left. But I just stood there; I didn't do anything. I could have done something, but I just didn't. I could have also stopped treatment with that psychiatrist when I saw that he was just bull-shitting me along. But I didn't. Instead, I just sat there and kept paying his bill. At this point, I said, It seems to me that you think you're responsible for all of this. And she answered, Yes, there's no question about that, and this is why I hate myself so much.

L: This is called blaming the patient, projecting all of the sickness onto and into the patient; and she'll get more depressed. Notice what you selected to say to her out of all the possible interventions that you could have made. Actually, this is an extremely common form of projection and projective identification utilized by therapists and analysts in which they attribute to and dump into the patient their own sickness and pathology. It's an extension of the belief that all the communications from the patient are fantasied and based on unconscious fantasies, in lieu of acknowledging the additional presence of unconscious perceptions. And since everything is the patient's fantasies and the patient is the sick one in the therapeutic dyad, it's very common at a time when the patient is unconsciously communicating perceptions of the therapist's difficulties, for the therapist to reproject these difficulties back into the patient. He dumps them back into the patient, adding to it his own sickness, and then attempts to cure himself through the efforts of the patient, or through his treatment of the patient's sickness that stems now in part from his projective identifications. This is one of the ways in which the therapist helps to create the patient's interactional neurosis and contributes to the patient's sickness.

Here, her mounting depression is such a neurosis and I think that the evidence is clear that in addition to the patient's intrapsychic problems, the therapist's interventions, and his failures to intervene, have contributed to this syndrome in the patient. And the therapist's intervention here is a subtle and not consciously intended effort of that kind. And as I said, you can see that it has this quality when you realize how he has focused on the patient's sense of responsibility, with a total neglect of every other aspect of her communications. That's why I said that she will feel even more depressed and guilty now, especially since she tends, as she said, to accept these destructive projective identifications into herself.

You can see here another aspect of a sado-masochistic misalliance. The therapist's intervention implies that the patient should take into herself, and accept, responsibility for the therapist's problems and sickness—even though this was not directly stated to her. That is the interactional implication of his comments. And there is little doubt that the patient has been struggling with efforts of this kind by the therapist for some time. It seems likely that he has been unaware of this aspect of his interaction with her and there is really no indication that he has been able to master and modify it.

And she says some very interesting things in the context of this kind of struggle with the therapist's projective identifications of his difficulties into her and her masochistic need to accept them. She says that she could have refused them and not accepted them, but that she did not do so. And this tells you something important about how the object deals with a subject's projective identification —it depends greatly on the nature of the projective identification and the object's own inner needs and pathology. A masochistic patient will tend to accept the badness and sickness of others into herself and become a pathological container for such contents. These contents are accepted unconsciously and serve to reinforce the patient's inner conflicts and neurosis. And many patients will permit themselves to become the containers for their therapist's projective identifications and, while they will ultimately become depressed and disillusioned through such experiences, they may temporarily feel better because of their capacity to contain the therapist's sickness. This is another form of misalliance cure.

I am hoping that this begins to help you understand the concepts of projective identification and containing functions, because once you recognize the interactional importance of projective identification, you are led to a study of both the contents that are projectively identified and the container for them—a point that Bion (1962, 1963) has called our attention to, although it has not been fully conceptualized as yet. There are, as I am indicating, appropriate and inappropriate, adaptive and maladaptive, containing function, and we will be a lot clearer about all this once we have more specifically studied the area. In fact, I think that this patient will help us with this project, because she has just now experienced another effort on the part of her therapist to put into her his sickness and "badness." We'll soon see how she reacts to these interactional efforts.

I think that all this also tells us something about the unconscious motives for becoming a psychiatrist. I suspect that they often involve unconscious needs to be a pathological container on the one hand, and on the other unconscious needs to projectively identify his own sickness into the patient and to make the patient the pathological container for that sickness. The therapeutic situation clearly offers unusual opportunities for these types

of interactional efforts, and there is little doubt that unless the therapist masters these maladaptive needs, his
therapeutic work will be quite unsound. And as I have
already indicated, this does not mean that he will not
provide his patients with misalliance cures, since these
mechanisms clearly can produce such results. It does
mean, however, that the patient will, by and large, have
the kind of therapeutic experience that this patient is
now so vividly describing for us.

Notice too that in order to understand the unconscious
interaction between this patient and therapist, as it is occurring within this bipersonal field, we have had to understand something of what is happening intrapsychically in both of them. While I am keeping my focus here on
on the patient who, as a component of this bipersonal
field, reverberates to the contributions from all parts of
the field—which is why we can actually understand aspects of what is happening within the therapist from the
patient's communications—in your work with patients,
you have the added advantage of exploring your own subjective responses. We can understand a great deal
through our focus on the patient's communications and
the occasional interventions from the therapist, but we
do not have the therapist's ongoing associations to complete our conceptualization of the interaction. Actually,
I have been impressed with how much we can indeed
comprehend despite this limitation, and I think it shows
you the extent to which the patient is embedded in her
relationship with the therapist, and the therapist in his
with the patient. But I have all along been emphasizing
the fact that you have to have a rather complete understanding of the therapeutic interaction in order to comprehend the intrapsychic stirrings within the patient—
and the therapist. Now, I am stressing the other side of
the coin: how you must understand in depth what is happening intrapsychically in both participants in order to

understand their interaction. The two go hand in hand.
   Well, this is really an intense moment in this treatment. Let's see what happens.

T: At this point I said, As you once said while you were here, you feel like a dishrag in a sense, because you are letting yourself feel like a dishrag. She said, Yes, and then she said, Do you know why I wanted to show you that I hate you so much? She said, Because I wanted to show you that I was strong, that I am not weak and that I am different here than I am on the outside, where I'm not able to tell people what I really want to tell them, where I'm not able to say no, and where I'm not able to refuse people things. But I'm so upset with myself. It makes me so angry at myself that sometimes I guess I just feel like smashing myself into a tree or driving a car into one, or something like that. It's just so overwhelming.

L: For one thing, you support my thesis that you are attempting to put all of your sickness into this patient. You blame her entirely for what she is feeling and for her sense of self-devaluation, even though there are powerful indications that in addition to her own responsibility, there have been major efforts to devalue her on the part of all of the physicians that she has been describing, and in a sense, even yourself. And she goes on, really rather exquisitely, to describe her struggle with her own masochistic needs, and with the destructive projective identifications that are being put into her. She wants to fight against them; she wants to refute the projective identifications and defend herself through hating others. If she cannot do this, she feels that she will be totally overwhelmed by her own destructive introjects, and by the further destructiveness that is being put into her, and that she will destroy herself. She is feeling overwhelmed by what you are putting into her, and her struggles to be rid of it. And you can see too the possibility of another kind of misalliance cure here, one in which the patient momentarily manages to control her masochism—her depression and her need to suffer—as a kind of herculean effort to fend off your hurtful projective identifications.

This is an interesting point for me, since I have had the impression that in every hurtful intervention and in every pathological effort to projectively identify into the patient, there lies a kernel of something good—a positive wish to help the patient. So, there is no such thing as an unmixed communication or unmixed interactional effort; no matter how overwhelmingly destructive, there is something curative in all of this as well. In part, it may be that by projectively identifying these disturbances into the patient, you are actually attempting to mobilize her adaptive potential, both in having her make efforts to cure you, and in her endeavors to constructively and adaptively refute what is being dumped onto her.

Now, please do not misunderstand. This is by no means the way to do psychotherapy with a patient, and it is far from the optimal cure. It has, as the patient is so vividly reminding us, some terrible dangers in that it can drive a patient to suicide or to some less deadly version of suicide. There are curative efforts that do not contain these risks, and it is that type of cure that we really want to offer to our patients. But on the other hand, I think that it is valid to appreciate that even in the most destructive therapeutic interludes, there is, however small, an effort to cure the patient contained within it. And it is very important to realize the presence of that positive element. It means that not only could you eventually turn all of this into the cure of the patient by realizing what has been going on, getting it under control, and interpreting at some length the patient's perceptions and fantasies in response to it, but also that you can find and magnify the small curative effort contained in this destructiveness and make therapeutic use of it.

I am reminded of de Racker's (1961) paper in which she describes paranoid patients who are filled with rage toward their therapists, and who destroy every intervention from them. She found that embedded in all of the hatefulness from these patients is a kernel of goodness, communicated in some form or another. And when she was able to tune in on this goodness and intervene in relationship to it, the patient accepted what she had to say and did not destroy it. She concluded that the patient feeds the therapist the ingredients that he needs to make his interpretations, and I believe that this is an extremely important observation.

Here, I am saying something similar about the therapist. That somewhere embedded in these hateful interventions is something good, and that if he and the patient can recognize it, they can build something out of it, especially if he can get the more destructive parts under control. After all, if he continues to be hurtful and to projectively identify into the patient all sorts of sick and bad contents, they will eventually overwhelm her in all likelihood. On the other hand, if he can find his curative intentions in all of this, he could build something therapeutic out of it. Not that we should pretend that all of this won't leave its mark on the patient—there is no substitute for nonhurtful therapeutic work—but it is a fact that the best we can do at this point is to get it all under control and to become helpful once again.

T: She said, I really think that that would be a brave thing to do. And I answered, It seems that it's easier for you to think of this, than to change the way you do things and stand up for yourself more. And she said, Yes, you are right.

L: So again, out of her masochistic needs, she accepts the projective identifications from the therapist. But in keeping with what I was just saying, notice that the therapist has also unconsciously attempted to encourage her to

struggle against the bad parts of himself that she has accepted to herself, and against her own destructive introjects, by standing up for herself. She also accepts that, so
there is one of your kernels of curative efforts in the
midst of so many hurts. And notice too, that this interface now contains a kind of therapeutic interaction that
is bilaterally unconscious, and that while it may shift, because the therapist has now said something that is more
appropriately empathic and timely, it will not do so as
the result of conscious insight derived from an explicitly
verbalized interpretation by the therapist. This will influence the nature of the interface which includes the patient's responses.

T: But why? she asked. Why does this happen so much to
     me? Why is it that I have to hate myself so much?

L: That's what she needs to be told—why: because you've
     been hurtful and you're not changing her hours—be-
     cause you hate her. Now, I'm not saying that this is a con-
     scious hatred, but it is the effect of your communications
     and interactions with her. She needs an interpretation
     that will bring together her experiences with you, in
     which you have doubted her, blamed her for her and for
     your sickness, and put some of your own inner distur-
     bances into her. And she needs to be told that as she feels
     hurt and frustrated by you, she turns it against herself
     and wants to destroy herself and the hurtful you inside
     her.

     So, once again, she first needs a clarification of a reali-
     ty problem—the situation with her hours. Next, she
     needs indications from you that you can get under con-
     trol your hurtful interventions to her. And then she needs
     an interpretation that will help her to understand her
     mounting depression—her current interactional neurosis
     —based on the unconscious interaction between herself
     and you, and its intrapsychic extensions.

     In this way, you will first of all relieve her of the struggle she is having over accepting your destructive projective identifications and wanting to refute them. That would already offer her a sense of relief, and it would also help her to manage her own depreciating and devaluating introjects and her devalued self-image. You could offer her both interactional and intrapsychic relief, and through some very specific interpretations, you could offer her the adaptive tools that she needs to manage her specific inner conflicts and disturbing introjects. This would be the road to inner structural change for her, while the present interaction is instead undoubtedly a repetition of the earlier pathogenic interactions that created her initial propensities toward depression and masochism.

And you can see how the present interaction also reinforces her neurosis, her pathogenic introjects, and her disturbed inner world. External reality corresponds for the moment to the disturbed inner reality on which her sickness is based. This is a neurotic vicious circle and what is most interesting about it is that we see unconscious efforts on the part of both the patient and the therapist to break the circle and to modify their misalliance. However, little in a lasting way will occur unless one of them becomes explicitly conscious of much of what is going on, and this, of course, is primarily the responsibility of the therapist.

T: I said that this was something we're going to have to work on here. And she said to me, But what if, even if I understand why I'm doing this, what if I'm still not able to stop it? What if those feelings just don't stop? You know, this fantasy I have of smashing myself into a tree just might take over and become reality.

L: This fantasy of smashing herself into a tree is again highly condensed. It reflects your uncontrolled comment— your attack on her; it reflects her rage toward you and her wish to smash you; it reflects the way in which your projections into her are smashing into her and destroying her; it reflects her identification with you and her wish to then destroy that part of your destructiveness that's inside of herself; and it reflects the culmination of all other contributions within herself to her own self-destructive impulses. You can see how complicated this all is, but again I think you have to emphasize the elements of unconscious perception that have set all of this off, and we should see how clearly we can conceptualize this patient's symptoms as expressions of the pathology of the bipersonal field and as an interactional neurosis. Unfortunately, your interventions, while you have been trying to be kindly and understanding, really have an assaultive quality that the patient perceives and then elaborates upon. Certainly, another patient, with another set of intrapsychic fantasies and introjects, would respond differently, but that response would also be comprehensible only if we understood what was within the patient, the therapist, and their interaction.

T: Then she said, I know in reality that I won't be there. And she said that in her fantasy, she dies, and her mother and husband and mother-in-law and her children, are all crying, and she's at the funeral. And she said to me that in the fantasy she dies and is at the funeral too, and is hearing all the people crying about how they mistreated her and how they weren't nice to her, and how they now blamed themselves for her death. And then she says, I know in reality I really won't be there, but I'm tempted to believe so. Here I said, It seems to me as though you are afraid to lose control. She said, Yes. Then she spoke about a friend who had started to behave bizarrely in a shopping center; she started with all sorts of antics that were ignored by the people who were passing by. She then told this to her husband and he said to her, just because she's thinking of it so much, she must be crazy. And here she said again that her friend was standing there, just going crazy and people were all passing her by and doing nothing. And that nobody, but nobody cared. And that was the end of the session.

L: How sad. Here we have not only her fantasies of revenge, but her own insight into the interactional nature of her depression. It's not that she is simply blaming others for her sickness, she has a valid point. And when the therapist touches upon an isolated fragment of her anxieties, without developing it within an adaptive context and with a long-overdue, meaningful interpretation, the patient responds by describing not only her own fear of going crazy, but her unconscious perception of the therapist's efforts to drive her crazy—a subject that Searles (1959) has discussed.

Do you have the beginning of the next session? You're leaving us hanging; did she get around to the question of the changed hours or not?

T: Yes, it was in the next session. And as a matter of fact, she started with it.

L: Well, thank you; how long could she wait? Could you briefly summarize that session?

T: The patient very directly brought up the question of whether I was going to change her hours. She also spoke again about her mother's discouraging remarks about treatment and described her masturbatory fantasies, in which she loved herself in the presence of a face that hadn't become clear. Now she revealed that the face was my face.

L: We can see again the great importance of the relationship between the patient and the therapist, and the way in which it plays an extremely significant role in psychotherapy. The whole issue that has been raised previously in the literature, as to whether one gets a transference reaction or a transference neurosis in psychotherapy as compared to psychoanalysis, loses its importance when we begin to realize the degree to which this patient is exquisitely sensitive to the interventions of the therapist; and she is exquisitely and unconsciously in touch with the therapist and what is going on within him, as well as what's going on within herself. And we see that in this interaction, the patient is constantly unconsciously perceiving the therapist and unconsciously accepting—introjecting—his projective identifications in terms of these perceptions.

My own work, as reflected in my book on psychotherapeutic technique (Langs, 1973a, 1974), has been criticized for not having drawn a sufficient distinction between psychotherapy and psychoanalysis. I think that most people have overlooked the fact that those volumes represented an empirical study, and that I expressed myself solely in terms of my clinical observations. And as you can see from this seminar, the material from patients in psychotherapy unmistakably indicates that in terms of interaction, the ways in which psychotherapy and psychoanalysis differ are relatively minor in comparison to the enormous ways in which they are similar.

After all, the patient in psychotherapy does not know that he is supposed to react differently to his therapist, or less intensely, or that he is not supposed to unconsciously monitor the therapist's communications, and that he should not introject the therapist's projective identifications. And he does not know that he is supposed to center his psychotherapy around his external life problems, rather than around his relationship with the therapist— a concept that I had been taught and erroneously articulated in my book, while the bulk of those two volumes clearly spoke against such a conceptualization, since they were deeply preoccupied with the therapeutic interaction. I was communicating something unconsciously there that I had not sufficiently crystallized consciously, although I have been able to do so now.

And when you take into account both the patient's perceptions and unconscious fantasies, you see that these are quite intensely centered on the therapist in psychotherapy, and that if you have a sufficiently sophisticated concept of the transference and interactional neuroses, they exist in psychotherapy as well as in psychoanalysis. And you can see that when the therapist has been hurtful and has made technical errors, and has failed to interpret properly, these preoccupations are enormously intensified to the virtual exclusion of other adaptive concerns within the patient for the moment.

In fact, you can see how one variable, of the many that determine the intensity of the patient's fantasies and perceptions related to the therapist or the analyst, can become an overriding determinant in the patient's transference or nontransference preoccupation with the therapist or analyst. Here, we see that a hurtful therapist and the therapist's countertransference problems, as they are put into the therapeutic bipersonal field and into this patient, are probably the single most important determinant of this patient's communications during these sessions, and of the interface of their interaction.

There is not sufficient time for me to go into all of the other variables that determine the intensity of the transference component of the patient's relationship to the therapist or analyst. Nor will I discuss the important ways in which analysis and therapy differ. I have considered these issues quite explicitly in the book that is now in preparation (Langs, in press a). Here I am trying to stress that basic clinical observation indicates that the patient's communications in psychoanalysis and psychotherapy, and the interventions that the patient sorely needs, are in many ways quite similar. In fact, I think that it is fair to say that the basic model of therapy prevails for both situations, and that the fundamental needs of the patient for a stable framework and for proper interpretations clearly predominate in both situations.

After a presentation such as this one, I am less concerned with the differences between analysis and therapy, than I am with the similarities. And because there has been a buildup of a kind of mythology in the literature, that the differences are more important, I have responded by unconsciously and now consciously, developing the similarities. Some of these erroneous contentions come from the intense renunciation required of the analyst with his analytic patients, and a human need to have available to him a situation where he can justify the surrender of principles, and the introduction of many modifications in technique that, whether they prove valid or not—and I am suggesting that most of them will, in the long run, prove not to be valid—gratify certain of his unconscious countertransference needs. I am by no means indicating that one decides issues such as this by determining their possible countertransference contributions; I think that these seminars have made it clear that the answers must come empirically, and from the patient. And I think that you can see that a patient has a great need to let us know this answer since it is in the service of his deepest wish for a curative therapeutic experience.

Once you become sensitive to this issue, I can assure you that the patient will consistently respond to unneeded modifications in the framework, and to inappropriate interventions, with negative reactions and with efforts to restore the framework and to help the therapist intervene properly. In fact, this is so universal, that I went back to Freud's case histories (Langs, in press, b, c, d) and was able to demonstrate from the sparse clinical material available—except in the case of the Rat man, where we do have some process notes—that every time that Freud deviated from today's accepted framework with adult patients, there were negative responses from the patient, and unconscious perceptions of these deviations incredibly similar to those communicated by our present patient. There were even indications of therapeutic efforts on the part of his patients toward Freud.

Lastly, I want to organize for you one aspect of the comments that I have made in regard to the interventions that this therapist should have made. In my bood on technique (Langs, 1973a, p. 364), I made an early effort to indicate that there is a hierarchy of therapeutic contexts by which I meant that certain types of problems have to be dealt with and interpreted in advance of others. As I think back to this early effort, I can see the seeds of my present thinking. I see many such seeds in those two volumes, most especially in my approach to countertransference problems, where I adopted what is actually an interactional approach—the understanding of the therapist's countertransferences from the syndromes that he evokes in his patients.

In any case, material like this indicates that the hierarchy of therapeutic tasks can now be put in something of the following order of importance. First, the therapist must deal with interactional resistances. Immediately, we see that the interactional approach reminds us that the resolution of resistances contained within the bipersonal field—that is to say in either the patient or the therapist—initially require modifications of the therapist's contributions. Then, if the resistance lies primarily within himself, he must resolve on his own his intrapsychic need for it. If on the other hand the resistance is primarily expressed in the communications from the patient, we must then analyze both the patient's awareness, consciously or unconsciously, of the therapist's contribution to his resistance, and the intrapsychic basis for it in the patient.

It is here that the second area of intervening arises, in that it relates to the interpretation of interactional mechanisms and interactional contents, as well as to containing functions. This brings to our attention both the con-

tainer and the contained, and the importance of dealing
with—by both modifying and interpreting—alterations
in the framework and the interactional pathology related
to both the therapist's and patient's containing functions. Here, I am referring to some of the earlier observations that I made related to pathogenic needs on the part
of the therapist to introject and contain the patient's
sickness in a nontherapeutic manner, and in addition, inappropriate needs on the part of the patient to accept into herself the pathology of the therapist who has a complementary need to use the patient as a pathological container. So, we stick to the basic maxim of dealing with resistances before content, to which I am now adding that
we must deal with the interactional sphere before the intrapsychic, and as part of that, the intrapsychic contributions to interactional resistances and contents, before
dealing with the primarily intrapsychic aspects.

It is only when the interactional dimension is under
control, that we are in a position to get around to the focus on the patient's intrapsychic conflicts and pathological introjects. But I think that I've made it clear that the
therapeutic work with the interactional dimension is by
no means a preliminary or second-order job, and that
such work offers the patient crucial cognitive insights
and positive introjective identifications with the therapist. Then, in working on this third level—the intrapsychic—in which the focus is on the patient's inner world,
we again deal with defenses and resistances, before content—core unconscious fantasies and introjects. In all of
this work we shift from the present to the past, and generally, we will tend to go back and forth from the interactional to the intrapsychic realms, stressing one or the
other, depending on the bipersonal field and the two participants. And it is, of course, in the depths to which this
work can be taken, and in the extent to which lasting
structural change can be effected for the patient, that

psychoanalysis shows its relatively greater potential than psychotherapy.

Well, I see that our time is up and I want to thank our therapist for a most interesting presentation. To say that it is I who have given him a great deal to think about would be to miss the point that I have spent these past two weeks translating the patient's unconscious communications into conscious supervisory and teaching comments. So if he has learned anything important, he has only his patient to thank. I hope he will return her efforts with some interpretive work of his own.

Chapter 5

THE ROLE OF RECTIFICATION AND INTERPRETATION IN RESTORING THE FRAME OF THE BIPERSONAL FIELD

THE INTRAPSYCHIC AND INTERACTIONAL CONSEQUENCES OF THIRD PARTIES TO THERAPY • INTERACTIONAL COMPONENTS TO ACTING OUT AND DEPRESSION • THE THERAPIST'S CONSCIOUS AND UNCONSCIOUS INTERPRETATIONS • HISTORICAL PERSPECTIVES ON THE CONCEPTUALIZATION OF THE FRAMEWORK OF THE THERAPEUTIC RELATIONSHIP • THE INTERFACE OF THE BIPERSONAL FIELD • THE THERAPIST'S USE OF THE PATIENT'S UNCONSCIOUS INTERPRETATIONS • AN EXCHANGE OF PROJECTIVE IDENTIFICATIONS

L: Today, we are going to study the nature of interventions and interpretations. Who will be presenting?

T: I will. The patient is a twenty-year-old, single young lady who had been hospitalized in another area, because of depression and episodes of panic during which she was afraid of hurting herself, and because of an incident where she had thrown herself in front of a car but had only been slightly injured. She was now being seen at an Outreach Clinic and was living with her family, except for her father who had died when she was four years of age.

I will begin by presenting the material from a session that occurred two sessions prior to the one that I want to concentrate on. Oh by the way, I guess I should also mention that I am the group therapist for this patient's boyfriend. He also had been hospitalized at the same hospital as the patient, and he is now being treated at the same Outreach Clinic. Actually, I had started to see the boyfriend first and began to see the present patient, twice weekly, sometime afterwards. It was she who eventually told me about their relationship, and I have noticed that the boyfriend seldom discusses it. I therefore referred the boyfriend to an additional therapist with whom he could discuss any of the feelings that he had about this particular treatment arrangement.

L: Another, oh by the way—let's look at it a bit. We'll see how peripheral it turns out to be. What are the principles we rely on for a situation of this kind? What do you do under these circumstances? What are your thoughts— before the patient answers these questions for us?

T: Well, we already went through this with a couple of other patients, in terms of referring them to another therapist, possibly in the same clinic.

L: Referring them?

T: Referring one of the two. Here it would be this patient since her boyfriend had been in therapy beforehand.

D: Had you discussed their relationship with each of them?

T: The relationship is really not very important to her. After all, she knows a lot of people in this Clinic, and I am treating some of them under other circumstances. This isn't really what I came to discuss.

L: Yes, I know, but . . .

T: We can discuss it; it's all right.

L: Well, I will put it this way: if I don't find this issue in these sessions, I promise to retire—quickly and to everybody's relief. Because it's the kind of problem that has to be on this patient's mind—it's related to the framework. And as I have been telling you, establishing the framework of the bipersonal field—creating a therapeutic container and an uncontaminated bipersonal field—is uppermost among therapeutic contexts—therapeutic tasks—for the therapist. And that is because it is a first order adaptive task for the patient, who will clearly let you know her need for a well defined frame.

Now, we have discussed a number of principles related to this issue and let's attempt to summarize them in anticipation of listening to this material. It is here again that we are immediately confronted with a reality problem related to the bipersonal field—a realistic issue with extensive intrapsychic repercussions for both the patient and the therapist, and one that will require the dual interventions that we have already defined for interactional difficulties: correction of the reality—the creation of a proper framework—and extensive interpreting of the meanings of the situation for the patient—and for the therapist is he has unnecessarily contributed.

Now, a situation of this kind may be such that the framework cannot, in actuality, be clearly established so long as you are seeing both of them. After all, it creates a very special situation where you are hearing about this patient from another source. And in addition, the two of them are sharing in reality something that relates to you that you are not in a position to modify. There is the potential for extensive transference and countertransference gratifications in such a situation, and it may not be feasible to forestall them. And to the extent that these pathological needs are actually gratified, this particular bipersonal field will be lacking in important therapeutic qualities. On top of that, you will have a therapeutic interface with each of these patients that is significantly influenced by vectors occurring outside your direct relationship with them, vectors with many unconscious implications that again may not be resolvable. On this basis, it would be my initial hunch that the optimal thing to do would be to refer them both to different therapists. I would not keep one as the favorite and exclude the other one.

Actually, the thing to do in a situation like this is, I think, basically to prevent it from happening, because when it does come up, you have an extremely sticky situation. It provides the patient with all sorts of unconscious gratifications and misalliances that are very difficult to deal with. Obviously, the only other alternative is that at the point at which you discover this involvement, you seriously consider referring the second patient. A certain amount of damage is done, but I think the second patient, as you said, should really have been immediately referred to somebody else.

The idea of dividing up the young man's therapy so that he can talk about this relationship with one therapist and about other things with you is totally naive. That's the only way I can put it. To think that this would modify the actual unconscious meanings and gratifications in some way is really an absurdity. It only plays into the misalliance aspects. And to think for example that his communications in the group don't pertain to his relationship with this girl is also an impossibility. That is, you can't tell the boyfriend to talk manifestly to somebody else about this patient and your seeing her, and agree with him that he is not talking about it in the group sessions with you. That is tantamount to saying that latent content doesn't exist, and it also implies that you are not capable of detecting it. In reality, you can be sure that the latent content of his every communication has some bearing on this adaptive context.

You can't tell somebody, Don't adapt here to that; just do it there. It makes no sense at all. And this is particularly inappropriate because you're the center of the whole interaction with both of them. So it's really an attempt on your part to deny unconscious processes and fantasies, and the actual consequences of this arrangement, and it permits a continuation of a pathogenic situation with the added denial on the part of the therapist.

The issue of what to do do is a really tough one. If the therapist is in private practice and learns, sometime after taking on a patient, that his patient is a good friend of another patient, he has a very difficult problem on his hands. If he learns that it is a relative, that makes it even more difficult. These are very tough issues. We have to see that under these circumstances the framework of the therapeutic situation has been basically modified. Remember that the defining therapeutic characteristic of the bipersonal field is the presence of a definitive and firm framework within which a unique interaction can take place. It is the frame that sets off the therapeutic interaction from all other interactions, gives it its unique qualities, and creates a situation where the patient can freely communicate the derivatives of his unconscious fantasies and introjects in his verbal communications and in his interaction with the therapist, knowing that there is a sense of safety, and that the basic ground rules and boundaries will be maintained. Then he can express wishes and impulses toward the therapist and toward others that can be analyzed, because he knows they will be handled in that special way. If he doesn't know that, he will not communicate freely to the therapist because the basic therapeutic hold will have been altered and he will not feel safe enough to put his pathology into the bipersonal field or therapist.

And this will interfere with the therapy on two levels— the two basic levels of therapy. The first relates to the image of the therapist, who is not holding the patient within a firm frame and who will be seen in some way as compromised—and as an inadequate, seductive and damaged container—even though he does and must maintain total confidentiality in the two treatment situations. Here the influence is on the patient's unconscious identificatory processes and those positive incorporative identifications from the therapist that help to generally build his ego structure, to reinforce his adequate superego functioning, and to aid him in managing his inner state.

This possible break in the frame also affects the second area of therapeutic interchange—that of the work with the patient's communications toward cognitive, ver-

balized insight. The patient will unconsciously repress
and keep to himself many derivatives of his unconscious
fantasies that he fears will be acted out with the therapist, whom he no longer trusts and whom he feels is not
maintaining definitive boundaries. The bipersonal field
will therefore not have available within it—and will not
be suited to containing—many important pathogenic
communications; they will be lacking in the therapeutic
interaction. This, as I said earlier, relates to the valid
meaning of the concept of transference as an illusion.
That is, the patient will experience as real and actual his
distorted feelings and fantasies toward the therapist, and
the derivatives of these; but he can do so safely within a
bipersonal field that guarantees their nongratification to
the greatest extent feasible. And it is only with such guarantees that he will reveal these important fantasies in an
analyzable manner.

As to what should be done here—and there is no easy
answer—you could, as I said, immediately refer the second patient to someone else, as soon as you learned of the
personal relationship. There are many therapists who
would be reluctant to do that, however. But in terms of
the framework, and the available positive identifications
for the patient, and the opportunity for therapeutic work,
you would be doing a great service to each of them. On
the other hand, if the treatment is under way and the
therapist feels that he can manage the situation and control the inevitable propensities toward acting out between
the two friends, some of which will be based on their belief that the therapist is joining with them in a misalliance, in a *menage à trois*—in a threesome that is filled
with potential for acting out and acting in—the therapist
can continue with one or both therapies until he learns
from his patients if it is workable.

If he in no way carries over anything from one treatment setting to the other, he can eventually let the two
patients know implicitly—not explicitly—that he can

maintain the boundaries. Once he has a need to explicitly reassure the patient, he's revealing a weakness and a need to modify his anonymity. This will be viewed unconsciously on the part of the patient as reflecting his concern that he can't manage this very difficult situation, and the patient will introject this sense of weakness from the therapist. On the other hand, if he does implicitly assure each of them their confidentiality, and if the therapist has the ability to explore and analyze all the ramifications of this particular arrangement, he might be able to handle it. He must recognize that any modification in the framework is a prime adaptive context for his patient, and that her communications will be filled with latent content related to it—in terms of unconscious fantasies, unconscious perceptions, and especially under these circumstances, possible unconscious misconceptions.

Here, the frame may have been modified in terms of the basic tenets of the total confidentiality of the bipersonal field. But if the therapist is not participating in any possible way in a break in confidentiality—for example, he is not using the material from one of these patients in his understanding of and interventions with the other—then he can treat these breaks not as his responsibility, but as the consequences of the behaviors of his patients. Actually, we would like to know a great deal more about how they became boyfriend and girlfriend, and about the interaction between their social relationship and the ongoing therapeutic experience of each of them. It really gets incredibly complicated, and you have to be quite a skillful therapist, and capable of managing your own inner propensities toward countertransference-based acting out, to deal with it. Remeber that it will only be feasible for the therapist to interpret the ramifications of this arrangement for this patient, and to link it meaningfully to her own intrapsychic conflicts and pathogenic introjects, if he does not participate and create a neurotic vi-

cious circle or misalliance. If he can do that, the patient
will unconsciously appreciate and understand his efforts
in this direction.

However, there are many risks, because these are realities and the patient may not be able to fully work
through and develop a certainty that his treatment is totally confidential. As I discuss this with you, I begin to
feel that a lot depends on the therapist, and on his ability
to maintain a secure framework under these circumstances. However, in a situation where you have a more
inexperienced therapist, where you have a great deal of
potential for leakage, where you expect that you will have
many difficulties in analyzing and working through the
implications of the modifications of this framework, I
would strongly recommend referral of the patient, immediately upon learning about her relationship with the
boyfriend.

One other point, I would recommend that you not
knowingly take into treatment a close friend or relative of
a patient that you have in therapy. Here, you would be
consciously participating in a modification of the framework in terms of the one-to-one relationship. There is a
negative quality here—it's not easily defined—but there
is a difference in the bipersonal field created for a patient
when a close friend is in treatment with the same therapist. Even if there is no leakage, the therapist has knowingly taken into treatment someone specifically known to
the first patient, and this will influence the therapist's
image negatively, and as I pointed out, it will then influence the very important introjective identifications made
by the patient and the opportunities for cognitive insight.

You know, when a therapist inadvertently takes into
treatment the friend of a patient of his, once the original
patient finds out that his buddy is in treatment with his
therapist, he usually will not know whether the therapist
did this knowingly or not. And especially when the therapist has only found out about the relationship between

his two patients sometime after beginning with the second patient, he will be strongly tempted to clarify the situation. because he will be under enormous direct and indirect pressure from the original patient in this regard.

After all, the first patient will feel that his privacy, and his right to some image of an exclusive hold by his therapist, has been modified, and that the framework of his treatment has been damaged. But this patient is entitled to express all his fantasies, and rages, and all the earlier life experiences that have been stirred up; and he is also entitled to the opportunity to know that the therapist can manage it all without any self-revelations. Remember, once you tell the original patient that you did not know of the friendship, you have modified the total confidentiality of the second treatment, and in a sense, you have even altered the one-to-one relationship. These modifications in the frame will have a lasting effect, something that is often overlooked. It is possible to so damage the framework that it results in a permanent alteration in the therapeutic qualities of the bipersonal field.

Well, I've gone on a bit because this is an extremely complicated and interesting problem. Now . . .

T: I plan to eventually terminate the treatment of the young man and to continue with this patient.

L: Yes, but you have maintained this arrangement for some time and there are a lot of consequences that you will have to set straight and explore with both of your patients. I think it's time to listen to some material, because I'm sure we'll get the answers we need from the patient herself, and she will tell us what to do.

T: Well, do you want me to just bring up the material?

L: Unless you have any other "by the ways." (Laughter.)

T: Well, it'll take about one sentence to describe what happened. Again, this is two sessions before. I might as well just start. Her ex-boyfriend—they weren't seeing each other regularly for the moment—wanted to see me in an emergency session . . .

L: Oh. It wasn't going to come up. It wasn't going to be mentioned.

T: In fact, once previously he had asked her—this was when he was going with her—if he could see me. In fact, what he did, he took a couple of minutes out of her session to come in and just make an appointment. He did this without my knowing about it ahead of time. He knocked, and I opened up the door; he was standing there, and I was dumbfounded. He walked in and I made an appointment to see him two hours later.

Well, at this present session, again there's a knock. He's there; he walks in and says that it's an emergency. he has to see me, and I say well, you know. She's standing there visibly angry and saying that it's all right. Anyway, I see him for a minute to tell him that I'll have to make an appointment to see him at another time. And so . . .

L: You see him for a minute with her standing there?

T: No; the door was closed and she was standing outside.

L: This was before her session or during the time set aside for it?

T: He came then because he knew that that was her time; so it was on her time. So then he leaves and she comes in; she's visibly angry. And she says it was okay. She says that things haven't really changed with her; she's still feeling depressed. She feels like she's right back at the beginning of treatment again.

L: It looks as though I don't have to retire. (Laughter.) Here, I thought that I am risking my career, and the first thing that we hear is that he came into her session. It's so unbelievable, and yet, if we recognize the importance of the framework, it is predictable. What is hard to anticipate is the specific means through which the patient will draw the attention of the therapist to the framework. Patients have an unconscious gift and great creativity in doing this, and the therapist has the job of understanding these remarkable communications. And they will always be there. Actually, the closest that I came to even anticipating something like this is that I was going to advise you to be sure to never schedule patients of this kind back to back.

So all this had happened on a previous occasion, and he had knocked on the door and walked in, and the therapist suddenly became inept because he didn't know how to deal with him. He talked to him and gratified some kind of special and neurotic need on his part to invade his girlfriend's therapy, and perhaps some neurotic need on her part to be invaded. And you can be sure, too, that the therapist also gratified some kind of countertransference needs of his own in that whole interaction.

And now, we can strongly suspect that the therapist was not able to explore and resolve the consequences of the original interruption and of the fact that he has both of them in therapy, and that this in part prompted this young man to repeat this particular piece of behavior. It is this that I would term *interactional acting out* and there are also qualities of a *menage a' trois*. The other patient is gratified . . .

T: I did get rid of him. I said I couldn't see him, and I made another appointment.

L: The way to get rid of him is to have gotten up, escorted him out into the hall and said, This is not your time. If you want to talk to me, you'll have to wait until this session is over. Period. Otherwise, you'll have a million e-mergencies. It becomes the emergency game: Doctor, I'm sick; don't talk to her, talk to me.

D: Our patients usually go to the secretary before knocking on the doctor's office.

L: It's a case of, you asked for it; it's interactional as well as intrapsychic. I told you that the patient would tell us the answer. Immediately you see the kind of situation you've created. I think it's intolerable for both of them—and maybe for you too. I certainly think that when it reaches this level, the answer is absolutely clear. The damage being done to both of them is insurmountable and it has to be repaired for both of them, by referring them to different therapists. It goes under the heading of an unfortunate major blunder. And if you discover it, you just have to face it with the patient and arrange for a referral.

And then we can only hope that the next therapist is competent and knows something about the importance of the framework for the patient and for the treatment, and can really help the patient work through all the traumas and damage that has been done in this first treatment setting. If he doesn't, then she's going to be terribly depressed for the rest of her life. It's a sad thing, and she already tells us that much.

So we don't know how the last situation was managed, though we do know that the therapist gratified this intrusive wish. Not only by possibly inviting it, but by accepting it even for one moment. Even without more data, we can suggest that the two patients are acting out both their own and the therapist's unconscious fantasies. You want a threesome; why mess around? Here's a threesome. You wanted it; you asked for it; you permitted it. You said to him: go to somebody else to talk about some of your problems. So he says, No, I'm not going to somebody else, I'm going to come to you—when she is here. It just happens that he gets his anxiety attacks when she's in the office. The timing is exquisite.

And what's so beautiful about it is that you could go ahead and say, Oh, look—he's acting out, and she's reacting, and they, the two of them, are really messing things up. Sorry. You're the director; you set the stage for this. So, however it was handled, we know it was handled in a way that didn't resolve it a bit. How long ago was the first interruption?

T: About three months ago.

L: And you can be sure that everything has been festering

ever since, and that there has been considerable chaos in both of their therapies. And now three months later he does it again. He barges in as you are about to get her for her session, and she's standing there, telling you that it's all right to use her time for him. But then she comes in and says that nothing has changed. You have a very evident adaptive context with which to formulate whatever is going to follow.

All of this leads me to reiterate some very basic ideas that we have gone over before and will have to review again and again until they are quite clear. It is here that the concept that the therapeutic relationship takes place within the bipersonal field once again becomes meaningful. As I told you, this is the term used by the Barangers (1966) and a variation on this concept has been offered more recently by Viderman (1974). The bipersonal field has a frame, and based on what I can determine from my extensive review of the literature on the analytic relationship and interaction (Langs, in press a), it has largely been the Kleinians who have considered the therapeutic aspects of the framework of the therapeutic interaction. And such a framework is, as I've said repeatedly, essential to psychotherapy as much as it is vital to psychoanalysis. And it has primarily been the Kleinians, with their interest in unconscious interactional mechanisms, and their stress on projective and introjective identification, who have been interested in the depositories for projective identifications and therefore, in containers and containing functions. As a result, they have had something important to say about the framework and have studied it analytically.

Actually, there is another avenue through which the therapeutic importance of the framework has been developed, and this derives from the writings of Winnicott (1965) who often wrote of the analyst's therapeutic hold and its importance for the patient. I do not think it is at all a coincidence that the "hold" concept conveys a con-

taining function—I think they are two different ways of
putting the same important idea.

For the Barangers, projective identification predominates so exclusively within the bipersonal field, that they
tend to disregard other contributions to the pathology of
the field. Because of that, I have borrowed their basic
concepts and some of the important ways in which they
elaborated upon them, but I do not take a position that is
identical to theirs. And in addition, I have elaborated
upon the implications of the bipersonal field in several
directions.

For me, the concept of the bipersonal field is an adaptational-interactional concept, and is one that can be integrated into the basic Freudian psychoanalytic position. It enables us to broaden the classical viewpoint to
include not only the intrapsychic phenomena within the
patient, and somewhat secondarily within the therapist
or analyst, but also the conscious and unconscious dimensions of the interaction between them.

In essence, if we view the therapeutic relationship as
occurring within a skewed bipersonal field in which one
polarity is the patient and the other polarity is the therapist, we can then see that the ground rules and the framework become crucial in that they define the limits of the
bipersonal field and they also create the conditions for
the interaction within the field. I've already alluded to
this, but I want to stress it: patients are exquisitely sensitive to the least modification in the framework. And
further, these responses are not entirely fantasies. This is
where reality comes into play, and these realities can
form the backbone for unconscious defenses, misalliances, and unconscious gratifications that really preclude any more insightful therapeutic work.

By seeing both of these patients in therapy after you
had discovered their relationship, and especially by not
being able to manage their inevitable tests of your capacity to maintain the framework in the face of this problem,

you have actually modified the therapeutic attributes of the bipersonal field for this patient. Now, it seems likely from the brief history that we have obtained, that this young lady is a borderline patient—and we will leave a-side any consideration of the boyfriend's problems here. It is just patients such as her, for whom deviations are so often advocated, whose fragile egos require an absolutely firm and solid framework, and a therapist who can maintain it in just that way.

This is not rigidity; this is the therapist's ego strengths being placed into the framework of the therapeutic relationship and expressed through the firm management of that framework and, subsequently, it is complemented by the therapist's offer to the patient to become a pliable and interpreting container for her pathology. And it is out of the containing functions of the framework and the therapist—and at this level, the therapist is part of the frame—that the patient would garner the ego strength that she needs not only for the other aspects of therapy—such as the exploration of transference distortions, but also for her general functioning in her outside life.

And these more fragile patients also express very blatantly what goes on more subtly in less disturbed patients. And so, this presentation begins not with an unconscious interpretation or with verbalized efforts to call the framework problem to the therapist's attention, but with an outlandish piece of behavior designed to accomplish these very same things. And here, too, we are in a position to recognize that even a blatant piece of acting out contains a therapeutic hope—a hope that the therapist will finally recognize that the effects that the modification in the therapeutic framework is having on these two patients, and that he will do something constructive about it.

And here, too, despite the therapist's best efforts, we see a modified field. There have been alterations in the necessary total confidentiality; the one-to-one relationship; confining the interaction to within the office; the anonymity of the therapist and his neutrality—to name just a few. Here, the therapist may have modified the basic framework of confidentiality and he has definitely modified the one-to-one relationship. And despite his best efforts, his patients immediately indicate the consequences of the alterations in the frame. They are confused as to who belongs where, and as to when each is to have his session.

And here, I would stress that this reflects the pathology of the field: the patient's reactions in some way mirror the therapist's contributions. And, together, they form an interface based on the interactions between the patients and the therapist. And when we look at this interface, we see that it's grossly disturbed and dislocated because the boyfriend has intruded on the patient's session. Now, as I told you, the Barangers (1966) called this pathology of the field a *bastion*—a split-off sector that is under repression by both the patient and the therapist. We will soon see the extent to which this is indeed the case. And as you know, I have called this a *therapeutic misalliance*, to indicate the unconscious collusion between the patient and the therapist, and the manner in which it disrupts both the therapeutic alliance and the analysis of transference expressions.

However we label such interactional pathology, it leads us to view every phenomenon in the bipersonal field as receiving contributions from both the patient and therapist—in reality and as based on each of their respective intrapsychic stirrings. In this way, we immediately consider the boyfriend's behavior as an unusual symptom of the bipersonal field within which he and the therapist work. The acting out of the boyfriend can be conceptualized as an interactional symptom and as an expression of the interactional neurosis of both himself and the present patient, and it undoubtedly includes shared interactional defenses between both of these patients and the therapist.

Viewing these developments in these terms directs us to explore not only the patient's intrapsychic difficulties, but those of the therapist as well—they direct us to consider all of the vectors contributing to this interface and to account for its most unusual qualities. Such an approach prevents us from being inappropriately biased, and from adopting a very limited and restricting view of the therapist as an observer or participant observer, and as a relatively inanimate screen—however sensitive—onto which the patient projects his intrapsychic fantasies and conflicts. In fact, one of the most important set of clinical observations that have led to the bipersonal field concept is the recognition of the extent to which the therapist is actively involved, consciously and unconsciously, in an interaction with the patient. It is here also that we shift from the model of the therapist as a screen to the therapist as a container. Our view of the therapeutic interaction becomes considerably more three-dimensional than previously reflected in the classical viewpoint, and it gives the therapeutic relationship a much more human and sensitive quality.

Actually, these concepts were developed when I discovered through presentations such as this that it is by no means unusual to find at a particular moment that the therapist has contributed as much to the patient's symptoms as the patient's own intrapsychic conflicts, and that at times, the therapist has even been the major contributor to the pathology of the field. In a well-run treatment, the disturbances in the bipersonal field should be dominated most of the time by the contributions from the patient, and the interface of the therapeutic interaction is correspondingly located closest to the patient's psychopathology. There will always be momentary and inadvertent pathological contributions from the therapist, and he must learn to recognize and detect these from the patient's material and from his own inner awareness.

In viewing the boyfriend's acting out, and the patient's participation in it, as a symptom of the field, we are directed to search for significant contributions from the therapist, and we suspect that, on the surface, this derives from his failure to be definitive in dealing with a similar interruption at an earlier time. This is in keeping with the patient's saying that she doesn't care about the boyfriend's using the time for her session. It is absolutely characteristic that patients will usually not protest directly against a misalliance. They accept the unconscious gratification and the shared defenses initially; then they later attempt to rectify the situation.

And I hope, again, that this patient will bear out this hypothesis, which is really one that I have seen confirmed repeatedly in previous studies. The patient will not protest directly; however, if the therapist listens to the patient with the modification in the framework and the pathology of the field as his contexts, the material will reveal the patient's unconscious responses.

I think that the patient's failure to protest directly accounts in part for the blind spot in many therapists and analysts regarding the importance of the framework. I think it's also a blind spot that is created by the therapist's unconscious pathological needs and the difficulties experienced by every therapist and analyst in maintaining an appropriate level of renunciation in their work with patients. So I must stress that direct protest will occur only under exceptional circumstances, while indirect protests will be abundant. And if the therapist picks them up, corrects the problems in the field, changes his own contributions, and explores the misalliance with the patient based on his ongoing associations—a considerable amount of valuable therapeutic work can be done.

However, this raised the issue of the point at which the bipersonal field is beyond repair, and this is why I said earlier that this situation may well be beyond that point. The pathology of the field seems absolutely enormous;

the contributions of each participant have been quite significant and unmodified for some time; and it may very well be that despite the therapist's best efforts, he will not be able to modify the many, many consequences of this situation. So it may well be that the field has been modified here to the point where referral is necessary.

Now, in an effort to anticipate the clinical material that we will be hearing, let's remember that it is quite characteristic of both patient and therapist, when they are involved in a misalliance and in maintaining a pathological sector of the field, to accept it on one level and to undertake efforts to modify it on another. So, let's listen further with these concepts in mind. And let's see how much they help us to understand what follows. So, back to that marvelously creative opening gambit.

T: She, in fact, remembers that it's like the beginning of her therapy; it's like back to the same place again. And there's an image which she refers to, of a dark parking lot, a scene of desolation which she remembers from an experience she had when she was in Texas about a year ago. And this always brings up images of bleakness and hopelessness.

Last Saturday night, she dared herself to commit suicide. She had argued with one of her sisters, and she wanted someone to talk with that evening. She thought of calling me; she didn't though. She was by herself and she took a razor blade and cut the skin of her wrist superficially. As she cut herself, she realized she couldn't go through with suicide and that that avenue was no longer open to her.

She then talked about receiving that day, a mail notice that her disability checks were cancelled. Still. she wouldn't be able to return to work because of her emotional problems and she had no money; she couldn't work and so she'd have to move from the apartment where she lives with one of her sisters and her husband.

L: She's sharing the rent—is that it?

T: Yes. And then she said, Well, I may not feel I have anything, but I may have more than other people. And I may
not have as much as some people have. And then she
asked if the people from the Disability Office had called,
and I said, No they haven't. She said, They will. She
talked of how demeaning it was to admit to them that she
was a patient and then she described the questions that
they asked her about her illness; whom she saw; how long
she'd been in therapy; why she was better? And she said
that my answers to the Office would determine whether
or not she'd get disability.

I said that it seemed that she wondered what I was going to tell them in terms of her disability and that she was
saying that it meant whether or not she was going to stay
in treatment. That if I didn't give the correct answers to
the Office, I didn't understand her; there was no reason
for her to continue. And that's essentially the essence of
the session.

L: All right. Who will comment?

T: I think that the adaptive context has to do with this guy
intruding on the session. I didn't even have it in my
notes. It came to me as I was going over some of this—
when she said, I don't have as much as some, but I have
more than others. I think, in fact, she may be describing
how she views herself in treatment: she may be coming in
more frequently than this guy, but she's not really getting
what therapy could be.

L: Any other comment?

D: Taking the intrusion as the adaptive context, it brought
to her mind feelings of helplessness and desolation, and
of abandonment too.

L: Why don't you tell us what the circumstances were at the
time of that scene in the parking lot.

T: Well, she had been in Texas and had gone to see some
friends outside of Houston. It was late at night. I can't re-

member—she may or may not have been using some drugs. But at any rate, she was walking back to the bus depot to go back to where she'd been living and she got lost. She found herself on a street, and then in this vacant parking lot that was dark, and she imagined all sorts of things such as being attacked, really being lost, not knowing exactly where to go.

L: So how do you connect that to the adaptive context?

D: The therapist is involved with this other guy, and she's lost, she's deserted—abandoned.

L: So, you're saying that his seeing this fellow for a minute before the session was experienced as a total abandonment?

D: Yes. I wonder whether she adapted to that and if she hadn't cut herself to prove that she was still there—that she existed.

L: Well, she had done that beforehand, so we have to put it a little bit differently. We can't say that the suicide gesture was a response to this particular incident since it occurred prior to it.

D: It sounded as though it had occurred as a result of that.

L: No, this was the session in which it was reported; it had already happened.

D: And the other thing, the other major adaptation was to the same adaptive context; it was the confidentiality bit. In other words, you're in touch with this boyfriend and the Disability people. Everything depends on them; not on you . . .

L: That's the point; it is so clear that I think the therapist should ask himself why he didn't see it.

T: Yes.

L: I've told you so many times that one ground rule problem begets another. And she comes back to the issue of confidentiality—she brings up the framework. She says, If you don't handle it right, I'm going to quit treatment.

This is something she's thinking of doing, and we have to attribute much of her decision to stay in therapy, in the face of the desolation that she is feeling, to her severe masochism—after all, she's suicidal.

Without knowing the prior material and what prompted this suicidal gesture in terms of contributions from within herself and from the therapist, it is difficult for the moment to sort out that aspect of the situation. But she is quite clearly saying that the continuation of her treatment, and of her life, has to do with your capacity to manage the framework, and with your ability to handle these issues of confidentiality and third parties to her treatment. And we have to recognize that you by-passed these problems completely despite our many discussions about how, once the boundaries come up, they become a major issue. So, there seems to be a blind spot here and one that we will expect to hear a great deal more about from the patient in the next session.

And notice too how her associations support my thesis that her surface acceptance of her boyfriend's intrusion into her session would be followed by major indications that she doesn't really accept it, and that she is disturbed by the break in the framework. In fact, her associations remind me that I could have been even more specific in regard to her response to the disturbance in the bipersonal field to which you had contributed, since you have given us sufficient background material to know that this patient tended to be severely depressed and even suicidal; however, I think I did say she'd be depressed.

And of course this is where the patient's own intrapsychic pathology and needs come into play, in that they will, along with the nature of the adaptive context, determine her responses. There is always an amalgam that combines the pathology that the therapist has put into the bipersonal field and into the misalliance, and the patient's own inner style of dealing with such disturbances.

So it was really no surprise that she experienced the

therapist's modification of the framework, and specifically, his taking some of her time to be with her boyfriend, as a total abandonment that recalled to her previous moments of utter despair and suicidal gestures. And before I forget, le me mention that technically it would only compound the trauma if the therapist did not clearly indicate to the patient that he was going to extend her session in order to make up the few moments that had been lost; without that, there would be an actual loss, in addition to the intense psychological hurts.

Now, I have found that whatever the patient's own pathology, she will express her responses to modifications in the framework in a fashion that derives from a kind of universal language. You have already heard communications from this patient that are not unlike those we heard from the patient who was last presented to us; after all, this similarity is even more apparent because they each have significant masochistic trends. There are differences of course, but we have not heard this patient out entirely. We will see what lies ahead.

Using the adaptive context of the modification in the framework, let's be specific about some of the more exquisite meanings that she has communicated through these associations: she feels abandoned and suicidal; she is in a rage and feels that the therapist is unavailable; she feels unable to function and yet despairingly expresses the hope that something good will be available to her; she feels demeaned and not in control of her own fate; and from what the therapist tells us of the experience in Texas, a bipersonal field into which a third party has been introduced and for which the frame has been damaged, becomes a place of enormous danger.

Some of this has been incorporated from the therapist through introjective identification, and so here let me indicate those aspects of her communications that I view as early attempts at unconscious interpretations to the therapist, and as an initial reflection of incorporative identifications from him. And I would say, despite the massive qualities of her own depressive and suicidal fantasies and impulses, that she is also indicating through these associations her impression that the therapist is profoundly depressed and that he needs the presence of an additional party to the bipersonal field in order to fill him in his emptiness. She also sees the therapist as destructive and attacking, and thus in part—and again I want to remind you that this is only a segment of the picture—the suicidal gesture relates to the incorporative identification of the therapist's destructiveness and depression.

From there, she goes on to speak of her own disability and of the Disability office, and this conveys, on the level that I am delineating, her unconscious perceptions of the therapist's inadequacies—his disability. And lastly, on this level, when she says that whether she is going to stay in treatment will depend on what the therapist tells the Disability people, she is reminding us that psychotherapy is not feasible within a damaged frame—especially when it has been damaged to this extent.

So, in her own way, these unconscious communications are filled with efforts to convey some of these difficulties to the therapist, and to offer him both some unconscious supervision and some unconscious therapy. I think that she has also to some extent confirmed in a preliminary fashion my impression that this bipersonal field is seriously damaged and may be beyond repair.

Despite the fact that we have now had the gloom placed into us by both the patient and the therapist, and we all feel somewhat depressed, let me point to one hopeful sign: while the therapist did not offer an adequate intervention, and while he missed the major adaptive context and the unconscious communications that could have been interpreted to the patient, he did offer her what I consider to be an unconscious interpretation, although it was actually rather limited. He was right in say-

ing to her that the way in which he handled the third party to therapy would be crucial to the outcome of her
treatment, and that his failure to have offered her some
correct answers—here I am attempting to read some of
the latent content of the intervention—did indeed indicate that he was unable to understand her for the moment. So he did agree with her, in a sense, that if he is not
capable of intervening more adequately, there would be
no reason for her to continue her therapy. These comments, however indirect, may offer her some hope, despite the absence of a valid conscious intervention by the
therapist.

What makes this situation so serious—and we can't
overlook it—is the risk of an actual suicide in the face of
the damaged frame and the therapist's failure to offer
some valid interventions. It is in this kind of a situation
that my clinical observations indicate that the suicide
risk would virtually disappear in the face of a clear-cut
and secure set of boundaries and a strong therapeutic
hold. Under these circumstances, the patient would have
an opportunity to put into the therapist, and into the bipersonal field, her suicidal fantasies and impulses; the
therapeutic situation, with the therapist as a part of it,
would readily become the container for these contents.
And together, these two functions—the therapeutic hold
and the containing function—would assist this patient
significantly in managing her suicidal impulses until the
specific derivatives of the unconscious fantasies and experiences that have contributed to this aspect of her illness become available for analytic resolution through
verbalized insight.

On the other hand, in the absence of adequate management of the framework, the patient becomes the container for the therapist's depression and inner difficulties, and is thereby overburdened. It is clear that she is
having difficulty containing her own impulses and fantasies, and that any additional input from the therapist

compounds these problems. In a general way, you can see why the therapist has to be unencumbered in order to serve as a container for the patient's inner pathology, and you can see what happens when the container is virtually full or spilling over—any further efforts to put sickness into such a containing-person will lead either to acting out or, I believe, other types of regression, including psycho-somatic illnesses.

Now, let's consider for a moment the opportunity that the patient is presenting to you, in dealing with the agency involved with her disability. Here, she again brings up a boundary issue and if you had found it feasible, for example, to indicate that you would not participate with additional third parties to her therapy, the effect on her would have been something close to miraculous. Oh, initially she would protest on the surface and probably even question your sanity, but unconsciously, she would offer you a tremendous amount of material that would not only support such a decision, but would add to your own understanding of it.

It is quite characteristic for patients, once the framework has been resecured, and especially when it entails some overt frustration to them as it would in these circumstances with this patient, to protest loudly on the surface; meanwhile, they add many other confirmatory derivatives of their positive unconscious perceptions and fantasies. They had failed to communicate this material earlier, because it was unsafe to do so within a damaged framework and with a therapist who could not be trusted. In fact, I will assure you that if you ever have the opportunity to secure a previously damaged framework, that you will learn how pervasive the influence of the framework is on the patient and on yourself, and how many fantasies and perceptions are defensively repressed when you have participated in this type of misalliance.

You see, when the issue of confidentiality came up, if you had used the principle of exploring all aspects of the boundaries when a particular framework allusion appeared, you would probably have gone back to the intrusion by the boyfriend and reviewed the patient's associations in that context. Then you could have pointed out to the patient that while she told you that she didn't mind the boyfriend using a few minutes of her time—and added right at that point that she would be having a full session—everything that she goes on to talk about indicates that she felt enormously threatened and angered by your having seen him under those circumstances. And then you could have spelled out, as I did just a little while ago, each of the unconscious perceptions and fantasies that she communicated in the light of this modification in the framework. Within that therapeutic context, you could implicitly convey to her how much you had learned from her in that session, by letting her know that you would certainly not talk to any third party about her therapy until the entire matter had been explored with her, and that, based on what she had conveyed to you, even the issue as to whether you would ever again discuss her treatment with a third person would have to be explored.

So you see, in two ways, you would benefit from her therapeutic efforts and your own insights: you would interpret adequately to her and you would, in reality, indicate your readiness to restore the framework. And on your own, you would go on to do two other things: first, you would terminate the treatment of the boyfriend, indicating to him that you felt it would be to his disadvantage to continue to work with you. After exploring this as fully as possible with him and interpreting his many unconscious responses to this decision—and they would then reveal many of the unconscious meanings of your modifications in the framework for him—you would then refer him to another therapist. And you would never share your decision with this patient or carry over in any way into her bipersonal field your experiences with him.

And second, with this patient, and under these circumstances, I would also advise you to continue her treatment on your own, entirely without supervision. Since you have started your presentation here, we will follow it through, because I think it is essential to assist you in restoring this framework and in convincing you of its importance. But once you are ready to offer her a secure framework, you should do it as completely as possible, without telling the patient; I can assure you that she will be able to experience it consciously and unconsciously in her subsequent interaction with you.

Well, this certainly is a vivid lesson in the importance of the framework. I'm reminded again of de Racker's (1961) comment that when you are participating in a vicious circle—and I would add in a therapeutic misalliance—you are not in a position to interpret it. On some level, both you and the patient are participating in a version of your respective past pathogenic interactions and confirming each other's pathogenic introjects and unconscious fantasies and memories. This makes it all the more striking—but you helped to arrange the threesome. On some level it must be unconsciously gratifying to you . . .

T: All I could see was that it infringed on her confidentiality. I didn't carry over the boundary problem of confidentiality in connection with the Disability office and relate it to what had just taken place.

L: Well, this shows how much you are embedded in the misalliance, and it reflects the difficulty that you had in understanding the patient's communications because of that. And this is really the kind of modification in the framework that affects the entire treatment and the patient's basic communications to you.

Now, this gives me a chance to point out that as we have been going along studying the framework and conceptualizing its containing functions, as well as the containing functions of the therapist, it has struck me that the framework metaphor is a bit too nonhuman and rigid, and that the same could be said about the idea of the container. After all, we have seen that what we are dealing with is a framework that has not only temporal-spatial qualities, but human qualities as well. For example, the therapist's neutrality and his anonymity are parts of the framework that cannot be visualized, but they are essential to a secure and therapeutic bipersonal field, in which analyzable transference expressions can unfold. And we have seen that when any of the ground rules are modified, it is not simply a matter of a break in the frame —a rupture in the hold—but that it actually entails unconscious communications, most of which are pathological, that are conveyed to and put into the patient.

In addition, we have seen that the therapist's functions as a container fluctuate with his own inner state, his capacity to manage his countertransferences, and the nature of the material that the patient is attempting to put into him. This is by no means our usual image of a container. It shows us that the particular container that we are attempting to conceptualize enlarges and contracts, is relatively open or relatively closed, may be passively receptive or actively inviting, and may process its contents adequately, poorly, or not at all—to name just a few of the qualities that would not occur to us if we stuck too closely to the container metaphor. I think that it is becoming clearer that as we get to understand these concepts better, we will eventually have to develop more adequate metaphors with which to describe them.

And here again, we see that we could revise one aspect of the framework and ground rules that I have repeatedly stated as the therapist's responsibility to maintain his neutrality, and to intervene with neutral interventions geared toward interpretations. What I have in mind is the way in which the statement of this tenet reflects the classical model of psychoanalysis and analytic psychotherapy, in which interventions in the verbal sphere that are designed to generate cognitive insight have received almost exclusive attention. Now that we are more sensitive to the therapeutic interaction and to the need for an appropriate bipersonal field within which the transference can be secured as analyzable and illusory, we come to recognize that there is another basic sphere of intervening—the management of the framework. And it is here that neutral intervention implies a sound management of the framework and the nonparticipation in sectors of misalliance—to the extent that that is humanly feasible. And in this context, a second basic and ultimate neutral intervention would come into play, one that I would term *rectification*—the modification of the therapist's participation in a misalliance or the actual correction of a mismanagement of the framework.

I am trying to stress in so many different ways that these actualities are basically not interpretable until they have been modified. Their intrapsychic consequences cannot be altered without rectification first. Misalliances and contaminations of the bipersonal field are realities and actualities; the appropriate intervention is rectification, after which interpretation can follow. And these actualities, if not modified, totally undermine the interpretive work, because they significantly influence the nature of the patient's communications to the therapist, the quality of their interaction, the patient's perceptions of and fantasies about his therapist—and himself—and the extent to which an analyzable transference neurosis or transference constellation will appear within the bipersonal field. To put this still another way, these actualities influence the extent to which the patient will feel safe enough to express his intrapsychic pathology, and put it into the bipersonal field and into the therapist. They affect the degree to which the patient experiences his inner disturbance as inappropriate and pathological based in part on the extent to which a healthy external reality is present in the therapeutic situation. And in addition, as you can see, these actualities also influence the way in which the patient will accept into himself and comprehend the communications from the therapist. They so completely influence the patient's image of the therapist that they color the meaning of every one of his communications. If he has not secured the framework or is participating in a misalliance, the implications of his verbal interventions for the patient will be distinctly different than they would be had his countertransferences not led him into such difficulties. Forgive me for repeating this over and over, but there is such a basic misunderstanding in this area, and such a disregard for the influence of these interactional realities on the entire therapeutic field and work, and on the patient and therapist, that I am making every effort to be as explicit as possible.

Now, if we return to this particular clinical situation, we can see that once the frame is broken, this patient's pathological inner world, and the outer world that's created by the therapeutic situation, become indistinguishable in certain respects; you lose what I would term *the therapeutic differential.* And in addition, the world outside of the frame, and the world inside of it, come to have the same rules in certain crucial respects. So, outside of the frame, in your everyday life, you fall in love, you express it in many ways, you want to go to bed with someone, you want to do this or that, or whatever. Now, maybe you can imagine what the therapeutic situation feels like to this patient without a clear-cut frame. And outside too, if you are angry or filled with hate you think of revenge or hurting back and the like. Inside the frame, such love and hatred is not expressed physically nor gratified directly—there are limits, controls and safeguards.

So, this is the kind of damaged bipersonal field that you have helped to establish for this patient and you can see that it has not been developed for her therapeutic needs, and she is making some attempt to let you know how frightening and dismal this therapeutic field is—undoubtedly in the hope of getting something better. And she even offers you the vehicle for the restoration of the bipersonal field in her reference to the Disability People. But for the moment it appears that you are so much of a participant in the misalliance, and that the alterations in the field are so in keeping with your needs, that you are unable to offer the necessary interventions: rectification and then interpretation. In a way, the three of you are there in bed together, so how could you be in a position to validly say that all of you shouldn't be doing this? And how could anything that you say be experienced as a valid interpretation from a positive or good object, when this is what you are sharing with them? Now we might suspect that in her image of desolation she is also expressing the wish that she could be alone and away from both of you and the boyfriend. As horrible as that is, she may be saying that she prefers it to what she has.

And so you see again how much we can learn from the patient. Unconsciously, the patient is a genius. This means that everyone who goes into therapy, somewhere has similar gifts. In a way, our basic job is to tune in on the unconscious creativity of the patient, and if we are capable of sitting back and listening in an appreciative way, we can do a great deal with the patient's communications. Unfortunately, in a therapeutic bipersonal field, there must be one conscious genius, so to speak, in addition to the unconscious genius, and that is the therapist. I have little doubt that the free associations of this therapist would reveal a deep unconscious appreciation of many aspects of this situation and of the material from the patient. But the therapist has the job of elevating these unconscious processes to a specific level of conscious awareness. And maybe much of the technical jargon and precepts that therapists are taught as they attempt to learn psychotherapy, just get in the way of this crucial process—the transformation of unconscious empathy and insight into conscious understanding and intervening. When we observe the incredible degree to which the patient is unconsciously sensitive, we are bound to give pause to reconsider how to best create a sound psychotherapist. However, I am beginning to drift off a bit. It's time to get back to this patient.

T: But I don't know what to do now.

L: Well, I think that it's becoming clearer that, despite your attachment to this girl and the extent to which you would like to work with her, you may have no choice but to refer her and the boyfriend to new therapists. I think that you have to be realistic as to where you are in your training, and face the likelihood that it would be extremely difficult, if not impossible, for you to rectify all the damage that has been done. However, before we come to any final conclusions, we should have a chance to listen to more of the material from the patient; once again, unconsciously she will show us the way.

T: Yes, but there is also the group.

L: I'm sure that if you looked at the material from the group, you would find that they too had been responding to the modifications in the framework of their treatment that have come from your involvement with this patient and her boyfriend. But, let me make another point, before the gloom descends on all of us. As I said earlier, there is always a positive or adaptive side to every communication and to every behavior. And if you want to see that aspect of the boyfriend's acting out, how could you put it? (Pause.) Well, he really is trying to do something adaptive and helpful for everybody. How?

D: Maybe he's trying to destroy this patient's therapy.

L: Yes, but that again emphasizes the destructive aspect. What is the constructive side? Well, I'd put it this way: he's trying to say, Look, damn it; Look what's happening. He's trying to bring it right to the center of your attention. How could he do it more effectively? In other words, I'm sure they both tried, subtly and not so subtly, to let you know that there's something terribly the matter, and that they're both suffering. And what happened? You didn't hear them! So what do you do, if somebody doesn't hear you? You knock on the door and walk in. Here I am, one, two, three—count us. And how do you respond? You lose count; you don't say anything. No wonder they have to go to this extreme. Then you wonder why patients attempt suicide and why patients do crazy things like interrupt a session. You see why? This is why.

Now, I'm not attempting to make you feel overly guilty —although a healthy sense of guilt and a healthy motivation to do something about this kind of situation is quite appropriate—nor am I trying to overburden you with the responsibility for the patient. So I'll say it again: the patient has to accept responsibility for her behavior, whatever the therapist happens to do. But there has been too much tendency to account for the unfortunate and hurtful or destructive things that happen in therapy by making them entirely or primarily the patient's responsibility, while overlooking what actually happened, and how the therapist also—and sometimes primarily—contributed to the disturbance.

And here, I'm simply trying to show you that we are dealing with an interactional neurosis to which you have contributed as well as the patient. And I'm trying to remind you that you have accepted certain responsibilities that are different from those of the patient, and that these include a conscious effort to avoid misalliances, to create a truly therapeutic bipersonal field, and to intervene through rectification and interpretation where needed. In a way, you could have accepted the responsibility of being the healthy container and contributor to the bipersonal field, at least to a significantly greater extent than the patient, while the patient is accepted as the one who will put almost all of the pathology into the field.

And you see, it is not surprising that the patient will feel exceptionally overwhelmed when you put significant pathology into the field and into her, since she is already overburdened, and since you had conveyed to her the expectation that, with absolutely minimal exceptions, this sort of thing would not occur. When the patient puts her pathology into you, there is hardly a feeling of disillusionment and rage; instead, this is what you're hoping for and this is where you can do some of your therapeutic work. In fact, it undoubtedly has something to do with the unconscious reasons that prompted you to select psychiatry as a profession. But the patient feels betrayed and hurt and mistrustful when the therapist behaves in a damaging way, and we can see why—despite our insistence that she maintain responsibility for herself. Nonetheless, the situation is particularly trying for her at times like this.

And this is what I mean when I say that we can most clearly conceptualize the communications from this patient by thinking of the bipersonal field, and by recognizing that any point in the field is under the influence of every other point, and that the experiences that this patient is having are influenced not only by her outer life and especially her intrapsychic life, but by her interaction with you. Not that this is entirely new; if you look at the recent literature on schizophrenia and adolescents— at Searles' (1965) concept of the therapeutic symbiosis, and at some recent studies of the adolescent's interaction with his family undertaken by Zinner, Shapiro, and their associates (1972, Berkowitz et al., 1974)—you will find their comments replete with references to introjection and projection, and to projective identification.

So we're back to basics again, and I think you can see clearly why you have to deal with the interaction and with actualities before you can understand and deal with the patient's intrapsychic conflicts and pathological introjects. Perhaps now you have a better feeling of how actualities influence fantasy, as well as how fantasy can influence actuality. There is a constant interplay, and we have always known that the way in which one behaves has a far greater influence than what one has to say. It has just taken us a long time to apply this fully to the psychotherapist. His behaviors and participation in any misalliance sector must be brought under control and his capacity to establish a sound bipersonal field clearly demonstrated to the patient, long before his verbal intervention will have their intended effects. But I think that now it's time to get back to some more clinical material before so much of what I have to say sounds like it's coming from me more than it's coming from the patient. But I see that our time is up; we'll stop here and continue with this presentation next week.

Chapter 6

THE INTERACTIONAL COMPONENTS OF THE THERAPIST'S INTERVENTIONS

THE ASSESSMENT OF INTERVENTIONS AND THE USE OF THE VALIDATING PROCESS • INTERACTIONAL COMPONENTS OF ERRORS IN INTERVENING • TECHNICAL PRINCIPLES RELATED TO THE DEVELOPMENT OF INTERVENTIONS • THE CONSTRUCTIVE NUCLEI WITHIN HURTFUL INTERVENTIONS • THE THERAPIST'S USE OF EMPATHY AND CREATIVITY • AN INTERACTIONAL PARANOID SYNDROME • THE TECHNICAL HANDLING OF ERRORS IN TECHNIQUE • THE THERAPIST'S MASTERY OF HIS COUNTERTRANSFERENCE DIFFICULTIES—INTRAPSYCHIC AND INTERACTIONAL DIMENSIONS

L: Please start right in.

T: All right. Perhaps to preface this session . . .

L: Not another preface! (Laughter.) Go ahead.

T: All right, I won't even tell you.

L: She'll tell us. Please do the session in sequence; don't spoil it for us; and first, please summarize the material to this point for us.

T: (The therapist reviews the prior session.) Now, she comes in for this hour and takes her coat off, and she looks on my desk as she's taking her coat off and putting it on the rack. Now, it's up to you to decide what she sees on the desk.

L: Well, if you know what she saw, I think we're entitled to know what you know.

T: I didn't know until after the session and after she had told me what she had seen.

L: In other words, she sees and you don't. That paradigm
     seems to be familiar now. So something was showing on
     your desk and you didn't know what it was. So I guess
     that we're stuck with your ignorance for the moment and
     we'll just have to accept it. But, whatever it is, what is this
     a reference to? Give me the broad concept.

D: Is it the boundaries—the problem of confidentiality?

L: Yes, she starts off another session with something about
     the boundaries. She has a therapist who has something
     on his desk, exposed. The framework is on her mind
     again. It took no seconds.

T: Yes. And the fact that I noticed that she even noticed
     something . . .

L: Yes, that's your unconscious response. You had better
     get in touch with it.

T: All right. The patient began this next session by talking
     about an internist she was to see the following day. Let
     me give you some background: she had been suffering
     from severe abdominal and chest pains, but there had
     been no positive physical findings. The doctors had sus-
     pected her gall bladder and her ovaries, and had some
     question about her heart, but had come up with nothing.
     She had been placed on high dosages of birth-control
     pills, but this had not alleviated her symptoms and had
     actually aggravated them. Her father had died from a
     ruptured abdominal viscus and heart failure, and an
     aunt had died in a similar way just prior to the patient's
     last hospitalization. The patient had also had some leg
     paralysis which actually was hysterical. She had been
     hospitalized for it, but she was discharged when she said
     that she wanted her upper abdominal pains treated. At
     another time, she was hospitalized when the upper ab-
     dominal pain went into her chest; there had been no
     physical findings then either, even though she had been
     put into an intensive care unit. She had been upset be-
     cause they had not explained to her why she had been

placed there, even though they said again that the entire work-up was negative.

L: Notice the allusion here to a rather totally crazy therapeutic situation.

T: I would agree and I can see what it means.

L: Yes, unfortunately it is a commentary on her current treatment.

T: Well, to continue with what she had said in the session: she was going to go to see a doctor the next day; she was afraid he wouldn't believe her. In fact, if she complained that she had stomach or heart pains, he was going to tell her that it was psychological; but if she didn't tell him . . . Then she said that she wouldn't tell him, probably. Even if he changed the medication, she probably wouldn't go along with it, because she didn't want to have the abdominal pain that was caused by the medication and by her ovulation when she was on it. And I remarked that the doctor seemed to be on the spot here, in terms of being in a kind of double bind. She remarked that her family had been quite concerned about her recently, although they . . .

L: We're learning about interventions. What kind of an intervention was that? The doctor's on the spot; he's in a kind of double bind.

D: A clarification?

L: Yes; it appears to be some effort at clarification—an attempt by the therapist to elucidate the implications of her associations related to the doctors. That is it's technical nature. However, it is important to recognize that in addition to this aspect, there is an interactional and communicative component to every intervention. It has major nonverbal qualities, and these are embedded in the contents of the intervention. And while we are discussing the ways in which we assess an intervention, let me point out that in addition to identifying its technical nature and stating the manifest therapeutic intention, we will attempt to formulate its implicit aspects. We will especially search out those implications that are designed primarily to help the patient, and those that primarily reflect countertransference problems in the therapist.

We will soon see that an incorrect intervention by no means rolls off the patient's back like water off a duck's, but instead, it communicates aspects of the therapist's countertransference and also serves as a vehicle through which the therapist puts his pathology into the patient and invites projective identifications from the patient as well. You will remember that we saw that communications involved in the mismanagement of the framework serve these functions. Now, we will be in a position to observe the ways in which missed and incorrect interventions have the same qualities. I think again that by understanding the maladaptive aspects of the therapist's communications, we will be able to recognize their adaptive functions more clearly, and thereby learn about appropriate interventions.

So, what are the interactional and communicative aspects of this intervention?

T: Well, let me say this. I didn't realize that I'm the doctor who is on the spot.

L: All right. The first thing that you communicated is that you didn't understand the latent content of her associations. At least, that is what you were conveying consciously, although I will show you in a moment how you were unconsciously indicating your appreciation that she is indeed alluding to yourself.

If we pause for a moment with this aspect of your intervention, we can see that it leads to a technical review of the session. You made your intervention without an adaptive context; and we can see that doing so is both being lax in your use of technical principles, and a psychologically dangerous procedure. And this is always the case: sound technical principles safeguard the interaction, while a keen sensitivity to the interaction will enable you to intervene in ways that will reflect sound technical

principles. In fact, we shall soon see that in considering
any intervention, we should always attempt to comprehend its interpretive and interactional dimensions. But
that again is a bit ahead of ourselves.

On this cognitive level, we can see that you failed to
identify the adaptive context that was organizing this
material. On the surface, she had a realistic problem in
approaching her physician; but on another level, it is evident that the adaptive context for these communications relate to the boyfriend's interruption of her previous session and undoubtedly to her anticipations that
the Disability Agency will be getting in touch with you.
More broadly, the adaptive context of this session is the
current problems with the therapeutic situation and with
the therapist.

Now, once this is confirmed as the adaptive context,
the therapist should be preparing his interventions and
subjecting them to the validating process as he listens to
further associations from the patient. By this I mean that
he would be checking out his formulations against his
own subjective impressions, his recollection of the previous and other recent or even remote sessions, and
searching out the manifest and especially the latent content of the patient's subsequent communications, for material that would support or refute his planned interventions. In principle, the therapist should intervene only
when this silent validating process has supported a tentative intervention.

And here, the therapist's preparation to intervene
would be based on thinking of this kind: he should be
aware of the unfinished business from the previous hour,
and might even begin to realize that the communications in the prior session related to her negative images
of him based on the inadequate ways that he had dealt
with the framework. Then, he would pick up the following themes: a doctor who doesn't believe her; her hesitation to communicate to him; her inclination not to tell
him the nature of her problems; her expectation that he

will put her off; and her anticipation that what he puts into her will cause her pain. And so, you can see that we would be preparing a series of unconscious perceptions of the hurtful therapist and attempting to understand their elaborations in the patient's intrapsychic fantasies, and their connection to her pathological introjects. And if the patient were to add some material that would bring her closer to the therapeutic situation or, as I would expect, directly to it, I would then be prepared to intervene by showing her the adaptive context and her responses to it.

Now, I want to pause long enough to also show you how the patient has validated one of the ideas that I have tried to establish in regard to the plight of any patient when the framework has been modified. I had put it into technical language, while the patient puts it in the form of rather plaintive associations. My technical comment was to the effect that the frame is necessary for the transference illusion experience—for the emergence of analyzable derivatives of the patient's intrapsychic transference constellations, as they relate to the core of her psychopathology. And I said that without a secure frame, the patient will not communicate in this way and will have reason to mistrust the therapist. Here I would suggest to you that in the adaptive context of a ruptured frame, the patient is saying exactly this in her own words —she is not only hesitant to communicate the nature of the sickness inside her, the responses of the therapist actually prevent her from doing so. Remember, this is something that we have heard over and over again; it is exactly out of this kind of situation and the responses of the patient that I initially made these particular formulations.

And she goes on and says even more about the influence of a modified and mismanaged frame. I had spoken of this complicated mechanism that we have termed introjective identification, and I suggested in a manner that might have sounded somewhat strange to you, that when the therapist mismanages the frame he puts his own sickness into the patient, and the patient suffers from an introjective identification of the disturbed therapist—from a pathological introject. In this patient's words, the idea is simplified by her saying that the bad doctor puts things into her that cause her pain—that make her sick. The image also has the quality of the container and the contained, so it may help you see why that particular metaphor also proves useful; the patient is complaining about being made to contain the therapist's sickness—it is too much for her to handle.

Are there any other communicative aspects of this intervention by the therapist?

D: He's also saying to her, Look what you're doing. It's bad; you shouldn't do it.

L: Yes, on the simplest level, he's identifying himself with this other physician and opposing the patient. So it is not simply a matter of the therapist being critical, he is unconsciously joining forces with the bad doctor. It is here that I believe that the unconscious communication of an identification with this other physician conveys to the patient an implicit acknowledgment that her associations are indeed related to himself. Remember, however, that the therapist has expressed this unconsciously and not explicitly, and it is of little cognitive use to the patient. And you can see that there are so many additional disturbing communicative facets to his intervention that any positive unconscious component will be overshadowed. The point is to recognize this component however, because it also again demonstrates that embedded in a bad or hurtful intervention is some good, or some effort at unconscious understanding. I have been extremely impressed with this type of combination in the communications from both the patient and the therapist: it seems clear that there is never a moment that they simply want to undermine the therapy and totally generate harm and neurosis. There is always embedded somewhere some sense of hope and some effort toward cure. Now while this may sound rather maudlin, it leads to a very important set of technical implications. I would stress one to you at this point, namely, that it fosters the search for good contents in the face of destructiveness, and permits the therapist to intervene not only in relation to the patient's resistances and efforts to destroy him, herself, or treatment—or all three—but gives him an opportunity at the same time to get in touch with the patient's good or healthy or constructive parts. Often, it leads to a much more sensitive and balanced intervention, and it modifies the image of the therapist as consistently critical and attacking, even when these efforts are done with tact and full control or sublimation.

As if matters were not complicated enough, this intervention is also a component of an actual unconscious interaction between the patient and her therapist, in which projective and introjective identifications are quite evident. Let me try to sort it out for you. As part of our formulations in the previous hour, I suggested that the therapist had possibly to some extent put into the patient aspects of his own depression, feelings of inadequacy, and need for a third party to their relationship. The therapist certainly conveyed a feeling of being overwhelmed by what was happening, and his failures to intervene in that hour added to that impression.

Now, in this session, in addition to the patient's conveying her unconscious perceptions of the therapist, we see the fate of these efforts by the therapist to put into the patient some of his own difficulties. On the one hand, the patient shows evidence of an incorporative identification with the deceiving and confused therapist. On the other hand, we could formulate her communications concerning the other doctor as an effort by the patient to put back into the therapist—to reproject—the pathological sense of confusion, uncertainty, and difficulty in managing that he had put into her. Now, it would be my contention that the therapist's comments about how the patient is putting the doctor into a double bind is an effort to handle the introjective identifications put back into him by the patient, by reprojecting them back onto her. This is not as confusing as it sounds: there is a back and forth struggle here with certain pathological contents that neither the patient nor the therapist seem to want to keep within themselves—to contain—and seem ready to put into the other. Both are serving as reluctant containers for these disturbed contents, and neither is connecting this struggle on a conscious level with the happenings within the therapeutic interaction.

Further, in making his intervention, the therapist immediately overlooks the patient's unconscious communication that *he* has been putting *her* into a double bind. This seems to be what the patient is actually trying to get across to him, and while the therapist unconsciously appreciates it, he utilizes his unconscious understanding in an inappropriate way by attempting to put the disturbing consequences of such a realization back into the patient.

Let me indicate the sequence again so that you have it clear: the therapist puts some disturbing contents into the patient in his mishandling of the framwork and of the patient's subsequent associations; the patient accepts the introjective identification and works it over by becoming deeply depressed and despairing, but then attempts to cure herself and the therapist by putting the disturbed contents back into the therapist through the vehicle of her expectations concerning the other physician. The therapist then receives these contents within himself and responds, not with an interpretation, but with further efforts on his part to project back into the patient these upsetting contents. In fact, this is a clear example of what Grinberg (1962) has called projective counteridentification: the therapist receives a projective identification from the patient and instead of metabolizing it toward conscious awareness and an interpretation, reprojects the contents back into the patient.

T: In fact, I must have been referring to the double bind that I was also feeling. I do find her in a double bind, but my own feeling as I rethought all of this is that I am also in a double bind with her.

L: Here you are describing a subjective association and feeling in response to your own intervention. This is one of the values of formulating interventions tentatively and then applying the validating process. Had you not intervened, you would have had an opportunity to explore the implications of the comment that you had thought of making, and would have had a chance to recognize that you were referring not only to your patient, but also to yourself. You could have then reconsidered the patient's associations, past and ongoing, for clues as to what it was that was placing you into a double bind, and in this way moved toward a discovery of the nature of the disturbed therapeutic interaction and the interventions that it required. Actually, you are now confirming one of the points that I made: you are putting back into the patient your own sense of inner difficulties.

T: Yes, I see.

L: If you have absorbed the interactional aspect that I have just described, I can add one more facet: in a way you were empathizing with one of this patient's inner objects —with the doctor who is, on this level, a representation of an internal object that is related to yourself on one level, and has important genetic precursors as well. This is a point that Deutsch (1926) and Racker (1957) have made in their studies of empathy: the therapist empathizes both with the patient and her objects. You can see that I am also suggesting that the patient will, in addition, projectively identify into you aspects of her internal objects, and that empathy is therefore best considered as an interactional experience—a point that Greenson (1960) had begun to develop in his paper on that particular subject.

But you must remember that empathic experiences such as sensing her plight and the plight of the doctors and yourself, has to then be processed and subjected to the validating process in particular. When something seems important, you focus on it and attempt to determine the adaptive context that is most related to it, and what it is that's going on within the patient and yourself, and in your interaction with her, that can best account for it. You want your interventions to be clearly adaptive and to consciously focus on the patient's struggles with an adaptive context and her intrapsychic responses.

After all of this has been considered, you can see that technically there is every indication that your intervention was incorrect and that it also modified the framework in that it was not neutral—it had a critical quality and in addition, unconsciously communicated to the patient aspects of your own confusion and inner disturbance. It was as I said, an effort to projectively identify back into her the disturbed, depressed, and devalued mental contents, fantasies, and affects that the two of you are unconsciously passing back and forth. On a technical or cognitive level, we would expect nonvalidation from the patient, while on the interactional level, we would expect her to now be under pressure to work over your projective identifications; she tends to incorporate them into herself and to elaborate them based on her own masochistic needs and depressive constellations.

Now we will go over this kind of thing again and again when we hear an intervention from a therapist, so I don't expect you to grasp every aspect of it for the moment. I want to stress two things before we get back to the clinical material. First, you can see that there is a great deal to be done before you make an intervention to the patient, and that your assessment includes both intrapsychic and interactional considerations. Similarly, once you have made an intervention, you search out its intrapsychic and interactional consequences for the patient. A valid intervention would be confirmed both intrapsychically and interactionally through fresh material on a cognitive level, and allusions to positive and helpful figures that represent the patient's incorporative identification of your good qualities as a helpful therapist. Incidentally, I trust that you understand that I am using words good and bad not in any judgmental sense, but more or less in the sense that the Kleinians have used the terms to refer to such things as the good and bad breast, or mother, thereby indicating a whole constellation of positive and negative fantasies and images. In any case, the patient's responses to an intervention are to be carefully explored on many levels for confirmation and nonconfirmation. In those situations where the intervention has been erroneous, you will find the patient responding without cognitive validation, and interactionally, often alluding to hurtful and nonhelpful figures. There often follows unconscious efforts to correct you, and once again to help you with your own inner problems as they prompted a nonvalid intervention. We will get to much of this later on once we've had a chance to observe the patient's responses to some of the therapist's interventions.

The second point that I want to stress is that we can now see that an incorrect intervention is an extremely meaningful communication and that it reflects aspects of the therapist's unconscious countertransference fantasies and his need for pathological interactions. In particular, this material has shown us that among the many functions of an incorrect intervention is an unconscious effort by the therapist to projectively identify aspects of his own inner sickness onto the patient. Once again, the interactional approach makes the therapeutic work seem more burdensome, but actually, I think it should be clear by now that it allows you to do more effective and sensitive psychotherapy. It simply means that you have to do a great deal more toward getting your own inner problems under control because you have recognized their extensive consequences in the therapeutic relationship. But this is certainly in keeping with the realities of the therapeutic situation—so it is all to the good.

Now, let's hear some more of the session.

T: Well, she went on: secondly, she wanted to say that her family, although . . .

L: So, she just ignored your initial comment?

T: Essentially, yes.

L: In assessing a patient's response to an intervention, we will consider both his manifest reaction and his latent communications. However, her nonresponsiveness to your intervention is an initial form of nonconfirmation, although it is by no means the last word on the validating process. Even an agreement with your comment would not constitute validation, since we would want to see whether the further material supported such an agreement and added truly fresh material. However, in general, when the patient tends to ignore an intervention, you have either commented on something extremely sensitive or you have said something that is basically not valid or helpful. We'll develop this aspect later on.

T: She went on, that her family, though they'd been concerned, they were not concerned in the right way. They were talking behind her back about her—all of them: her brothers and sisters and her mother. Not only did one of her sisters and her mother talk to each other about her, but her sister had a boyfriend who talked about her behind her back. Then she recalled a poem she had written for me, which she hadn't read to me; and how she read it to her sister who, in turn, told her boyfriend about it. And she hadn't given her permission to do this.

L: Yes, well, I hope there isn't anybody in this room who doesn't hear the message. She herself comes back to the issue of confidentiality, and we begin to see the development of some paranoid symptoms. In fact, we see exactly how they can arise interactionally in a situation where the therapist has not maintained confidentiality and is expecting to violate it once again when he calls the Disability office. She immediately lets you know what a betrayal this is, and her paranoid symptoms have to be seen as an interactional neurosis—or perhaps, a reflection of a more severe syndrome (I tend to use the term neurosis very broadly in these seminars). Once again, they are based on paranoid mechanisms within herself, but they have, as do all paranoid symptoms, a significant kernel of truth in them. You could hardly think that this patient is totally out of her mind because she is upset and suspicious about what her therapist tells the Disability people, and even her boyfriend, especially since the therapist has not given her the necessary assurances in regard to his capacity to manage such matters.

Notice one other thing which I think is very important: the patient conveys here something else, that I have tried to say to you in various ways. She wrote a poem for the therapist, that is, she tried in some creative way to put something that is in her eyes good and beautiful into the therapist. Now, this represents again her wish to reach the therapist in some good and curative way, and also her wish to make him understand both her inner disturbance and her inner creativity. You'll notice too that she did not read it to the therapist, once again indicating the way in which she is keeping out of the bipersonal field for the moment not only her sickness, but her most creative parts. Incidentally, did you find out what the poem was about?

T: I don't know. It had something to do with death and her feelings of depression. At this point, then, I said to her, It reminds me of last week's session and the insurance policy, and you were worried about what I would say to the people at the insurance company.

L: Isn't it a Disability office?

T: Yes—Disability. But she ignored that also.

L: Well, it is the kind of intervention that tends to foster her use of denial. But remember, even if she directly ignores the intervention, it may influence her subsequent associations and you may find some confirmation. Technically, your intervention reflects a not uncommon problem seen in therapists in training, so let me briefly discuss what you have said.

First, on a formal level, you have made a general interpretation. That is, the spirit of your intervention reflects an effort to link a manifest association involving betrayal and a lack of confidentiality in her relationship with her mother and sister, to similar concerns in her relationship with you. You are therefore attempting to make something that is unconscious within the patient at this moment conscious for her. And I call it a general interpretation because you are not attempting to identify a specific unconscious fantasy and for the moment, you are also not considering any specific genetic contributions.

And on the positive side of this intervention, you are implying to the patient that her concerns about the confidentiality of her therapy is a prime adaptive context, and while this is only partially true—she's actually concerned about a number of specific problems in her relationship with you, and especially about the intrusion of the boyfriend—you are at least dealing with her associations by relating them to what is undoubtedly their most significant implication. So, through this intervention, you reveal your sensitivity to an important concern of the patient's, and connect her associations to the therapeutic relationship and to an issue related to the framework. These are among the positive assets of this intervention, and I suspect that the patient will respond favorably to them, although there are, in addition, some difficulties that she will also have to deal with.

So, now for the other side of this intervention, some of the problems that it reflects. First, on a technical level, the intervention is clearly a verbalization of an association of your own to the patient's material. As such, it does not bear the hallmark of a sound interpretation in that it does not directly identify the specific adaptive context, nor does it clearly indicate the patient's unconscious fantasies, even though you are attempting to elevate them to consciousness. The intervention is a bit too vague and general, even though it does in an important way identify a central concern of the patient's.

And on the technical level, it is also premature. This gives me a chance to indicate again what the therapist should do with his own associations to the patient's material before he intervenes. Here, you have a valid association and you should have utilized it to make a silent formulation. You then subject this formulation to the validating process, which, as I said, would entail reviewing your own subjective feelings and fantasies toward the patient and your recollections of earlier associations from her—all in an effort to find support for your hypothesis. And as you are doing this, you are also monitoring the patient's subsequent associations for confirmation of your ideas as well. It is then, at the point where the patient's associations lend support to your formulations and actually add some further depth and dimension to them, that you should intervene to her.

In this situation, having now identified the central adaptive context, and having seen some of the connections between the patient's associations and the therapeutic interaction, the patient might have gone on to talk about her boyfriend, or about somebody barging in on her in her bedroom or in the bathroom. In some way, she would have further developed her unconscious perceptions and fantasies that relate to the adaptive context concerning the therapeutic interaction, and her associations would have permitted a much more sensitive and extensive intervention, one in which you could have used some of her specific associations as building blocks. Remember, we have already seen that unconsciously the patient feeds the therapist the interventions that she herself needs—a formulation that has been rather nicely developed by de Racker (1961). You can rely on this feeding process; the major skill to develop is the ability to comprehend what is being put into you, and to make use of it for interpretations.

To show you briefly what I mean, her associations already contain references to boyfriends, although these are clearly what I have termed *remote derivatives*—that is, well disguised versions of the patient's unconscious perceptions and fantasies. In most sessions, the patient will tend to move from remote derivatives to derivatives that are closer and far less disguised, and much more readily utilized in intervening.

One last point before we continue: I want to remind you of a principle that I developed earlier in our discussion, namely, that when dealing with an issue related to the framework, rectification comes before interpretation. This is a very cryptic way of indicating that no matter how precise your efforts at interpretation are in the area of her concerns about the confidentiality of her therapy, so long as you do not create a confidential therapeutic situation, these will have little effect on the patient. After all, you're in the peculiar position of betraying her need for total confidentiality, while asking her to trust you. You can see the absurdity of the situation, and the patient will see it in exactly the same way. She will see you as a hypocrite and she won't really trust you, and there will be a whole sector of her unconscious fantasies and perceptions that she will split off—with your assistance. This will create a bastion of the bipersonal field that will be impenetrable because of your modification of the confidentiality of the field and the patient's need to split off important contents related to that issue within herself. And while you may be able to continue to do some type of therapeutic work in other spheres of the bipersonal field, this type of misalliance does tend to influence all of the therapeutic work, since it entails the modification of the frame and a basic impairment in the therapeutic quality of the field.

These are really very important considerations in these times where releasing information to disability offices, insurance companies and other third parties has become accepted practice. I am indicating to you that there are deep and valid reasons to question this practice, and to strongly object to it as a detriment to psychotherapy and psychoanalysis. No matter how necessary it may seem for other reasons, modifications in confidentiality and the revelations involved in releasing information of the kind that would be involved with your patient are actualities that create bastions of the bipersonal field, that modify the therapeutic qualities of the field, and result in a compromised psychotherapy. Such a release of information puts negative incorporative identifications into the patient, as you have already seen with this patient. What is more difficult to demonstrate to you is the manner in which these alterations in the frame alter the therapeutic quality of the bipersonal field. It is only when you have participated in such a modification of the frame, and have then rectified it, that you discover that the patient has been extensively repressing crucial material and has been indeed struggling with deeply disturbing, valid negative introjective identifications concerning yourself as a therapist who has modified the frame. The change in the material from the patient is astounding, and not only that, the state of the patient is also remarkably changed. You discover that your own alteration in the framework has provided her with a framework cure that has sealed off significant aspects of her psychopathology and offers her a noninsightful means of managing it. You discover you have actually been involved in a misalliance cure, and you also find that as long as the framework is modified, the patient will characteristically begin to develop important themes, only to break off for reasons that are entirely unclear to you. The therapy usually becomes quite erratic; the modified frame becomes the backbone of relatively unresolvable resistances in the patient.

I really don't want to go on discussing this area until we have more material from the patient. I've said a little because I think it is one of the most seriously misunderstood aspects of psychotherapy and psychoanalysis today. For whatever reasons, therapists and analysts have denied the major consequences of modifications in the framework related to releasing information to third parties such as insurance companies, and much of this stems from a failure to recognize the extent to which actualities influence the therapeutic qualities of the bipersonal field and therapeutic interaction. As far as I have been able to discover, only Szasz (1962) and Haplert (1972)—in addition to myself, Langs (1975b)—have even hinted at these important considerations.

Szasz (1962), in considering training analyses and the modifications in the confidentiality of such treatments, made a statement to the effect that once there is a violation of confidentiality, the treatment can no longer be considered psychoanalysis. He goes on to say that it can still be a therapeutic relationship, but his definition of psychoanalysis includes total confidentiality. It was not a point that he developed more extensively, but it seems evident to me now that he had made observations quite similar to my own, although he did not specifically detail them in that particular paper.

Halpert (1972), on the other hand, described the analyses of two patients for whom the treatment, for a period of time, was paid entirely by insurance. He found that the reality of total coverage of the fee by an insurance company reinforced certain intrapsychic resistances in his patients and offered them a variety of actual gratifications that rendered them essentially unanalyzable under these conditions. All that I can say is that the conscious and unconscious motives in therapists and analysts that prompt them to accept and even seek after insurance payments for psychotherapy and psychoanalysis, without investigating scientifically the implications for their therapeutic work, must be enormous because, once you do study this area in depth, there is absolutely no question that these conditions modify and compromise the therapeutic field. This may be an unpopular view and it may even have unfortunate social implications, but it is a valid scientific statement. You cannot change scientific findings to suit social and personal unconscious needs; instead we must make use of these findings in some way or another to more appropriately answer the needs of our society. Social protest does not make a scientific observation disappear, nor will it change the nature of the findings. Well, at the point where I begin to philosophize, I think we had better get back to some clinical material.

T: She said that there was a third thing she wondered about. She wanted me to tell her, person to person, what was wrong with her, and not using medical terms. She wanted to know how serious, i.e., how crazy she was, and if she could be helped.

L: Everybody know what that is?

D: She is saying that the therapist can't help her.

T: She wonders if I will be able to help her.

D: He's been breaking boundaries all over the place.

L: It's the boundaries, yes; and now she is asking for a nontherapeutic intervention—a modification in neutrality, and perhaps, since it would reflect the therapist's assessment, anonymity as well.

D: He's talking behind her back, so she says, Talk to me, tell me what's wrong with you.

L: Yes, in a way he is telling her what's wrong with him. I think there's almost a shift here to the treatment of the therapist. What is the question she's raising? How crazy am I? What's the latent question?

T: How nuts are you? She's referring to me.

L: Of course, she's really wondering now, just how crazy you are. I'm sorry, but that's what she says. I get blamed for things patients say, but that's what she's really wondering. We know the adaptive context—the things that have been going on in therapy—and they get crazier and crazier. She says, My mother and sister, my sister and my boyfriend, they're all talking behind my back; and you say, That must have to do with the disability. But the next thing you know the boyfriend will be knocking on the door again: I'm here to collect the insurance (Laughter.) Her craziness—yes; but yours too.

As I said, I think the interface of this bipersonal field has now shifted toward the pathology and cure of the therapist, and that the patient's communications are centering on that effort. She has three things on her mind: the doctor whom she doesn't trust and who will make her suffer even more; the violations of her confidentiality by her family members; and, last, her diagnosis. If you look at the sequence, you see allusions to the sickness of the physician, its expression through the alteration of the framework, and then an attempt to establish a diagnosis—these are respectable therapeutic efforts. Again, I feel that they overshadow for the moment reflections of the patient's own inner disturbances, and while these are certainly present, and we very much want to get back to them in order to do some sound psychotherapy with her, they cannot for the moment be our focus, because they are not the focus of this therapeutic situation. There are large nontransference elements in these efforts which have to be appreciated long before we can get to the transference components.

There is a great deal to be said now, so I will elaborate a bit. We have here a therapeutic situation where the therapist's disturbances and his blind spots, that led to failures to rectify the framework and to offer some valid interventions, have had some significant effects. For one, it has created a chaotic situation in the therapy, and unless the therapist is cured there will be no treatment. I think that the question, How crazy am I? reflects the patient's introjective identification of the therapist's craziness. Now she has it inside her and she feels under the obligation to cure the sick therapist inside her; that becomes tantamount to her own cure. She can communicate the threads of this, the building blocks, unconsciously, but again, she needs the therapist to make them conscious, to interpret them. But first, she needs the therapist to be able to respond by changing the actual situation, so that it's not crazy and does not put crazy things into the patient.

I hope too that my hypotheses regarding the importance of the framework have been validated sufficiently for all of you. Notice that the patient repeatedly comes back to issues related to the framework. She also conveys the sense of hopelessness that patients experience on some level when the framework has been modified. Patients unconsciously and intuitively, based on their own use of a validating process, sense both the damage that is being done to their therapeutic hopes, and the problems in the therapist who has failed to maintain the frame.

So, within the adaptive context of a modification in the frame, the patient returns to this theme again and again. And she does so for a number of reasons. First of all, there is her hope for the unlimited gratification that she derives from the misalliance, and from the pathology of the interactional field. She also wants to test the limits of this gratification—how far the therapist will go. And she wants to see how much she can derive both in the way of gratification and in the way of defense. Here the misalliance is protecting her from dealing with her own neurosis; it enables her to put her sickness into the field and into the therapist. The shift here is to the pathology of the field and to the primary contributions from the therapist.

Now, in the usual psychotherapeutic situation, we would hope and expect that the patient would largely determine the points of interface and of interaction, and would contribute most of the pathology to this interactional interface. We have here a situation where the usual vectors have been reversed, and the therapist is the primary contributor to the pathology of the field. As a result, the patient unconsciously addresses herself to the pathology of the therapist, in an effort to assist him in modifying it within himself and within the field, with the hope of creating a proper therapeutic framework.

So here we see that within the interactional field, when the greater disturbance stems from the therapist, the focus of cure will be on the therapist. This is not by any means the way psychotherapy should be developing under optimal conditions. But these are hard realities. When the therapist is contributing to the pathology of the field, the patient will unconsciously incorporate this pathology and attempt to cure the therapist. So you can see that her coming back to issues of the ground rules is also an effort to let the therapist know that there are problems in this area, to generate related anxieties in him, and to create within the therapist an experience of the symptoms of the field. This could then alert him subjectively to his own problems, and to his contributions to the disturbed interaction with the patient, so that he is mobilized toward cure—of himself and then of the patient.

We have to recognize that the entire therapeutic situation has been distorted because of the modifications in the boundaries. And it is in this context that we should turn to the patient's symptoms. They are somewhat paranoid and previously, we would have immediately thought of the patient's paranoid pathology. We would have looked for the intrapsychic basis for this pathology and you can be sure that we would have found it. But now there is more: there is the disturbance in the field and in the therapist, as they are perceived by the patient. These are elaborated according to the patient's own intrapsychic needs. To consider this as an intrapsychic symptom exclusively, or even primarily, would be to miss certain realities and external inputs that are immediately called to our attention through a study of the bipersonal field: the symptoms of this patient are based in part on unconscious perceptions of the therapist. The therapist is indeed not to be trusted; he has betrayed her; he has hurt her; and he has misunderstood her. He has conveyed his own unconscious awareness that he is in difficulty, and the patient has perceived it, has incorporated it, and has thereby incorporated the pathology of the field. It would probably be more adaptive if she could resist this introjection or deal with it without becoming ill—that is where her vulnerabilities come in. But this symptom has not only an intrapsychic basis, it has an interactional component. It is a symptom of the field—a neurosis, or possibly even a psychosis, of the field. It is, in part, an interactional illness. The symptom is located for the moment in the patient, but we must recognize that there have been two types of compromises to create this symptom: one is intrapsychic within the patient, and the other is interactional within the bipersonal field. So you can see that much depends on the field, which can be influenced by internal and external occurrences, and that the outcome in turn depends on how the therapist and patient manage these occurrences.

We see too that the patient, as one of the polarities of this field, echoes and mirrors its pathology and that the point at which the patient and therapist meet, the interface, reflects contributions not only from the patient but also from the therapist. The patient's earlier suicidal feelings also may well have been interactional symptoms. Her sense of hopelessness, and her destructiveness, are all more than reflections of her intrapsychic conflicts, guilt, and masochism. The same may be said of her ego dysfunctions, and the impulsive quality of her behavior. They also represent the helplessness of the therapist, his unconscious aggressions, his failure to be helpful, his difficulties with controls and management, and the hope-lessness of the total interaction—in a word, the depression of the field.

And so you see that the patient's concern with crazi-ness alludes to both herself and to the therapist, and to bipersonal field and its interface for the moment. And I think that this material shows you something else: that in addition to the unconscious and pathological compo-nents of the exchanges of projective identifications be-tween this patient and therapist, these projective identifi-cations also serve adaptive and curative ends. The patient puts her sickness into the therapist, not only to be defen-sively rid of it but to have him cure her of it. And the therapist in return puts his sickness into this patient, not only out of his countertransference-based failures to pro-perly metabolize and interpret these projective identifica-tions, but with the hope that the patient will generate curative endeavors. In fact, in writing of the subject based on my study of the literature (Langs, in press), I suggested that pathological projective identifications by the therapist contained within them a component of ther-apeutic intention, and I think that this interchange de-monstrates that idea. Again, I am not suggesting that this is the optimal therapeutic *modus vivendi*; I am sim-ply trying to demonstrate that out of the most disturbed interaction, one can still extract a modicum of hope and potential for therapeutic gain.

Well, I trust that this synthesis has been helpful; now, I think, it's time to hear more from the patient.

T: Then she made reference again to last Thursday and whether I thought of her suicidal threats as serious. And I said at that point that she seemed concerned that I didn't understand her.

L: Yes, while that is, once again, an emphatic response, it will not prove to be too helpful for several reasons. First, it is a subjective reaction that should be subjected to the

validating process and developed around a central adaptive context. Your interventions are now becoming scat-
tered and without organization; in my book on technique, I called this type of work "trivia therapy" (Langs,
1973a) in an effort to devalue it and to promote therapeutic work built around major adaptive contexts. This business of saying something to the patient whenever you
have a thought that might be helpful does not, in the long
run, offer very much to the patient. And this is even when
you have been empathic, because the patient needs something more than that—she needs a valid interpretation.

And here is one other extremely important consideration in respect to this intervention—it indicates that you
were not trying very hard to assess the patient's responses
to your earlier interventions, and to understand the apparent absence of validation. Whenever you intervene,
you should really, as a general principle, sit back for
some time and attempt to assess in depth the patient's
responses. And if the material is not deepening the ideas
you presented in your intervention, you should attempt to
reformulate, using both your own subjective efforts and
the patient's associations—she will attempt to help you
there too.

T: Yes, right. To continue: she wondered *on a spectrum*
where she was at in terms of being crazy. Did thinking
about suicide . . . was that serious? Or talking about it?
Or doing something about it . . . She believed that she
thought too much about it. Then she referred to the
thoughts that stopped her from attempting suicide. And
then, there were her thoughts that life did not end after
the death of the body. She knew that in fact, it did, but
she really just couldn't feel it. And then she related this to
what she was told earlier in her life—that her father did
not die, but that he had just gone to heaven where he
continued to watch her and judge her. Then she wondered about alternatives that she'd be faced with if she

didn't have suicide as an alternative. At that point, I
stated that there really weren't any alternatives after suicide, and, of course, it couldn't be taken lightly.

L: You know, that's a very interesting comment that you
just made. I was wondering what she was trying to tell
you and I thought that it had to do with her feelings
about your depression, and her efforts to offer you hope
and some kind of cure. Now, I was mindful of her own
depression and its genetic foundation in the death of her
father, but I was also thinking interactionally in terms of
some type of unconscious effort—perhaps a general
genetic interpretation—to get you to think about the
earlier sources of your own sense of depression. And of
course, I was attempting to subject my formulations to
the validating process through following the patient's associations. And now I also have your intervention.

And you know, it is my impression from your intervention that you misunderstood her, and I think as a result
you have confirmed both my formulation and her own
unconscious perceptions of you. I will take this step by
step. First, I suppose we could formally label your intervention as a confrontation, although it is a special type in
that it does not entirely confront the patient with her own
communications, but adds a stern reminder from yourself. On another technical level, we can think of this as
what has been termed in the literature, a supportive intervention, and an effort to mobilize her ego strengths in
assisting her to deal with her suicidal impulses.

And as is always the case, I have little doubt that she
will respond to this seemingly kind and supportive effort
in some negative way, and will feel that her autonomy is
being encroached upon, and that you have some special
fear of her suicidal impulses; especially since you have
been unable to interpret their basis for her. What has
been termed supportive therapy in the literature becomes, through a study of the bipersonal field and the

therapeutic interaction, a kind of myth; actually, it is
based primarily on misalliance and framework cures that
have little adaptive value to the patient. But I do not
want to go too far afield, so let's continue our assessment
of this intervention.

Communicatively and interactionally, you chose to
speak at the moment when she said that she was now exploring alternatives to suicide. Notice that, because it is
crucial. It brings out the interactional component of your
intervention, and your need to intervene at a specific
point. Here, at the very moment where she shifts to other
considerations, you remind her that there is no alternative after suicide. And so you see that you were saying . . .

T: What alternatives are there in the treatment situation?

L: No; I'm talking about it differently. She was saying
something quite different from what you said, therefore
your comment seems to reflect your own conflicts in this
area.

T: Yes.

L: Now, how can we also relate this to the difficulties that
have been going on in the therapy?

D: She did not question the alternatives after she committed
suicide.

L: Yes, but we can now place this in a broader context. I
would say first that in a sense your intervention confirms
the patient's unconscious interpretation to you. After all,
if the interface of this bipersonal field is now loaded with
vectors from your own pathology, and the patient is attempting, on one level, to therapeutically work them
over, your own comments will provide us with an opportunity to determine the extent to which you have unconsciously confirmed her work. I stress all of this because
I want you to see that within the bipersonal field, the
therapeutic efforts may quite definitely focus on the therapist from time to time, and that the same basis principles related to the validating process will prevail. In fact,

your intervention is confirmatory, in that it expresses your own resolve to master your depression, even though it was manifestly intended to offer such strength to the patient. In a way, then, you are letting her know that you have benefitted from her therapeutic efforts, but you have still not shifted the therapeutic direction and interface of this bipersonal field back to the cure of the patient. A better means of indicating to the patient that you have been helped by her communications would be to make such a shift, and offer her a valid interpretation of her associations.

Let me pull some of this together. We are approaching these associations from the patient based on a view of the bipersonal field that does not immediately assume that these communications are primarily distorted or primarily transference-based; we will search out each aspect. I am suggesting that the material contains important, relatively nondistorted, unconscious perceptions, and valid, similarly relatively adaptive, unconscious therapeutic efforts directed toward the therapist, and only secondarily designed for the cure of the patient. So I am indicating that at times, under special conditions such as those that prevail within this bipersonal field, the patient may indeed become the primary therapist and the therapist become the patient—a conclusion, as I told you before, that Searles (1965, 1975) has also reached. And if we focus on this material solely in terms of the patient's intrapsychic pathology and its disturbed contents, we will miss the therapist's contributions to the pathology of the bipersonal field.

Now, to place all of this in the broader context of the recent problems in this therapeutic situation, the patient seems to be indicating that the need for an additional person—the boyfriend—in this bipersonal field is based not only on her own depressive constellation, but also on that of the therapist. While I think that there are additional factors in the situation, for the moment the pa-

tient, again out of her own need and those of the therapist, is focusing on this sector and attempting to cure the
depression that the therapist has in part put into her.
And incidentally, all of this seems to validate my earlier
comments about the exchange of projective identifications that has been taking place between this patient and
therapist, as they each attempt to develop unconscious
therapeutic efforts in the face of a lack of their conscious
presence.

Let me use this material to make some further general
comments which will be an elaboration of my earlier discussions. Projective identification is certainly the most
predominant mechanism in the bipersonal field—just
as repression is the central mechanism intrapsychically—projective identification with its complementary
process of incorporative identification. This does not imply that the patient is under obligations to accept projective identifications. She will incorporate those that
fit in with her needs; she will reject others; and she will
process all of them according to her intrapsychic needs
and fantasies. And when I say projective identifications,
I'm talking about an interactional mechanism through
which one person puts contents, inner contents, out of
himself and into another person. I'm not talking about
projection, which is an intrapsychic mechanism, in which
somebody imagines a content within himself to be in
someone else. That's an imaginery and internal process;
it is not designed to evoke an interactional effect, or to
stir up a response in another person. So projection is
intrapsychic; projective identification is interactional.
And both occur along a continuum, from primitive uses
with loss of ego boundaries, to those that are less primitive and occur in the face of intact ego boundaries and
in the context of relatively mature object relatedness.
Each of these mechanisms may be utilized in a primarily
defensive or pathological way, or each may be used in
nonpathological and adaptive ways. And as we have seen,

there is often an intermixture of both adaptive and mal-adaptive implications when these mechanisms are utilized.

Now, as for the specific intervention that you could have been formulating and planning to offer here, I would suggest something like this. You could have pointed out to her that she seems to feel, based on the recent intrusion of her boyfriend into her session and on her concerns about your modifying the confidentiality of her therapy, that treatment is hopeless. And that she further feels that you don't understand her and have accepted these modifications of the privacy of her therapy because of some lack or need within yourself. It is then that you could add that this has served to reinforce her own self-destructive needs and depressive feelings. And you could add one more comment: that she perceives these recent activities on your part as a desertion, and is experiencing this abandonment as a repetition of the loss of her father. Now, while I would probably stop at this point, we ourselves should see that her comments about the loss of her father, which she deals with through some kind of pretense and denial, may well be a sound commentary on the spirit with which the damage to the therapeutic situation is being handled—again, it has both intrapsychic and interactional implications.

In this way, you would be moving from her unconscious perceptions to her unconscious fantasies, and you can see that you would be dealing with the interactional neurosis first, and then with her own intrapsychic disturbance. And you would be implicitly indicating that you are prepared to handle the situation differently, and to create a sound framework for the therapeutic field—a point that you could then make explicit when these problems arise again.

This material also gives us a chance to review the principles needed in dealing with an incorrect intervention by the therapist. We have already established that these are self-revelations on his part, and that they contribute to the pathology of the field by putting the therapist's problems into it and into the patient. And he can discover this by listening to the patient's responses to what he has said, and by subjectively reassessing his comments as well. If he gets validation of his intervention, he can be assured that he has said something that reflects the unconscious processes of the patient and that is in the service of the needs of the patient. When he does not get confirmation—that is, new material which adds to his insights, and, second, allusions to constructive functioning and helpful people—he must then undertake several important jobs. The first is a cognitive one—determining where the error came from, what is going on within himself. In doing this, he explores the patient's associations that occurred before and after his intervention. Those associations that occurred before the intervention offer clues as to the adaptive context for his idiosyncratic comment. They indicate the stimulus that prompted him to make an error. And the patient's associations after the intervention will give him clues as to what he is missing in the patient's material, and indications of the patient's unconscious perceptions of his difficulty. In all, he can pick up the sources of his problem from a subjective self-scrutiny and a search for his countertransference difficulties, and from a study of the patient's material. Remember, the patient is in that bipersonal field mirroring the therapist's difficulties and giving the therapist important information that he can utilize to understand the source of his errors.

And then, lastly, the therapist must explore what he has revealed through his erroneous intervention, and determine what he has put into the patient—and how she deals with it. Once more he does this using the resources of the field—his own subjective associations and the subsequent associations of the patient. And he uses all of this information to deal with the error, not by confessing it, and not by directly admitting it, but by implicitly acknowledging its presence and meaning through his subsequent interventions and management of the frame.

With this patient, we see that the general antecedents of this intervention have to do with the modifications in confidentiality, and the patient's mounting suspiciousness and concern about craziness; while the immediate adaptive context was the patient's struggle with suicide and the depressive contents that she in part put into the therapist. Now, if confirmation does not follow his intervention, the therapist could identify these contexts and reassess his own inner state and the communications of the patient, in an effort to understand what it was within him that prompted an error in intervening. Remember, just as transference expressions are based on unconscious fantasies, countertransference-based errors derive from unconscious fantasies as well. I am attempting here to help you develop some of the means through which the therapist can get to these unconscious components. And in particular, I am suggesting that in addition to the usual efforts at self-analysis, the patient's associations can be of help to him.

One other point: ultimately, knowing yourself and your own personal equation proves crucial in so many ways. It is the key to the validating process, and it is the ultimate standard by which you test inner and outer reality—for yourself and your patient. It is therefore the basis for your assessment of the transference and nontransference elements in the patient's material, and also the means by which you distinguish between your own countertransference and noncountertransference functioning.

In this context, I want to point out that there has been a tendency toward an inappropriate imbalance in certain aspects of the therapist's assessment of the patient's communications as compared to his own. With the patient, there is a constant search for distortions and for the unconscious implications of his material, and the depths are rightly treated as significant. In contrast, the therapist's communications are searched for their undistorted and surface implications, without a similar acknowledgement of their valid unconscious meanings. While many therapists maintain a defensive stance of this kind— they're the ones who see virtually every communication from the patient as distorted and transference-based— the patient, as you can see, is not so inclined. In her own way, she experiences the deeper and indirect meanings conveyed by the therapist's interventions, and she responds accordingly. This is a bias that cannot be justified.

I hope too that you realize that I have formulated the reference to the father in these associations, not primarily as a transference component but as largely stemming from an nontransference-based perception of the therapeutic interaction. I want to stress that, because this aspect of the material is often misunderstood. This is not primarily a situation where the patient is perceiving the therapist in some distorted way, based on earlier memories and experiences with her father, and even less so on the transactions between herself and the therapist. It is instead, based primarily on valid unconscious perceptions of the therapist's failure to be available to her—an emotional and actual loss of the therapist. This characteristically comes up when the therapist has failed in his responsibilities to maintain the framework or to interpret correctly to the patient. So here the reference to the father points primarily to the manner in which the present interaction with the therapist is repeating a version of the traumatic and disturbing experiences with the father in the patient's earlier life. Now, let's finally get back to the patient.

T: She said there were two questions: how these suicidal thoughts came when she panicked, and second, how she stopped them. But she felt that really life was worth living, and she said that she was satisfied to *know* that, but that she didn't *feel* it. I mean, there was part of her that still didn't feel that.

L: You see, again this is also a comment about you. She feels you're saying something about suicide, but there's a hollow quality to it. In addition, notice, she's saying to you: life is worth living. And she tells you that she is divided—and you are too: There is the side that has the suicidal impulses and there's another side that should offer and have controls. It's as if she's virtually appealing to you to restore the boundaries and the framework—the external means through which she could obtain from this kind of an institution some aspect of control. Remember, this has to be supplemented by cognitive insight and by the assumption of your own personal controls, which is related to the way in which you manage the boundaries. There is now also an appeal to you to help her to manage, and for you to manage better yourself. I can only go back to her suicidal gesture and I seriously suspect that this too was a symptom of the interaction of the field, and part of the situation and difficulties that we're picking up in these two sessions. Go ahead.

T: Well, I just say to her at this point: When questions like this come up, I'm glad that you can talk about them here in the sessions. At times, you have done that.

L: What kind of an intervention is this?

T: I thought of it as a supportive intervention.

L: Yes, but let's identify its properties.

D: It's an attempt at reinforcement through gratification. As if for example, you're rewarding her for something. If they say, Oh, I'm talking about suicide now, we say, Oh, I'm glad that you can do that. The patient is supposed to feel rewarded and happy and should continue to do that . . .

L: In terms of the ground rules of treatment, what kind of

intervention is it? (Pause.) It's an extratherapeutic gratification, for one thing. What else is it; what other ground
rule does it affect?

D: Well, it affects the therapist's anonymity . . .

L: Yes, the anonymity of the therapist—it's a self-revelation. And it's also a modification in his neutrality, so it
modifies the framework in several different ways.

And you know, when we think of the extent to which
this patient needs a sound intervention, the fact that all
that you were able to offer her at the moment was a bit
of encouragement will, I think, make her feel quite sad.
And I think that also it is interventions of this kind, in
the face of such intense and deep communications from
the patient, that have led her to perceive you as quite
depressed and empty. And this is typical of the circumstances under which a so-called supportive intervention
is made. So much is being missed by the therapist, and
he offers this type of comment at a time when he is unable to make a much-needed interpretation. He also offers this kind of intervention as a kind of desperate effort to rectify a whole series of missed interventions and
mismanagements of the framework, only to find that he
has compounded the difficulties, because of the disturbing interactional communications contained in this so-
called supportive effort.

In this situation, your comment is also an expression
of relief on your part that she really doesn't want to kill
herself, and that you won't be burdened with her suicidal
impulses. This is part of what she's doing now—she's
trying to please you. The way in which she's not com-
mitting suicide for the moment is that she knows that
you don't want her to. And yet, if you just push her too
hard, then she'll hate you for it and destroy you in herself. So, if you really wanted to be supportive, you would
restore the frame and make a tentative interpretation—
and she would show her deep appreciation for all of that.

T: Next, she said that I was not available when these thoughts did come to her . . .

L: That you were not available?

T: Yes.

L: So, she's telling you that if you want to break the boundaries, you should be with her all the time. What kind of deal is this?

T: Right.

L: You're being supportive, then why aren't you always there? And how come you're always there for my boyfriend? Explain that one to her. See, now that's what she was talking about, when she said earlier that she wanted to call you, but didn't. He wanted to see you and he just walked in on her session. And you don't say anything; you see her point?

T: Yes.

L: And if you want to gratify her inappropriately, this is what happens. It's Langs' rule: one neurotic gratification begets another; one deviation leads to another. After all, if you really want to cure her with love, then, why do you do it partway? How frustrating that is.

   And in the context of my earlier discussion, we can even add this: she is not only talking about your unavailability in terms of further extending the boundaries, she is also unconsciously alluding to your absence as an effective therapist for her. This has been a repetitive theme, and it is understandable in terms of the adaptive contexts that we have been developing; and it is in keeping with her relatively valid unconscious perceptions of you. She has a considerable awareness of the hollowness of your interventions, and as she puts it here, your unavailability as a healer of her disturbing inner thoughts.

T: She said that I wasn't available when these thoughts of panic and suicide came to her, but that other people were there. But she realized that even though they offered help, she withdrew from them, and wouldn't tell them how she felt.

L: Do you hear that? I said the same thing just a while ago —the patient doesn't want support. She's threatened by it because it's offered out of weakness and she knows it. And this is so characteristic: you offer a direct, personal, nonneutral effort at support and the patient doesn't want it. It invades her autonomy; it reflects difficulties within you in understanding her and in managing your own difficulties as well as managing hers, and so she puts you off. Patients don't welcome these kind of interventions.

In addition, there is another point to be made. Her comment about not accepting help from others is also based on an unconscious perception of the therapist's failure to accept the help that she's attempting to offer him. This too is a cause of depression for patients, who realize on some level, and most of this is usually unconscious, that they're attempting to help the therapist and that the therapist fails to listen and fails to comprehend. So you see, again, the confluence of her intrapsychic reactions and fantasies, and the consequences of her unconscious perceptions of the therapist.

T: Then, she said that she had a cousin whom she felt that she could help.

L: Who could help—the patient?

T: Yes, she felt that she could help this cousin. She said . . .

L: See about the therapy—who's getting the treatment? She's really feeling a tremendous need to help you and that she can. So, once again, we find confirmation of the concept that when the therapist is in difficulty, expressions of the patient's unconscious need to cure the therapist and to cure the sick therapist inside of her consistently appear. And it becomes the fulcrum of treatment. The working through of this kind of a misalliance and this kind of a disturbance within the therapist can be curative for the patient, who can ultimately have the satisfaction of having helped the therapist and of seeing him change for the better. And then the therapy can be restored to its proper perspective, so that it deals primarily with the pathology of the patient, and to a far lesser degree with that of the therapist.

T: She was told that because she was seeing a psychiatrist it invalidated her objectivity, and that this was part of her illness. And that they'd just say that she was crazy if she tried to make any comments about this cousin. At that point I said, Come back after you've seen the psychiatrist and if your heart's still beating, tell us if it hurts.

D: Who said that?

T: I said that. This is what the internist had been telling the patient—she'd been preoccupied that there was something the matter with her heart.

L: This is an intervention; how would we identify and assess it?

D: It's certainly confusing.

L: Yes—it has the qualities of a non sequitur. But there's more to it.

T: Well, first of all it comes down . . .

L: What did you have in mind?

T: I was thinking of what she had said early in the session about the doctor she was going to see—the doctor she would ask about her heart. Now she talks about not being able to be objective about what she sees, because she's seeing a psychiatrist.

L: Perhaps you should finish the session.

T: She smiled and she said she liked that, and she added that she needed . . . that she knew that love was important for her. She thought about something that went on with her father, and said that she wanted to talk about that at our next session—that we didn't now have time for it. Well, there were a few minutes left and I told her that this was so. She said that when she saw her boyfriend last weekend some things came up with him that she was afraid to talk to him about, because she was afraid of what he'd say. And that was the end of the session, essentially.

L: Did she say anything about whom he would talk to?

T: Well, no. In fact, my last intervention was, Afraid of me, or of your sister? I was implying that she was afraid of what I would say.

L: Okay, now, you promised us a surprise at the end.

T: What? Oh . . . (Laughter.)

L: You don't think I forget such things, do you? I know you forgot already, but I didn't. What was . . .

T: Oh, yes, on the desk was a notepad that had part of a patient's name and "paranoid schiz." written on it—you know, an abbreviation for schizophrenic.

L: So, the session ends with the reference to not trusting the boyfriend. Well, let me conclude by saying something about your intervention. There is a real element of creativity in it. It really seems to come largely out of your own primary process thinking, but it shows a certain quality of beauty. However, it is also not directly relevant to the understanding of the patient. It's a personal communication and the patient experiences it as an act of love and as an expression of your need for love; it's a kind of loving comment that expresses your wish that she would love you and your wish to love her. To love her, not through the appropriate ways that the therapist can in a sense love the patient—by helping them, by interpreting to them, and by maintaining the framework; but by offering little bits of gratification, inappropriate gratification, which then frightens the patient. And then again, after the intervention she comes back to her father and to her fear of saying something to her boyfriend. She comes back to the threesome and to the way in which she has introjected the therapist's fear of establishing boundaries and of setting the bipersonal field straight. And this is where the hour ends: there's no confirmation of the intervention and there's no flow in the session.

The group was rather startled by the therapist's intervention. It seemed to come out of nowhere and it's hard to define formally. However, let me emphasize this: creativity of this kind in a therapist is a gift. If it's mastered, if the therapist learns to use his subjective imagery in order to understand the patient, to formulate properly and to eventually interpret and interact properly, he can be an extremely sensitive and helpful therapist. This is not just simply countertransference. It is a kind of unconscious understanding of the patient's difficulty, of the way in which she's feeling disillusioned and of the way in which she feels at a disadvantage in treatment. But the therapist's responsibility is to communicate consciously and directly, not through his own unconscious fantasies, made conscious to the patient in some derivative form. That will lead to a mutually seductive misalliance, or to efforts in that direction by the therapist which the patient may or may not accept. Here, I think the patient reacted in a mixed way, wishing for the love and yet recoiling from it, and ending up with a statement of fear.

Well, this is an interesting moment and more could be said about it, but our time is up. I suggest that we hear more about this patient in our next seminar.

Chapter 7

THE INTRAPSYCHIC AND INTERACTIONAL ASPECTS OF DREAMS IN PSYCHOTHERAPY

PREDICTING THE MANIFEST AND LATENT CONTENT OF A DREAM • THE POTENTIALLY CURATIVE DREAM • THE PATIENT'S ATTEMPT TO RESOLVE THE INTERACTIONAL PATHOLOGY OF THE BIPERSONAL FIELD • PSYCHOTHERAPEUTIC TECHNIQUES RELATED TO DREAMS • THE COMPREHENSION OF THE LATENT CONTENT OF A DREAM • DREAMS AS REFLECTIONS OF UNCONSCIOUS FANTASY AND UNCONSCIOUS PERCEPTION • THE FUNCTIONS OF DREAMS WITHIN THE BIPERSONAL FIELD

L: Today, we continue with the patient we were discussing last week. As I hope you will remember, this was a most interesting sequence and we are eager to hear more.

T: (Here, the presenting therapist briefly summarized the previous session.) She came into this next session and immediately related a dream which she had had the night after the session I have just described. She said that her dream went as follows . . .

L: Now, let's attempt an exercise. I want the group to tell me what this dream is going to be about.

D: I would expect that the patient would have a frightening dream.

D: I think that it will deal with incest.

L: Yes, it could deal with incest, or in that connection, with the primal scene. And what else?

T: I think it might help them to guess what the dream might be, to know something more about the patient.

L: Thank you, but we really don't want to know more about
    her. Certainly, there may be features of this dream that
    we may not be able to guess, since they are based on
    things that we don't know about her, but we have heard a
    good deal of material and we want to see what we can do,
    based on just what we know. Because if you tell us some
    specific feature, you're going to be feeding us something,
    and we're not sure that we want that feeding. So you're
    saying that there's a specific issue that we probably don't
    know about; but that's okay.

D: She may appear disappointed and depressed.

D: And she may feel seduced.

L: Yes, what you are all saying is, to organize it, that you
    anticipate a dream in which the adaptive context will be
    the relationship with the therapist. That, if . . . Well,
    you're already giving us a signal, so I can't offer to retire
    if it isn't so . . .

T: No, I'm just saying that that's correct.

L: I'm going to have to teach you how to play poker; keep a
    blank face for a while. We're saying that we would antic-
    ipate that the adaptive context for the dream will be the
    therapeutic relationship and especially the recent ap-
    pearance of the boyfriend—all of which is unfinished
    business. Is this the first session of the week that you're
    going to be describing?

T: No, the last.

L: So, it was just a week ago that day that he had broken
    into her session. And the therapist hadn't really under-
    stood most of the ramifications of his appearance, and
    hadn't interpreted them. So, we feel that the dream is
    going to be replete with the unconscious communica-
    tions—perceptions and fantasies—related to that inci-
    dent. And in trying to identify with her, I would think
    that the lack of protection that she felt would be a very
    important thing. Here's this fellow—he breaks in on the

session and the therapist doesn't protect her. Now sure, the experience also has all sorts of incestuous and seductive meanings, and it has created disappointment, anger, and frustration in the patient. There is also the lack of barriers, and if we were to review the previous session more carefully, we would have other predictions in keeping with the formulations we made last week.

But the dream is also going to be something else. I'm varying a phrase of Winnicott's (1947) who described what he called curative dreams that he would have when troubled in his work with a patient. He would be in the midst of a countertransference problem and finally crystalize a dream, which is curative once it is unraveled —analyzed. Now, this implies that the therapist or analyst, when he finds himself in difficulty—when in some way he senses a disturbance within himself and in his therapeutic work and in the bipersonal field—will take such a problem as an important adaptive context, and generally work it over in an effort to resolve it. He'll try to do this consciously by allowing himself time to free-associate, and he turns to his self-knowledge and uses self-analysis, in order to detect within himself his contributions to the disturbance in himself, in the patient, and in the interactional field. And one important means of this type of therapeutic work is based on the analysis of the so-called curative dream.

Now, we can see that such a dream can and should occur in the therapist, and that the therapist who is sensitive to the things that are disturbing him, to his own adaptive tasks, will tend to associate to this type of dream —and to any of his dreams—with the particular therapeutic problem in mind. He will take his therapeutic dilemma as an adaptive context for his associations, and in this way he'll try to get at his unconscious countertransference problem. Because after all, that's one of the difficulties. Countertransference problems are based on unconscious fantasies and unconscious interactions, and the therapist has the responsibility of attempting to make these difficulties conscious, just as he has that responsibility to render the patient's unconscious fantasies, interactions and introjects conscious to him. This is one of the significant differences between the patient and the therapist. The patient can communicate these threads unconsciously and indirectly; it is the therapist's responsibility—one that he hopes the patient will eventually share with him—to make these fantasies and perceptions conscious. The therapist cannot be satisfied with unconscious communications; they do not afford the patient either the cognitive tools to master her conflicts nor the necessary positive incorporative identifications with which she can build up her ego.

So, when there is a disturbance in the bipersonal field, both participants may be expected to have potentially curative dreams. It's really very important to recognize that it is at the very moment that the patient is most depressed and most angry, and possibly even attempting to give the therapist a very difficult time, that there is also an unconscious curative wish present—both for the patient and for the therapist. So the curative dream may occur to both so that the therapeutic effort is bilateral and is a shared attempt to, in a sense, cure the interaction and the bipersonal field. I would predict that it is a curative dream we are going to hear, in that it would particularly emphasize the attempt to cure the therapist who needs it most of all at this moment. She has been talking about her ability to help others, so I think it's going to have that quality. Okay; let's see what happened.

T: You got carried away with the last part, but essentially that's correct.

L: Where did I get carried away?

T: I think that dreams tend to be . . . I don't want to talk out of the context of the material, but I think that dreams tend to be more curative, not of somebody else, but of the person who's having the dream . . .

L: Oh, the ultimate purpose of this dream is to cure the patient; of course. I need a background sign that would remind you that treatment is, of course, ultimately designed for the patient; the primary goal is the cure of the patient. But, unfortunately, if the therapist can't do it, he has to be cured first. I'm not saying that that means that his cure is a primary goal.

You see, when you read the analytic literature, you find that those writers who emphasized the constructive use of countertransference, or wrote of the therapeutic effects of positive introjective identifications of the therapist by the patient, were immediately criticized by many classical analysts. The classicists pointed out that the ultimate goal of treatment is to generate cognitive insight within the patient, and to enable the patient to get to know his inner self and sort out his inner distortions, thereby mastering his neurosis.

But what is distorted and what is nondistorted cannot be determined until we have a valid picture of the patient's communications. Similarly, what is contained within the patient and what is contained within the therapist cannot be clearly distinguished until we know the truth about the therapeutic interaction. And the basis for all of this lies ultimately in the therapist's self-knowledge.

So—the ultimate focus on the patient's inner disturbances can only come about when the therapist is not putting his own difficulties into the patient, and when the therapist's pathology does not dominate the bipersonal field. It is only under those circumstances that the therapist is capable of offering valid cognitive insights; it is only then that he will be positively introjected by the patient. Both processes go hand in hand, and there is no need to devalue one or the other basis for adaptive inner change in the patient, so long as these interrelated processes are properly integrated, and the limitations of each are recognized.

And as I have said repeatedly, at this moment in this therapy, the first step toward the resolution of the pathology in this bipersonal field is the cure of the therapist and the cure of the sick therapist within the patient. Now, you're saying that you think that this dream will focus more on the cure of the patient. I am saying that a sensitive reading of the current therapeutic situation indicates otherwise: it is more likely to focus primarily on the cure of the therapist—and only secondarily on that of the patient.

Let's not lose sight of some fundamental principles that we are using in making this prediction. We are basing it on our belief that the dream will be a response to the major adaptive context with which this patient is dealing—the problems in the bipersonal field. Once that has been established, it seems clear that the manifest and latent dream content will be part of the patient's efforts to deal with this adaptive context. And beyond that, based on our previous discussions, we have suggested that the patient will unconsciously perceive the problems within the bipersonal field and within her therapist in a variety of ways, elaborating each according to her own intrapsychic fantasies. I will not repeat our expectations of the manifest and latent content, except to note that these relate both to the actual modifications in the framework itself and to the meanings of these modifications—for example, the implications of the acceptance of the boyfriend into the bipersonal field.

Your remark prompts one last comment that occurred to me as you reviewed the previous session. I was reminded of a point Greenson (1971, 1972) has made about those analysts who, as he terms it, only analyze, and his description of how they give the patient the feeling that he is crazy by implying that everything he says has to be sick and distorted. And you may recall that the patient had made the comment in the previous session that because she goes to a psychiatrist, everybody thinks she's crazy. This was really her way of making exactly the point that Greenson had established. She had felt that the therapist was treating her communications as fantasies and distortions, at a time when she was on some level very much aware that she was communicating valid perceptions of the therapist, and expressing largely nontransference responses, including some that were intended to be quite therapeutic. Now, however, she extends these perceptions that valid core has to be recognized and implicitly acknowledged in your interventions. And when this is not the case, the patient not only feels that she is viewed as crazy, but she will also interactionally experience your failure to accept what is valid in her associations as an attempt to undermine her inner reality testing, and as an effort to drive her crazy—a topic that Searles (1959) has considered.

So when you anticipate that the main potential in this dream will be the cure of the patient, I was reminded of those therapists who enter sessions with the fixed anticipation that most, if not all, of what the patient will convey will be neurotic, distorted, and primarily transference-based. The study of clinical situations where the therapist is having unmistakeable difficulties enables us to recognize beyond any question that patients are quite capable both of primarily transference and primarily nontransference communications, and that a major job of the therapist is the sorting out of these two components. And in this way, we come full circle and get back to the therapist's own capacity to sort out these distorted and nondistorted aspects of her functioning and awareness; and we recognize that if this capacity is impaired in any way, it will interfere with the totality of his therapeutic functioning.

And so, I end up saying what I said at the beginning of my comments—when the therapist is in difficulty, his cure is essential to the restoration of a therapeutic bi-

personal field, and to a return of the focus on the cure of
the patient. I will grant you this: once we have conceptualized her therapeutic endeavors on your behalf totally,
we will also have a full opportunity to discover in this
dream aspects of the patient's efforts to achieve her own
cure. In fact, if you happen to make sound use of the
dream for the purpose of restoring the framework of this
bipersonal field, and of conveying some understanding of
what has been disturbing her over the past weeks, you
will have the rare experience of seeing the shift of this interface to the patient's pathology, and of seeing additional associations to this dream that will enable you to
do some effective therapeutic work for the patient. So I
think that it is now time to hear the dream.

T: She began by saying, I had a dream the night following
     our last session that I think I want to tell; I feel that it in-
     dicates that I'm getting better. So, the dream was this:
     She was at a party with a boyfriend, and it was a boy-
     friend she had met in New Jersey. This is a little back-
     ground on this guy: she had met him several months be-
     fore; she'd gone down twice to see him; and there had
     been a falling out in the relationship. In the dream she
     was at a party with this boyfriend; in fact, she was at the
     same party where she met him originally, and at this par-
     ty the situation was exactly the same as it was originally
     but all that had passed, all that had gone on between them
     had actually taken place, including the falling out. And
     at this party, instead of paying attention to her, he was
     paying attention to another girl; there was someone else.
     And he came up to her and she told him off. She just told
     him off; she said to him, Get lost. Then she went on to
     say she was very happy about last week's session . . .

L: That's the dream?

T: Yes.

L: Well, we have heard the manifest content of the dream,
     and listening to it in whatever adaptive context we think

is relevant, we have our own associations, and we search for schematic threads. I want you to think about this dream while I offer some remarks about the use of dreams in psychotherapy. And even before I do that, I want to make one initial comment: she says that this is a dream that indicates that she is getting better. I would submit that this indicates, among other things that we will discuss later, that it is indeed a curative dream in the sense that it contains somewhere in its latent content the material that the therapist needs to offer an interpretation to the patient that would help to resolve some of her symptoms. Her little addendum to the dream was so much to the point of my previous discussion, that I want to comment on it before we get involved with many other important issues.

So, as I offer this brief discussion, try to organize the dream and, using the adaptive context, attempt to read some of the latent content that the manifest dream, as a derivative of the latent dream thoughts, is conveying. This is only a first step because we do not as yet have the patient's associations to the dream, but it is a valid one and will generate some initial formulations and potential interventions that can be subjected to the validating process as the patient continues.

In regard to the use of dreams in psychotherapy, I work under certain specific assumptions that I have derived from my own clinical experience and from seminars like this one; and I want to make them explicit here. The first and most basic principle is that the psychotherapist can analyze dreams in psychotherapy within the limitations that derive from the therapeutic modality itself, and that he need not accept in advance any restrictions in his work with dreams, nor should he modify his therapeutic techniques basically in dealing with dream communications. There are, as you may know, many therapists who advocate setting dreams aside, so that they are virtually never dealt with in psychotherapy. There are others who restrict their work entirely to the manifest content.

But there is no inherent reason for such approaches; in fact, to advocate such restrictions is to turn away from the fullness of the patient's communications and to ignore important aspects of his adaptive and therapeutic efforts. We would certainly not ignore any other type of communication, so it is a great mystery why with dreams, of all of the patient's communications, one should disregard the search for the patient's intrapsychic conflicts, and unconscious fantasies and perceptions. There is no logical sense to it, although some of it may stem from irrational fears of dream communications. It is well known that since dreams are experienced in an altered state of consciousness, they contain on some level important and often primitive unconscious material. In fact, as is true with any communication from the patient, if you allow the patient to go on and to associate, and if you can appreciate in depth the implications of these associations, the patient will teach you that quite often dreams are indeed very significant communications and that there is much therapeutic gain to be derived from them.

I am reminded again of Winnicott's (1965) comments that the therapist should face the fact that ultimately, he learns everything from the patient, and that this is as it should be, even to the point of learning when not to intervene. This applies especially to the moment when a patient recounts a dream. I have noticed a tendency among young psychotherapists to intervene immediately, either with a question, or with a commentary on the dream itself. Technically, it is inadvisable to immediately jump in and say, Well, what does the dream bring to mind? Even when you get around to such a query, be certain that you do not ask the patient what the dream means, or her thoughts about the dream, since these are common ways of promoting intellectualization in the patient. And while it is often best to initially investigate the day residue, and the events that prompted a particular dream, I am suggesting that technically the best approach is to sit back and let the patient proceed.

Now, if you do this, you will quickly find that the dream is still an excellent means of ascertaining unconscious fantasies and introjects, and unconscious perceptions, and that while they are, indeed, special communitions, they can also be used as a kind of defensive decoy and in the service of resistances. In allowing the patient to go on, you see what he does with his dreams, and you learn something about his ego functioning, the ways in which he deals with more primitive instinctual drive contents, and his basic cognitive style in handling his dream experiences. We will observe if he associates directly to the manifest elements of the dream, or if he goes off in other directions. And when he does shift, do these associations appear to connect to the dream and clarify its implicit meaning? Related to this we observe the extent to which the dream itself—and with its associations— appears to illuminate the current adaptive contexts with which the patient is dealing. There are lots of other questions that we ask, including whether the dream points to an additional adaptive context, and whether, in the face of a known adaptive context—which is the case with this patient—the manifest dream itself seems to illuminate that context or suggest strong defenses. The therapist should also remember that his interests extend beyond the patient's direct associations to the manifest elements of a dream. While these associations might be quite helpful, whatever the patient talks about—his indirect associations—may have relevance, and he should be given the freedom to show the way.

While it is impossible to spell out every technical principle related to dreams in psychotherapy, we certainly can establish the importance of the therapist's initial silence. We want to remember that while dreams may serve very important communicative functions, there are times when their presence primarily serves resistances.

Then too it is well to realize that dreams and their associations reveal not only instinctual drive components, but aspects of ego functioning including the patient's defenses, as well as superego manifestations. A great deal depends on whether you have ascertained the central adaptive context to which the dream relates, or whether you are waiting to determine it. Much depends too on your developing a clinical sensitivity for identifying when the dream is serving primarily as a distraction from the central issue, or when it appears to have the potential to illuminate it. So long as you remember that you are seeking both unconscious fantasies and unconscious perceptions, and that you are working with the basic technique of establishing an adaptive context, and dealing first with resistances, the situation is not as chaotic as this general discussion may make it seem.

Dreams can be quite helpful in assisting you to get to the unconscious fantasies that relate to the patient's resistances, and can also facilitate their interpretation. Interactionally, the dream can furnish important clues regarding fantasies and perceptions of the therapist, of the bipersonal field, and of the state of the therapeutic interaction. You should in part approach the dream with a totally empty mind, allowing the patient to fill it with the manifest dream contents, and his associations. At the same time, part of your mind should be filled with the content of the recent sessions, and there you should be attempting to ascertain the most important adaptive context for the patient at the moment, and especially those adaptive contexts that are connected with the therapeutic relationship. In a sense, then, in working with dreams we utilize the same basic principles that apply to any of the patient's associations, although we certainly do it with a greater intensity, and in a special state of mind that complements the patient's dreaming state of consciousness.

Because it's a sensitive point, let me stress again that

it is not the therapist's place to impose limitations on therapeutic work with dreams in psychotherapy, and to restrict the patient. These limitations, as compared with analysis, derive from the nature of the psychotherapy situation, based on the usual twice-weekly frequency of the sessions, the use of the face-to-face mode, and whatever limitations these create for an analysis of the patient's communications. These are inherent limitations; they mean that you won't usually get an extensive network of unconscious fantasies and unconscious perceptions; you will get something more restricted. You won't get the build up that you get in analysis; you won't get the depth of regression; you won't get the pervasiveness of unconscious communication seen in analysis; but you will get modified versions of all of this, most definitely; and you can be very helpful to the patient in this more limited way. And besides, the patient will not appreciate being shut off. The patient in psychotherapy doesn't accept some notion in the therapist that he should not explore his dreams, and that he should not get the benefit of what his dreams communicate.

So altogether, while we mustn't overvalue dreams, we mustn't neglect them either. Empirically, they are a unique form of communication, and quite often a session in which a dream is recounted will turn out to be very meaningful and productive. This is a point that Greenson (1970) has made for psychoanalysis, and I think that it is valid for psychotherapy as well.

On the other hand, in working with a dream, the therapist should not modify his basic framework or technique. He follows the patient and searches for his most meaningful communications, and he is prepared at all times to deal both with resistances and central fantasies, and with unconscious perceptions as well.

Beyond these general principles, we will develop some more specific ideas from this patient's material. Returning to the present moment, we heard the manifest dream and while we are very interested in hearing the patient's associations, we should already be making formulations. We have established that one crucial adaptive context relates to the recent interactions with the therapist and within the treatment situation. And we begin to think metaphorically and in a primary process mode, responding to the various manifest elements in this dream to search for possible latent threads and to determine whether there could be any connection to the adaptive context. That is, even before we hear the patient's associations, we have the responsibility of deciding whether the manifest dream in a particular adaptive context sheds light on the patient's unconscious fantasies and perceptions as they relate to that context. And more broadly, we begin to wonder what the dream tells us about the therapeutic interaction and the patient's views of the bipersonal field. But before I say more, who would like to offer a comment?

D: In the dream, the boyfriend pays attention to someone else. She may feel that the therapist was more interested in the boyfriend than in herself, because the therapist decided to see him on her time.

L: Yes, she dreams of a situation in which there is indeed a threesome and she is slighted. And we hear that the setting is that of a party, and this, we suspect, represents not only her struggle with sexuality, but may also indicate her use of manic defenses. Already, the manifest dream and the adaptive context of the recent therapeutic interaction indicate that the patient is struggling with unconscious sexual fantasies, and is attempting to use manic and denial types of defense to cope with them— and with the underlying depression that we have seen. And along these lines, we can further see that these defenses are failing and that the patient is beginning to feel depressed and rejected. In a way, the dream already suggests that the appearance of the boyfriend in her session had shattered certain romantic fantasies that the patient was having about the therapist.

At the same time, these elements reflect unconscious perceptions of the therapist, in that she is attempting to alert him to his own use of manic defenses and denial, which she suspects accounts for the way in which he ignored the intrusion of the boyfriend and her intensely depressive response. As for the bipersonal field, in a sense this patient is indicating that she feels that both her therapist and herself share the need for a third party, who will provide them with some type of defense against their own sexual stimulation, with some type of denial of depression, and along different lines, with a great deal of stimulation that has sexual qualities for both herself and for the therapist.

You will also notice that the patient says that the dream takes her back to the time she first met this boyfriend, and yet it covers all that has actually taken place between them since. This is a reminder of the patient's first words after the therapist had seen the boyfriend, to the effect that she was experiencing something akin to the beginning of her psychotherapy. Certainly, we could say more if we knew the specific conditions under which this patient began her treatment, but you can still see how much can be said about a manifest dream once we know the adaptive context. The reference to the third party and to the falling out seems quite evident, as does the patient's anger and wish to be rid of the therapist. But at the same time, these elements contain additional unconscious perceptions of the therapist, who has so clearly rejected her, and seems to wish to be rid of her altogether. Already we can sense that this is a curative dream on a number of levels, and that the dreaming experience and its communication to the therapist contain within them efforts to cure both participants in this bipersonal field.

veloping, this dream seems to convey the patient's unconscious perceptions of having experienced some type
of initial closeness or fusion with the therapist—and here
the concept of fusion is certainly my own, since the patient is far from indicating that for the moment—and
that the incident with the boyfriend and the problem of
violations in the confidentiality of her therapy with the
Disability agency has, in a sense, shattered that feeling
of union. It may well be that her efforts to restore her
manic defenses have something to do with another interpretation of her comment that she felt that the dream
meant that she was getting better—she was mobilizing
her manic defenses. We'll have to see what her associations tell us about that comment. She also apparently
feels better, because she tells the boyfriend off. This leads
me back to another point about this dream: he is with
another girl—what are your thoughts about that?

D: She might be saying that the therapist has something else
    in mind. He cannot be ready to devote time and attention
    to her, because there is someone else on his mind. Never-
    theless, he goes to her or approaches her, so he really
    shows that he wants to, but he can't because there is
    something else on his mind.

L: Yes, but you've made that much more general than it is.
    It's a specific image: he's with another girl . . .

D: The girl is her boyfriend.

L: Yes, but what about that? This girl is a representation of
    her boyfriend—what does that imply?

D: How do you get that?

L: If the dream is about the adaptive context of the treat-
    ment . . .

D: Oh.

L: So, you see it. There are three people involved. In the
    therapy, there is the therapist, the patient, and the boy-
    friend, who is also in treatment with this therapist. In the

dream, there is a different boyfriend, the patient, and another girl. And the patient has already indicated that she has known the boyfriend from New Jersey for some time and that there has been a falling out. So there is some indication of communality between the therapist and this boyfriend. This has to do with the dream's use of metaphor and the therapist's responsive shift to thinking in terms of analogy and communality when he attempts to reach latent content from a manifest dream, the associations to the dream, and the relevant adaptive context. For example, the fact that there are three persons in the dream points to a parallel to the threesome in therapy, and readily supports the thesis that the dream has to do with the adaptive context that we had postulated before having heard the dream report.

So, actual reality has presented one threesome, while for the patient, within her psychic reality, there is another threesome. Now, this is actually tantamount to saying that in her latent dream thoughts, the patient is dealing with a particular trio and that one of the participants has been transformed through the dream work into the girl to whom the New Jersey boyfriend pays attention. Now, what do you think about that?

D: It's unacceptable to her that the therapist will have a boyfriend.

T: The patient is upset that the therapist pays more attention to him than to her.

L: Yes, all of that is unacceptable, but is there anything else that this could imply?

D: It could imply her perception of her relationship to the therapist—that she has sexualized that relationship. Therefore the other relationship is seen in the same terms, and it's not acceptable to see it as homosexual.

L: Yes, the dream reflects her fear of homosexuality, but what else then?

D: It may be her perception of the relationship between the therapist and herself.

L: Right, it's both: it's the patient's struggle with homosexuality on some level, and this aspect of the dream represents her heterosexual conflicts too. Now, we can now see that having identified the adaptive context for this dream—and we are making no claim that this is the only adaptive context; it is the one that we have at hand for the moment—we can learn something of how a dream is created. Even further, we can see something of the kind of dream work that Freud (1900) described, through which a latent unconscious fantasy is translated into a manifest dream element. This is an important clinical model, because it relates to the kind of thinking that you will do when a patient reports a dream, and it will also help you to develop your capacity to discover within any of the patient's manifest associations, the dream's latent elements.

So, let's follow this carefully: the adaptive context and therefore the day residue for this dream is, to simplify it a bit, the intrusion of her boyfriend into her session. In a sense, she has been attempting to work over this adaptive context within herself and within her relationship with the therapist for some time, and the therapist has not been able to understand her unconscious communications. Now, her adaptive efforts shift to the experience and report of a dream—she tries a new medium of communication. And the first thing that we notice is that the patient is dreaming about a threesome, thereby affording us an initial confirmation of our hypothesis that the dream does indeed relate to the intrusion of the boyfriend. But the patient, in her manifest dream, disguises the situation—she changes the sex of one member of the trio. Now, this is not simply a matter of disguise, it is a form of unconscious communication, and it already expresses certain unconscious fantasies and perceptions of the patient. It is because the patient has modified this aspect of the day residue that we look to within the patient for its meaning. We ask ourselves, what could she be telling us in this way?

And of course, since we are classical therapists and analysts, our first thoughts turn to the patient's intrapsychic fantasies, and that is all right, so long as we do not stop there—a point that I will get to in a moment. So, we think first that the New Jersey boyfriend may actually represent a part of the patient, and since he turns to a girl, this is a part that contains homosexual fantasies. This is a reasonable assumption and in a way constitutes our own version of the general hypothesis that every person in a dream, on some level, represents an aspect of the patient's inner self. For the moment, we know very little about the patient's homosexual anxieties and conflicts— their defensive and gratifying dimensions—but this bit of analysis alerts us to their presence, and we will look for their manifestations in the patient's further associations.

Now, it is another aspect of this manifest dream that suggests the patient's heterosexual conflicts, namely, the upset between herself and her boyfriend from New Jersey. Again the patient has taken the adaptive context and disguised or modified aspects of it that give us clues to the latent content, and to the dream work that has produced the manifest dream content. Remember, Freud (1900) indicated that there are certain basic mechanisms through which the patient processes his latent dream thoughts into a manifest dream. In the main, he described these as the primary process mechanisms of condensation, displacement, symbolism, and visual representability, though it is my impression that today analysts would consider all of the patient's intrapsychic defenses as contributing to the dream work. And already we are suggesting that the patient has condensed and displaced aspects of her relationship with the New Jersey boyfriend with those of her therapist and of the boyfriend who came into her sessions.

But to return to the point that I was developing, the manifest dream indicates heterosexual conflicts in her struggle with the New Jersey boyfriend, who abandoned her and whom she tells off. This aspect of her conflicts she represents more directly in the manifest dream, and this indicates that she is less defensive about her heterosexual conflicts than she is about her homosexual problems. And regarding her heterosexual problem, her recent material indicates that one of its genetic sources is the early death of her father, though again we know little more for the moment.

Now, what we have done so far is to take the manifest dream in its adaptive context and to search out certain aspects of the dream work and the latent dream thoughts that constitute an approach to the patient's unconscious fantasies and introjects. I am sure that you recognize that this is only a rather general effort, and that we will need the patient's associations to this dream to fill it out and to identify more specific fantasies. But we do have some important clues, and if we were to relate them directly to the adaptive context at hand, we could say so far that the intrusion of the boyfriend in some way has stirred up the patient's own heterosexual conflicts, and in a less evident manner, something of her homosexual anxieties as well. Perhaps, the incident has stirred up some longings for a woman in the face of the hurt by the two men, or the homosexuality is a defense against her heterosexual longings. But here we become speculative for the moment and will leave off this trend in our thinking.

So, having attempted to search out some latent intrapsychic fantasies detectable in this material, we now have a second job to do—one that, to my knowledge, has not been identified in the literature in connection with dreams. Right now, I suspect that you can anticipate me, but to be clear, it is the effort to comb this material for unconscious communications to him based on these perceptions. And what is most interesting about this particular search is that our findings actually fit the material even better than did our formulations related to the patient's inner struggles. Of course, there is a condensation in every dream, and in its extended structure, of both unconscious fantasies and unconscious perceptions, and the two elements intermix. It is only for teaching purposes that I am isolating them in relatively pure form, but I want to stress that I am not indicating that a patient is capable of an unconscious fantasy totally without influence by reality, nor is he capable of an unconscious perception without some effect on it based on his own intrapsychic fantasies and set.

Actually, in some ways this manifest dream within its adaptive context offers a general interpretation to the therapist, to the effect that he accepted the boyfriend into this patient's therapeutic situation because he had major heterosexual and homosexual conflicts. Now, how did I arrive at that? Well, we take the adaptive context and we see what the patient has done with it in her dream. First, she conveys a struggle between herself and a boyfriend, in which she is rejected. As an unconscious communication, which the dream serves *par excellence*, this conveys the patient's perception of the therapist's behavior—he has rejected her in favor of someone else.

Now, again you could say that it is the patient who is sexualizing the therapy, but there is really no inherent reason to restrict this to the patient, even though this is her dream. This is also an unconscious perception of the therapist, and an effort on her part to develop an hypothesis that would explain his behavior. As you know, it is my contention that technical errors stem from a condensation of lack of knowledge and countertransference needs. Within the patient, there is a great need to understand the therapist's inner motives for his error, and as we have seen, to help him to rectify it. Certainly, the patient has her own heterosexual conflicts, but she has also incorporated those of the therapist. And if you think of it, the hypothesis that this therapist has some type of heterosexual conflicts with this young lady, that are disturbing his work with her, is a perfectly reasonable one. In fact, I was much more tentative in offering such an idea than this patient has now been, but she is becoming impatient with the therapist and has become bolder in her unconscious interpretations. So, this dream constellation reflects both the patient's intrapsychic conflicts, her unconscious perceptions of conflicts within the therapist, and a mixture of the two.

In addition, there are the indications of a homosexual theme in this material, and it is here that the patient is also offering an unconscious perception of the therapist's involvement with the boyfriend who came into her session, and suggesting far more subtly, that the therapist also has conflicts in this area that are disturbing his work with, actually, both of his patients. And the hypothesis of the therapist's homosexual conflicts fits much more clearly with the evidence at hand than that related to the patient, since he has accepted a man into the therapeutic situation. If we follow the patient's lead, this action suggests to us both the therapist's unconscious homosexual wishes directed toward the young man, and his use of the presence of a man as a defense against the anxieties related to his heterosexual conflicts with this patient.

So, our initial impressions, based on first hearing the dream and identifying the adaptive context for it, is that this is indeed a curative dream, with certain self-curative trends, and with extensive curative efforts directed toward the therapist. And already, most of the initial predictions that we made, even before hearing the dream, have been borne out, and the patient has been quite explicit about it. And I hope that you have some feeling of how to go from an adaptive context to the manifest dream and then to some of the latent content; and that in addition, you are convinced that your search must be not only for the patient's unconscious fantasies, but for her unconscious perceptions and even her unconscious interpretations to the therapist. And lastly, though I will not try to illustrate them here, the manifest and latent dream also contains unconscious self-perceptions—of the patient regarding herself.

I would account for what I call the exquisiteness of these communications from the patient by pointing to the extent to which the therapist has resisted appreciation of the ramifications of the incident with the boyfriend, and the patient's anxieties regarding further violations of her confidentiality with the Disability people. Now, technically, all of this discussion would represent silent hypotheses developed by the therapist, to be borne out by the patient's subsequent associations. And yet, while we have them in mind, we are prepared to reserve another part of ourselves in a blank state, ready to hear of additional adaptive contexts and unexpected unconscious communications. This should be our usual way of listening—partly organized and partly empty and ready to be filled.

T: Can we go back to the two sessions after he had walked into the office? She said that she felt depressed; she felt as if she was back in the same place again; and then she brought up the imagery of the parking lot.

L: Right, that was the time that she had felt so desolate . . .

T: That was right after he had come into the room.

L: Right, but now you are going back to the patient's struggle with her—and your depression, and her efforts to deal with those problems. These depressive conflicts are also present, but they should not take us away from the evident sexual conflicts that are beginning to emerge, again, in both the patient and yourself.

Your comment about the depressive element also reminds me that in a way, in attempting to be supportive, you were, on some level, offering her the use of manic and denial defenses, so that even there we can see an interactional component. The evident denial in this dream is an interactional defense, with contributions from both yourself and the patient, who, of course, welcomes them. However, when the therapist offers the patient a pathological defense, it need not correspond to the patient's own usual defensive armamentarium; of course, when the therapist and patient share the same defenses against their respective intrapsychic conflicts and anxiety, there is an intensification of their use within the bipersonal field. However, I have seen patients introject defenses from their therapists that have not been their usual means of defending themselves, so we will have to await further material before deciding on the vectors contributing to this aspect of the patient's response.

One last comment: these communications occur in the face of a therapeutic misalliance, and of a view of the therapist as hurtful and dangerous. There is therefore not only an intrapsychic need for disguise and defense, but an interactional need of this kind as well. It is not the patient only who is having difficulty managing her own inner impulses; it is the therapist also who is having problems in managing both his patient's communications and his own inner state. At such times, the patient's defensiveness will be quite strong, and will be balanced against her need to communicate, and to get well.

So, you can see how complicated it is to be a psychotherapist, and how much work can be done not only immediately after we have heard a manifest dream, but even in anticipation of it. I can assure you that there will be even more to do as we hear the patient's associations. But there is hope—once you learn how to organize the material from the patient, and something of the relationship between an adaptive context and the communications that follow, your work can be made much easier. Of course, that's on the intellectual side; as you have seen, emotionally it helps to sort out your own conflicts and get them under control. Now, let's hear more.

T: So, she said that she was very happy about last week's session—the last session. She felt much better about it and toward me . . .

L: What had you said to her in that previous hour?

T: It had to do with what I said toward the end. The statement that nobody believed I'd said. It was about her appointment with the doctor. I paraphrased what he might say to her: Come back after you've seen a psychiatrist and if your heart's still beating, tell me if your heart hurts. She said now that she knew from what I said that I understood her and that I believed her, and that she was worried before that I didn't. And then she asked me if I had any thoughts about this. I said that I was wondering what I was doing the other three months of her therapy. And . . .

L: Wait. What does that mean?

T: She was glad that I understood what she said. I was wondering: she finally knows that I understand her, then what have I been doing for the last three months?

L: All right. We're studying interventions. I gather that this isn't the interpretation you planned to present. (Laughter.)

T: No.

L: Let's discuss this intervention for a moment; how would you identify it?

T: I'm not finished with it.

L: Oh, you have more to say. Sorry.

T: I just reiterated what she had said. That it was important for her to have someone that understood her.

L: Okay, how would we identify it?

T: The way that she asked the question was very complimentary, Oh, I'm so glad that you understand me. And I said, You know, I wonder what I was doing the other three months.

L: All right. What kind of intervention was that?

D: A defense.

L: What else?

D: Before, she was not doing well; now she says I feel better, you're doing the right thing. The therapist wants to tell her that's what I was doing those three months, but you were not able to see it.

D: I get something else from it. If I were the patient here, I would feel that he is being sarcastic in questioning what he had been doing all that time. It's as if he was wondering if he had done something magical that she felt so well. He also sounds impatient and as if he doesn't feel that he has anything to do with her feeling better, that it all comes from inside her or from her neurotic conflicts. It's as if he's saying that from what he's doing, he wouldn't expect her to be so well.

D: Is this a misalliance cure?

L: It could be a misalliance cure, but that does not identify this intervention. Actually, we don't as yet know what has prompted her to feel better; we're going to have to see. It's reasonable to suspect a misalliance element, since we have no reason to believe that it is based on any insight or constructive intervention offered by the therapist. And it may be that the point that you were trying to make is that this intervention invites a misalliance with the patient, and we will get to that in a moment.

What I find most interesting about this intervention is that, despite the fact that I wrote a book (Langs, 1973a) in which I followed the classical lines in elucidating interventions, I really can't classify this one. Oh, it is certainly a question asked of the patient, but it is not the usual kind of question that comes from a therapist in an effort to clarify the patient's associations and to build toward an interpretation. I think that this intervention shows the extent to which formal classifications of the type that I offered have their limitations, and how important the interactional and communicative functions of interventions are. So, once again we will have to look to those areas if we are to anticipate how the patient will experience this intervention.

This comment comes, in part, from the therapist's idiosyncratic style of intervening, in that he consistently says the unexpected and the difficult to classify formally. Here, he is somewhat less creative, although he is certainly being spontaneous and sincere. Perhaps, this patient will teach us that these qualities, however admirable, do not necessarily serve the patient, and that, in fact, this intervention was once again far from neutral. It is, as one of our discussants indicated, virtually a confession of your confusion about your work with this patient up to the present moment. It is really a modification in your neutrality and, in its widest sense, your anonymity.

Now, unconsciously, it has another quality that is extremely pertinent to our discussions of this patient. We are fortunate that you made this intervention before you presented this patient to us here, because it reveals your own unconscious wish for therapeutic help. You are virtually asking this patient to help you to understand your confusion and the difficulties that you have been having in treating her. You are asking that the bipersonal field be devoted for the moment to your therapy, and while the patient may welcome such a request, since it is in keeping with some of her needs, she will also ultimately resent it.

The patient's comment that she was gratified by your intervention at the end of the previous session is also very important. Initially, we can see that she is indicating that she was actually cured by your unconscious identification—probably an overidentification—with her, and by the manner in which it was expressed in the name of empathy and concern. You offered yourself as a container for her grief and confusion, and invited an introjective identification that afforded her a moment of relief. Perhaps her initial remark in this session, to the effect that she was feeling better, can be understood on this level as being related to your accepting the patient's sickness into yourself and momentarily freeing her of it.

However, there are some drawbacks: you are not aware of what you had done; you didn't metabolize the introject in order to understand the patient; nor did you intervene based on such a comprehension. As a result, the patient did not develop cognitive insight through the experience. It shows, however, how powerful these mechanisms can be, and it does indicate that, for the moment, this patient is feeling better based on a misalliance cure.

Technically, your intervention, related to her heart, reflected your introjection of the patient's contents, and constituted an expression of a projective counteridentification—that is, you accepted and invited a projective identification into yourself that occurred without your conscious insight and understanding. I am impressed with the extent to which such a process—a pathological introjective identification—can gratify the patient and offer her momentary symptomatic relief. I wish I could say more, but now I feel some of the limitations of attempting to formulate this material before we begin to hear the patient's associations. Such efforts have both advantages and disadvantages. The main thing is that we are prepared to listen to her associations and will allow her to direct our further thinking.

Now, we can come back to the dream. We had said initially that the adaptive context—the day residue—for this dream was the intrusion of the boyfriend. Now we listen to the patient's first association. What is she saying about the immediate day residue for the dream? This is a basic question.

D: The first thing she talks about is the intervention that he made. That may be the day residue.

L: Yes—his intervention. She said, I had this dream the
    night of our last session. In other words, the boyfriend's
    interruption was only the long-term day residue. You see
    how you must always listen to the patient's associations.
    She says, You know, what you said to me last session re-
    ally made me feel good; I really felt understood. Now
    she's also saying that's what prompted this dream. So,
    while we have one very tentative understanding of this
    dream, based on the day residue of the intrusion, we now
    have to go back over the whole dream, based on this oth-
    er day residue. To do this in a sensitive way, you have to
    understand your intervention; you have to know your
    personal equation. The intervention in question was in
    the form of an empathic statement. It seemed to have el-
    ements of countertransference in it, in that it just con-
    veyed an identification with the patient somewhat with-
    out a proper context, and it didn't really deal with the
    issues disturbing the patient. Some empathic statements
    can be quite appropriate; here there was something that
    was appropriate but somewhat idiosyncratic as well. Cer-
    tainly, our discussion of last week emphasized our feel-
    ing that it came out of nowhere, didn't deal with the
    main adaptive context . . .

T: All right, in that context then, she perceived that play-
    back as really not dealing with the adaptive context re-
    lated to the intrusion.

L: Well, yes, that's one thing; there was a shared avoidance.
    In her dream, she brings you back to the intrusion. But
    she also brings you back to your intervention. What is
    she trying to communicate? I haven't thought this out
    yet. The second day residue for this dream is the thera-
    pist's empathic identificatory comment; and she played
    it back to you. Oh, there's another way that your remark
    was revealed as a somewhat countertransference-based
    identification. The way you said it—you were speaking
    for her. You had really merged with her. You didn't say,

you feel that the doctor will say such and such; you just said it directly for the patient. That style revealed something too. You just said it as if she had said it. You had come back with exactly her words, her feelings, her tone; this shows that it was very important for you to identify with her.

Now, let's examine the dream in the context of that particular day residue—it gets so interesting. She's at a party where she first met this fellow; it's like it once was, and yet it's different. Now you get a feeling: the bad part of you accepted the boyfriend and the intrusion; the good part of you merged with her. You see, now I get a feeling of the mixed image. It was like our first meeting, the excitement and the chance for love was there, and yet everything transpired so that it wasn't like that. In other words, the bad part—the bad qualities contained in your letting the boyfriend into her session—spoiled the momentarily good experience and her sense of fusion.

So, this second adaptive context helps us to understand the party, and the manic-like qualities in that the therapist had offered himself as an object of fusion for this patient. She accepts the excitement and the gratification of that experience and even feels better based on it, but then she is reminded of the hurts that have come from the therapist, and the dream ends on that note. So, we see that the adaptive context of an empathic intervention that indicated an unconscious need on the part of the therapist to identify with and merge with the patient, was worked over by the patient into a manifest dream in which she is at a party with a boyfriend and is remembering the excitement of their first meeting. The patient is indicating that unconsciously, she experienced this intervention as a sexual expression, related to the image of boyfriend and girlfriend, and sexual feelings were also stirred up within her.

I hope that you see now how we follow some basic principles. First, following the patient's lead, we identify the adaptive context for the dream, and then we explore the manifest content within the framework of that context, in an initial effort to detect some of the latent dream thoughts. And once again, we search out not only the patient's intrapsychic fantasies and introjects, but also attempt to identify her unconscious perceptions of the therapist and of his intervention. There is again a quality of an unconscious interpretation in that the patient is trying to convey to the therapist her reading of the unconscious implications of his comment, but the main quality is that the intervention raised a sense of hope in her that brought with it the fear of further hurt; or perhaps it already contained the hurt, because of its inappropriate and noninsightful qualities.

T: Then, my intervention about wondering what had gone on in the past three months . . .

L: Oh, you're up to your second intervention, while I'm still discussing the first one. I am attempting to stress that once you know a specific adaptive context for the dream, you both reassess its latent content and you attempt to determine the unconscious content of your intervention, doing so through your subjective awareness and the clues in the patient's dream. Day residues have manifest and latent content, as does every adaptive stimulus and every association from the patient. I wrote about that in a paper on day residues (Langs, 1971). In addition, when a patient selects a particular stimulus as the day residue for a dream, it is her way of telling you that that particular event had important unconscious meanings for her. Now, who would like to say something more in this area?

D: He made the correct intervention. Being nice to me now isn't going to undo what you did to me.

L: No, there's something else here. He made an intervention that wasn't entirely correct. His intervention, while in words, was basically an identification with the patient—an incorporation of her anxieties, her concerns, her paranoid thinking; he shared them with her. How did she react to that? In this dream, what does she do?

D: She rejects him.

L: She rejects him. She could have had anything she wanted in this dream—she has a rejection. She starts off by saying I loved it; it was the beginning of the promise of love, but no, I have to push you away. Here, I'm taking the dream not as an unconscious perception of what the therapist did, but as unconscious fantasy and as her reaction not to his accepting the boyfriend, but as her reaction to his identification with her. She says, It's too much; it's too close. I have to push you away. We have to know that in order to sense the climate of this session. And we can only know it if we know the day residue for the dream.

We now get to understand the dream by knowing the day residue or precipitating event. And we also have a feeling for what she experienced and how she experienced it. That came in part from self-knowledge—from self-analysis of the intervention. If the therapist doesn't understand the nature of his intervention; if he thinks he made a correct interpretation, then he'd think, Well, she's rejecting me because I made a correct interpretation. It's much more intimate than that. There was a very intense identification with this patient. She experienced it and she had the need to repudiate it.

At the same time, if he had been preoccupied with the business of accepting the boyfriend into the session, he would have missed what the patient is telling him. Notice what I did: I had a context and I was going to work on the dream in that context. Then, the patient gave me a communication, and I listened to her. I added it to what I was developing. I didn't say, No, it has nothing to do with the intrusion. Obviously it does. But I did examine where she directed me to look. This is the way you should listen as a therapist. You have to be able to break your set. You can't be married to it; you shouldn't be narcissistic about your own formulations.

Now, I can make one other observation and it is typical. In this dream, there is a clear reference to the hurt and the rejection, right? It doesn't refer so obviously to the loving; notice how that is more disguised in the dream. It appears in the dream—she says it was like when we first met—but it's quickly put aside. And most therapists, having overidentified with a patient, would be very glad to have a little bit of distance now, because she was getting too close. And they would interpret the anger about the intrusion, and ignore the fact that she's also dreaming about the way in which the therapist moved closer to her and overidentified with her—and expressed his love through an identification. You see, they would have the need to defend themselves against that loving quality.

So, you have to listen to the patient. Decide what is primarily defense and what is not. When I hear a day-residue like this and I can go back to the dream and integrate the two, then I know she's not simply trying to get away from the incident of the intrusion; she's trying to tell me that two things happened. First the therapist hurt her, and then he loved her. See? And in the dream, the patient reverses it; she uses the mechanism of turning into the opposite—a not uncommon primary process mechanism.

Now, when different aspects of the material and your formulation of it begin to synthesize like that, and you can bring pieces together that you didn't realize were related, then it is likely that you are on the right track. It is important, however, to continue to apply the validating process to your formulations. It was actually by doing precisely that that we modified our assessment of the situation with this patient, and recognized that she felt both hurt and loved. She experienced the therapist as moving away from her and pushing her away, and then as drawing extremely close to her. Here, the interaction-

al concepts of *closeness* and *distance* take on important
meaning and help us to understand both the patient and
the therapist. And because each of these interactional
processes were expressed unconsciously through the therapist's interventions, the patient viewed them as reflections of his poorly managed inner state and as a personal
threat.

Now, we have developed a conceptualization of the
therapeutic interaction up to the point of your last intervention. True, we have had to go back and rethink many
of the antecedents, but this aspect of the validating process should be initiated whenever the patient implicitly or
explicitly directs you to do so. And once again, we find
that your intervention contains far more that is implicit
than explicit. It is far from merely an interpretive effort
that gives the patient insight; and it is much closer to a
countertransference expression that once again will call
for the therapy of the therapist.

And if we follow the sequence of the interaction, we
can develop some tentative ideas about the difficulties
that the therapist was having. It was at the very moment
that the patient said in this session that she felt that he
understood her because of his empathic response, that
the therapist interrupted her associations to ask, if I may
paraphrase it, What the hell have I been doing for the
last three months? Instead of busying himself with the
many therapeutic tasks that we have discussed, and instead of waiting for more associations, at a point where
the patient is beginning to reveal important unconscious
processes, he made this intervention. Now, think about
that and tell me, what is the main quality of this comment?

D: I don't understand what I'm doing.

L: Yes, and what is that? How would you describe it?

D: I'm confused; I don't know what I'm doing.

L: Yes; give me some descriptions of that comment. What

categories could we put this response into?

D: Frustration.

L: Frustration. Give me some more categories.

D: Incompetency . . .

L: Yes, you're describing implications of the content. What else can we say?

D: Is it an interrogation?

L: It's not really an interrogation. Tell me what it is.

D: She feels sad . . .

D: I think he's saying that at last we've got it together.

L: Fine, but what more can be said?

D: Unconsciously, he perceives that he cannot do his job.

L: See how fixated you all are—you keep giving me content. There are other dimensions.

D: It's a self-revelation.

L: That's what I want. Of course, it's a self-revelation. I wanted to stress that it was a personal statement. Don't you see? It's another reflection of his personal involvement with this girl. You can see from it that he is involved in an exquisite interaction with this patient, and that this patient is in touch with it too. You know, you'll hear people say, Oh she's crazy, you can't put her into insight therapy; you can't see her twice a week; you can't interpret to her. Meanwhile, the material to shape your interpretations is pouring out of this girl. And you should be intervening—as she is unconsciously—not only in regard to the interruption, but also in connection with your interventions as well. She's telling you that she has to cure you of those two problems; it is interesting because they're interrelated. Your need for a third party comes out of the way in which you relate to her. Accepting the intruder goes with your overinvolvement with her; you're much too close. I don't know if you're conscious of it or not, but it's there and I'm sure that you can appreciate it now. At least I think you can; it comes out of your words. Now there's nothing the matter with that, if you get it mastered. Being able to respond with real affect to a patient is important. However, it must be controlled and in the service of the treatment.

Once again, however, you have made a self-revelation and now it tells the patient that you have been too involved with her. And your intervention, interestingly enough, can serve two contradictory interactional purposes: to push her further away by confessing your ignorance, and to bring her closer to you by revealing a hurt and uncertain part of yourself, and by asking the patient to help to cure you. Interactionally, you have not established a proper and therapeutic distance between yourself and her; she will react to that.

So, we again see that incorrect interventions are filled with unconscious communications, many of which are related to the therapist's countertransference difficulties. Because they put the therapist's pathology into the bipersonal field and into the patient—in terms of their content and the distance between the two poles of the field—they become important adaptive contexts for the patient. We will undoubtedly see this when we continue with this session. After all, once again you have modified the framework through this intervention, and you have done it through what primarily appears to be defense against the growing closeness between yourself and the patient. You can see now that the poles of the bipersonal field are not fixed; they move toward or away from each other at the behest of one participant, and in keeping with the reactions of the other. The bipersonal field is a basically human, ever-changing field, and the closeness and distance of the two polarities have many important interactional implications.

We'll take a short break now and then resume our discussion.

Chapter 8

A PATIENT'S ATTEMPT TO CURE HER THERAPIST—AND HERSELF

THE THERAPIST'S INCOMPLETE INTERPRETATIONS • THEIR INTRAPSYCHIC AND INTERACTIONAL IMPLICATIONS • THE INTRAPSYCHIC AND INTERACTIONAL CONSEQUENCES OF AN ONGOING UNREPAIRED FRAME • SECTORS OF THERAPEUTIC MISALLIANCE AND THE DEVELOPMENT OF A MISALLIANCE CURE • THE THERAPIST AS A PATHOLOGICAL CONTAINER FOR THE PATIENT'S CONTENTS • COMMUNICATED MEMORIES • THEIR RELATIONSHIP TO UNCONSCIOUS FANTASIES AND UNCONSCIOUS PERCEPTIONS • A SHIFT IN THE BIPERSONAL FIELD TOWARD THE PATIENT'S INTRAPSYCHIC CONFLICTS • THE PATIENT'S EFFORTS TO PROJECTIVELY IDENTIFY INTO THE THERAPIST

L: Let us continue. Are there any questions?

D: Yes. Isn't it also possible that the therapist's interventions have something to do with the dream and that he may have unconsciously reacted to the contents contained in the dream communication?

L: I would agree. It seems likely that, in addition to any conscious assessment, he would also unconsciously process the dream and would be responding to its contents as they have been put into him. Part of our job in understanding dream communications is to become aware of impressions that are initially unconscious. We really don't know what was going on in this therapist; we have only the patient's associations.

However, even within that limitation, the dream conveys that mixture of loving and hurt, of closeness and rejection, that we had discussed previously. And the patient seems to be attempting to establish a more loving element; and the therapist seems to be trying to push her away again, although, as I said before, on a deeper level he is actually drawing her even closer to him. Certainly, the therapist's associations would help us here, but that is beyond the province of this seminar, and requires an entirely different setting. We have to restrict our inferences regarding what is going on in the therapist, and we can only base them on his interventions and the patient's conscious and unconscious perceptions of him.

Still, in being critical of this intervention I again want to point to the marvelous kind of potential that it contains. Perhaps it won't be helpful to this patient, because the therapist does not appear to have mastered his own creativity, but it would really be unfortunate if he lost the spark and the genuine sincerity reflected in his interventions. We see an unusual cognitive style of intervening here. Everybody has his own way of relating to a patient, and of making comments to him. There is something very special, and very difficult to define, in these very human and almost soulful interventions. I certainly would not like to see them replaced with a more mechanical and overintellectualized manner of communicating. It would be far better if the therapist could maintain his individuality, but learn to manage the pathological components of his particular style of intervening.

It may very well be that it is the somewhat exciting sparks of concern that are helping this patient to maintain herself. Of course, this would constitute a form of misalliance cure that has considerable danger to it, since this patient is struggling with suicidal impulses; but I wanted to stress some of the positive qualities contained in these interventions. The consistent effort should be made to sort out the noncountertransference and countertransference components of the therapist's interventions; they are always intermixed. So, on one level, this intervention is a self-revelation, and on another level, it confirms his comprehension of her wishes to have somebody who understands her, which again has to do with this whole business of the sharing between him and her.

T: Well, in the situation with the boyfriend, it was not understanding her.

L: Yes, not understanding is also involved—it's both. The patient, in asking you what do you think, is also testing you out; are you going to shift the situation again into one in which you make a self-revelation? There's no intervention called for at this point. Her question as to what you think should be responded to either with silence or with a comment like, Let's see what more comes to your mind. But you have a need to respond to her, to tell her how pleased you are, in this indirect way. Here I would have waited to see what more came to her mind, and if she drifted away from the dream, I might have asked her what some of the elements of the dream brought to mind; we don't have to ask her what prompted the dream—we know that. Sure there are other day-residues, but we've got enough to deal with in this session . . .

D: Wouldn't you ask her, What are your thoughts? . . .

L: Not, What are your thoughts? . . . If she drifts away from the dream, I would listen to where she goes. I'll tell you later if and when I would say to her, Well, what else comes to mind about the dream? It depends on many factors. But I can tell you already that you know something about therapeutic work at hand—the therapeutic contexts. There is plenty of work to be done on the intrusion and her reaction to his self-revealing comments; that's a session's work. You don't have to worry about other day residues and other contents; that's where the work has to be done for now. Let's continue.

T: Okay, she then said that she appeared motivated to start bringing up . . .

L: Your comment would get her going; that's for sure.

T: She wanted to bring up what she had mentioned last time, last session, toward the end. She now tells me the story of a girlfriend that she had when she was very young. This girl had a father . . . he was divorced and this girlfriend was staying with him. And she was very distressed with both the girlfriend and the father figure. She identified him as being such—a father figure—for her. She just remembered that one day she was over at their house and they had to go to the basement. She and the father of the girlfriend were in the basement together and he made a pass at her.

L: So you see, that didn't take very long, did it. You see what I mean? So where does this material come from? It comes from the unconscious perception of your intervention—and her elaborations of it.

T: But there's more.

L: Oh, I'm sure there's more. (Laughter.) But look at how rich this material is when you understand it. It takes us back to the intrusion and tells us more of what that meant to her—and to you. Perhaps she is now helping you to become aware of your need for the threesome—allowing the intruder into the session as a protection against seductive feelings.

     Everyone in this room can empathize with your position, and it tells you something about why doing psychotherapy is such a wearing undertaking. You're in a situation where all of your emotions and fantasies are repeatedly stirred up, and you have the basic responsibility to achieve as close to total renunciation as is humanly possible. And we are now adding a dimension that has been largely overlooked by most analysts—and you can really sense why they have done so—the patient is unconsciously perceptive of much of your plight and is consistently communicating these perceptions—and their elaborations within her—to you. You can see how great the burden is for the therapist. His is an extraordinary job, and the patient's sensitivity to his unconscious communications—which has a positive side that we should not forget—makes it all the more trying.

You should all be thinking of what prompted this particular memory, and what light it sheds on the initial intrusion of the boyfriend, the intervention of the therapist in the previous session, and his intervention in this hour. I will just remind you of this sequence as the first bit of data, so that you can all think about it as we hear more from the patient. The intrusion, of course, came first and had set the tone for the subsequent sessions. Then, the therapist made his intervention about the patient's plight, which, as we have seen, reflected an intense over-identification with her; and it was immediately following that comment that she brought up this memory and decided not to tell it to the therapist—an important point, since I have been stressing that the therapist who modifies the frame is not an object of trust to the patient. Then, in this next hour we heard the patient's dream, a reference to the end of the previous session that I have just described, and then the intervention from the therapist about his doubts over what he had been doing since the beginning of this patient's therapy. It is at this point that she turns directly to this recollection and describes it. The sequence alone reveals a great deal, not the least of which is the way in which these two interventions, which we formulated as modifying the framework and as containing more self-revelations than understanding, each brought to her mind one particular incident. Let's hear more.

T: Anyway, she said that after he had made the pass at her, they went upstairs together. She didn't really know what to say to him. And the girlfriend asked her, What were you doing downstairs? Her next thought was that she had tried to call this man last weekend and that he'd been married twice since then. She also remembered other times when she was abused by him.

L: It just so happens that she tried to call him last weekend, do you know why?

D: The therapist's intervention had stirred her up.

L: The intervention was after the weekend.

T: The intervention was Monday, but the intrusion of the boyfriend was the Friday before she made the call.

D: Did she call after the dream?

T: No, before the dream.

L: So, why did she suddenly call this man?

D: The therapist is still threatened by this close relationship with her.

L: Yes, and the patient is also threatened by her overly close relationship with the therapist—it's both. The patient is trying to manage the improper distance between herself and the therapist. The intrusion of the boyfriend into her session had also reminded her of the earlier experience with this man—a father figure. It prompted her to call him, and we can speculate that in part, she was attempting to deal with the anxieties and memories that the experience in treatment had stirred up within her. And you can see from the telephone call that it certainly is not simply the therapist's problems, and her unconscious perceptions of them; in addition, she has her own intense needs to act out the perceptions and fantasies that were being stirred up in her through the therapeutic relationship. It would appear that she was struggling with the wish for incestuous gratification.

Had she seen this man, and had there been any type of sexual involvement, this would have been termed acting out, in that it would have been a living out of fantasies related to the therapist. In the past, this would have been conceptualized as an acting out of unconscious transference fantasies, but you can now see that acting out is usually much more complicated. In fact, it is my impression that an important facet of acting out is that the therapist often participates in it unconsciously and through contributions not unlike those we see in this present vignette. So, the acting out even at the level of the telephone call relates to unconscious perceptions and fantasies about the therapist, and reflects not only the patient's difficulties in managing what is being stirred up, but the therapist's difficulties as well. So here we arrive at a concept of acting out as both an intrapsychic and interactional symptom—a syndrome of the bipersonal field.

And now we see that the patient has brought together all three interventions that we have been studying: the handling of the intrusion, and the two verbal comments of the therapist—about her heart still beating and what has he been doing until now. The intrusion had prompted the phone call, while the verbal interventions had prompted the memory. In a way, the patient is saying that the unconscious meanings of each of these experiences are strongly intermeshed.

Now, let's see what she's communicating through this recollection. For one thing, she's saying that with the man's daughter present, everybody is safe. Right? In that case there wouldn't have been any pass, and nothing would have happened. Alone with him something happened. Now, I think that I can venture to say that before you presented this patient to me, you were making the same kind of interventions that you're making now. So, the qualities of your intervening, with its seductive aspects and the need to overidentify with her, have been present for a while—and she's been aware of this on some level. And she's trying to understand why you allowed this fellow into her session, and she's really formulating that without his presence, you would not be able to control your seductiveness—just as she would not be able to handle it. I'm not trying to say by any means that it's only you, though you are involved; it is also herself.

I do not join her in her exclusive view of the situation, either then or now, as one in which she was entirely the victim of a seduction. While that is valid, it is only one level of what is happening, and only one part of the contents of these associations.

On the next level, she wants to seduce you; that's why she too has allowed this fellow into the sessions. Believe me, she could have told him in two seconds, Look, damn it, get the hell out of my sessions! But she didn't. Just as you didn't. You both need his presence. So, she's conveying her unconscious perception of the bilateral sexualization of her treatment, and offering this memory as an intervention regarding both herself and you. She even finally conveys her participation rather clearly through the phone call. But it all came to her mind again after you made this comment, You know, what have I been doing for three months? See? How quickly your remark mobilized that association.

This gives me an opportunity to stress an aspect of the material that is usually much more in focus in the course of treatment, and which you may have begun to believe I ignore. I refer here of course to the patient's fantasy that she is the victim of an inappropriate seduction, to the exclusion of all other possibilities. With my marked focus on her capacity for unconscious perception, and on the valid core of such a fantasy, it has never been my intention to overlook or exclude the patient's contributions to such a communication, and especially its pathological component. It is for that reason that I want to stress here that we can see in this material the patient's own unconscious wish to be seduced, and her defensive use of projection through which she attributes this to the behaviors and intentions of others—the girlfriend's father and, unconsciously, the therapist. In the usual therapeutic situation, this component would come to the fore as a distortion and would be readily assessed as a transference response, were it not for the therapist's behavior, through which some degree of actual repetition has occurred.

But the point that I want to make is that the communication from the patient is highly condensed and contains both unconscious perception and unconscious fantasy. The discovery of one component by no means excludes the other, and in our usual clinical work we are constantly sorting out each of these aspects.

Actually, it is for two reasons that I have stressed the unconscious perception dimension in these discussions. The first is, of course, the presence of many disturbances within the bipersonal field, to which the therapist has significantly contributed. The second is a general tendency among therapists and analysts to neglect this particular aspect.

But here, when the patient stakes a claim for a valid unconscious perception, to which she would like to think she has made no contribution, I have an opportunity to stress the patient's own part in the situation. I will say it one more time: the understanding of the unconscious perceptions and valid cores of the patient's material is by no means intended to set aside the intrapsychic distortions contained in these associations. After all, ultimately the therapist must be in a position to isolate this pathological component in order to be able to demonstrate to the patient that it does not in fact correspond to the actualities of the therapeutic relationship. He can then interpret its source in the patient's unconscious fantasies and memories as related to her intrapsychic conflicts.

Now we're in a position to recognize more clearly that your difficulties and her difficulties coalesce into the psychopathology of the bipersonal field, and that underneath her unconscious interpretation, related to your common homosexual conflicts is, as we anticipated, another crucial level—your respective fears of not being able to manage heterosexual impulses. Now we have evidence that they patient has these difficulties in herself and that they relate to a whole range of unconscious fantasies with strong incestuous overtones. Remember, somebody here predicted that the incestuous element would come through. In addition, the patient is suggesting that there are similar conflicts in yourself for whatever reasons, which you should, as the therapist, attempt to identify, self-analyze, and resolve. But here we won't enter that province. The two of you have together created the psychopathology of the field, and each of you has a responsibility for resolving it.

And now we also see more readily that the dream and her indirect associations—she is not as yet directly associating to the dream elements, although her association clearly relates to them in terms of the memory of another threesome—indicate that she is indeed attempting to adapt to and alter the three major modifications of the framework—based on the intrusion and the two self-revealing comments that we have already identified. And we have further evidence that your intervention in the previous session enabled her to feel better through the closeness and gratification gained from your overidentification with her. In addition, she may have experienced some sense of inner relief through the consistency with which you are putting your own pathology into the bipersonal field. We can make some interesting observations about this aspect of the material, in that this recollection indicated that the patient, in the presence of a seductive father figure, can for the moment view herself as the less disturbed person in the dyad.

Hopefuly, you can see from this what we mean when we speak of the therapist's offering himself as a pathological container for the patient's inner disturbance. And while we can finally identify some of the patient's specific psychopathology through this last communication, we would have a difficult time interpreting it to her at a moment when the therapist is actively contributing to and intensifying it—and even overshadowing her own difficulties.

So, in all, we have seen an instance of a misalliance

cure that has evolved not through insight or adaptive inner structural change, nor through positive incorporative identification, but through a variety of maladaptive mechanisms. Here, I would include the shared seductive gratification afforded to both of you, your offers of fusion and manic denial-based defenses that were met by the patient's own needs in these areas, and the active putting of your own difficulties into the bipersonal field, through which the patient was able, for the moment, to dispose of her problems.

Now, notice again what happens once the patient has achieved the gratifications offered through such a misalliance cure. Initially she accepts it and even tries to exploit it by putting her difficulties into the therapist and by gaining some momentarily defensive relief through it. But soon she becomes anxious about it; it's filled with disturbing unconscious meanings and she now attempts to modify it—she attempts to cure the field and to cure the therapist.

I know that I'm repeating this, but the sequence is very important. Patients do accept misalliance cures, and if you don't assess the basis for their symptom relief, if you simply take it face value—and say, Well, the patient's feeling better; that's marvelous; let's not explore it—you will be doing a great disservice to the patient. We must examine the antecedents of a feeling of relief and understand them. If they've come out of a constructive interpretation and an accompanying constructive identification, that's one basis. If they've come out of some other type of effort, you should know that too. These have been called countertransference and transference cures. I prefer to call them misalliance cures because both patient and therapist participate in them. We should know what has happened, so we can understand when things turn sour. We can also understand the therapeutic work that the patient subsequently undertakes, and we can then set things straight with her help. You could then get onto the right track in terms of offering her valid interpretations geared toward insight.

So here I think is an illustration of a misalliance cure —momentary relief from symptoms based not on the constructive insight developed between the patient and the therapist (the insight of the field), but based on the pathology of the field and a possible bastion. It is also a framework cure in that the frame has been modified. And how quickly the patient turns against it and begins to convey the seductive and inappropriate qualities of this type of cure, and how she tries to do something about her own and the therapist's participation in it.

Lastly, recall her words: he made a pass and she didn't know what to say to him. The patient will not communicate within a modified frame.

T: The thought of the man came to her after I made that intervention about coming back after she's seen a psychiatrist.

L: The so-called empathic statement.

T: The countertransference-based counteridentification.

L: She had then thought about this man?

T: That's what came to her mind, and she said that she would talk about it next week.

L: Okay, so you see, she was already working on that intervention. It was a prelude to the dream too. You had made the intervention; she had thought about this man who had been seductive; and then she had the dream about the boyfriend. But, please continue.

T: The patient went on to talk about how she had indeed been abused by men at least three or four times in her life. One incident occurred when she was working at the same job as her sister, and the boss was a father figure for both of them. When her sister quit the job, the patient realized that she was having sexual thoughts about her boss. Now, the woman who replaced her sister at work was very attractive and the boss became interested in her, and the patient grew quite jealous. The patient was upset when the boss got involved with this woman and chased after her in the evenings after work. Eventually the patient left the job.

The second time was when she had been dating a fellow and felt he was quite sick—he wanted her to beat him. And there was still another fellow. She had been on a trip with a cousin and this fellow had tried to rape her. And because of all this, she hated men and she couldn't have an orgasm.

At this point, I said something to the effect that she had said that with the first man she wanted understanding, and saw him as a father figure, and he took advantage of the situation. That was the intervention.

L: Who will identify its formal nature?

D: I would say that it is a confrontation.

T: Actually, I was attempting to lead her up to the theme of her relationship with myself. I had begun to sense that she was talking indirectly about me.

L: That's an important moment, in that it has taken you a long time to recognize that this material is filled with derivatives of her unconscious perceptions and fantasies about you. While I don't think we can really object to a confrontation of this kind, so long as your intention was to eventually get to yourself, the patient might misunderstand it. I don't think that the timing was optimal. She was beginning to communicate a wealth of derivatives related to the therapeutic relationship, and there are both major transference and nontransference elements. These are closer derivatives than the earlier communications that were relatively more disguised; and they are intensifying both affectively and in terms of their content.

She may feel that you have once again failed to understand the many facets of her communications, when you intervene at the point where she is talking about her ha-

tred of men and blaming them for her own failure to have
an orgasm. It seems inadvisable to select one set of derivatives, while ignoring all the other rich communications
from this patient. This selection reflects something that
is possibly defensive on your part, and at the same time
may indicate to her that you are more identified with her
girlfriend's father than with the other men through
whom she was conveying her impressions and fantasies
about you.

I would have waited until the material seemed to level
off, and then would have made use of each of these memories by specifically demonstrating to her the ways in
which they reflected specific fantasies and perceptions
of yourself. I would also have attempted to clearly demonstrate her own contributions to this material, in an
effort to ultimately redirect the therapy back to her own
intrapsychic conflicts and pathogenic introjects. And as I
have said to you in earlier seminars, I would have intervened specifically at the point when her associations finally came around to the therapeutic relationship in
some direct or relatively undisguised way. And I can assure you that in almost every instance, this is a subject
that she would return to once again in this session. And
if she did not do so, and the session was drawing toward
its close, I would simply utilize the sequence of her association as a means of showing her that each of these
memories came to her mind after an intervention by the
therapist, whom she saw as threatening and seductive.
Notice again that I would state it in terms of this being
her view of what the therapist had done, rather than
through some direct acknowledgment or confession on
your part of having actually behaved seductively. The
implicit acceptance of her perception of the therapist as
seductive will enhance her capacity to test out inner and
outer reality, and there is no need to do more than that
for her.

Now, once I was ready to intervene, I would make use

of each of the incidents that the patient remembered. And I would be quite candid in my comments, because that is the way in which the patient is now communicating. And I would say something to her that is quite close to the ways in which I have formulated this material. If we take it in the sequence that she offered, I would put it something like this.

In the first incident, the patient is indicating that she views the therapist as a boss and as a father figure, and that she is in competition with her boyfriend for his favor. She has also indicated that she is having sexual fantasies about the therapist, who is rejecting her and who is turning sexually toward the boyfriend—another reference to the therapist's homosexual conflicts as perceived or fantasied by the patient. The final threat here is that of terminating the therapy.

Now, let's pause for a moment and recognize that there are both transference and nontransference components in these derivatives. There seems to be some element of an erotic father transference, but this is somewhat overshadowed by the actual relationship with the therapist, in which he is, on some level in reality, reliving with the patient an aspect of a seductive interaction that we must now postulate to have occurred with her father. Of course, we can expect her to have had sexualized longings for him upon his death, but in addition, I would suspect some type of actual seductive interaction. This we could discover as the patient went on, since under the circumstances of an early loss, it is possible that much of this stems from reparative sexual fantasies within the patient. However, in seeking out the truth about the patient's past, we have there too the job of sorting out reality and fantasy, and their intermixture.

While the reference to her boss's attraction to the other woman is certainly, on one level, a defensive projection of the patient's sexual interest in the therapist, we can see that it is also condensed with an unconscious perception of her therapist, based on his handling of the intrusion of her boyfriend into the session. And I want to also stress the manner in which the patient communicates her perception of the modification in the framework, since it shows that this is a subject that is not only important to me, but that it is important to patients—and it enables me to say again that I actually learned all of this from patients. She does it by mentioning that the boss chased after this women after hours—he, and possibly she, modified the framework. It's at that juncture that she talks about leaving her job, and by implication, therapy. The atmosphere is again one of mistrust and hurt, and there is an erotization of the therapy; the therapist is seen as pursuing the boyfriend and perhaps other women, while the patient indicates that her erotic fantasies involve the therapist.

We can already sense the richness of this material, and appreciate that the patient is both acknowledging some of her own intrapsychic difficulties and making efforts to alert the therapist to his, and even assisting him with them. Next, comes the reference to the fellow who was quite sick and wanted to be beaten by her. Again, there is undoubtedly a projection onto this fellow of her own illness and her own masochism, but condensed in this communication there is also a largely nondistorted perception of the therapist, and possibly an important insight into the unconscious motives for his nonhelpful interventions. We do not know enough about the therapist to test out the validity of the patient's unconscious perception and interpretation of his masochism—his wish to be beaten—so we will not pursue this question here. However, I want to stress the way in which, at a time when we have formulated the patient's intensification of her therapeutic efforts toward the therapist, and we have suggested that he has put a great deal of his own pathology into the bipersonal field and into the patient, she makes comments that indicate her unconscious awareness of his sickness and of the state of the total therapeutic situation. Sure, there are distortions here, but she is also richly perceptive.

Lastly, there comes the fellow who attempted to rape her, and her statement about hating men and blaming them for her inability to have an orgasm. Once again, we may formulate this in terms of unconscious fantasies and conflicts within the patient, but we would also have to readily acknowledge that she has, in addition, valid reasons for her rage with men and her orgastic difficulties. Here, I suspect that what she is saying is that both her fantasies and perceptions of what men attempt to put into her are filled with violence and harm, and they evoke intense hatred. Here, she is commenting on the therapist's overidentification with her, and his efforts to put some of his pathology into her, and to ask for her help. In her own way, she indicates that such interventions by the therapist are as inappropriate as rape and she describes her need to fend them off. The rape also refers to the therapist's uncalled-for projective identifications into her and his misuse of her as a container for his sickness. Certainly, too, there is in this last communication, as with that about the girlfriend's father, the patient's own perception of the bipersonal field as being centered on the inappropriate gratifications of the therapist, and as being intensely threatening.

Now, please remember that these efforts to delineate the patient's valid unconscious perceptions—and these must be established first—are not intended to disregard the degree to which the patient not only misperceived the therapist to some extent, but also the ways in which she elaborates upon her perceptions in terms of her own intrapsychic fantasies and disturbances. After all, we do not as yet have a specific indication that the therapist is endeavoring to be sexually involved with the patient, and certainly he has not attempted to rape her, either sexually or mentally. These are some of her elaborations, although again, to keep things in balance, they are not

entirely distorted unconscious speculations about the
therapist. On some level, there is a great deal of truth to
these perceptions. Once again the therapist would have
to turn to his knowledge of himself, and to his efforts at
self-analysis, to sort out those aspects of the patient's
communications that are ultimately valid on some level,
and those that are essentially distorted and stem from
her own pathological unconscious fantasies and memories. This is by no means an easy task, but it is one that
the therapist would undertake as soon as he began to
hear this material. The tone of his subsequent intervention and its success would depend a great deal on the outcome of these efforts. So, at times such as this, the therapist is busily involved in both formulating the patient's
material and in understanding himself. He will then subject all his initial formulations to a validating process
based on further material from the patient and further
self-scrutiny.

At this point, we can also think back to the patient's
dream, and recognize that these memories are actually
associations to the dream and that they illuminate the
latent content of the dream. For example, the reference
to the past being like the present would have as its latent
content the manner in which the current interaction with
the therapist is in some ways like these earlier experiences, and especially resembles the incident with the girlfriend's father. The element in the dream that has to do
with the boyfriend being interested in another girl, and
thereby hurting the patient, appears to have as its latent
content both the hurt from the boss who ignored her and
the incident of sexual molestation. We also begin to recognize masochistic wishes in this patient, and these may
possibly be related to guilt over her incestuous fantasies
and wishes. We see too how the patient's rage at men is
interfering with her achieving mature sexual gratification. So, in many ways, these associations provide us with
additional clues to the latent content of this manifest

dream, in terms of the patient's unconscious fantasies and memories.

At the same time, we see that the latent content of this dream is filled with added unconscious perceptions of the therapist, and their elaboration. I have formulated these a number of times and won't belabor them for the moment. I simply want to stress that we are observing a very rich and meaningful session, one in which the material is coalescing and deepening, and one that would benefit from a major interpretation by the therapist. And I want to repeat again, that the dream and these associations are serving as a vehicle for the illumination of both the patient's unconscious fantasies and her unconscious perceptions.

This patient is now working quite hard to deal with the psychopathology of the bipersonal field, and of both the therapist and herself. We see that unconsciously she is very gifted and creative, and we might postulate in assessing the therapist's last intervention that, to some extent, she seems to be helping him get around to the central problem—her relationship with him. Whether he will be consciously able to identify the components of the interaction between himself and her remains to be seen, but you can see that through her help, and through whatever self-analytic work the therapist has done, he's beginning to move toward the therapeutic relationship and situation.

I'll stress one last thing: this is a productive session, but if the therapist doesn't understand the adaptive contexts and doesn't have these unconscious fantasies and perceptions in perspective, he could only do a very poor job in interpreting to the patient; then there will be new hurts and disillusionment. Now, please continue.

T: The patient said that she could remember often looking for father figures, particularly in her relationships with men. She didn't know if she had done that lately.

L: Certainly, her father is the key genetic figure in her relationship with the therapist for the moment. But we will have a lot of work to do to sort out how much of this material can be identified as transference—and as indicating that the patient is searching for the father who died early in her life, in her relationship with the therapist—and the extent to which the reference to the father relates to the therapist's having behaved in a hurtful manner that on some level repeated the traumatic abandonment and loss of the father, and mobilized a renewed search for him. This is an important distinction since it will affect the way in which the therapist intervenes, while for the patient it will be crucial in that a repetition of the hurtful relationship with her father would offer her virtually no therapeutic opportunity to work through the intrapsychic conflicts evoked by that earlier experience. An inappropriate search for the father in the therapist would on the other hand provide such an opportunity.

T: Well, she went on to talk about how she had always searched for a hero type who could give her anything that she wanted, and that she'd feel guilty afterwards, guilty because her father had died and she had been so young at the time. As a child, before he had died, she'd often called for help from him at night, and he would get up and help her, and her mother—for some reason or other—blamed her for her father's death.

L: The patient now seems to be shifting toward her own intrapsychic pathology, and away from that of the therapist. This material leads me to think that the patient found something constructive in your confrontation about her wish for understanding and the betrayal by her girlfriend's father, and that she had some idea of what you were getting at. I say this because a positive image of her father appeared in her associations and, if you think about it, it is the first image of this kind that we have heard in this material. Actually, that particular intervention was the first neutral communication that you offered her, and in its small but crucial way, it helped to restore the framework and some of the therapeutic qualities of the bipersonal field. So, after several interventions of a much more disturbing type, this confrontation has had a significant positive effect on the patient.

T: Then, at this very moment, a spider crossed the floor in front of the patient and myself, and she told me to kill it. I got up and escorted it back into the corner with a piece of paper, but the spider again started across the room. The patient then said, Well, let it be. This time I picked it up on a piece of paper and tossed it out of my office. The patient then said, You can't kill anything.

L: This is a remarkable moment. Weiss (1975) has written a paper on incidental events in the course of an analysis —an interruption of a session or the patient's overhearing an inadvertent remark made by the analyst before a a session—and he pointed out the need to explore and analyze these experiences. Here you can see that this remarkable incident with the spider really plays into the unconscious fantasies and perceptions that the patient— and maybe the therapist—is struggling with. And the therapist again responds behaviorally and probably unconsciously when the patient directs him to kill the spider—to become the killer. And she asks this of him at the very moment when she is struggling with an image of herself as such a killer—the killer of her father.

In this light, her request that the therapist kill the spider is an effort to projectively identify into him this troublesome image of being a killer. And notice what the therapist does: he does not intervene and interpret to the patient the meaning of her request, possibly then linking it to the recent adaptive contexts and associations of the patient. He responds behaviorally. He might have said to the patient that she seemed to be feeling guilty over some kind of destructive impulse toward her father, and that she was attempting to put this destructiveness into him and to have him enact a version of this hurtfulness for

her. I say this only to illustrate the type of intervention
that can come from understanding an effort by the patient to projectively identify contents into the therapist.
If I had intervened, I would have continued and dealt
with the other issues that we have discussed.

But here, you have a unique opportunity to observe a
refusal on the part of the therapist to accept a projective
identification and to become a container for this aspect
of the patient's inner conflicts and contents. It will be
difficult to anticipate the patient's reaction, since on the
one hand she has not obtained immediate relief from her
conflicts regarding the death of her father, while on the
other hand she has had an opportunity to observe the
therapist behave in a kindly way. She will also react to
the therapist's failure to intervene verbally; the situation
once again becomes rather complicated. Let's see what
happens.

T: The patient went on to say that before her father died,
she found out that he had actually had a number of affairs, and that when she learned this, she was furious.
But then she felt glad because at least he had had some
pleasure before he died—he had really gotten nothing
from her mother. Here, I said to her, Your father had affairs; you're talking of men taking advantage of you.

L: Now, we have an intervention that approaches an effort
at interpretation.

D: Perhaps you could define an interpretation as you view it.

L: Well, as you have read in my book (Langs, 1973a), an
interpretation may be formally defined as an attempt to
make conscious for the patient some inner contents of
which she is unaware—in brief, to make that which is unconscious, conscious. Even on a formal level, generating
an interpretation is a complicated matter, especially if it
is to be specific rather than general. An interpretation is
not made in isolation, but should be made within an
adaptive context, so that the patient knows what he is

dealing with and has some idea of what has mobilized the particular set of unconscious fantasies, memories, and introjects that are being called to his conscious attention. Currently, I would include within the realm of interpretation, efforts to make the patient aware of unconscious perceptions as well, since their conscious identification are also essential to the resolution of the patient's intrapsychic conflicts and essential to his very basic capacity to differentiate outer and inner realities: in essence, to perform the function of reality testing and to resolve his neurosis.

As you know, a specific interpretation will include references to the derivatives that reflect the central unconscious contents, and will delineate the relevant instinctual drives and wishes, defenses, and superego contributions. It will relate to the present situation and current precipitant, as well as to the relevant genetic components.

But in addition, as we have seen earlier, interpretations are the vehicle for unconscious communications that extend beyond the verbal elements. This will be reflected in the style of the intervention, its timing, its tone, and other nonverbal qualities. An ill-timed, though correct verbalization will have a number of effects in addition to producing insight, and some of them may be quite disruptive.

This brings me to the intervention that we just heard. The therapist said that he was approaching what has been termed a transference interpretation and we will accept that as his intention, although we have clearly indicated that the patient needs both a transference and a nontransference interpretation—an intervention related to the the totality of the therapeutic relationship. And notice what the therapist has done in speaking of the father and of men taking advantage of her; he has left himself out. While he may again justify this, based on his wish to approach the patient's relationship with himself very slowly, there are a number of dangers in this omission. It is not only a matter of not being sufficiently specific, this intervention may shift the patient away from the therapeutic interaction and in this way, serve as an invitation to a misalliance—an invitation to create a shared blind spot in the field, a bastion. In the face of such intense derivatives related to the therapist, this is very risky, even if you had in mind intervening in two steps.

If you wanted to intervene here—and if it were late enough in the session, I would have done so—you could have included many of the formulations that I suggested to you earlier. This would have made it more adaptively relevant, and far more pertinent for the patient. Actually, if it were late enough in the session, I would have intervened at some length here, and built it around the formulations that I have discussed earlier. I would have no criticism of a lengthy intervention at this point, since there is a great deal to be done in the areas of unconscious fantasy and memory, unconscious perception, and the framework. And the derivatives are so thinly disguised, I would feel that the patient would benefit greatly from the interpretation of their latent contents.

To give you just a small sampling of the kind of approach that you might have taken: you could have told her that she was talking about men who took advantage of her, and that you suspected that this had something to do with her current picture of you; and then you could have indicated from her associations some of the fantasies that she seemed to be having about you. Some of this has to be tentative since she has not directly brought you into the material, although she has done that several times indirectly. That is why I would have waited until she did refer to you specifically, because I could have been even more explicit then. However, to continue: you might have gone on to indicate that her perceptions of you seemed to have been based on your accepting the boyfriend into her session without comment or without exploration with her; and in addition, on your having left some of your papers on your desk; and lastly on your recent interventions, which she seemed to have experienced as somewhat self-revealing. From there, you could have detailed the specific unconscious perceptions and fantasies contained in her recent associations, and concluded with your belief that these experiences had stirred up recollections of her father, including her responses to the affairs that he had had.

T: The patient then told me that she could remember a job that she had had. She was interested in a different boss who also was a father figure, and then she got interested in him sexually. When he went chasing after some of the other women, especially one who had left the job, she decided to leave also, and see if he would follow her. She felt that she could only satisfy men sexually. She had called this boss recently.

L: Notice how this patient is really hinting at thoughts of leaving treatment, and also how she feels that turning away from somebody has tremendous seductive potential. Her fantasies of leaving treatment are related to the death of her father and to her conflicts about wanting to get involved with the therapist. They are also related to the damaged frame and her unconscious perception of the therapist. The recollection also contains an unconscious interpretation by the patient to the therapist, to the effect that his rejection of her is an effort to attract her to him.

T: She went on to say that she saw now that she was concerned about how she'd present herself to the boss and it all kind of fitted together. And I said, You saw this boss as a father figure at first, and then you saw him sexually. You were disappointed that he didn't chase after you.

L: Now, we're getting very near the end of this session, and I can't help but feel that the therapist is joining with the patient in a sector of misalliance. For her part, the patient doesn't quite get around to clearly indicating that her associations have a great deal to do with ther present relationship with the therapist. She could have done this indirectly by producing associations related to the therapist or the treatment, and, under these circumstances, she could also have done this by saying something directly to the therapist about her mistrust of him. Or she could have in some other way of her own, directly linked her associations in this session with thoughts and fantasies about the therapist. But she doesn't take her associations to that point, and as we have already formulated, this is undoubtedly not only a reflection of her own intrapsychic defenses, but also because the framework has been modified and the patient continues to mistrust the therapist. This mistrust is reinforced by her conscious or unconscious observation of the therapist's own avoidance of the therapeutic relationship, and his own failure to connect these very rich associations to the recent events in the treatment situation. As a result, we are observing an interactional resistance—a shared misalliance, in which specific references to the therapeutic relationship are split off into a bastion by both members of this therapeutic dyad, and thereby avoided. We have, in a sense, both a reluctant patient and a reluctant therapist.

T: The patient went on to say that she didn't know how she felt about this now. She wished she could get to the point where she didn't need men, even therapists. And that was the end of the session.

L: So, you never did get around to specifically connecting this material to her relationship with you, and she waited to the very last moment to say, Even therapists. I think this accounts for the sad tone of her final association and the return of her depression. She's also saying in those final words that she deeply needs an intervention from you, and that she is quite disappointed in not having obtained it. It also contains an image of self-cure through isolation and self-fulfillment which, in one sense, is one of the few avenues left to her in the face of your failure to adequately deal with her material.

And so we see how the prediction that this would be a therapeutic dream—a dream of cure—in the service of the modification of the psychopathology of both the patient and the therapist, has been borne out. We have seen that this patient not only produced a potentially curative dream, but a potentially curative session. And it is inevitable that she would feel disappointed, as we do and as I am sure the therapist does in retrospect, with his failure to utilize her curative efforts in the service of her treatment.

This final note also helps me to remind you once again that it is because we are observing major unneeded modifications in the framework, and significant failures to intervene, as well as crucial incorrect interventions, that I am led to focus on the patient's unconscious perceptions and curative efforts, to the relative neglect of the usual focal point of therapy—the patient's psychopathology and the therapist's conscious curative efforts. However, it remains an important clinical principle that before we can deal with the patient's internal dangers, and the anxieties derived from her intrapsychic conflicts and her pathological instinctual drives, we must deal with and resolve the external dangers and real fears with which she is confronted. While we have not seen a good illustration of this, although the patient is beginning to move in that direction in this session, valid psychotherapy should actually center largely around the patient's inner problems, rather than her difficulties with the therapist. But when it is in reality otherwise, we must recognize it and deal with it accordingly. And I think that you can also see that it is much easier to be unconsciously perceptive and to offer creative unconscious interpretations, than it is to be consciously aware and to offer specifically verbalized, conscious interpretations. In that respect, the job of the patient is far easier than that of the therapist. This is again not to say that there are not great burdens for the patient in psychotherapy, because there are many; it is merely to offer a perspective on the observations that we have made from this material.

I hope that one other thing has been accomplished through this material. Since, for some reason, it is a point that still appears to be in dispute, I hope that I have demonstrated that the therapist can work with dreams in an effective and rich manner within psychotherapy, and that such work can and should include the utilization of the patient's associations and efforts to determine the latent content of the dream—both in regard to unconscious fantasies and unconscious perceptions. In fact, in a session such as this, in which the dream network is so deep and rich, one could hardly point to a limitation in psychotherapy as compared to analysis, when it comes to the exploration of dreams. As I said earlier, I have no doubt that one can do considerably more with such material in the course of an analysis than in the psychotherapeutic situtation, but a session such as this clearly demonstrates that at any given moment, a dream in psychotherapy may be the pathway to very rich unconscious material and insights. This was a deeply communicative dream, in which the defenses and the resistance aspect was minimal, so there would have been little need to deal with that component, while great use could have been made of the dream and the associations in the adaptive contexts that we have discussed.

Since there are a few minutes left, would you please briefly tell us what happened in the following hour.

T: Well, the patient started again by saying how her friends were talking behind her back.

L: I hope you remember what I told you earlier: when there has been a modification in the framework that has been unexplored, and when the framework has not been clearly restored, the patient will come back again and again to some derivative related to the frame and to the psycho-pathology of the bipersonal field. As I said earlier, quite often this will be contained in the opening communication of the session. We are still in familiar territory.

T: Actually, I intervened here and said to her, Well, you mention this kind of thing with others, I wonder if you are having any thoughts that I might be doing something like that?

L: Well, it will certainly be a relief to your patient and to yourself to have you finally attempt to link some segment of her fantasies and perceptions to her relationship with you. But there are a number of problems with this intervention. In fact, this is a rather common sequence of interventions by therapists who are having countertransference difficulty and uncertainty in dealing with the patient's material. For a long while, you failed to make the connection between a myriad of derivatives related to yourself and their specific link with the patient's relationship to you; then suddenly, the patient says a couple of words, and you jump right in.

To be brief because the hour is late, if you had already begun to develop a silent hypothesis that this material had a great deal to do with recent events in the therapy, and more specifically with yourself, when the patient again began to talk about her fear of what others say behind her back, you should have known that she was still working over these same adaptive contexts, and that the material would readily unfold along such lines. You then should have sat back and allowed the associations to develop, so you could observe which specific aspects of these recent incidents in the therapy were most on her mind, and which of her unconscious perceptions of you, and their elaborations intrapsychically within herself, were most central. Then you could have intervened with a great deal of specificity, and probably at some length, in a manner that could have been quite effective.

Instead, by intervening quickly, you do not permit the patient to give you the necessary bridges between these outside suspicions and her relationship with you, and furthermore, you are restricted to a general comment. You can see that you failed to link these fears she has of your talking behind her back to either adaptive context that we know it connects with—the intrusion of the boyfriend and the impending communications with the Disability agency. In intervening, you should try to be as specific as possible and you should wait for as many specific derivatives from the patient as it seems feasible to obtain, since this will help you to be precise with her. Remember the basic principle of formulating silent hypotheses in the early parts of the session, and then subjecting them to the validating process, in terms of recent sessions as well as the patient's ongoing associations and your own continued subjective reactions. Once you have worked over such formulations and found a communality of confirmation, you can feel quite confident in intervening.

T: Her answer to me was that she was only concerned about important people talking behind her back. She could tell things to her boyfriend and, well, she was just concerned about how he would react. She didn't want to make love to her boyfriend. And there was another fellow that she didn't want to stay out with—she was hoping he would just go back home. And she had even told him, Look, please, stay away from me; don't press me, and she had felt good about it.

L: Because of the hour, we must stop here. I would appreciate your continuing to present next week.

I will conclude the seminar by pointing out that the patient's response to your intervention is very much in keeping with the comments that I just made. Once again, they express her unconscious efforts at supervision, and they reflect both an endeavor to help you and an effort to manage her own inner anxieties. She develops her re-

sponse around the unconscious perception of the suddenness with which you had brought yourself into the interaction, and the pressure you had created within her. And
again, she experiences it as a sexual kind of pressure and
a lessening of interactional distance, and handles it by
devaluing you and telling you to stay away from her. For
the moment, she repudiates the contents that you are attempting to put into her, and this is only partly because of
the suddenness of your intervention and your failure to
allow her associations to develop to the point where their
connection to you would have been unmistakable. In addition, there can be little doubt that it serves her own defensive needs and that she is frightened of closeness with
you and of what she perceives as your sexual penetration
through any type of intervention, valid or not. For her,
dealing with her relationship with you poses an enormous
sexual threat and this is all the more reason to wait until
her communications present clear-cut derivatives related
to the therapeutic relationship. Then at least on a cognitive level you are on firm ground and in a position to interpret her subsequent resistances if she attempts to fend
off a valid interpretation. In any case, we see that the
whole matter of the recent therapeutic interaction remains confused and unresolved, and we can certainly expect to hear more about it from the patient—and hopefully from the therapist.

Among the more important lessons of the past hour I
would stress the manner in which this patient and therapist have demonstrated that every communication from
the patient has to be measured against the background of
the therapeutic relationship and interaction. I cannot
stress this enough; it is one of the most crucial realities
of psychotherapy. This does not imply that the therapist
is always intervening in this area, but it does mean that
it is invariably one aspect that he must consider before
and after each of his interventions. And he will find that
there is an element of the therapeutic relationship in

every aspect of his patient's communications to him, and of course, in every communication that he makes to the patient in turn. And you will find that even when there are crucial adaptive contexts outside of the therapeutic relationship, and important interventions to be made in such connections, the material will eventually funnel back into the therapeutic relationship. This is where the patient is and if you will turn to your own empirical observations, I'm certain that you will find confirmation of this basic concept.

Without reiterating the differences that nonetheless prevail between psychotherapy and psychoanalysis, I simply want to point out that this is why I have developed my discussion of dreams within the context of the bipersonal field, and have done the same in exploring the nature of the therapist's interventions—valid and invalid. In this way, interpretations come to be understood within the total context of the therapeutic interaction, and insight is seen as a product of the bipersonal field—with contributions from both patient and therapist—a point made some time ago by the Barangers (1966).

In the midst of all of this criticism it is well to add that once again, despite the poor timing and distinct limitations of your intervention, it had a constructive and good nucleus. By this I mean that your effort to introduce the patient's relationship with yourself was clearly a step in the right direction, and the patient's associations indicate that she appreciated it. This is reflected in her describing her own capacity to be firm, and in a sense, maintain boundaries and limits, and in her feeling good about something she had done. Here, she quickly introjects the good qualities of your intervention and uses them to reinforce some of her own more constructive functioning. Actually, when an intervention has mixed qualities, both sound and unsound, the patient's response to it will characteristically include both constructive and nonconstructive qualities.

So, on this positive note, we will conclude for today. I look forward to hearing more next week.

Chapter 9

A MAJOR INTERACTIONAL SYNDROME

INTERACTIONAL SYMPTOMS AND RESISTANCES • THE THERAPIST'S INTERVENTIONS AS PRODUCTS OF THE BIPERSONAL FIELD • ATTEMPTS TO RESOLVE A MISALLIANCE • THE THERAPIST'S ATTEMPTS TO DRIVE THE PATIENT CRAZY • THE ADAPTIVE AND MALADAPTIVE ASPECTS OF THE THERAPIST'S CONTAINING FUNCTIONS • PSYCHOSOMATIC SYMPTOMS AND CONTAINING FUNCTIONS

L: We will be continuing with the patient who was presented to us in the last two seminars, and we will pick up the material in the session last reported to us. I suggest that we get directly to the clinical material.

T: What had happened was that for the first time there had been a confirmation of the fact that she was concerned about my talking about her outside the sessions. Well, the session began . . . She came in and said that there were some friends and relatives of hers who had been talking behind her back and that it disturbed her that they did this. Also, they really didn't understand her even after knowing her for so long. They didn't understand her if they could say behind her back that she was too much of a city girl for this boyfriend who was kind of a country hick. (Laughter.)

L: Well, I guess that hurts a little—she certainly has picked up your rural accent.

But, to turn to more serious matters, you may remember our discussion of the first part of this session at our last meeting. To orient us again, notice the rapidity with which the patient develops several important themes—related to people not understanding her and talking behind her back, and to her relationship with her present boyfriend—all themes with which we are familiar. And so, once again, the basic tenet that when the framework is an unresolved issue, the patient will come back to it again and again, most usually in some disguised form, is quickly borne out. The patient is concerned with not being understood—the problem of sound and neutral interventions; with people talking behind her back—the problem of confidentiality; and with her boyfriend—the issue of the third party to her therapy. So, she has rather quickly returned to some very basic unfinished business —the reestablishment of a sound frame for her treatment. Let us see the extent to which this does indeed prove to be important in the material that follows. Was this the beginning of the session?

T: Yes, this is the beginning of the session.

L: Did your intervention come after this material?

T: Yes, my intervention followed this and a bit more. Actually, she first went on to say that they had told her that she really shouldn't be associating with somebody who wasn't a city type, and that she felt this as an insult because what she wanted to do was to live in the country and raise horses; and so she felt that they really didn't understand her at all.

It was here that I said, You've been talking about people in New Jersey talking behind your back. Also, in the past, you've talked about your sister and your mother talking behind your back. I wonder if in fact you might also be worried about what I might be saying behind your back?

And then she went on and said, I only wonder about what people say behind my back if they mean something to me. And she talked then about these two instances: one where she told her ex-boyfriend that she didn't want to make love with him, and the second when she was on a date with, I guess a new boyfriend, but anyway a different guy, and she didn't want to stay out any longer on the date. She said she wouldn't have been able to do that before; that she was finally being herself; that she didn't care what Billy, or her friends, or other people thought as long as she felt progress was being made. And she did feel that progress was being made in our sessions.

And then she said, So much for the good.

She went on to say that she had a suit—a law suit—with a hypnotist related to this chest pain and . . . First, here's a little background information: she had gone into the hospital with a hysterical . . . well, a paralysis of the left arm, and a hypnotist was called in to evaluate whether this was an organic illness. And she was consciously faking the paralyzed arm so that . . .

L: This is all background, it didn't come up in the session . . . ?

T: Right. She faked this arm so that the doctors would evaluate her chest and abdominal pain; she was really concerned about that. But anyway, he saw her twice and then charged her something like $150 for the two consultations, and one of them was just to tell her that she couldn't afford his fees. And since then, he has brought suit to get this money from her.

Anyway, in this session she said that the court rulings, which this referred to, went against her. She had more bills to pay, and these were realities; these were also realities, besides her ability to tell these two fellows what was on her mind. She wondered if she'd been concentrating too much on one aspect and neglecting other aspects. There were parts of her life that involved problems that remained as great as they did before.

L: Yes, what she does is interesting: she splits you up again; she splits your image and communications into the good and bad. The good she identifies inside of you and the bad she splits off—here onto the bad hypnotist who overcharged her. And she apparently does that in order to maintain a loving image of you, because she has this fantasy of marrying you and going off to your farm, to raise horses and things like that.

Actually she initially condenses you with the boyfriend through the reference to the quality of the country hick. Once again, this hints at her own unconscious erotic fantasies toward you, and in addition, at her unconscious perceptions of your seductiveness. Later in her associations, this is expressed on a somewhat different and probably more primitive level, through the reference to the hypnotist. There the imagery has to do with fusion and surrender, and includes a sense of failure and anger, so that the quality of the communications soon shifts back to that of an inappropriate and destructive therapist.

Now this is based partly on the fact that your intervention had both good and bad qualities, because of its relevance and yet its incompleteness and the prematurity of its timing. I think that the patient is also experiencing you as both a kindly and dedicated therapist, and as someone who is having significant inner difficulties—especially in regard to offering her the specific interpretations that she so very much needs.

And while she does split off and disguise some of her positive and erotic fantasies about you, such as the marriage fantasies, she even more intensely splits off her negative and destructive images of you. In the face of this destructiveness, she tries to preserve your good qualities and in a sense, she tries even to protect them. But then your destructiveness comes to mind and spoils her moments of pleasure—which had, again, some qualities of manic defensiveness—and we hear next about this charlatan-hypnotist who charged her for doing absolutely nothing.

Now, she too is faking things and so we hear of a misalliance in which there is mutual deception, and this once again is so unconsciously perceptive and, on one level, really—and I'm sorry to say this—reflects what has been going on here. So again we hear of the blackness and the disillusionment, and even of the ultimate dishonesty of the therapist who puts his own problems into a therapeutic relationship and who is unable to be significantly helpful in an interpretive manner.

And I stress again the specific means through which the therapist can be helpful, because I think it is very evident that you are a kindly person and that you are trying to the best of your ability to be helpful to her. And as I said, I think that she knows this, and that is why I believe that this material indicates exquisitely the patient's ultimate reaction to a therapist who attempts to be supportive while he is unable to intervene properly, not only out of ignorance, but also out of a variety of countertransference difficulties. This is not the kind of help that the patient wants, and ultimately, with a significant grain of truth, the patient sees this as defrauding her.

Now here again we may be seeing an aspect of the intrapsychic elaboration of an unconscious perception—in the patient's indicating that she had been behaving fraudulently. She may be implying that she deserves to be ill treated. But you'll notice something else, her deceptive behavior was a response to what she had perceived to be inadequate medical care and it was an act of desperation. Of course, we are not in a position to know the extent to which this is a valid perception, or the extent to which it is essentially a distortion of her picture of her doctor. It is here that we need more material in order to establish the validity of her perception—an important step in sorting out unconscious perceptions from unconscious fantasies. There is also contained here an intense appeal for help—for a proper diagnosis or tuning in on her problems, and for some type of medical care that will properly alleviate her symptoms.

Now undoubtedly, on some level, a division of you into good and bad reflects aspects of her own inner objects—her introjects. But you see again how reality mixes with fantasy, and how conscious and unconscious perception mixes with unconscious fantasy and introject. And the influence of actuality on her intrapsychic processes is brought out again when we recognize that this is the first time in these sessions that we have heard any clear-cut indication of positive perceptions and fantasies within this patient, related to yourself. It is no coincidence that this occurred after an attempt to offer an adequate interpretation and, in fact, if I remember correctly, we saw hints of such positive imagery before, at the time you had made your first neutral intervention. So once again, when we follow the sequence of events, we see the extent to which conscious and unconscious realistic perceptions generate introjective identifications, mobilize responses within the patient, and stir up related intrapsychic fantasies and introjects.

So she goes from the good to the bad, and she especially displaces the negative fantasies, which is rather characteristic of patients. And we see again, that the formulation of a central adaptive context for the patient's associations and reactions, as related to the continued concern with the damage to the framework, enables us to deeply and significantly organize this material in a meaningful way.

And you can also see how, depending on ongoing realities and the like, the patient will find one or another means of conveying her continued unconscious fantasies, perceptions, and concerns to you. Here you see something of a patient's effort to find mediums of expression, the materials through which she can communicate to you. And as I said before, if reality does not lend a hand, she will create a dream or a fantasy, so long as she is endeavoring unconsciously to communicate meaningfully. And we see that this patient is indeed making such efforts, and we can see how intense they are. And so it is because of this that the theme of destructive professionals returns, and you'll notice that it now appears in a form that indicates more clearly than before the destructiveness of the professionals involved.

Listening to this material also brings up a number of other more general thoughts. For example, the feeling that people are talking behind her back reflects an extremely common theme heard in clinics. We have an added element in that the therapist is seeing this patient's boyfriend which certainly brings it very much to the fore, but again, this is a paranoid fantasy of the field. It occurs within the patient, but the therapist contributes to it significantly and so does the clinic. Clinic settings are notorious for revealing names of patients and other facts. There are secretaries calling out names, charts and reports on the desks of secretaries and therapists, and even the mention of supervisory personnel—let alone the patient's own awareness of them. There are tremendous amounts of leakage and there is little doubt that even in the best run clinic, unless the therapist can in actuality assure the patient of total confidentiality, there is a significant modification in the framework—especially in the basic need for a one-to-one relationship with total confidentiality. And as a result, the basic therapeutic hold and container are somewhat impaired, and this will limit the therapeutic accomplishments.

Now, as I have been talking, I have been thinking about this patient and the various modifications of the framework that she is attempting to work over. My thoughts turn again to that intervention about her coming back with a broken heart—the one that reflected the intensity of the therapist's overidentification with her. And in her own way, she has found a remarkable means of returning to that issue, by talking about this hypnotist. Certainly, we are once again faced with some of her own unconscious fantasies and longings, but we are also seeing striking condensations with some valid unconscious perceptions of the therapist.

And there is really an unconscious interpretation for the therapist contained in these associations, among its many other implications. After all, she talks about someone who has decided to be a hypnotist and who goes about, hopefully for sublimated and therapeutic reasons, merging and fusing with his patients, and momentarily modifying the self-object boundaries between himself and his patient. And in a way, of course, this is a model of overidentification and it conveys the patient's indications to the therapist that this reflects in him some need to merge with her.

Now again, I'll continue to stress that I'm not attempting to indicate that this is the only meaning of these associations, because there can be no doubt that they also reflect very important aspects of this patient's needs and pathology. But once more, I want to emphasize those aspects of the associations that have been overlooked by others, and it is these very aspects that have to be both rectified and interpreted before we can get to the patient's own nucleus of pathology.

And I hope that you can see by now that it is no coincidence that the patient found this very exquisite way of communicating this condensation of unconscious perceptions and fantasies, and that it is no coincidence that this material reflects her unconscious perceptions and working over of the therapist's need to inappropriately overidentify with her. So again, this patient is attempting to modify the misalliance between herself and the therapist—you'll notice that she did not cooperate with the hypnotist. And she is again, in her own simple way, reminding the therapist that misalliances and the imposition of countertransference difficulties into her therapy are actually quite destructive.

Now we can also see that the patient not only divides

up her image of the therapist, but that she, to some extent, is doing this with herself. She accepts into her self-image some of the good things she has done lately, basing them as we have seen on a positive introjective identification with the helpful aspects of her present therapist. And she is displacing some of her own badness and destructiveness onto the hypnotist, and may even be projectively identifying some of her own destructive and sick inner contents into him. In addition, this aspect of her self-image, however unconscious, is based on a negative introjective identification of the inappropriate qualities of the therapist's intervention and behaviors.

You will remember too that whenever a patient talks about unfinished business, and with not dealing with important problems, you should take this as a signal that possibly something is not being properly understood and analyzed within the therapeutic situation, and you should attempt to reassess the interaction and the nature of your understanding and interventions. Such a communication need not always be based on a valid unconscious perception of difficulties in the therapeutic interaction, but it quite often turns out to be the case. So, there is a great deal of therapeutic work yet to be done here.

T: By the way, this session occurred after we had already begun to discuss some of the problems in her therapy here.

But here, I said to her that there was another reality, namely that her boyfriend Bill—I'll call him Bill—was in therapy with me. And I said that I wondered if there was any connection between her feelings about people talking about her and Bill being in treatment with me.

L: Now, this comes under the heading of unbearable pressures from supervision—from my discussion of this therapy. How could I have been so stupid for so long, and I'd better change very fast. That is, the correct way to deal with an area that you feel you've neglected is to sit back and wait for the material from the patient. All you have to do is tell her that you've been wondering about the treatment situation—or even think about it to yourself—and she'll suddenly tell you more about it than you ever dreamed was in her little mind.

So, you are in the right area, and I gather that she had already mentioned in passing something about this boyfriend, Bill. And it will help her if you are beginning to recognize where the problem lies, although you do it rather suddenly and without allowing the derivatives to build. If you begin to have faith in your patient's need to communicate to you, and if you develop the capacity to recognize the crucial adaptive context, you will learn that the patient will put into you the good interpretations that you have to make to her. She does this unconsciously, in order to have you process them toward consciousness and intervene.

Now, while I would have strongly preferred continued silence on your part, if you had decided to speak, you might have said something more like this to her: You seem to be feeling some kind of inner strength and are bringing up the question of mistrust in your relationship with other people and especially with men. While you are talking about how you feel that you're getting stronger from treatment, and have better controls and all, you are also moving on to some very unpleasant things about therapists who have been destructive. So in a way, you seem to be dividing up your image of me and you seem to be saying, even though you don't want to put it more directly, that you feel that there is also something destructive that I'm doing. What comes to mind about it?

You see, in this way you are working at the level of the patient's associations and not introducing too much from yourself. This is a good example of what happens when you become convinced that a supervisor is right, and it also occurs at times when you suddenly recognize a major blind spot. You want to avoid intervening too quickly, and by delaying in this way, you have the opportunity to subject your revised formulation to the crucial validating process. You don't want to reach the point where she comes in and says, Good morning, and you say, Good morning, Bill's in treatment with me and what have you been thinking about it? Yes, she'll have something to say about it because the intervention is long overdue, but if you develop this theme out of current derivatives, she will have a different kind of experience. Otherwise, what you're saying to her is, You know, it just suddenly occurred to me out of the fog that I've been in all these months that there is something crazy going on in here. This has a different kind of impact than a more measured intervention.

And one last point: once again, you did not make use of the specific associations from this patient. This is a very crucial technical point in that, having chosen to intervene, you should build your intervention from the available material from the patient. Use her medium; use her communicative productions; and be as specific as possible. Here, the crucial communications related to the hypnotist are omitted, and we can rightfully suspect that there is a countertransference contribution to this oversight. After all, it is here that she most vividly conveys some very negative and hurtful perceptions—and probably fantasies as well—of you, and we can sense something dynamic about your avoidance of them.

So you can see again that it takes a relatively unencumbered therapist to make full use of what the patient puts into the bipersonal field and into him. Otherwise, you generate a new misalliance with her by sharing the displacement. The two of you agree that the bad doctors are out there, and the good doctors are in here; and you decide that this is a very nice way to put things and attempt to keep it that way. As a result, you have a bastion of the bipersonal field and a subtle undermining of the entire therapeutic qualities of the field.

You look a bit puzzled, so let me attempt to clarify.
What I'm trying to stress is that the therapist attempts
to deal with the material at the level at which the patient
has presented it in the session at hand. The therapist
should follow the patient, and not feel a need to introduce too much from himself. Of course, an interpretation
always includes a contribution from the therapist, but
even that is shaped by the patient. I think that here it
would have been sufficient initially to recognize that the
patient is bringing up the whole issue of good and bad
therapists—helpful and destructive treatments—and to
point out that this is on the patient's mind. This could be
justified here because the therapist has been avoiding
this subject and he's known about it from previous sessions. This is a rather simple confrontation—a repetition
of what the patient is talking about. There's no effort
here at interpretation for the moment; nothing unconscious is being made conscious.

In contrast, the intervention that I suggested earlier
included an interpretive component in showing the patient that unconsciously she is dividing up her image of
the therapist. But even a simple confrontation would implicitly convey to the patient that the therapist is prepared to listen to more material in this area. And hopefully the patient would then go on to say something about
her conscious thoughts about the therapy and therapist,
and then go on to indirect associations that would give us
her unconscious fantasies and perceptions.

So here, I am stressing the nonverbal components of
the therapist's interventions. An intervention is a product
of the bipersonal field; it's built out of the material from
the patient and the subjective reactions and perceptions
of the therapist. And it has an effect on this field. An intervention in which the therapist now says, Look, let's
talk about our relationship, opens up that bastion, that
misalliance, that area which has been defensively sealed
off as relatively forbidden, as an area that the two of

them should not be talking about. The therapist now opens that up, and reestablishes free communication in the field.

And in terms of his containing function, the therapist is saying to the patient, Look, I'm willing to allow you to put this material into the field and into me, and I'm prepared to deal with it. Besides, I will contain my own pathology and will not put it excessively into you.

So, once again I'm stressing that in addition to the verbal contents of your intervention and its cognitive effects, there are important implicit and nonverbal communications that are very relevant to the therapeutic interaction and to the functions of the bipersonal field. Please continue.

T: She said that Bill was not important; why should she care? I was the one who was important, and that it was my problem that I was bringing it up now. It didn't bother her in the least.

L: And you said, No it's not my problem; it's Dr. Langs' problem. Have I told you about him? Of course, we must see what follows, but you presented all of this in a way that played into her use of denial. And notice the extent of her denial. Can you imagine somebody saying that it's not important to her that her boyfriend is in treatment with her therapist? But, if you bring it up out of nowhere, you then enable her to initially utilize the denial.

T: I can see that.

L: You offer her something that she can deny. See how you set it up? Now, we'll just continue to listen; the last word isn't in. She's saying you're wrong and that you've got this terrible problem. I'd say that was true before, but it is less true now. Her conscious perception has a basis, but there is a significant element of distortion and defense.

Patients will characteristically deny that they are consciously concerned about the boundaries. And I think that this has fooled a lot of therapists and analysts. And it has produced a number of papers in this area that are basically related to manifest observations, without listening to latent content, so that therapists have come to think that modifications in the boundaries can be helpful in nonemergency—or even emergency—situations, and they have not listened to the patient's indirect communications. So in a way I welcome this patient's denial because we'll see if it holds up in her subsequent material.

But I also want to use this sequence in a second way. As I said before, to the extent that the therapist has indeed intervened prematurely, he has contributed to the patient's denial. So once again, we find it helpful to treat a defense that appears in the patient as a phenomenon of the bipersonal field. By doing this, we recognize that therapeutic efforts must not only be directed toward the patient, but toward the therapist as well. And we see that the therapist is trying to open up this particular area related to the therapeutic relationship, but that his timing indicates a certain amount of reluctance. And the patient once again lets us know that this is the case and as a result, for the moment, the bastion is not resolved.

While we will still await what follows before making a final decision, you can see how this patient, with her own needs for denial, unconsciously exploits the therapist's own uncertainties and needs for defense. And I think by now you have come to realize that this relates to a very basic therapeutic principle: that every defense and resistance that appears in the course of a therapeutic interaction should be treated, on one level, as a product of the bipersonal field, and that the therapist should scrutinize himself and his recent work with the patient, in an effort to detect any contribution that he has made to the patient's defensiveness. And similarly, when the therapist finds himself with a blind spot in resisting the exploration of a particular area, he can look to the patient's contributions to his own difficulties. You will find in these ideas the key to the resolution of many resistances within the patient; often they are unconsciously fed by the therapist and cannot be modified until his contribution is rectified and subsequently interpreted. Remember again that these actualities within the bipersonal field and therapeutic interaction call for both rectification and interpretation.

I think that this approach offers a much more realistic picture of what is actually going on between the patient and the therapist. It brings the therapist fully into the therapeutic interaction and acknowledges that this is the case. And it allows us to understand the contribution from the therapist to the patient's difficulties, as much as to the patient's cure, because the therapist is deeply involved in both. And it leads us to the important task of locating the interface of the therapeutic interaction, and detecting the intensity of the vectors from each participant.

For example, it would appear to me that the interface here is somewhere in the middle of this bipersonal field, and that it derives significant contributions from both the patient and the therapist. So we have here an excellent example of an interactional resistance, and an opportunity to understand the intrapsychic contributions from the patient, as well as the interactional elements that have derived from both the patient and the therapist. We can only assume for the moment intrapsychic contribution from the therapist—he has not revealed sufficient derivatives of his unconscious fantasies—though this is what the classical study of countertransference has tended to focus on.

But the point to be stressed is that the bipersonal field concept includes both interactional and intrapsychic components; neither one nor the other is excluded. There are many analysts who have studied the therapeutic interaction, but have excluded the intrapsychic components or have viewed them solely in terms of primitive intrapsychic mechanisms. Unfortunately too many other analysts have studied the intrapsychic components within the patient, but have tended to neglect the interactional dimension. We need a complete conceptualization, and it is my belief that the bipersonal field approach offers such a vehicle. And I would add, offhand, that until now, it is Searles (1965) who has come closest to this kind of approach, basing it on a study of what he called the interpersonal and intrapsychic realms.

So, now let us see what follows this patient's denial. While we must be prepared to find some valid core in her negation, we are entitled to be equally prepared for indirect communications that undermine and contradict this denial. In the meantime, too, we will be scrutinizing the basis on which we made such an intervention, or felt that it had valid aspects, in an effort to verify what has been said. In all, we are once again subjecting an intervention to the validating process, through a study of the therapist's subsequent considerations and the patient's additional associations.

T: All right. She said that I had promised her confidentiality and that if it wasn't so, she would sue me for $350,000, and that . . .

L: That's an interesting number . . . (Laughter.)

T: Well—I said, $350,000? And she said, That's the amount that that guy was sued for, and Bill said I should sue you for that much.

L: Parenthetically, for those of you who are not familiar with the situation, some months earlier a psychiatrist had been sued for damages by a patient who claimed that the psychiatrist had had sexual relations with her on a number of occasions; and the jury found him guilty as charged and awarded her a sum to that amount.

But notice that the patient is implicitly undoing her denial with this first additional association. While not explicitly reversing herself, she shows that thoughts of suing the therapist have been on her mind, and that un-conscious perceptions related to his sexual abuse of her on some level, and to his sexual conflicts, have also been on her mind. And once again, I would not simply accept this as a communication of an unconscious perception, without recognizing the manner in which it offers clues regarding her own need for the denial and for her need to accept the presence of the third person—the boyfriend—into the treatment situation. You can see that the boy-friend protects her from the therapist and that because of this, she denies any concern. This is another reason for the denial. So her associations continue, and they be-gin to illuminate the unconscious motives for her partic-ular defense.

T: She said, I told him that he was sick, that he had a sick mind, and that's what it's at now. And then she asked what I thought. At which point I didn't say anything. She said that she thought that he had a thing with au-thority, that he wanted to break therapists down—any authority figure, whoever it was. She felt superior to him; he had been in the hospital four different times and he'd probably be there again. And his friends were also quite sick, she felt. She'd been in the hospital only once, and she felt she wouldn't be back in the hospital again, and that it was a mistake for her to have gone in the first place. Then she went on, she said that she knew that it was my problem. That she thought that the problem might arise that Bill would need private treatment. And then again it would really be my problem.

And I said, You in fact said that he wasn't doing very well now, and, Yes, I do feel that it's important for me to see him privately—in individual sessions—right now because I think that he is having some difficulties. And I told her that I felt the difficulty in maintaining con-fidentiality with both of them in treatment . . . that I found it hard to maintain confidentiality for both of them, and that it presented a problem right now because

I would like to see him in individual sessions.

L: Is that where you stopped?

T: Yes.

D: What are the arrangements right now?

T: Well, I am seeing him individually at present because he
      is in an emergency type of situation . . .

L: Look, first of all, it is well to realize that there are motives
      on every conceivable level for her wishing to have the
      threesome. She describes one; let's just identify it. Why
      does it gratify and serve her for you to treat them both?
      What did she just say?

D: He's the one who has the need to put down the thera-
      pist—not her. So she maintains herself by splitting off
      the bad things to the outside, while the good things are
      in her and in here.

L: That's part of it. What else?

D: The thing about the psychiatrist who was sued. This goes
      along with something we had hypothesized before: that
      she needs a third party for protection.

L: All right, so we have that. What else? (Pause.) That allu-
      sion again shows the unconscious sexualization of thera-
      py for her, and reflects her speculations about you. She
      says more though. First of all, Bill expresses the aggres-
      sion, not her—again she can deny it. She can dump or
      put all of her hostility toward you into him, and never
      have to deal with her own anger at you. She never will
      analyze these hostile feelings and fantasies as long as he's
      involved. That's number one. And number two, she says,
      He's crazy; I'm not. I was hospitalized by mistake; not
      him, he's going to go back. Thanks to you, good doctor,
      you're so great, he's going to be rehospitalized. She can
      dump her craziness into him too. And as a result, she
      feels good—superior; she has her framework cure. This
      is why she wants the threesome.
            Now, what happens next? She says that confidentiality

would only be a problem if you were seeing him privately, by which she means in individual sessions. We all heard what the therapist then said; will someone please comment perceptively? Would you read your intervention again?

T: That one, specifically?

L: Yes, your intervention. Do you want to fake it? (Laughter.) You want to change it now? Well, you can read the original intervention and then tell us the one you would like to offer now.

T: I just want to say that if you are going to address yourself to that, it certainly will be a problem for me to maintain confidentiality when . . .

L: Now, I would suggest that you not attempt to outguess me, because you're only half way there . . .

T: Well, I do know that this is a problem for me and that you said that Bill probably wasn't doing very well now. That is true, and it presents a problem in that I want to see him for individual sessions right now. And it will be difficult for me to maintain confidentiality for both.

D: I think what struck me immediately was that what the therapist was saying is . . . The confidentiality is not going to remain intact . . .

L: If I see him, it won't remain intact. What else strikes you?

D: He's also denying, going along with her denial of her craziness and reinforcing the defense. He is saying that Bill's crazy, you're not; that's why I'm seeing him individually.

L: That's one level, which is true. He is saying by implication, Yes, you have a very sick boyfriend and I'd like to see him individually. What else is he doing? The issue is related to confidentiality; what is the therapist doing in that area? What's implied in his intervention?

D: He's telling her that he's having difficulty managing the situation.

L: Well, yes, that's something else—in terms of his anonymity and his containing functions. You are now telling her you have a problem maintaining the boundaries and in doing therapy—which she already knew earlier in the session. But what else is he doing about confidentiality?

D: He's telling her very openly that it cannot be maintained any more.

L: Yes, but he's doing something else. It's so important to hear it.

D: He's breaking it.

L: How?

D: By telling her what he's doing with the boyfriend.

L: Exactly! That's the point. He said to her, I want to see him individually; he is having some difficulty. That's a violation of the confidentiality of his treatment.

D: I said he was troubled about confidentiality.

L: Yes, he said that he wouldn't be able to maintain confidentiality if he saw them both privately. That's one thing. But I'm talking about the statement: I want to see him individually; he is having difficulty. That is a confidence related to his treatment, and you shared it with her. At the very time you're talking about maintaining confidentiality, you violated it. Also, you pretty much implied that you were having some special difficulties with him; that is also a violation of the confidentiality of the other treatment. Now, that's very important to realize. And you're puzzled by it. What's puzzling you?

T: Well, I won't even bring in the fact that there are other supervisors involved with this who suggested that approach. But I really looked at it as important for her to know that this had to be discussed with him, and that I had talked to him about it individually.

L: Okay, so you felt it was important for her to know something about his treatment; that it was important to her that you violate the confidentiality of his treatment.

T: Yes, yes.

L: Perhaps it's beginning to dawn on you that if you violate the confidentiality of his therapy, then there will be the inevitable question of what you will do with her treatment. And in the meantime, you are attempting to help her to explore a sickness that she has. You call it something like paranoia, and you want to indicate that it works in the following way: she has these crazy ideas that people are talking about her and these distortions cause her a great deal of grief. And you want to tell her that she has the nerve to think that you might do something like that. And there is the fact that you are actually doing something like that, so . . .

   Of course, you realize that what I'm getting at is that her internal reality, however distorted, once again corresponds to a disturbance in outer reality. And once more, you have put a piece of pathology into the bipersonal field, and you have, through your self-revelation, modified the framework not only of Bill's therapy, but also of her own treatment.

D: Are you saying that you would not do something like that?

L: Yes, that is exactly what I'm saying. I would never do anything at all like that. Look at how it sounds: By the way, do you know what I've been doing with your boyfriend's treatment?—Well, let me tell you. And he's paranoid too; he thinks that I talk about this therapy. (Laughter.) You know, it's a crazy world we live in.

   All right. This is how the therapist can drive his patient crazy. At the very moment that you're trying to interpret to her that she has a distorted fantasy, you are secretly confirming that very fantasy and indicating that it's a reality. The contradiction is maddening.

   As some of you may remember, I mentioned that Searles (1959) has written a paper on this very subject—

efforts to drive the other person crazy. As I said a while ago, he appears to be the analyst who is most in touch with the types of discoveries that I myself have made empirically, and he deserves full credit for them. I want to stress that even when it comes to efforts of this kind by the therapist to drive his patient crazy, I came to this empirically, although I knew exactly where to look for the literature once I had recognized the phenomena—that is, I turned immediately to Searles and found that he had indeed written a paper on the subject. I mention all this largely to stress the independent sources of these important formulations.

And here we see such an effort: on one level there is a communication directed toward establishing a sense of trust, and the framework related to confidentiality; on another level, the therapist almost immediately violates a tenet of confidentiality. This is of course a means through which he can create a double bind and convey totally contradictory messages to the patient. In addition, such a sequence of communication is designed to undermine her testing of inner and outer reality. The patient is without a sound anchor among these realities, and will experience an impossible conflict both within herself and the therapist. She will introject the therapist's craziness as well as experience some of her own. This is the road to a significant emotional disturbance and I don't at all mind using the phrase, driving the other person crazy, to describe such an interaction, since it gives us an opportunity to then specify some of the components of the experience. I think that you have once again created a significant modification in the framework, and are in the process of offering the patient a new version of the misalliance that the two of you have been sharing.

Your intervention shows us something else that is quite important. When the therapist is under the influence of a significant countertransference difficulty, based on a variety of unconscious fantasies, memories, and introjects, he will tend to express this pathology in his interventions. You can see that at the very moment you became aware of certain expressions of your countertransference difficulties and attempted to rectify them, you exposed these inner problems in a fresh way. This reminds us that there is really only one solution to the therapist's countertransference: self-analysis, insight, working through, and inner change. Failing that, he closes the hole in the dyke at one point only to immediately find another leak. This is inevitable.

Now, in the light of the advice that you have received from other supervisors, you can see why it really is not therapeutic to treat these things lightly or to think of them superficially. Your intervention is filled with unconscious and interactional meanings, and we have seen in the past that the patient is quick to unconsciously perceive them; she is deeply influenced by them. And notice too that once again you are unconsciously, and nearly consciously, asking this patient for help. And she will react to this aspect as well.

And you can also see how difficult it is when you are under countertransference pressures, to sit back and allow the patient's associations to unfold, and to utilize her communications constructively and synthesize the fragments and derivatives into an ultimately sound intervention, derived from the contents that she unconsciously puts into you. As a result, you have put her boyfriend's therapy into the bipersonal field that exists between you and her—again his presence is felt—and there are bound to be repercussions.

Now certainly all of this is overdetermined. There are, I realize, contributions from your supervisor and from me. There are also contributions from your own particular cognitive style of intervening and your efforts to find a manner of relating to this patient, and her cognitive style of communicating to you, so that there can be an effective therapeutic interaction. But it seems to me that it is crucial not to overlook the additional contributions from your countertransferences.

There is of course a continuum from an adaptive and personal mode of working with and communicating to your patients to those aspects that are maladaptive and reflect your own inner disturbances. And you can see how your own particular style of working may be distinctly different from that of a given patient, while with others it may complement the patient's mode of working quite well. The point here is to recognize that whatever your individual style, and this certainly is precious and should be preserved, so long as it is uncontrolled, it will consistently get you into difficulty. This is important for you to realize because you tend to reveal too much about yourself to your patient. It's fine to be natural, but when you learn that you're conveying far too many pathological unconscious fantasies that the patient will collect and misuse—and suffer from—you'll realize that you're not doing her a service. You have to modulate and rectify your style of working a bit further. You remember your comment, What have I been doing for three months? What you are saying now is a different and more intellectualized version of it.

Based on the patient's associations, it would appear, then, that you have an unconscious need to be a pathological container for this patient's sickness, and to accept her unconscious image of you as the sick one within the bipersonal field. It's almost as if you can't resist offering her the kind of misalliance cure that her boyfriend offers—permitting her to feel well and superior by experiencing and mastering your disturbance.

You may feel that I am making an extraordinary fuss over this intervention, particularly since it was suggested to you by a supervisor, but I do believe that we're going to see a major change in the tone of her communications now, and a renewed effort on her part to work over your sickness. And I cannot help but feel that there is something very crucial going on within yourself, when, at the very moment when you have cleared away some of your own pathological contributions to the bipersonal field and have reestablished the framework, that you have a need to undo these steps.

It appears that there is a great need for you to do some therapeutic work within yourself related to your anxieties with this patient and your own fears of a secured framework. Because of the importance of this point, let me put it still another way: at the very moment when we are beginning to focus on the patient's intrapsychic conflicts, defenses, and fantasies, you offer her an intervention that will immediately relieve the patient of her inner pressures and shift the focus back to yourself. So in this context, there appears to be an unconscious need on your part to utilize her therapy and this particular bipersonal field, to work out your own problems rather than those of the patient; you have shifted the interface again.

So this is going to be another crucial moment for this patient, who will immediately and unconsciously perceive your own confusion, craziness, your effort to drive her crazy, and in a sense, your unconscious efforts to make her paranoid. And I think that she will be frightened of you and maybe she will say in one way or another that she'd like to get back into the hospital, or, if aggravated to an extreme, develop symptoms that might necessitate hospitalization.

So you see how exquisite the interaction between yourself and the patient is, and the extent to which a comprehension of it can lead us to make predictions. Turning this around within the therapeutic situation, if you had been able to very quickly recognize what you had done, then, as her further associations unfolded, you would be in a position to rectify the trauma and reestablish and secure the framework. But you know, when we see a situation where every effort to secure the frame is rather quickly followed by its undoing, we do have to wonder whether it is feasible for you to create a therapeutic bipersonal field with this patient. I am sorry to take it this far, but I do believe that the material points to such a question.

Please continue, and this time I would hope that you won't leave things out, such as you did toward the end of our last seminar. I really don't remember your mentioning the country boy routine. (Laughter.) You can see how significant seemingly innocuous associations can be, and you all might as well learn this from the beginning: you really can't conceal your unconscious from your patients or from sensitive supervisors—that's the nature of this work. So you may consciously or unconsciously omit some aspect of your interaction, but we will pick it up somewhere else anyhow. Okay; please continue now.

T: She said that she had had confidence in me when she came into the sessions, that she trusted me and that I was special to her because she could trust me. She asked, Isn't that important for me? Or should it be as it was with me in the past, that when I've trusted someone, I become vulnerable—and then become hurt? Now she isn't sure that she trusts me since I've brought this up to talk about.

L: And you thought this came up just because of your surface question. Now she doesn't know if she can trust you; she's known that all along. She can't trust you; she really can't. So the idea that she's trusted you all along is . . . Well, this girl uses so much denial that it just fits in beautifully with your own defenses and needs. And now that you've made this new hurtful intervention, she will consciously begin to question her feelings about you. That's one way of getting material, but it's not the way you really want to do it. But we must wait for more material; much of this is well rationalized—and projected—for the moment.

D: Could you have predicted that there would be such immediate conscious expression of this?

L: It's difficult to predict the level at which these communications will appear, and the extent to which the patient will utilize disguised derivatives, or express herself more directly. I hope that you're impressed with the fact that this is a conscious expression, even though it is well defended. However, I am looking for a much clearer form of confirmation, and will be patient until we hear more material. I think that these thoughts are becoming conscious within this patient because of the sensitive areas to which they relate, and because of the therapist's repeated problem in this regard.

T: That's the end of the session.

L: So it ends on a note of her trusting you and her concerns about being hurt, and her feelings that she trusts you less. Let's move on to the next session at this point. These are good summaries and I expect that there will be more for us to deal with.

T: The next two sessions have choice segments.

L: Please—no advance notices.

T: She began by saying that she wanted to finish the discussion that she had started last . . . Oh, first of all, she was sick the remainder of the week, and missed the second session of that week.

L: Another, Oh by the way. Please, first things first . . . (Laughter.) It's so important to have the specific sequence.

T: Well, she had not come to that session.

L: So, she had been sick. It's really very important to observe the conditions under which your patients get sick. They will stay healthy when they are well mothered by their therapists—within certain limits of course. But here we see that the mothering has been damaged repeatedly by this therapist, and she gets sick.

Now, I want to take this observation, even before we

hear some material from the patient, and develop it a bit further. It relates to a hypothesis that I have discussed briefly with you before, namely that the containing functions of the framework and of the therapist contribute to the patient's capacity to deal with his intrapsychic problems on a psychological level, without a significant spill-over into the somatic realm.

Many analysts and therapists have observed that their analysands seldom become physically ill during the course of treatment, and most have thought of this in terms of the basic and implicit nurturing and mothering functions of the therapist or analyst. I want to stress here that by this I do not mean explicit and direct efforts to behave in a mothering or supportive manner; I am alluding instead to the analyst's and therapist's basic stance of maintaining the ground rules and boundaries, and in offering the patient a proper and sound therapeutic hold.

What I am adding here is my impression that this holding function of the therapist, reinforced by a secure maintenance of the framework, offers the patient an opportunity to put aspects of his inner disturbance into the bipersonal field and into the therapist, and to safely work over his intrapsychic disturbances within such a setting. And it is this containing function of the therapist and therapeutic setting—and here, the therapist is functioning as a living part of the framework—that is, in addition, silently introjected by the patient, thereby serving to reinforce his own containing capacities. In a way, I am elaborating upon the concept that the framework offers the patient an external structure and matrix through which his own ego development can be resumed and enhanced.

Here, I am adding that one aspect of this ego development is related to the patient's containing and controlling functions, which are also reinforced through introjective processes related to the therapist's handling of the framework. However, I think that you can see that this has wider implications, because physical illness is not inherently an issue of control, but relates to the working over of intrapsychic conflicts within the psychic realm as contrasted to spill-overs into physical sphere. And it may well be that it is because this therapist has been having difficulty in offering this patient a secure framework, and in offering himself as a healthy container for the patient's inner pathology, that the interaction has in some way weakened the patient's own containing functions and her ego capacities to manage her intrapsychic conflicts and other inner difficulties. The sequence is such that physical symptoms may also relate to a mounting sense of depression within this patient, but I do believe that the pathology in the containing functions of both the patient and therapist may well play an important role in this illness—and in her depression as well.

Now, I am well aware that I am assuming that the patient's illness occurred largely because of the disruptions in the holding and containing functions of the therapist, and the damage to the framework of the bipersonal field. And the material may or may not bear me out; we shall see. Physical illness may however be another implicit way in which the patient directs the therapist's attention to the framework.

Now, whether this concept has general applicability to psychosomatic illnesses or not, I leave for you to explore. By extrapolation, for example, this thesis would suggest that patients who develop psychosomatic illnesses do so in part out of failures in the containing functions of their parents. Well, it comes up and I think it's worth thinking about and seeing if additional observations will bear it out.

In any case, this is an important area to study, particularly in regard to the therapeutic situation—we must learn more about the consequences of impairments in the containing functions of the therapist. And, after all, a break in confidentiality indicates that the therapist can-

not contain and hold within himself the contents of the
sessions with the boyfriend, including this boyfriend's
projective identifications into the therapist. There has
been spillage and in fact, the therapist's comments to
this patient indicate an awareness on his part of a need
to offer the boyfriend a more specific and selected, individual container. In a sense, the difficulty is being conceptualized in terms of individual versus group therapy,
while on this level, the problem appears to have a great
deal to do with difficulties that this therapist is having
in carrying out his various containing and holding functions with his patients.

I am quite aware that I am talking about the containing function in a number of different ways, and that actually I have involved you in a very complicated and unusual area of study. Actually, we need a great deal of
clinical research in order to conceptualize the implications of the therapist's containing functions, and its role
in psychotherapy and psychoanalysis. As you can see,
there are a number of dimensions. This therapist has
been unable to hold the contents of his other patient's
within himself, and to confine them to his interaction
with the boyfriend. He has been unable to contain the
craziness of the boyfriend; he's been unable to contain
the erotic transference and communications from this
patient; and he has been unable to contain his own erotic
countertransference and to manage it intrapsychically
without significant spill-over into his interaction with the
patient.

And as if this were not enough, there are other aspects
of the containing function with which this therapist has
had difficulty. This includes his inability to contain and
adequately process—containing implies processing at
some point—the projective identifications from each of
his patients and on another level, to offer a secure container in all of these ways.

So, this is quite a complicated area, but one that I think is basic to the development of the therapeutic relationship and interaction. And I am suggesting that the spillage into the somatic area may have been a function here of the therapist's difficulties in these various aspects of his containing functions. And please try to understand, I am not suggesting that this is the only factor in psychosomatic illness and that the patient's vicissitudes vis-a-vis her own containing functions do not play a role; clearly, psychosomatic illnesses, as is true for all psychophysiological and psychological disorders, are overdetermined. As you have gathered, I am making an effort in these seminars to stress aspects that have not been sufficiently considered in the past.

I have wandered a good bit, and I think that now is the time to return to the patient and to hear from her.

T: This is how she began: she wanted to finish the discussion that she started a week before. She was sick with a fever and she wanted to come in but . . . to finish this discussion, she said that she thought that this was my problem; that I had brought it up. She wanted to say a few things. That in reference to Bill, I had brought up this problem; that he meant nothing to her; that it could be anyone, not necessarily Bill; that she used his name because I happened to know him, but that then she referred to other people, for instance the people in New Jersey or her family, she didn't use their names; and, once more, that seeing him was my problem.

L: Notice, in line with my previous hypothesis of how patients come back again and again to the boundary problem when it's unresolved—and actually that's more of a clinical observation than a hypothesis—notice that this patient does indeed once again bring up this particular issue right at the beginning of the session. It's unfinished business. The fact that these are her first associations may lend some support to my suggestion that the damaged frame and hold were important factors in her getting a fever and missing the session. And notice too that she clarifies how the boyfriend is indeed the therapist's problem.

T: Secondly, she said that I was everything to her; that she trusted me completely; that they talk . . . that she . . . something about . . . she talked . . . she said something about talking about the relationship. I don't understand exactly what she said. Then something clicked with her, and it reminded her of relationships in the past where she had trusted men and they took advantage of her. And that was why she didn't like me to talk about the relationship between us. And I remember now what she referred to, what she meant by talking about the relationship: she was referring to us talking about me, talking about the relationship that we have . . . It upsets her. Here, I said to her that this has something to do with Bill and with my talking with him in individual sessions.

L: Now, before we get to the patient's response, let's formulate another aspect of this material. The patient is saying here that the situation regarding confidentiality is the therapist's problem, and that it disturbs her when the therapist talks about their relationship. And in a way, I think we can see in this additional evidence of an important phenomenon that I want to discuss a little bit; namely, that the therapist—and possibly with the advice of his supervisors who were involved in a similar mechanism—is dumping into the patient the problem that he is having in maintaining confidentiality under these circumstances. We know from the therapist's comments and the boyfriend's behavior that things aren't going very well in his treatment. We know nothing about the reasons for this, but as you would expect, my first hypothesis is that it has to do in a significant way with the modifications in the framework of his treatment. At least we know that the boyfriend has shown up twice at this patient's sessions, so he's made two major communications in this particular direction.

In any case, the treatment with the boyfriend is not going well; the therapist is having difficulty. He then brings this difficulty to the patient; he says that he wants to share this problem with her, and wishes to talk about it frankly. Freud (1912b) in one of his very early papers on technique, said that the rules that pertain in psychoanalysis—the way things happen in treatment—are different from what one would expect in ordinary life. And I think that too many analysts and therapists forget this very early piece of insight. So, in ordinary life, wanting to talk over something very candidly with a person who's involved in a particular problem makes a great deal of sense, and in ordinary life, sharing such an issue and discussing it frankly also makes sense. But the rules of psychotherapy are different. While therapists of all kinds forget this, patients never do—which is actually where these rules come from in the first place. These rules are not inherent to the therapist who in fact, struggles to adjust to them; they are inherent in the patient—they come from his needs. I think that over the years the basic rules of adult analytic technique, and their counterpart in the basic ground rules of psychotherapy, evolved into their present form because patients taught those therapists and analysts who were sufficiently sensitive, where the line should be drawn, where the boundaries should be established, and how the therapist could offer to the patient an optimal hold and container.

And I think that once again this patient is showing us the need for a proper framework for psychotherapy. Her response to the therapist's efforts to frankly discuss the problems that he's having in the boyfriend's treatment indicates her recognition that the therapist is having a problem and that he is trying to put it into her. So, once again, interactionally, the therapist's effort to convey to the patient something of his own difficulties is experienced by the patient as a projective identification, and of course, this is exactly what it is.

The therapist puts this problem into the patient, and asks her implicitly to work it over, and she is disturbed by it. She immediately feels that the therapist is taking advantage of her, and in terms of the conditions of the bipersonal field of psychotherapy, this is a valid unconscious perception. As I have said so often, the psychotherapeutic field is not the place where the therapist should put his problems, nor should he be asking the patient to assist him with them. It is for this reason that she feels taken advantage of, and is disturbed by what is happening. In this way, the patient indicates that she had to some extent introjected some of the disturbing qualities of the therapist's difficulties, while at the same time she appears to be rejecting aspects of his projective identifications into her. She does this last by saying that it is the therapist's problem and, in a sense, that he should work it out himself. From this you can see that the patient is not bound to accept the therapist's projective identifications, and that she will respond to them according to her own needs.

In this context, let me briefly review for you the concept of projective identification—hopefully, it will all sound clearer now. This process is an interactional mechanism and we must remember that it is not the same as projection. Projection is the process of attributing mental contents from within oneself to another person; it's an intrapsychic mechanism. The patient—or therapist—has the inner fantasy or belief that somebody else is experiencing something, and upon analysis, it turns out that actually he is the one who's experiencing it. Now, projections are often built from kernels of truth, but the essential experience is going on within the subject, and by-and-large is not occurring in the object. And a patient's projection may be told to the therapist—it may be communicated—that is still not a projective identification, although it may be at that point.

A projective identification is an interactional mechanism through which one attempts to put into the other person some set of contents, good or bad, and this can be done through a projection, though very often it is done through other means. Here for example, no projection is involved: the therapist is simply saying to the patient that he has a problem and he wants to tell the patient about it, to have her experience it and by implication, to have her work it over. In this instance you can also see that there is an attempt here at an evocation of a proxy, the kind of effort related to projective identification described by Wangh (1962). In effect, the therapist is attempting to evoke some type of response and functioning from the patient in the face of his own difficulties. Even if this is not his conscious intention, it is unconsciously conveyed to the patient. In his own way, the therapist is attempting to have the patient mobilize ego capacities that he lacks in dealing with the boyfriend, and it may well be that he has chosen this patient not only to assist himself, but also to become an assistant therapist for the boyfriend. Of course that becomes speculation, but I am attempting to show you the extensive repercussions of interactional mechanisms of this kind.

And notice too, in keeping with the continuum that I described earlier, from very primitive to sophisticated uses of projective identification and proxy evocations, that this particular example of these mechanisms is taking place in the presence of clear-cut self-object boundaries, and in the context of an object relationship that ranges somewhere from narcissistic to mature on the part of the therapist. In this particular instance, I think we are observing a pathological form of projective identification, in which the therapist has put some of his inner difficulties into the patient and into the bipersonal field, but we should remember that there are healthy and adaptive forms of these mechanisms as well.

Remember too that these efforts can entail the placing of both good and bad contents, and one may through such means put healthy functions and fantasies into the other person. In this context, you might remember that incident when the patient asked the therapist to kill the spider and he set it free. This behavior might be viewed as an effort on the part of the therapist to put into the patient certain forms of kindness and control of aggression, through which she might be able to master some aspects of her own destructiveness.

Parenthetically, projective identification by therapists into their patients is an extremely common mechanism, and most of the time it has important pathological components. In fact, it appears that the opportunities for the therapist to projectively identify his sickness into patients is an important unconscious motive for entering the profession. Special efforts have to be made to remain on the alert for inappropriate uses of this mechanism within the bipersonal field.

Here, the projective identifications of the therapist have to do with his difficulties in managing the problem of confidentiality, while on a deeper level, there is an implicit request that the patient assist the therapist with his unconscious sexual conflicts, and with his own difficulties in maintaining adequate boundaries with this young lady. There also seems to be some problem on his part in establishing sufficient separateness from her, and perhaps some difficulty also on a symbiotic level. And remember too that much of this culminated in this patient's illness, suggesting that pathological projective identifications can be a factor in such occurrences.

You know, it occurs to me that there might be a lot less confusion if we used the term *interactional projection* instead of "projective identification." There isn't time to elaborate—I'll leave that for another day. Here for the moment we have developed some hypotheses and the time has come for a search for validation. We'll get to that task after a ten minute break.

Chapter 10

TRANSFERENCE AND NONTRANSFERENCE IN PSYCHOTHERAPY

THE INTENSIFICATION OF AN INTERACTIONAL SYNDROME • ERRORS IN INTERVENING • THEIR FUNCTION AS PROJECTIVE IDENTIFICATIONS AND THE TECHNICAL PRINCIPLES RELATED TO THEIR MANAGEMENT • THE INTERACTIONAL DIMENSIONS OF THE THERAPIST'S COUNTERTRANSFERENCES • A SECOND POTENTIALLY CURATIVE DREAM • THE PATIENT'S UNCONSCIOUS CREATIVITY • RESPONSES TO A SECURED FRAMEWORK

L: Let's hear more about the session that you were describing.

T: I had just said to her that her mistrust of men and not wanting to talk about our relationship had something to do with my talking with Bill in individual sessions. She then said that he could be anyone with problems that she involved herself with.

L: Notice that comment—anyone with problems that she becomes involved with. That could readily apply to the therapist.

T: At this point I realized to myself that she never used the name of this guy in New Jersey, and . . . well, I'm kind of surprised, because it's here that she actually mentioned not using the name of the guy in New Jersey. In any case, I said, You want me to understand you, and a couple of sessions ago, I said that about you and the doctor. She shook her head vigorously when I told her that she felt that it showed that I understood her. But, I went on and said: The next session you described getting close to someone, your girlfriend's father, and he took advantage of you and made a pass at you. And you also spoke of the guy on your vacation who tried to rape you. So, for you, closeness implies seduction.

L: When you mentioned your comment regarding the doctor, she shook her head—that would be a no; nodding her head would be a yes.

T: Okay, she nodded her head.

L: An interesting slip. So—what about this intervention?

D: His intervention doesn't seem to have to do with the problem of confidentiality. After all, he had done something in talking about Bill, and then she missed a session; then she comes back and she's still talking about how she won't mention Bill and the names of the people in New Jersey. In other words, that's still the adaptive context on her mind. And this intervention does not include any reference to it.

L: What else is rather striking about this intervention?

D: It is a complete change of subject.

L: Which means it comes from where?

D: From supervision. (Laughter.)

L: Yes. Often enough the supervisee will try to put it into the supervisor. But in terms of the session with the patient and the therapist's responsibility to respond to the material from the patient and to the content of her associations, it is evident that for the moment this comes entirely from within the therapist. Granted that it is based on material from earlier sessions; for the moment it has no basis in the ongoing material from the patient. And for that reason, it sounds like a confessional.

It's as if the therapist is now telling the patient that the reason he needs to have other people around is because for him, closeness is tantamount to seduction. While it is couched in terms of an intervention related to difficulties within the patient, and while it even is derived from her earlier associations, at this moment this once again constitutes a projective identification into the patient.

And the main clue that this is indeed an erroneous intervention, and that it conveys aspects of the therapist's unconscious fantasies and anxieties, and that interactionally it is a further effort to put his specific sexual conflicts into the patient, is that the therapist shifted from the immediate problem related to the issue of confidentiality—the one that the patient was concerned about—to the earlier problem involving his erroneous interventions—the one that reflected his own pathological overidentification with the patient. And notice too, that the therapist selected the material related to the patient's sexual anxieties as her central response; and while this was certainly a large factor in her reactions, it was not the only component.

But the main point is that the therapist decides not to deal with the immediate adaptive context and problem with the framework, but shifts to an earlier one; this reflects his own preoccupation with this sector and his avoidance of the issue of the third party to therapy. In a sense, this implies that the therapist is willing to keep the boyfriend as a participant in the treatment and that he prefers to deal with other issues.

So, once again, we see that an erroneous intervention reveals a whole range of pathological unconscious fantasies and introjects that lie within the therapist, and that it constitutes as a rule an effort by the therapist at projective identification into the patient.

T: Well, in light of what we're talking about, I would have given a different interpretation to her . . . I mean in terms of . . .

D: In terms of breaking more boundaries related to confidentiality.

L: No, I don't think that this intervention can be viewed as
     a violation of confidentiality; the therapist does not con-
     sciously betray any aspect of the boyfriend's treatment
     and certainly, he is not consciously or directly offering
     the patient confidential information—even about him-
     self.

D: Isn't this a violation of anonymity?

L: It is important to recognize the extent to which a partic-
     ular ground rule has been modified, and the extent to
     which an intervention remains within the framework
     though it is essentially countertransference-based and re-
     flects unconscious self-revelations and pathogenic inter-
     actional mechanisms. In this sense, this intervention is
     not a violation of anonymity in the usual sense of the
     word, although if you wish to indicate that anonymity has
     to be maintained consciously and unconsciously, you
     might be able to say that it had been modified. I don't
     think that much is served by broadening the concept of
     anonymity in this way, and I think that we have a suf-
     ficient place for this type of intervention by identifying
     it as not coming from the material from the patient, and
     as therefore deriving from the intrapsychic conflicts of
     the therapist.
         In the context of this patient's associations to this
     point, you see a demonstration of something that is very
     basic in terms of technique; something that stresses the
     importance of listening to the material from the patient,
     of not being in such a rush, and of allowing the patient
     to help you to develop your interventions—to put them
     into you bit by bit. I think it shows you that the need for
     activity on the part of the therapist may come out of a
     countertransference sense of urgency, rather than from
     the needs of the patient. Again, this is not an attempt to
     suggest that the therapist should never intervene early in
     a session; it does stress the fact that he should have a de-
     finitive reason for doing so and that it should be shaped

by the patient's current associations. And from all of this, you can see just how much work the therapist has in establishing an adaptive context and in formulating the associations around that context. And this is not a brief for passivity or for becoming the silent therapist-analyst. I'm simply emphasizing that it's important to understand the material from the patient and to get the derivatives from her; then do the necessary job with it.

Instead, you step in so quickly. Here, she's saying, Look, he means nothing to me, I only mention his name because you know him. He's special. I never mention names; you're the only one that's important to me. All right. That's for openers. Now let's see where she goes from there. Let's formulate and attempt to validate; there's time. But suddenly you pop in with, You know, you felt close to me, and you felt it was like being raped and seduced by a dirty old man. Closeness is sexual, for you . . . Where does this come from? Now just imagine her sitting there. Here she was trying to set you straight about confidentiality; what's all this stuff about sex? What the hell is going on?

T: I see.

L: You know, I keep waiting for the shift to the patient's psychopathology, and for the interface of this bipersonal field to receive its most significant vector from the patient's inner problems. I would then give you my lecture on the patient's projective identifications into the therapist, and the ways in which this creates a special burden for the therapist and has a great deal to do with the anxiety-provoking and draining qualities of being a therapist or an analyst. That is another side of the therapist's motivation in becoming a psychiatrist—the wish to take in, contain, and work over the mental sickness of others. It is a wish that can be sublimated and brought under control in an adaptive manner, so that one becomes a creative therapist.

But we see here that this particular therapist is having a great deal of difficulty in accepting the material from the patient, and the pathology that she wishes to put into him. In fact, by intervening so quickly, he is unconsciously involved in an effort to cut the patient off, before she gets into her own difficulties and begins to put such contents into him. He seems refractory to serving as an appropriate container and metabolizer of her sickness. And as you can see, for many reasons, this is very distressing to the patient, who has come into therapy to legitimately find an opportunity to put her sickness into the bipersonal field and into a therapist who can help her resolve it. She is feeling overburdened by the therapist's difficulties in accepting these contents and his need instead to put his pathology into the field and into her.

You can also see what I meant when I said earlier that so long as a countertransference difficulty remains unresolved, it will crop up first in one place and then in another. Here, with the therapist still unable to work out and resolve his underlying erotic countertransference, and possibly his underlying needs to make use of this patient as a therapist, he continues to express these difficulties almost each time that he intervenes. And I'm sure that the patient will experience this as an intensification of his efforts at projective identification, and as his search for more specific interventions and curative efforts on her part. The pressure is for her to be the container of the pathology of the therapist—it will drain her.

Now, I have not overlooked the patient's renewed expression of trust in this therapist. I have not addressed myself to this; I have not done so because this manifest comment does not appear to fit in with my own assessment of the therapeutic interaction and of the material from the patient—and from the therapist. Now, it is not that I exclude those communications that do not fit in with my hypotheses; instead, I keep returning to them in an effort to understand them—either by making them fit in with my ongoing ideas, or to have it exert pressure on me to revise my conceptualization. As I have said before, this is how the validating process works.

And, it seems to me that her manifest comments of trust are best viewed as an effort at denial and as an attempt to maintain a fragment of a benign or good image of the therapist. I share this thought with you because it is one that I hope to have tested out in the patient's subsequent associations. If I am right, the material will once again indicate, through its latent content, that the patient is unconsciously and actually deeply mistrustful of this therapist. Of course, I have already had a small validation of this thesis in the patient's comment that she really didn't want to talk about her relationship with the therapist, because it would bring up her feelings about men whom she trusted and who then disappointed her. But, for the moment, this is how I would integrate the material from the patient, and I hope that you will join me in attempting to subject these assumptions and formulations to the validating process based on the patient's continued associations.

Before we get back to the material, I want to say a few more words about the therapist's intervention. First of all, the therapist is implying that he had made a sensitive intervention that the patient inappropriately experienced as sexualized closeness. This again goes under the heading of the patient as the one who distorts; the patient must be crazy. It of course leaves out the patient's unconscious perceptions and the kernel of truth in the situation —as we later validated it—that the therapist had actually behaved in a seductive way. So, a communication from the patient is being treated here primarily—and essentially—as a transference distortion, even though it contains a large measure of perceptiveness. This is also going to confuse the patient and undermine her capacity for inner and outer reality testing.

This is an excellent example of a characteristic way in

which the distinction between transference and non-transference is not maintained clearly within the mind of the therapist, and is not reflected in his interventions. And you can see that in addition to the conceptual confusion, this distortion by the therapist of his assessment of the contents of the patient's communications stems from his own countertransference difficulties, and from his need to put into the patient his own sexual conflicts. In this sense, this intervention includes both a projection —of the therapist's own possible sexualization of treatment—and a projective identification—here, entailing an effort to put his sexual anxieties into the patient in order to have her work them over.

Now, once again, I am not overlooking the veridical components that facilitated this therapist's projections and projective identifications. As you can gather, reality and fantasy constantly intermix, and there is valid reason to believe that this patient is sexualizing the treatment situation and is involved in efforts to deal with her own intrapsychic sexual conflicts. The point that I am stressing is that for the moment, these sexual problems are not in evidence and the therapist's intervention has to be seen as containing more of his own inner problems than those of the patient. It is always a matter of proportions, and there is never a situation in which we will observe a pure intrapsychic projection without some component of reality contributing as well. This is why we say that there is no such thing as pure transference or pure nontransference, nor is there any such thing as a purified unconscious fantasy or unconscious perception. Reality and fantasy are always intermixing, but nontheless, it is crucial to know what predominates at any given moment, and furthermore, to intervene based only on a valid assessment of the proportions involved.

So, once again we want to get back to basics: wait for the establishment of the adaptive context for the patient's material; wait for sufficient associations so that you can understand the patient's unconscious fantasies and perceptions; and accept the patient's communications into yourself as a means of building your understanding and of developing your interventions. And remember that in assessing any intervention, we view it in terms of its manifest content, the material from the patient on which it was based, and its unconscious communications to the patient. We pit it against the therapeutic interaction.

Remember too that an erroneous intervention is filled with unconscious communications and interactional pressures in your relationship with the patient. In this way, you will be prepared for the patient's subsequent reactions and associations. And utilize your own inner validating process, self-knowledge, and the mirroring aspects of the patient's associations—through which they reflect veridical components of the nature of your intervention. And so you listen to the patient after you have intervened; you assess the associations for cognitive confirmation and nonconfirmation. And you are always prepared to revise your formulations and to rectify your errors—you will seldom be able to rest on your laurels.

You also attempt to understand what the patient has taken in from you, based on the intervention. Here you attempt to determine the contents that the patient has introjected and how she processes them; and of course, you explore within yourself the fantasies that you have endeavored to put into the patient. And when an intervention is valid, there will be fresh material, and new and meaningful turns to the patient's associations. And there will be allusions to people who are helpful, good, and kind, and to ways in which the patient is functioning well and constructively. And when an intervention is not essentially valid, there will be no confimation and the material will remain flat, although eventually the patient will make unconscious efforts to alert you to the true nature of her conflicts and to the basic meanings of her associations. But she will also talk about people who are hurtful, harmful, and who lack understanding, and she will begin to become depressed and self-critical. And in addition to these more general responses, the patient will, especially with an invalid intervention, make efforts to work over the specific pathology that you have put into her, in an effort, as I said before, to cure your sickness in her and to thereby cure a piece of herself. So, now let's see what happens.

T: She said that was why she called me Doctor. Because she didn't like doctors. And she wanted me to be less than a doctor; she wanted me to be a friend and a doctor too.

L: You can glean several implications from this response. Of course, these communications are an expression of her own erotic transference. But it also relates to your erotic countertransference as we have formulated it. That is, we could see this simply as an expression of her own wishes to be more involved with you, but we could also add that this material reflects an introjective identification with your own wishes that she be both a patient and a doctor as well. So in a sense, this confirms the formulation that I made, although it is certainly just a beginning.

In addition, for the moment, she is willing to accept the full burden that you have placed into her, and to take full responsibility for the erotic psychopathology of the bipersonal field. We have already seen that she consistently responds in this way, and that she maintains a denial of her perceptions of you as seductive, and accepts all of the badness into herself.

But, while she initially accepts the therapeutic misalliance that you have offered her, and also accepts your projection, in that she communicates her own responsibility for the sexualization of the treatment, you can expect that she will eventually shift her response. She will soon either repudiate the introjection and misalliance, or more actively attempt to cure you. But here, she shows that in a way her first effort is to remind you that you're a doctor. It is as if she's telling you, You're starting to get a little edgy; you're moving too close to me. Remember, you're a doctor. That's the Hypocratic oath—hands off; that's what it says. She is attempting to reestablish a proper distance from you.

D: The $350,000 lawsuit.

L: Right. That relates to something that she never clarified for you—why it was that they were talking about hard times and the boyfriend told her that she should sue you. So, you shouldn't be fooled too easily by her readiness to accept what you put into her. We will have to see where she goes from here.

    Remember that unless you know yourself and your personal equation, you are bound to misunderstand the patient's communications and to misperceive them as well. It is an important component of the validating process. Otherwise, without appreciating the interaction and the things that you have put into this patient, you might be feeling that here she is agreeing with you, and the sessions are going along just great. Now, I expect that something negative is going to happen—I just expect it. Let's see.

T: Okay, so I said that she used "Doctor" to put distance between us. She said that she had never considered that, but she would though. She thought that I expected her to be more than just a patient, and she was angry that her whole life revolved around coming here. And I saw many other people here. And she felt that I wanted her to fall in love here, but she hadn't. With the other therapist . . .

L: You know, it's just so incredible . . . I just have to emphasize these points because you should all learn them. Think of Freud sitting with a patient who falls in love with him; and he immediately calls this transference.

Now such love does sometimes come primarily from distortions and misperceptions, and therefore from within the patient. But, if you look at real life and what really goes on in a therapeutic interaction, you can see that there are many other things that may go on. And she says, You expect me to be more than a patient to you; you want me to fall in love with you. Now, is this transference or nontransference? Is it distortion or reality? Is it unconscious or conscious fantasy, as compared to unconscious perception? Again, there is clearly an admixture, in that the patient is certainly including her own intrapsychic elaborations of what she has perceived. But at bottom, there is a great deal of truth in these words; so much so that I would not describe these communications as primarily transference distortions. I would think of them as nontransference-based, unconscious perceptions that have been elaborated to some degree intrapsychically by the patient.

The validity of what she has perceived is crucial here, and it strikingly confirms my own conscious perceptions of what has been going on, and of what you have been communicating to her. She has picked it up and we really don't know—and this is something that you can check out personally and within yourself—whether her belief or fantasy that you want her to fall in love with you is based primarily on her own inner contributions, or whether it represents something that is essentially true.

In intervening with this patient, if you were to tell her that she has this crazy or unjustified idea that you want her to be more than just a patient to you, you would be undermining her capacity to perceive and to test out reality, both as it pertains to yourself and as it relates to her inner fantasy life. Her crucial ability to distinguish between reality and fantasy would be destroyed, and along with that her capacity to resolve her neurosis. Once again you would be embarking upon efforts to virtually drive her crazy.

And unfortunately, there are many therapists who would do exactly that. As soon as the patient expresses some belief or fantasy that the therapist wants more from her or wants her to be in love with him, he will immediately step in and interpret this as a projection and as a distortion based on some earlier relationship. And he will totally obliterate and deny the therapeutic interaction that has prompted these communications, and the valid perceptions that they contain. In fact, it is exactly those therapists, with unconscious needs of this type which prompt them to become involved with their patients in this kind of way, who will be lacking in the self-awareness and the sensitivity to the therapeutic interaction that would enable them to deal with these associations in a more realistic and therapeutic manner.

T: Yes, I have realized something else. I read Racker's (1957) article about countertransference and I thought her comment that I really expected that she would fall in love with me was as though she was first of all saying, that she hasn't fallen in love with me. And my reaction was: You are a son of a bitch for not falling in love with me . . .

D: She's supposed to.

L: That was your reaction to it; that's how you felt?

T: Yes; I can detect now in thinking about what you said . . . at least, I could feel at the end of the session, of course I don't want you to fall in love with me; I just want you to have a "positive" transference.

L: Yes, that is called the rationalization. (Laughter.) You should also read some of Searles' (1965) collected papers; they are quite pertinent to your reaction.

But the point that I want to get across is that these expressions come out of the therapeutic interaction. You are in reality creating a lot of pressure on her for love and care; and you are asking her to be something other than a patient. In fact, you are also asking her to be your therapist; she comes to that very quickly.

What I am trying to stress here is not that we should neglect this patient's transference components—her own intrapsychic conflicts about sexuality, her own unconscious and even conscious sexual fantasies and the conflicts that they are creating. They are there, and they are contributing to this bipersonal field, and they're contributing to the interface of this interaction. What I'm trying to show you again is where the therapist has also contributed to this bipersonal field. And hopefully you can once more see why the field concept is so crucial: it tells us to look in both directions.

And further, I want to point out that when the patient says, I call you Doctor to have some distance, that's an attempt to solve a problem in the field—to offer boundaries for the therapist as well as for herself. And when the patient says, You want me to be something more than a patient, she not only conveys that she unconsciously perceives something about the therapist wanting to have a seductive relationship on some level; she also has unconsciously picked up the projective identifications from the therapist and realizes that he is asking her for help.

Now, the therapist's awareness of his disappointment that the patient doesn't love him is very important. It was brave of him to tell us about it. Let's make use of this, because it gives us a chance to talk briefly about the therapist's subjective reactions to the patient. When the therapist becomes aware of such a thought, it should serve as a signal to him that there is a countertransference problem in this area—that he does indeed want too much from this patient. And again, if he undertakes some self-analytic work, if he listens to the patient's material and uses it in part to direct him to his problems, if he knows that he's in a bipersonal field where the patient is mirroring his difficulties, then he can begin to comprehend not only what's going on in the interaction, but also what's going on within himself.

In addition, I want to very briefly point out that your angry fantasy about her failure to fall in love with you confirms the various formulations that I made about your erotic contertransference. It shows you that you must take such passing thoughts quite seriously, and subject them to self-analysis, and in addition check out your interventions for the various ways in which they unconsciously transmit such needs. Also I think that your fantasy confirms my formulations related to this patient's unconscious perceptiveness, and my demonstrations of the various ways in which you have conveyed your erotic countertransference to her, both through your interventions and through your problems in managing the framework. Well now, we are most interested in seeing what happens next.

T: This is the next session.

L: Oh, how did she end this hour?

T: She hoped that I was not offended if she didn't fall in love with me, and said that I might be expecting her to.

D: She certainly has made an accurate perception.

T: Well, this is the next session. She told me that Monday night, the night after the last session, she had a dream, and before I said anything, she wanted to tell me . . . (Laughter.)

L: So, she's saying, Look, let this be my session for once. Now, we attempted to predict the content of a dream from this patient once before, and I think we can do the same thing here. I'll be brief because I think it's rather evident what I will predict. The adaptive context has not changed very much, and has even been intensified. We still have an unresolved problem with the framework, and we still have an unresolved series of projective identifications by the therapist into the patient. I expect the patient to work these over through her dream.

So you see again how you enter a session with an awareness of what has gone on previously, especially in the therapeutic interaction and intrapsychically within yourself and the patient. You almost know what to expect, and again let me stress that this does not mean that you are overly biased and prejudiced, and that you will not listen for other communications. I think I've demonstrated that half of our mind remains blank and prepared to hear the unexpected, and to be freshly filled by the patient.

Now, we could add to our prediction some specific anticipations related to the erotic qualities of the therapist's projective identifications and the patient's efforts to defend herself against these contents and against her own erotic transference. In a way, you can simply take my discussion of the previous session as a prediction of where the patient will pick up in this hour. Rather than elaborate, I think we should hear from the patient.

T: She was anxious about what was said on Monday and she had trouble getting to sleep.

L: See, we immediately get to the sad and serious part. Also—the dream, she is indicating, was prompted by the events of the previous session.

T: She was trying to decide if she had the thoughts about me or if I was putting thoughts about me as a therapist into her head. Before she went to sleep, she finally convinced herself that I was not interested in her sexually. And then she had the dream.

L: Notice again what seems like a really crazy thought: were the thoughts hers, or were they the therapist's? And notice too her need to convince herself that the therapist is not interested in her sexually. How many therapists would wonder about where these crazy ideas came from, and why this patient is regressing now? How many therapists would write this off as part of the patient's borderline pathology, without ever recognizing their own contribution?

On the other hand, I'm sure that you will remember

our discussion and immediately recognize the extent to which we anticipated exactly these communications. She is now working over consciously many of the comments that I previously made. If you know the adaptive context, this patient doesn't really seem so crazy, and in fact at this point, when to other eyes she would seem on the verge of a psychotic break, we are in a position to appreciate her great sensitivity. Not that this will guarantee her capacity to avoid a serious regression; only the therapist's consistent understanding of the actual meanings of these communications and his interpretations to her on that basis can help her to restore her controls.

But what is particularly interesting about this regression, is the extent to which it reflects the therapist's continued difficulties and actually shows the degree to which the patient is being disturbed by the therapist's projections and projective identifications. After all, the therapist has attributed to her what were, for the moment, quite clearly his own sexual fantasies and conflicts. As I said before, this will undermine the patient's capacity for reality testing, and she is quite dramatically confirming that formulation.

And as the response of the patient becomes more intense, I want to stress again how impossible it is to understand a patient's communications without knowing the adaptive context and the unconscious implications of the prior therapeutic interaction. Once again, knowing the actualities takes precedence and is the only basis on which you can separate fantasy from perception, and distortion from reality. And to whatever extent the patient is indeed attempting to get under control her own erotic transference fantasies, you can see that long before we could deal with that, we must deal with what the therapist has put into her. And there, in terms of the therapist's projective identification of his sexual conflicts into her, we see her respond with anxiety, and we also see her efforts to contain and work over these sexual contents. As a result, she convinces herself that he is not interested in her sexually and communicates that back to the therapist, as if to put back into him the resolution of his sexual conflicts, namely, that he should establish a conscious renunciation of his sexual wishes toward her. This is a most moving therapeutic effort and proxy offer.

And forgive me for being even more somber in pointing out that my earlier formulations, that the therapist's mismanagement of the framework and his erroneous interventions constituted attempts to drive this patient crazy. We see here that she is on the verge of an interactional psychosis and we see her struggling to master it. We notice the manner in which the therapist contributed to this, by ascribing to the patient fantasies within himself that were active and unresolved for the moment. And the therapist not only put his own sexual conflicts into this patient, but also his confusion, and we see the patient's introjection of these contents and processes.

And in fact, this patient rather exquisitely identifies the process of projective identification since she has experienced it first hand. She puts it this way: she was wondering if the therapist was putting thoughts about himself into her head. And you can see that this is exactly what I felt that the therapist was doing, particularly in his last intervention. And she goes on to indicate to the therapist the outcome of her own processing of his projective identification—I'll say it again—namely, that the solution lies in renunciation of his sexual interest in her and in conscious control. Freud could not have said it better.

Now, I will only add that I am fully aware that her own psychopathology and distorted fantasies, and her own ego dysfunctions, have led to the particular way in which this patient has processed her introjective identification with the therapist. There is no question about this aspect, since each patient will process or refute projective identifications in keeping with the nature of their own intrapsychic structures and functioning. And ultimately, I would hope to interpret aspects of the patient's inner problems to her, but as I said a moment ago, it will be necessary first to modify the actualities of the therapist's contributions to them, and to analyze this patient's unconscious perceptions and introjective identifications. Then, we would be in a position to get to her contributions to the pathology of this bipersonal field.

So, we have a rather sad but exquisite opportunity to learn something about interactional syndromes, and the ways in which patients regress in the face of their incapacity to adequately contain the psychopathology put into them by a therapist, who himself has failed in his own containing functions. And so you see that this situation is one in which this therapist has for some time been impermeable to the patient's efforts to put her pathology into him, and he has had difficulty in functioning as a therapeutic container for her sick contents. In addition, he has actually dominated the scene—the bipersonal field—by repeatedly attempting to put his sickness into the patient. And as I predicted, sooner or later the patient becomes overtaxed with these burdens, and I think we are witnessing again her efforts to once more turn to the therapist and mobilize him to become the container of her sickness at long last. Her regression is both adaptive and maladaptive.

T: Do you want to hear the dream?

D: No, I don't. (Laughter.)

L: All right, and after the dream, what happened? See now —that's a good example of projective identification. You sure as hell don't want to tell the dream. So we sure as hell are not supposed to want to hear it, but for many reasons—mostly constructive, I hope—we're not going to let you get away with that.

No, but again, aside from the much needed levity, let's begin to appreciate some of the seriousness of this situation. It's often said—and this is an example that would be used to justify it—that in psychotherapy you can't deal with the transference; if you do, the patient regresses. And some who know of my work criticize it because I don't make sufficient distinction between analysis and psychotherapy. Now, I have a very simple answer to that criticism, and that is the material from this patient. The patient is indeed quite preoccupied with what's going on with the therapist. It is where the patient is at, and it is there that you must intervene or it will be not only meaningless, but will again convey to the patient that you are unprepared to deal with her anxieties regarding the therapeutic relationship. She will feel that you are pushing her away and refusing to contain these new contents, and she will be right; and she might regress even more.

The fact of the matter is that this material illustrates not that you can't deal with transferences, but that you must properly conceptualize the therapeutic relationship to include all aspects—transference and nontransference, unconscious perception and unconscious fantasy, distortion and reality. And once you recognize the totality of this therapeutic relationship and the extent to which every communication from the patient has a bearing on this relationship, and even more, the degree to which there are interactional sequences in which the therapeutic relationship is overwhelmingly central to the patient, then you realize that much sound therapeutic work can be done in this area.

You're showing us not that you cannot deal with the transference in psychotherapy, but that you must know how to deal with it, and that the problem lies in conceptual confusion and in countertransference difficulties, rather than anywhere else. First, you have to understand the patient's communications; you have to know what's going on and you have to know what you're doing. And all of this implies that among the many reasons why

transference—and here what I really mean is the therapeutic relationship—is not dealt with in psychotherapy is
that the work is done by unanalyzed psychotherapists
who have great difficulty especially in managing the relationship with the patient. And as for the vast majority
of analysts who feel exactly the same way, I can only say
that much of this seems to stem from their own needs to
relax the boundaries of their relationship with patients
in psychotherapy after the stringent controls that they
maintain in analysis—and I assure you that there too
they make many unneeded modifications in the framework, and quite a few erroneous interventions and efforts
at pathological projective identifications into the patient.
And matters get even more complicated when we realize
that most psychoanalysts have been analyzed under conditions in which the framework of their own analysis has
been modified; and I think that this accounts in part for
the extensive general blind spot in regard to the meanings of the framework, and the neglect of the vast implications of erroneous interventions, that prevails in the
psychoanalytic literature.

But I do not want to get too far from this patient's material, and basically I want to indicate that serious work
must be done in the area of the therapeutic relationship
with this patient. And I want to suggest that this is not
the exception, but the rule. Even in those situations
where the therapist has not behaved traumatically, there
are many inevitable hurts, anxieties, and disturbances in
a relatively sound therapeutic interaction to preoccupy
the patient for many hours.

This patient has not read the books and does not know
that she is not supposed to be preoccupied with this unusual figure—her psychotherapist—who can offer her
one of the most unique cures known to man—inner
structural change and new adaptive resources that are
established within herself and offer her a means of handling conflicts and affects in ways never known to her be-

fore. The patient in psychotherapy invests heavily in this unique relationship, and intuitively, using her own validating process, I am sure, senses what she needs and responds when it is lacking. And while I repeat that I am not advocating exclusive therapeutic work within the realm of the therapeutic relationship, I am stating that it is an extremely significant arena and that, ultimately, the patient's communications filter again and again through to that relationship.

D: I had this discussion with someone just yesterday—who told me of a study, perhaps not very well researched, that showed that it doesn't matter whether the therapist has been in therapy or not. And I said, I just can't accept that.

L: Yes, I know; Look: denial exists and you're never going to prevent it. All I ask is that you look at the material from your patients, and attempt to formulate it as deeply and as carefully as you can. Look at the material that we have explored in these seminars, and you will see that despite the most sincere and best efforts of these therapists, who have not been in analysis or intensive psychotherapy, their own pathology is repeatedly put into the bipersonal field and disturbs the therapeutic process. It is only by not attempting to explore the patient's material in depth, and by insisting that the sickness always lies within the patient, and that nearly everything that the patient communicates is based on distortion, that you can deny these observations. Such denial at times can reach delusional proportions, and I'm not going to worry about that. Some years ago I shared that delusion, because it had been taught to me and had been well rationalized, but you people taught me otherwise very quickly; a year of supervising here and I knew it wasn't true.

So what I'm trying to get at is a very serious matter. You see, if you avoid this issue, the therapeutic interaction, especially now as the patient consciously struggles with it, there's no treatment, no treatment at all. But if you're going to deal with it, you have to get back to the basics. Let the patient talk. You're under such pressure to do so much. Let it unfold. Try to understand what she's perceiving, so that you can help her understand where these feelings are coming from. Recognize that they stem from your interventions and from that damn business of your violating a confidentiality at the very moment when you're telling her that you want confidentiality to exist. To the extent that so much of this is coming from your inconsistencies and from your modifications of the framework, this constitutes what I would term a *framework psychosis*—a sickness in the patient generated by the therapist's inconsistencies in his management of the framework. And I can assure you that this is a surprisingly common syndrome.

So, listen further to her and work within yourself on your countertransference and use her communications to assist you. Recognize the difficulties that you are having in managing, and that for the moment the patient is stressing the sexual difficulties; but don't miss the fact that there is also an aggressive component here. While both of you are putting it in sexual terms, realize that there is something very destructive here too. And, once the patient's material becomes clearer, and you can sort out her perceptions and fantasies, you should intervene; intervene so you can help her to cognitively master the growing disturbance within her, and intervene to show her that you have gotten matters under control and that you can manage things better. Once again, you will at such a moment offer her the dual gifts of cognitive insight and a positive introjective identification. Please continue.

T: This is the dream. We had had our session and she was anxious because of it. And then, at night, she decided to come and tell me her decision, the decision about whether or not I had put the thoughts of her being interested in me sexually into her head, or whether they came from her. I was in my office and as she started to tell me her decision, I interrupted her and said or did something.

You might not believe this, but the phone rang at that moment. And she said, Hurry up. She was very very angry. Afterwards, I commented that she seemed angry about the phone call. And she said that she didn't want to interrupt her train of thought, about the dream, that we were having an affair, a sexual affair.

L: What a moment. I would never have answered the phone at that point.

T: You would never have?

L: Never. No, I don't answer the phone. I don't at all . . . there's no need to.

T: Well, what do you do?

L: Basically, I don't think there's any need for the therapist to answer the telephone. First, I would suggest a preference for an answering device, since it maintains total confidentiality. One can check and call back immediately after a session and in this way prevent unnecessary interruptions. And even if you do answer the telephone, there are certain times when you just tell yourself, Not now. You know, in itself, it's like a piece of acting out already. You're trying to interrupt what is really . . .

Look, I hope everyone in the room begins to appreciate how the therapist is feeling as this dream starts to unfold. If you're capable of any kind of anxiety, you've got to be experiencing it. If you're capable of reasonable guilt, knowing your own thoughts, that's inevitable too. You try to control it, but you feel it in response to the intensity of her reaction. You see the intermingling of the countertransference communications, her transference reactions, her perceptions of you, and her psychopathology. Her response borders on a delusion . . . is he trying to control me, put things into my head? The kernel of truth is there. These are personal styles of reacting; another patient would not do it in this exquisite, excruciating way.

And then comes the manifest dream. All of this could be misunderstood. Actually, you brought yourself into it, now she's dreaming about you. This is how erotized transferences often arise. The literature doesn't quite say that; Blum (1973) does say that occasionally it can occur this way. But believe me, it happens more often than not. Rappaport (1959), who wrote one of the original papers on this subject, described how one of his patients was upset because he was eating his lunch while the patient was associating, and that she developed an erotized transference. He did not for a moment consider that his eating lunch was a modification in the framework and a significant reality precipitant for this transference, nor did he ascribe any relevance to the therapeutic interaction in general.

However, clinical observation has indicated to me that quite often, though certainly not always, an erotized transference is in actuality an interactional syndrome and reflects failures in management on the part of both patient and therapist. Now again, don't misquote me by saying that I insist that this is the only factor in an erotized transference. Again, the patient's own inner dispositions play a significant role; however, careful clinical observation has indicated that these syndromes are quite common in response to mismanagements of the framework of the bipersonal field and as reactions to other disturbed communications from therapists. It's another literature that I think we have to restudy in the context of a more careful understanding of the therapeutic interaction.

But coming back to this moment, the phone rang; at such a point, I know that I have to be listening to the patient. And an interpretation doesn't make that go away, nor can it easily—if at all—be rectified. Okay. So, you told her she was angry; she goes on with the dream.

T: Yes. We were having an affair, a sexual affair. Well, she didn't say sexual affair—she said affair. And that all of the thoughts about the relationship, her interest in me, were hers. That I had initiated her interest, but she had continued the feelings herself. That she was giving all; and I was giving nothing in return. The only way that she feels she can satisfy a man is sexually.

L: Now is this an association?

T: Yes.

L: She was giving all and you were giving nothing.

Notice too how the patient now turns to a new and highly pliable medium of unconscious communication—the dream. While the therapist is mainly projectively identifying, the patient is attempting to work with derivatives of unconscious fantasies. Often, these are alternate means of expression for a patient.

T: That was in the dream.

L: You know, you talk about patients and distortions and craziness; I just think so differently. Here's a girl who says to you that you had stirred her up and then she carried it on from there. Who could ask for more from a patient? Here, she so clearly appreciates that you had indeed evoked an erotic response within her, and she goes on to say that then, because of her own needs, she responded and was stirred up by it and that she took it from there.

In her dream, she dramatized my lecture and she made the point that I have developed so often: the sequence is one of unconscious perception, introjective identification, and elaboration according to the patient's needs. You see how creative and perceptive the patient is unconsciously; how, through her immediate experiencing of the therapist's difficulties and of the things that she put into him, she is able to unconsciously offer such incredible insights. And again I remind you that it is the therapist's responsibility to make these exquisite insights conscious; but you'll notice that all you need do is to take the rich unconscious understanding of the patient and present it back to her in conscious, direct form. It looks so deceptively simple, doesn't it?

And there is another thing that is so remarkable: at the very point when we are faced with some of this patient's ego dysfunctions and inner disturbances, we see an extraordinary capacity for unconscious understanding and a remarkable sensitivity. This patient is communicating rich derivatives that are quite analyzable and workable. There is contained in these communications an intense wish to put both her sickness and her own therapeutic efforts back into the therapist, for processing and for interpretation—and I must add, for a good bit of rectification as well.

And as if all of this wasn't enough, I am struck by the contents of her dream that allude to the therapist's interrupting her prematurely. I have made this point to you several times before, and suggested that your latest intervention has been quite premature. And so again, I can point out that the patient is your unconscious supervisor; if you can truly understand your patient's communications, you really don't need me at all. And in fact, every patient should legitimately serve this function for every therapist and analyst; all we need do is to recognize this capacity within the patient and to make use of it.

If you read the Kleinian literature, you will find that they write a great deal about projective identification and the manner in which it is followed by an introjective identification and a reprojection. The main problem with this literature in the context of our discussion today is that they seldom refer to the realities that contribute to these processes, and they especially avoid the projective identifications of the therapist or analyst. However, you have here a very good illustration of exactly that kind of sequence. It begins in a manner that we really can't identify at this point; I can't tell you who initiated the first sexual projective identification—the patient or the therapist. In any case, much of our discussion began with several instances of the therapist's efforts to projectively identify into the patient his own sexual conflicts, and we are following a sequence at this moment that began with such an intervention. And so the patient has this dream and processes his projective identification in keeping with her own pathological and adaptive needs. Through this dream, she puts both the therapist's and her own sexual conflicts back into the therapist—she reprojects the introjected contents. And while these seem like complicated words, I think that you can recognize this process and see that it is a very basic and important one.

And what is the main adaptive outcome of her own inner processing of this sickness of the therapist within her? She tells him that she is giving all and that he is giving nothing in return. This is a profound truth, unfortunately, but again, the therapist is in a position to appreciate its validity and to rectify these conditions. Here again, only rectification can modify the situation, after which interpretation can add a great deal. And she goes further, and states that it seems that the only gratification that the therapist wants for the moment is sexual, and because of her own needs, she is struggling with her own inclinations to comply. How clearly she is stating things.

You can see how exquisite this situation is and how much we can already comprehend about this dream by knowing the adaptive context and the therapeutic interaction. Well, let's hear what she went on to say.

T: She felt that the only way that she could satisfy a man was sexually. That either way, she didn't like it; that if I put the ideas into her head, then how could she trust me? That it was my problem and she would lose faith in me. That I'd be just like any other man with her that she'd known before. And that she'd be afraid to make herself vulnerable here in the session; that she'd be taken advantage of.

L: Once again, this patient, using her own idiom, is repeating so many of the things that I have said throughout these seminars. Here, she says that if the therapist is contaminating the bipersonal field, and if he is projecting his sickness into the patient and inappropriately modifying the boundaries, then he becomes like any other man. The therapeutic situation is no longer a unique one, and transference is no longer possible, nor can there be any trust or any cure. The therapist is no longer a therapist but is a sexual object—a man; and the patient is afraid of her vulnerability. And she says even more: under these conditions, there is no guarantee of controls, there is no certainty that the interaction will take place within the proper boundaries, and no assurances that direct gratification of these inappropriate sexual wishes will not occur. The situation becomes totally dangerous, and is in some way a repetition of past pathogenic interactions.

I am reminded of something that I have repeated many times: a sensitive patient—and this applies to most —can, when working over a particular issue, write the entire chapter related to that issue. Remember her message: pathological projective identifications by the therapist, in whatever form they are expressed, undermine and may even destroy the therapeutic field. And on another level, of course, they destroy the therapeutic alliance; and here we see the major influence that these interactional pathological mechanisms have on the therapeutic alliance—the extent to which they can undermine it when they are pathological, and the extent to which the alliance can be reinforced through a sound interaction.

T: She went on: If, on the other hand, it was from her, then it was no good either. That was like that with her former therapist: she just clammed up after she began having feelings about him. She wanted this place to be a haven from all her other problems, but if she had the same problems here, then she didn't know what good treatment was going to be for her.

L: So, here again, she says if treatment repeats past pathogenic interactions, it cannot be therapy; she cannot solve her problems under those circumstances. All right, let's continue.

T: At that point, I said that I'd also thought of what she said last Monday, that I might want her to have feelings about me. And that I'm in the process of exploring this myself now.

L: Whew! That's a toughie; that really is tough. I don't know who taught you that style; I know it exists. What are you saying? Let's appreciate the unconscious communication, which is . . .

D: What he's saying is that she's absolutely right, her perceptions of him; that yes, he has problems; that he did stir up something or wanted to stir up something; and again, he doesn't deal with the adaptive context, the confidentiality issue, or even the missed session.

L: I'm not any longer sure about the most central adaptive context. I would have interpreted this in two ways, which I'll get to in a minute. But, by saying what you did, at the time . . . Here is a patient who comes in and says, My ego functions are kind of failing me; I'm really not sure of reality and I'm getting very scared. Either I'm stirred up about you because something in my sexual feelings are getting out of hand, or you're trying to stir me up. And I don't know which it is. Either way, it's not good, but after all, if it is coming from her, you're at least the therapist who could help her with that part. If it is coming from you though, she has no way of trusting you, and treatment is destroyed. And if it's coming from her, well, that just frightens her because she's afraid she's going to clam up.

Your response is, I don't know either. I'm looking into it; I'll let you know when I know—that's number one. Number two, you're saying, It is very possible, it seems likely that I have been trying to stir you up. So you do have reason to be frightened of me and not to trust me. Now, of all the things to do at that time! You know, you talk about supportive therapy and think of this sort of intervention. But supportive therapy comes from the strength of the therapist who doesn't get swept up in the pathology of the patient. And here, you're just becoming part of the sweep. If you had said anything . . .

T: Like what?

L: Well, first of all I would not have intervened and would have waited, listening to her further associations and doing a hell of a lot of work in formulating what was going on. If you felt the need to say anything, you could have asked her what had prompted the dream and what it brought to her mind. I'm not in any hurry to intervene, but, if you feel you must say even more, you could have indicated to her that this dream followed upon the previous session, and seems to have been a response to your intervention regarding the issue of confidentiality in her therapy, the intrusion of her boyfriend, and your suggestion that she was in some way sexualizing her relationship with you. But, I think that this would be premature and that I would have been formulating this intervention as a silent hypothesis and subjecting it to the validating process. I can assure you that the patient's associations would have moved in directions that are related to this line of thinking, and that there would have been ample opportunity to make interventions of this kind.

I keep thinking of a possibility that I see less and less evidence of, while my alternate notion seems more and more substantiated.

D: It's not about confidentiality at this point.

L: Perhaps. Let me say what I'm thinking. This dream and reaction could come from two sources: one is your failure to maintain confidentiality and your projective identifications; the other is the threat that you might establish a confidential situation. If you offer this girl one-to-one treatment—and you were suggesting a while back that you might—then she's telling you that she's afraid she'll go crazy because of her sexual fantasies about you; their ramifications undoubtedly are quite anxiety-provoking for her.

In fact, this is probably as close as you have come to securing the framework, and it gives me a rather questionable opportunity to make several points about the patient's response to a secure framework. And while I freely acknowledge that this seems at best to be a weak hypothesis that would need considerably more material to confirm it, I think that the patient is actually perceiving your efforts in the direction of securing the frame, and that this accounts for one of the two possibilities that may be on her mind.

You see, when she says that maybe the problem is entirely in her, I think she is responding to those few efforts that you have made to create a secure and confidential therapeutic field. And this gives me, as I said, a chance to point out that at that juncture where the therapist does indeed secure the framework, he should not be surprised to find that the patient becomes anxious and defensive. At such times, one frequently observes a regression based on the upsurge of the patient's own psychopathology, which can no longer be put into, or concealed by, the therapist's difficulties in managing the framework, nor justifiably defended because the therapeutic situation is not secure. However, this type of regression is essentially therapeutic, in that it is the means through which the patient's relatively uncontaminated transference neurosis and intrapsychic pathology is communicated to the therapist in an analyzable form: it is the primary vehicle for the intrapsychic resolution of the patient's symptoms.

In this context, you may remember my comments about the anxiety-provoking qualities of a secure frame. As you can see, when a patient regresses and begins to be concerned about his inner fantasy life, you must assess the sequence to see the basis for this response. If it follows an effective securing of the framework, you can be fairly confident that you are observing a response to that measure. At such times, there will be a period of defensiveness that is designed primarily to protect the patient from the unfolding of his inner anxiety-provoking fantasies and memories, and if this is effectively analyzed, the deeper pathology will appear.

So, remember that a secure therapeutic hold offers a patient not only safety, but the conditions under which his deepest sickness will emerge. The patient will deeply appreciate and welcome such efforts, but he will also dread it, and these anxieties will have to be explored and worked through. So, coming back to this patient, when she addresses herself to her fear of her own inner fantasies, she may in part be responding to an unconscious perception of efforts by this therapist to secure the frame.

Simultaneously, this patient continues to respond to the defects in the frame and to your projective identifications. It is in this area that she strongly mistrusts and fears you, and sees you as putting into her your own sexual difficulties. And this is based on your telling her that you want to see her boyfriend individually, and by your adding that you're not sure if you can maintain the confidentiality of the two therapies. In addition, your latest intervention which prematurely and inappropriately introduced the concept of the sexualization of the therapy in a manner that entailed both a projection and a projective identification, also burdened this patient.

And so, for the moment, I would center my therapeutic efforts on these latter aspects, since I would recognize that my first therapeutic job is to continue the rectification and reinstatement of this damaged frame and to interpret her unconscious perceptions, fantasies, and anxieties in this area. So, your first job would be to let her continue to associate and to lead you to interventions in this area.

And once you had sufficient material, you could convey something like this to her: you had expressed to her rather directly your concern about maintaining separate confidential treatment situations if you were to continue to see both her and her boyfriend individually. And you could point out that you had said something about his treatment to her, which she seems to have taken as a kind of violation of the confidentiality of his therapy. And in addition, you could review the intervention that you had made in the previous session, in which you brought up the sexualization of the therapy. And after having alluded to each of these interventions—so long as her associations pointed toward them—you could then suggest that she had experienced these interventions as pressures from you to bring her closer to you, to involve her more with you, and even, to introduce sexuality into your relationship with her. Only then could you add that on her part, she is responding on her own with very intense, sexual fantasies that are frightening and disturbing her. And that as a result of all of this, she seems to feel dislocated and mistrustful of the therapeutic situation and of you, and uncertain as to what is going on both within herself and within you. Finally, once further material permitted, you could get around to her anxieties about your establishing clearly separate treatment situations for both her and her boyfriend, and her fears of her own inner fantasies when she is no longer in a position to put the sexual problem into you and is no longer protected by the boyfriend's presence.

Again, let me stress that I would not have done this in one step, but would have taken it little by little as her material permitted, and that I would have added considerably more along the lines of my previous discussions as she helped me to shape these interventions. And you can contrast this with your intervention, where you made little effort at rectification and even less effort to identify the basis for her unconscious perceptions and introjections, and to clarify the muddled bipersonal field. And certainly, you are not assisting her in regaining her controls by avoiding the delineation of these realities and by adding that you are becoming aware that you yourself have been having difficulties. Now, while this might be viewed by her as a step in the right direction, I think it carries with it many liabilities that could have been avoided.

Remember, her dream conveys her unconscious perception of your mutual seductiveness, and yet, a good deal of the sexualization is coming from her. And in the dream, she does address herself to the framework, because she dreamed of seeing you at a time when there is no session or for an extra session; she's coming in the evening. She is showing you that the boundary problem is quite crucial and that it is because the boundaries have been extended, that she has perceived the therapeutic situation as unsafe, seductive, and nontherapeutic. But all of this is coming through in a very blatant way, and it's disturbing her. And that is why I say that your intervention will, for the moment, largely place new burdens into her; it is another form of projective identification even though it is well-meaning.

Remember, we have seen some disturbing consequences to your self-confessions to the patient, and have come to realize that they are appropriately experienced by her as an effort on your part to put into her some of your own difficulties. Another effort of this kind is bound to disturb her and to further disrupt her functioning. Your method may be one way of offering this patient a misalliance cure by saying to her, Okay, I'll be the crazy one for a while. But once again, in the long run, she's not going to appreciate or really benefit from it.

T: Well, actually you said something in your book (Langs, 1973a, 1974) about using that type of intervention.

L: Yes, I probably did, because I was under the influence of that way of thinking at the time. I have so modified my position in that respect that I had forgotten. I apologize for it; I have been trying to set it straight in the new work that I am doing.

Actually, this was a position that Greenson (1967, 1972) had advocated, and on the surface it really seemed to make a good deal of sense. If he has made a technical error and the patient perceives it, Greenson wrote, then the therapist should acknowledge it and analyze all of the ramifications of both the error and the acknowledgment. And he added that in making such an acknowledgment, the therapist might indicate that he was working on it within himself, but he should not in any way burden the patient with his own inner difficulties.

Now, even if you had based your intervention on such a position, this type of stance has to be used with sensitivity and discretion. Unfortunately, you picked a moment when this was not the intervention that the patient needed, and it served more your own need for relief than it did as a means of reassuring the patient. If you think about the implicit communications contained in your comment, the timing indicates that this could be quite disruptive to the patient.

I also want to make clear to you that once I began to investigate this particular approach to technical errors, and to analyze in depth the patient's unconscious perceptions and introjections of it, I quickly realized that such a response constituted a modification in the framework—a violation of anonymity through a self-revelation—and that the patient responded adversely to this disruption in the frame, much as he would to any such alteration. And you'll find my revised position in my recent papers on the framework (Langs, 1975b) and *Therapeutic Misalliances* (Langs, 1975a). There, I stated that when the therapist recognizes the patient's veridical conscious and unconscious perceptions of his errors, and he wishes to acknowledge them to the patient, his own contributions should be stated in terms of the patient's perceptions of him, thereby *implicitly* accepting their validity, rather than offering any explicit acknowledgment. This implicit acceptance, in which there is no suggestion that the patient has been distorting or is in any way crazy, is quite sufficient for the patient's need to separate reality from fantasy, while explicit acknowledgment modifies the frame and unduly burdens the patient.

Here, for example, you could have pointed out to the patient that she has viewed your acceptance of the boyfriend into her sessions as inappropriate and as a modification of the therapeutic situation; and that she had viewed your comments about the boyfriend's treatment as inappropriate and as a violation of his confidentiality; and that she had seen your introduction of the sexualization of treatment as premature and without basis in terms of her more recent associations—and you could point out these perceptions without in any way questioning them. And you would then build from there an understanding of the patient's responses to these perceptions and their intrapsychic elaboration within her, while at no time would you question the valid aspects of these perceptions. And I assure you that the patient would understand that she had not distorted aspects of these experiences, and that you would thereby be helping her to sort out her valid perceptions from those that are invalid.

Well, let's see how much of this is borne out in what follows.

T: She said, What did you find out? She paused and then went on: If I don't find out myself, I'm going to feel . . . if I don't find out for myself, then I will feel that our time has been wasted.

All right; do you finally want to hear an interpretation?

L: Oh, this is the interpretation you were leading up to? Okay. But first notice: you reveal one personal fact, and she immediately wants more.

T: I said that I'd been trying to put all this together with what went on in the session before. That with Bill coming several times into the sessions with us . . . and I said, Last time I mentioned his coming in and my seeing him for individual sessions; and I think that you feel that I have been pressuring you and putting thoughts or feelings into you that you may find that you have to protect yourself from. And I think that Bill's involvement in our therapy is a safety valve; he's being used as a safety valve in therapy. Okay, that's the end of that.

L: Well, you are attempting to deal with the central adaptive context and to identify some of her unconscious perceptions—all without indicating that they are sheer craziness. And while you are somewhat ambiguous and have introduced Bill into this material even though the patient had not brought him up, this is an attempt at a general interpretation that has considerably more neutral qualities than your previous interventions. You want to be so careful about introducing your own associations into your comments, and about this matter of informing the patient that you have difficulties and are investigating them. So much of this can be motivated by your own appropriate or inappropriate guilt and your need to put difficulties into the patient. You must constantly review your wish to add such elements to your comments, and subject them to self-analysis so that you are capable of refraining or of being certain that they are truly relevant.

Since the hour is late, could you quickly summarize the balance of that session?

T: Well, the patient said that she still didn't know if the thoughts were hers or not, and if not, I had put them in her head. And she was really afraid of talking about her relationship with me so much. If there was a problem outside and it was similar inside, there was just going to be a lot of difficulty. She didn't want to tie it all to what was going on in treatment because, after all, how could she trust me if I had problems? And she wondered if she should return at all.

I told her that I couldn't decide for her. She'd been dissatisfied with her previous therapist, and leaving meant not exploring and facing her problem with men. The patient said she wanted to see me as a doctor, not as a man, and she agreed to return.

Briefly, in the next session the patient was very angry with me. She added a part of the dream that she hadn't mentioned; namely, that there was a wall between herself and me that had been torn down, that I was naked, and that we had had sexual relations—she had been active, while I was passive. She was concerned about enjoying it and it was a lot like what she had felt about her previous therapist and about treatment now, because she was giving and she was getting nothing; and she wanted to know what I thought about it. Actually, later in the session, I called attention to my nakedness and she said that I had let the wall down and had revealed things about myself—that's why I was naked in the dream.

L: Well, unfortunately, our time is nearly up and I must conclude this seminar with a few final comments. First, I want to point to those associations from the patient that echo once again some of the basic principles that I have been teaching you. For example, there is her comment that if the problem inside of therapy is similar to the one outside therapy, there will be a lot of difficulty—to which I will add, once more, that therapy will not be feasible and that the therapeutic situation will simply constitute a repetition of past pathogenic relationships. Of course, she's again appealing for a bipersonal field, and a therapeutic situation, that is secure and distinctive, so she can get the therapeutic help that she needs.

Now, there is also the reference to the barrier that would have prevented this patient from having had intercourse with the therapist. In her dream, the therapist has shattered this barrier and has revealed things about himself. She conveys here the need for secure boundaries and adequate distance between the patient and the therapist, and the intense sexual meaning of the absence of such boundaries and distance. Further, her reference to the

therapist's nakedness is a not uncommon communication from patients following modifications by the therapist of his own anomymity, especially self-revelations.
Once again, she spells out in so many different ways her
valid conscious and unconscious perception that the therapist has filled her and the bipersonal field with his sexual conflicts.

Notice too that the therapist's confession to the patient
about his own difficulties led to another response, that
she still did not know whether the sexual thoughts were
hers or his. In addition, when the patient raised the question about termination—a question that often comes up
when the boundaries have been modified and the therapist is having other difficulties—the therapist once again
altered his basic therapeutic stance and offered an intervention that could not be characterized as neutral. As we
would expect, the patient once again experienced this as
some type of undue pressure from the therapist, and re-
stated her preference to see him as a doctor rather than
a man. Lastly, her reference to being the active sexual
partner in the addendum to the dream certainly has a
basis in our observations of the therapeutic work within
this bipersonal field: the patient has certainly been the
more active therapist of the two participants. While I do
not think that she is receiving nothing at all, she certainly, for the moment, has given a great deal more than she
has received.

Perhaps it is most important to stress in conclusion the
chaos that comes from unneeded modifications in the
framework. With a patient who has the potential for very
disturbed responses, failures in the area of the framework, added to failures in interpreting, will create what
I've termed a iatrogenic—therapist-evoked—regression
(Langs, 1974), and what I would now identify as a syndrome of the interactional field. When neither participant is really carefully grounded in reality, and when the
therapist is not carrying out his proper functions and not

maintaining the boundaries and the framework properly, you can see that the patient's ego functioning begins to regress. And the instinctual drive-based conflicts that are stirred up within her further that regression, as does her guilt and other superego responses. So again, we've ended up really focusing on the framework. To some extent we've had something to say too about the pathology of the bipersonal field. We've seen a dream come up and notice once more, that the dream played a crucial role in this sequence of sessions and that the addendum to the dream was also important.

There is a great deal more that could be said about this most moving sequence, especially in regard to the therapeutic efforts and hopes that are contained in the patient's regression and in her dream, but the hour is at an end. I would like to conclude with an expression of gratitude to this therapist for his most candid and sensitive presentation. It has been a humbling experience to have shared with him the travails of learning to do psychotherapy—a variant of what Freud (1937) so perceptively called one of the impossible professions. My main hope is that I have showed you something of how there is hope and the potential for cure contained even in the most despairing therapeutic interlude, and that you will extrapolate from that the realization that, out the morass of confusion about valid psychotherapeutic techniques with which your minds are now filled, there is the possibility of an effective resolution and synthesis. I really hope that I have pointed you in that direction. Sound psychotherapy is not only feasible, it is also richly and appropriately rewarding for both patient and therapist. Thank you again for helping us to forge the way.

REFERENCES

Baranger, M. and Baranger, W. (1966). Insight in the Analytic Situation. In *Psychoanalysis in the Americas*, Ed. R. Litman, New York: International Universities Press, pp. 56-72.

Berkowitz, D.; Shapiro, R.; Zinner, J. And Shapiro, E. (1974). Concurrent Family Treatment of Narcissistic Disorders in Adolescents. *International Journal of Psychoanalytic Psychotherapy* 3:379-396.

Bion, W.R. (1962). *Learning from Experience*. New York: Basic Books.
_____ (1963), *Elements of Psycho-Analysis*. New York: Basic Books.

Blum, H. (1973). The Concept of Erotized Transference. *Journal of the American Psychoanalytic Association* 21:61-76.

De Racker, G. (1961). On the Formulation of the Interpretation. *International Journal of Psycho-Analysis* 42:49:54.

Deutsch, H. (1926). Occult Processes Occurring During Psychoanalysis. In *Psychoanalysis and the Occult*. Ed. G. Devereux. New York: International Universities Press, 1953, pp. 133-146.

Freud, S. (1900). The Interpretation of Dreams. *Standard Edition* 4 and 5.

_____ (1905). Fragment of an Analysis of a Case of Hysteria. *Standard Edition* 7:3-124.

_____ (1909a). Analysis of a Phobia in a Five-Year-Old Boy. *Standard Edition* 10:3-49.

_____ (1909b). Notes Upon a Case of Obsessional Neurosis. *Standard Edition* 10:153-320.

_____ (1912a). The Dynamics of Transference. *Standard Edition* 12:97-108.

_____ (1912b). Recommendations to Physicians Practising Psycho-Analysis. *Standard Edition* 12:109-120.

_____ (1913). On Beginning the Treatment (Further Recommendations on the Technique of Psycho-Analysis I). *Standard Edition* 12:121-144.

_____ (1914). Remembering, Repeating, and Working-Through (Further Recommendations on the Technique of Psycho-Analysis II) *Standard Edition* 12:145-156.

_____ (1915). Observations on Transference-Love (Further Recommendations on the Technique of Psycho-Analysis III). *Standard Edition* 12:157-171.

_____ (1918). From the History of an Infantile Neurosis. *Standard Edition* 17:3-122.

_____ (1919). Lines of Advance in Psycho-Analytic Therapy. *Standard Edition* 17:158-168.

_____ (1920). Beyond the Pleasure Principle. *Standard Edition* 18:1-164.

_____ (1926). Inhibitions, Symptoms and Anxiety. *Standard Edition* 20:77-174.

_____ (1937). Analysis Terminable and Interminable. *Standard Edition* 23:209-253.

Greenacre, P. (1959). Certain Technical Problems in the Transference Relationship. *Journal of the American Psychoanalytic Association* 7:484-502.

Greenson, R. (1960). Empathy and its Vicissitudes. *International Journal of Psychoanalysis* 41:418-424.

_____ (1967). *The Technique and Practice of Psychoanalysis*, Volume 1. New York: International Universities Press.

_____ (1970). The Exceptional Position of the Dream in Psychoanalytic Practice. *Psychoanalytic Quarterly* 39:519-549.

_____ (1971). The "real" relationship Between the Patient and the Psychoanalyst. In *The Unconscious Today*. Ed. M. Kanzer. New York: International Universities Press, pp. 213-232.

_____ (1972). Beyond Transference and Interpretation. *International Journal of Psycho-Analysis* 53:213-217.

Grinberg, L. (1962). On a Specific Aspect of Countertransference Due to the Patient's Projective Identification. *International Journal of Psycho-Analysis* 43:436-440.

Halpert, E. (1972). The Effect of Insurance on Psychoanalytic Treatment. *Journal of the American Psychoanalytic Association* 20:122-133.

Kernberg, O. (1969). A Contribution to the Ego-Psychological Critique of the Kleinian School. *International Journal of Psycho-Analysis* 50:317-334.

Langs, R. (1971). Day residues, Recall Residues, and Dreams: Reality and the Psyche. *Journal of the American Psychoanalytic Association* 19:499-523.

_____ (1973a). *The Technique of Psychoanalytic Psychotherapy*, Volume 1. New York: Aronson.

_____ (1973b). The Patient's View of the Therapist: Reality or Fantasy. *International Journal of Psychoanalytic Psychotherapy* 2:411-431.

_____ (1974). *The Technique of Psychoanalytic Psychotherapy*, Volume 2. New York: Aronson.

_____ (1975a). Therapeutic Misalliances. *International Journal of Psychoanalytic Psychotherapy* 4:77-105.

_____ (1975b). The Therapeutic Relationship and Deviations in Technique. *International Journal of Psychoanalytic Psychotherapy* 4:106-141.

_____ (1975c). The Patient's Unconscious Perception of the Therapist's Errors. In *Tactics and Techniques in Psychoanalytic Therapy*, Volume 2: *Countertransference* Ed. P. Giovacchini, New York: Aronson.

_____ (In Press, a). *The Therapeutic Interaction*. New York: Aronson.

_____ (In Press, b). The Misalliance Dimension in Freud's Case Histories. I. Dora. In *Freud and His Patients*. Ed. M. Kanzer and J. Glenn. New York: Aronson.

_____ (In Press, c). The Misalliance dimension in Freud's Case Histories. II. The Rat Man. In *Freud and His Patients*. Ed. M. Kanzer and J. Glenn. New York: Aronson.

_____ (In Press, d). The Misalliance Dimension in Freud's Case Histories. III. The Wolf Man. In *Freud and His Patients*. Ed. M. Kanzer and J. Glenn. New York: Aronson.

Little, M. (1951) Counter-Transference and the Patient's Response to It. *International Journal of Psycho-Analysis* 32:32-40.

Malin, A. and Grotstein, J. (1966). Projective Identification in the Therapeutic Process. *International Journal of Psycho-Analysis* 47:26-31.

Milner, M. (1952). Aspects of Symbolism in Comprehension of the Non-Self. *International Journal of Psycho-Analysis* 33-181-195.

Racker, H. (1957). The Meanings and Uses of Countertransference. *Psychoanalytic Quarterly* 26:303-357.

_____ (1968). *Transference and Countertransference*. London: Hogarth Press.

Rappaport, E. (1959). The First Dream in an Erotized Transference. *International Journal of Psycho-Analysis* 40:240-45.

Sandler, J.; Holder, A.; Kawenoka, M.; Kennedy, H.; and Neurath, L. (1969). Notes on Some Theoretical and Clinical Aspects of Transference. *International Journal of Psycho-Analysis* 50:633-45.

_____ ; Dare, C.; and Holder, A. (1973). *The Patient and the Analyst*. New York: International Universities Press.

Searles, H. (1959). The Effort to Drive the Other Person Crazy—An Element in the Aetiology and Psychotherapy of Schizophrenia. *British Journal of Medical Psychology* 32:1-18.

_____ (1965). *Collected Papers on Schizophrenia and Related Subjects*. New York: International Universities Press.

_____ (1975). The Patient as Therapist to his Analyst. In *Tactics and Techniques in Psychoanalytic Therapy*, Volume 2. *Countertransference*. Ed. P. Giovacchini. New York: Aronson.

Stone, L. (1961). *The Psychoanalytic Situation*. New York: International Universities Press.

Szasz, T. (1962). The Problem of Privacy in Training Analysis. *Psychiatry* 25:195-207.

Viderman, S. (1974). Interpretation in the Analytical Space. *International Review of Psycho-Analysis* 1:467-480.

Wangh, M. (1962). The "Evocation of a Proxy:" A Psychological Maneuver, its Use as a Defense, its Purpose and Genesis. *Psychoanalytic Study of the Child* 17:451-472.

Weiss, S. (1975). The Effect on the Transference of 'Special Events' Occurring during Psychoanalysis. *International Journal of Psycho-Analysis*. 56:69-76.

Winnicott, D. (1947). Hate in the Counter-Transference. *International Journal of Psycho-Analysis* 30:69-75.

_____ (1965). *The Maturational Processes and the Facilitating Environment*. New York: International Universities Press.

Zinner, J. and Shapiro, R. (1972). Projective Identification as a mode of Perception and Behavior in Families of Adolescents. *International Journal of Psycho-Analysis* 53:523-531.

INDEX